State Shrinking

Special Publications Series
Institute of Latin American Studies
The University of Texas at Austin

STATE SHRINKING
A Comparative Inquiry into Privatization

Edited By
William P. Glade

Office for Public Sector Studies
Institute of Latin American Studies
University of Texas at Austin
Austin, Texas

INSTITUTE OF LATIN AMERICAN STUDIES
THE UNIVERSITY OF TEXAS AT AUSTIN

Library of Congress Cataloging in Publication Data

State Shrinking

1. Privatization—Latin American. 2. Privatization.
I. Glade, William P.
HD4010.5.S73 1986 363 86-10631
ISBN 0-86728-016-6

Printed in the United States of America

First Edition, 1986

CONTENTS

Foreword

Privatization, it is said, is an idea whose time has come. Whether or not this is so, it is certainly a policy about which one hears a great deal these days, sometimes in the most unlikely places. In any case, the notion of extracting the modern state from some of its many involvements in the operations of the economy--state shrinking, as it were--runs so counter to the main drift of history in the twentieth century that having a look at it seemed, to the researchers at the Office for Public Sector Studies (OPSS), a project whose time had come.

The OPSS, an adjunct of the Institute of Latin American Studies of the University of Texas at Austin, was established in 1976 to help pursue the research interest of a number of scholars on the UT campus who had been exploring the role and impact of the state in one or another of its activities. The group has been multidisciplinary from the outset, as befits the requirements for studying the extraordinary complexity of the contemporary public sector. Not all were directly involved in this particular inquiry, but at one point or another most of them contributed, at least indirectly, to such insights as may inform the volume at hand. From the Lyndon Baines Johnson School of Public Affairs the OPSS has drawn on the work of David Eaton, Chandler Stolp, Sidney Weintraub, Robert Wilson, and, before he moved on, Victor Arnold; from the Department of Government, Henry Dietz and Lawrence Graham; from Economics, Michael Conroy, William Glade, and Wendell Gordon, as well as visiting professors E. V. K. FitzGerald and Thomas Trebat. Robert Malina of Anthropology and Antonio Ugalde of Sociology have for years codirected a graduate seminar on health policies and planning, the oldest instructional effort of the OPSS. This seminar, along with their research, has yielded key insights into the dynamics of the policy process in developing countries. Emile McAnany of Radio-Television-Film and Patricia Wilson of Community and Regional Planning have likewise contributed much of value in both research and teaching. So, too, have three other visiting professors: Carlos Estevam Martins, Luciano Martins, and Enrique Saravia. In History, the current research of Richard Graham promises an instructive new perspective on the development of the Brazilian bureaucracy, and Susan Deans-Smith will soon publish a useful study of an early public enterprise in Mexico.

Given this widespread campus interest in the public sector's role in development, in Latin America and elsewhere, it was probably inevitable that the most recent policy inflection in these matters, privatization, should excite considerable scholarly curiosity. Research embodying a comparative international perspective seemed in order, to catch the phenomenon in the early, and presumably formative, phases of its evolution. To assist in the effort, and to reduce possible ethnocentric bias, three foreign scholars, two of whom had, in fact, participated in the founding of the OPSS, were recruited to join in the design and implementation of the project. A senior United Nations specialist on public enterprise, V. V. Ramanadham of India, was not only generous in providing frequent counsel along the way but also carried out that part of the research focused on Africa. Horacio

Boneo of the Center for the Study of State and Society (CEDES) in Buenos Aires, like Dr. Ramanadham, had been in touch with the OPSS from the outset and returned as visiting professor during the year leading up to the conference at which the papers in this volume were presented. (A colleague at CEDES, Oscar Oszlak, who had likewise helped to launch the OPSS and who lent a hand in project design, was unable to participate in the conference as by then the new Alfonsin government had drafted him to shape up Argentine public administration.) We were singularly fortunate in having with us a visiting social science research associate during the last year of the project, Felipe Ortiz de Zevallos, a Peruvian economist who had recently headed his country's National Development Corporation, the agency charged with overseeing much of Peru's parastatal sector. The insider's view Dr. Ortiz de Zevallos was able to bring was buttressed further by his former role as chairman of the board of the key development financing entity of the Peruvian government. In these posts, he had been party to the highest-level policy discussions on the issue of privatization.

One scholar who could not be with us for the final stage of the project was Alfred Saulniers, coordinator of the OPSS. At the time he was on leave in East Africa, working with an ILO team to improve the management of state-run companies in a number of countries. (He found that the problems of parastatals there were astonishingly similar to those he had investigated in Latin America.) For most of the project, however, his contribution was invaluable, not least because of his participation in a World Bank mission that studied the possibilities of privatization in Peru. Like Dr. Ramanadham, moreover, Dr. Saulniers was able to bring a cross-cultural perspective to bear on the research problem on account of the extensive fieldwork he had done previously on development in West Africa as well as Latin America.

Our aim in this project was to take a systematic look at the apparent reversal of historical policy represented by privatization, to understand its origins, its varied manifestations, its viability or "life expectancy," and its implications for the policy environment with which U.S. policymakers, in business no less than in government, have to deal. Would, for instance, the redimensioning of the state turn out to be a mere historical blip, or does it constitute a more enduring sea change in public policy? While the defining concern of ILAS is Latin America, we knew that much of relevance to these questions would be missed if the inquiry did not examine cases of state shrinking in other regions where different cultural, ideological, and situational factors could be influencing variables. Thus, a decision was made at the beginning to cast the project in a broad comparative analytical framework, one that would also avoid the somewhat polemical tone that discussions of privatization have tended to take hitherto. All too often, those favoring privatization have been inclined to liken the present policy course to a conversion experience: government officials and electorates, having seen the error of their erstwhile interventionist habits, vow to mend their ways and seek in the magic of the market the social solution for a widening range of problems. For those of this persuasion, the so-called rationality of the market (notwithstanding its magical appellation) invites objectivity and efficiency into allocative patterns. By the same token, those opposed to state shrinking have seen it in terms of subversion and conquest: an insidious redefinition, and eventual overwhelming, of the general interest by private goals. For those of this persuasion, the reassertion of market criteria amounts to a sort of social recidivism. In point of fact, the personal policy preferences of the participating scholars were varied. This did not, however, hinder a fruitful collaboration at any point. On the contrary, it was the general judgment that the diversity of view enriched the sensibility of the group as a whole, just as the cross-national element was critical to the success of the overall project.

Further, although most participants, in common with economists everywhere, accepted annual increases in GNP as the central metaphor of development studies, we opted to employ an interdisciplinary mode of analysis so as to recognize the interplay of economic and non-economic factors that determine both the configuration of the public sector and the characteristics of its interaction with the private sector. In this we were guided by a common conviction: the value of interdisciplinary study lies in the fact that, in a scholarly sense, it greatly enhances peripheral vision; thereby it enables researchers working from the more confined focus of an individual discipline to avoid being caught unawares by phenomena that might come swimming into the disciplinary field of vision from adjacent parts of the social order.

Last, along with mustering academic resources from several fields and countries, we felt that it would be eminently useful to bring into the final deliberations the experience of persons directly involved in business management. American business executives know that in the past half-century a formidable participant has entered the business arena in other countries, the state-owned enterprise; foreign business leaders are, for the most part, on even more intimate terms with these public enterprises. In Latin America, as in Africa, Europe, and parts of Asia, governmental companies dominate the economies of many nations by controlling such key sectors as communications, transport, energy, banking, and even mining and heavy industry. In the business systems of country after country, the government-owned firms sometimes called parastatals often play, at least formally, the role of a fulcrum, balancing diverse national interests against those of the local private sector and multinational corporations and the operations of the world market generally. What is more, this important form of business ownership has steadily increased its reach, through foreign trade and investment, into the U. S. economy. All the while, the operating environment of business the world over has been witnessing the emergence of baroque regulatory schemes that affect private sector management decisions at virtually every point.

To tap this experiential dimension, we were able to enlist the cooperation of experts from three major corporations, Dow Chemical, Esso Inter-America, and IBM. These corporations along with some particularly generous individuals, composed the membership of a support organization known as the Friends of ILAS. It was the financial backing of the Friends that made the whole project possible. In addition, the intellectual contributions of the corporate members of the Friends strengthened, in significant degree, the quality of the final product. Arguable though the point may be in other contexts, the collaboration between the public and private sectors that occurred in this project was, we think, immensely productive. It was also, perhaps atypically, devoid of acrimony. We could not have asked for better colleagues from the business community.

William P. Glade

Part I

INTRODUCTION

Chapter 1

Sources and Forms of Privatization

William P. Glade

State shrinking, which is what this book is all about, has taken on an assortment of guises: deregulation, liberalization, government budget cutting, debureaucratization, and, occasionally, decentralization. Privatization (or denationalization, as the process is called in Europe) has in several forms come to figure especially prominently among the measures that have been taken to dislodge the state from its preponderant position in national economic organization and to reverse the modern tendency to look to government to remedy all sorts of persisting social and economic problems.[1] The paternalistic solicitude manifested in the expanded role of government as provider of a whole array of social services, as owner and manager of varied economic undertakings, and as regulator and planner has not been without its blessings. But in an apparently growing number of cases, the activist state has been judged inefficient, or even perverse. The combination of the state-shrinking policies actually used to set matters on a different course has varied from country to country, but the net result has generally been to place greater reliance on the market than did the policy packages they replaced.

Without much doubt, one of the most arresting policy developments of our times has been the more-or-less simultaneous appearance (at least as historical evolution is reckoned) of these changes in the relation of state to economy in three sets of societies: the centrally planned economies, the mixed industrial economies of the West, and the less-developed economies of the Third World. Although the incubation of some of these changes runs back a bit earlier, it is during the past two decades that they have gathered momentum. To one degree or another they have interrupted, if not halted, the dominant policy trend of the previous hundred years or so. Whether the new policy orientations will be enduring--and therefore a basis for, say, long-term corporate planning--remains to be seen. The fact is that at the moment we have firm evidence on neither the chances of the new policy orientation's spreading further nor a systematic tracking of the paths by which state shrinking has already been diffused.

In the course of this inquiry we shall cover a great many of the charges that have been leveled against what is perceived as overloaded if not self-aggrandizing government. What may be noted at the outset, however, is the striking change that has taken place in the climate of opinion in which issues involving the public sector are now being debated. The intellectual establishment is no longer nearly so unified as it once was behind the welfare state. Both empirical studies and conceptual-theoretical advances have led to a newer and more sophisticated assessment of the operations of the public sector--and more generally of the social architecture of the modern age wherein bureaucrats defined as public servants in fact wield considerable actual power. The public, too, has come to share this more clearheaded appraisal, tinged, at times, by a probably justified skepticism if not cynicism. Coupled with widespread disappointment over the limited results of social welfare programs, this skepticism has made the public much more cautious than it once was about reposing its faith in government's ameliorative action.

Save for the most doctrinaire Marxists, prevailing views also show scant attachment to the principle of public ownership, and it is evident that there has been a considerable expectational deflation regarding what may be accomplished through successive increments in government intervention.[2] Indeed, so vast and complicated are the patterns of intervention today, to say nothing of the labyrinthine political processes that underlie them, that in the public's eye no less than in the scrutiny of the scholar there has been a significant blurring of the distinction between public welfare programs designed to alleviate genuine social distress and governmental measures that merely protect or advance the interests of particular privileged groups, including the functionaries of the public sector itself.

In the newly industrializing nations, additional forces are, as we shall see, at work in undermining the faith in state-driven or policy-led development. Here, even more than in industrialized countries, acute budgetary stress has been brought on by mounting social expenditures and the problems of adding capital-raising and the operating deficits of the parastatal firms to the public sector borrowing requirement. Confronted with an increasingly complex state apparatus and more subtly articulated and refined economic structures, the "*estado rector*", to use a currently popular Mexican term, has simply fallen down on the job. By trying to do too much, it has ended by not doing anything very well. The magnitude of the challenge, arguably, has finally surpassed the reach of the state at the same time that, in the mixed economies, a maturing private sector has felt up to shouldering more of the task of development. (In Latin America, the harshness with which autocratic rule has been applied by several statist regimes has impelled even followers of the Left to contemplate the desirability of shrinking the state so as to provide a wider discretionary social space for dissent and more room for private action not controlled by the state.)

Such has been the erosion of confidence in the beneficence and capability of the state that proposals for government retrenchment have clearly gained in popularity, cashing in on the ambivalence with which the state is now viewed. Undoubtedly it is this that has heightened the resolve of some political leaders to strip the public sector of many of its economic enterprises and pare back its social programs. The cumulative costs of interventionist measures, introduced and assessed piecemeal for their service to particular policy ends over the course of many years, have in most cases remained indeterminate, with the shifting incidence of costs and the proliferation of cross-subsidies and other transfer payments becoming so complex as to preclude any comprehensive evaluation of the total impact of such policies. Though there would seem to be a prima facie case that they are, on balance, counterproductive, the empirical evidence for this judgment is not altogether conclusive. Nevertheless, the melange of regulatory and support measures has become simply too shapeless to be readily defensible anymore, and the hope is that, freed of some significant portion of its comprehensive responsibilities, the capacity of the state for ordinary administration, for social relief, and for macroeconomic management ought to be enhanced.[3] Such, for example, is part of the message being conveyed today by the IMF and the World Bank in their structural adjustment programs that reduce tariffs and quantitative restrictions on trade, remove price controls on agricultural products and other goods and services, and replace administered or political prices of all sorts with market prices designed to signal relative scarcity and productive opportunities.

To put the matter into some sort of historical perspective, it must be recognized that privatization is not altogether new. An early version appeared in the nineteenth century in countries like Honduras, Rhodesia, and India, where the emergence of plantation economies and mining enclaves in a certain sense arrested the growth of the public sector; perforce the capitalist enterprises operating in such remote areas had to take on the provision of infrastructure and a modest range of public services, there being no duly-constituted public authorities capable of doing so. Closer in logic to the modern form, however, was the investment policy practiced by the Japanese government in the two decades after the Meiji Restoration. There, the state's pioneering investments in industrial development were turned over to private persons, partly in compensation for landholdings expropriated during a thoroughgoing agrarian reform, while welfare expenditures were largely confined to a heavy investment in free universal education to build up a literate working class.[4]

Oddly enough, the first three twentieth-century experiments with privatization appear to have occurred in the centrally planned bloc. First, of course, was the famed New Economic Policy (NEP) episode, which followed the period of wartime communism in the Soviet Union, but in the years following World War II, two presumably more durable injections of market guidance were effected. Soon after the break with the Soviet Union, Yugoslavia began, in 1950, its highly original experiment with a type of market socialism, which to some extent had been theoretically described by the Polish economist Oskar Lange. By 1965 central planning had been ended and the self-managed enterprises that constituted the cornerstone of its distinctive system were allowed to respond to market forces. Under quite different circumstances, Hungary began in 1968 a reform that, with further modifications in the 1970s, installed the policy package known as the New Economic Mechanism.[5] Of all the Soviet satellites, Hungary has remained the most market-oriented, though several of the others have gone as far as to permit a type of joint venture, known as co-production agreements, with Western firms. Even more startling in dimensions, of course, has been the grandiose venture into market economy launched since 1979 by the leadership of the People's Republic of China. Fascinating though these cases may be, however, the kind of privatization on which this volume focuses is that carried forth by the sundry mixed economies of the noncommunist world.

Tour d'Horizon

By all odds, the premier example of privatization in a Western context is the case of the United Kingdom. Thanks to the maturity of its private-sector institutions--the breadth and organization of the capital market, the availability of experienced private management, and the rich supply of supportive business services--the field was ready-made for the exercise of the political will necessary to get the process rolling. Impelling the government to embark on this controversial policy direction were circumstances that bred a spreading malaise, especially the sluggish macroeconomic performance that seemed virtually to define the term "stagflation."[6]

Excessive growth in the nonmarket sector, chronically unsatisfactory industrial relations and union rigidities, unimaginative management, disincentive taxation, and the preservation of obsolete industries as nationalized firms are some of the problems to which Britain's inadequate performance has been attributed. Which of these, or other factors, must bear the chief blame for the country's chronic economic woes is far from settled even yet. Be that as it may, public attachment to nationalization has grown notably weaker as ailing operations have become more costly, and public sympathy for labor unions in the nationalized industries has tended to be somewhat less than overwhelming. Certainly, to judge from the Thatcher government's programs, people have, on the whole, felt much more aggrieved by cutbacks in the various types of social payments than by switching the ownership of enterprises from the public to the private sector as government has cast about for ways of relieving its financial burdens. No less significant, in view of the role of organized labor, in tandem with certain circles of intellectuals and Labor party politicians as the main constituencies for public ownership, has been public support of more restrictive labor legislation, which has helped to dampen labor protest.

The progress Britain has made in carrying out its privatization program has been so well publicized that at this point we probably need only to mention the major operations that have been hived off: over 750,000 units of council (i.e., public) housing, Associated British Ports, Amersham International, BR Hotels, British Gas Onshore Oil, British Aerospace, Britoil, British Sugar, British Telecommunications, Enterprise Oil, Ferranti, Inmos, Cable & Wireless, Jaguar, National Freight Company, Sealink, assorted shipbuilding enterprises, a promising biotechnology venture known as Calltech, plus innumerable municipal services besides the aforementioned housing projects. In the offing, as of mid-1985, are the proposed sales of British Airways, the National Bus Company, Rolls Royce, Royal Ordinance, the British Airports Authority, British Gas Corporation, and two lesser-known state-owned firms, BL's Unipart subsidiary and Shorts Brothers. No other government has come close to the scale of these transfers, and throughout, with varying degrees of success, the state has continued with efforts to shape up British Airways, British Steel, the National Coal Board, and other nationalized producers. Significantly, though, even in a regime as dedicated to the mandates of the market, public-interest restrictions have been placed on some aspects of the sales. For example, the state has declared a maximum size for initial shareholdings and set limitations on foreign purchase or even joint venturing with foreign companies--to stave off allegations, no doubt, that privatization was equivalent to denationalization in the sense of relinquishing national assets to foreign interests.

Elsewhere in Europe, divestiture has also been making headway. In West Germany, where the federal government had over the years built up shareholdings in some 487 companies, the finance minister began in 1984 a program to reduce the government's stake in Veba (West Germany's largest company), Lufthansa, Volkswagen, Vereinigte Industrie-Unternehmungen, and seven other firms. If, on the one hand, the German flirtation with state shrinking seems excessively cautious compared with the boldness of the policy change in the United Kingdom, Hungary, Yugoslavia, or China, the country's experience also provides evidence that pervasive state involvement and comprehensive social insurance schemes are not necessarily antithetical to stunningly successful economic performance. The same, for that matter, may be said of the modest steps Austria has taken along the privatization path, giving tighter supervisory control to the minister of state industries and the holding company in charge of the most important of the state firms, laying off redundant workers at the Voest-Alpine steel works, and placing parastatals generally under stricter market discipline. The Dutch government, too, began in 1985 to review the possibilities of some divestments, in chemicals and other industries, but in this case, unlike in Germany and Austria, welfare interventionism has not gone hand in hand with outstanding economic accomplishment. Italy, where the subsidiary firms of IRI, the state holding company, and ENI, the petroleum combine, sprawl into nearly all parts of the economy, has moved less forcefully into privatization, but even so an outstandingly successful divestiture by IRI of Montedison was, after an interval, followed by projects to sell Alfa Romeo, a portion of IRI's interest in Alitalia, a substantial part of the Banca Nazionale del Lavoro, and an ENI subsidiary named Saipen. At the same time, another state concern, Italtel, made singular gains in attaining profitability and divising promising strategies for growth under the leadership of Marisa Bellisario, the country's most acclaimed female entrepreneur.

Two particularly interesting cases are Sweden and Spain, the former as the very avatar of the welfare state and the latter because of its adoption of state curbing, if not state shrinking, policies under a socialist government. In the former, dissatisfaction with the increasingly sclerotic quality of Swedish social and economic organization brought a more market-oriented government to power in 1976, halting the forty-four year rule of the Social Democrats.[7] Worsening economic circumstances, however, inhibited efforts to contract the scope of intervention, and public enterprises even expanded. It remained, ironically, for the Social Democrats, when they regained power in 1982, to institute measures--chiefly devaluation and wage restraint--that would begin to reinvigorate the private sector and, unintentionally, to build up its legitimacy by galvanizing private business leaders into action through the institution of the wage earner's funds. By the end of 1984, the Palme government had also ended subsidies to a number of large concerns, enjoined the relatively few nationalized companies to become profitable, and sold off the government's shareholdings in businesses worth around $170 million.

Spain's socialists were much newer to power but went to some pains to reassure private investors that their policies would shore up the economy and actually improve the business environment. Several state-operated firms--for example, the television monopoly and the national telephone company (which announced its plans to seek a listing on the New York Stock Exchange)--moved into a better financial status, and others, such as SEAT (an automobile manufacturer) and ENP (a petrochemical company), began to introduce cost-cutting programs (including layoffs) designed to lift productivity and profitability, even at the expense of employment. At the macroeconomic level, austerity was the order of the day, while several small firms acquired by the state in the failure of the Rumasa conglomerate were sold back to private investors. It seems no exaggeration to say that the Gonzalez government has gained an enthusiastic backing from the Spanish business community.

In some respects, though, it is France that represents the bellwether case for Europe, for, in addition to its deeply embedded statist tradition (a policy bias with monarchical roots), it had at first moved, under the Mitterand government, sharply counter to the general trend. In what many took to be the country's characteristic idiosyncrasy, the country took a tack opposite to the drift of policy elsewhere and, in a spate of socialist exuberance, nationalized both key industrial combines and the lion's share of the private banking system that remained after several major banks were socialized in the aftermath of World War II. By the end of 1984, however, a significant degree of doctrinal backfilling had occurred and there were no more forays of this sort. More and more, in fact, the government began to talk in pragmatic terms of fiscal prudence and productive performance, an aboutface masterminded by a new prime minister, Laurent Faubius. Consequently, a new note of restraint came to characterize fiscal policy, payrolls in state industries were pruned, and public-sector managers were encouraged to develop new, commercially viable financial, production, and marketing strategies. They were, for example, authorized to seek infusions of private funds through the sale of minority interests, to set up joint ventures with multinationals, and undertake more active overseas investment. Some fields were deregulated, and the government went so far as to allow private television to compete with state-owned channels. Increasingly, too, it was expected that a new conservative government would pursue the policies of "destatization" more aggressively still.

In the Middle East and Asia, significant policy changes have been observable in several countries, the most publicized being, perhaps, Japan's decision to privatize the Nippon Telegraph and Telephone Public Corporation and open the telecommunications field to competition, India's almost reluctant liberalization of its policy vis a vis foreign capital, and the self-proclaimed (but only partially realized) free-market policies of the Ozal administration in Turkey (where the state employs almost a third of all workers). In a few instances, Thailand being the main example, the private sector has been leading the way to an impressively high aggregate growth rate for years, notwithstanding the seventy-odd state corporations that operate in the country. In many more (Sri Lanka and Egypt spring to mind), the more capitalistic growth strategy is a product of recent years, the former since 1977, the latter after President Anwar Sadat began to phase out Nasserian socialism.

Surprises are in store for students of this part of the world quite as much as in the case of Europe. New Zealand's embrace of free-market policies after mid-1984 came about, for example, under the aegis of a labor government. The Singapore economy, often cited as a market success story, includes around 490 companies that are controlled by the government or by one of the statutory boards. Though both Singapore and neighboring Malaysia have put up for sale their governments' shares in a number of public and mixed enterprises, the fact that they have enjoyed so much economic success while operating substantial parastatal sectors (particularly Singapore) provides yet another caution against jumping to conclusions in making associations between state-sector size and systemic economic performance.[8]

African development experience was generally disappointing in the 1970s, filled with ill-conceived and poorly administered projects, characterized (sometimes grotesquely so) by mostly inefficient and bloated governments of various degrees of corruption and a penchant for intervention that was very nearly always counterproductive in the extreme. By the dawn of the 1980s, and indeed somewhat before, country after country had to turn to the IMF for stand-by arrangements and help under the Extended Fund Facility, over and beyond their long-standing reliance on external financing for trade and capital formation. So grim was the situation that the Fund and the World Bank together had, in effect, to mount a massive salvage operation.

Prompted by the Fund and the Bank, fiscal policies were revamped to generate additional revenue, wherever possible, expenditures were curtailed, and efforts were made to increase credit to the private sector, which had suffered from crowding out due to the subordination of monetary policy to fiscal needs. Special attention, in many cases, was given to rectifying the mismanagement that had become so pervasive in some, though not all, of the parastatal sectors of the continent.[9] Measures were implemented to improve the efficiency of some public enterprises, while others were scheduled to be closed down as hopeless in what amounted to an economic triage program. No one would expect these reforms to have enjoyed an unblemished success, but in at least fourteen countries some type of privatization project has been partially implemented: Burundi, Guinea, Guinea-Bissau, Kenya, Liberia, Malawi, Mali, Mauritania, Mozambique, Rwanda, Senegal, Somalia, Swaziland, and Togo. Even Tanzania, by mid-1985, had begun to ponder the advisability of returning its now run-down state-owned plantations to private entrepreneurs.

Not a few of these countries, as might be imagined, have required assistance from USAID, the ILO, and other entities to get their privatization programs moving and to begin to rehabilitate their public enterprises. In contrast to Europe, where the state-shrinking route appears as one among several policy options and in any case is implemented as an in-house affair, in Africa the restructuring of the economies seems much more imposed by circumstances, particularly the relations of the local economies with the rest of the world, and foreign or international institutions loom considerably more intrusive. The chance that the policy option and the process itself will ever become "indigenized" is, accordingly, rather more problematic. Whereas even in some European cases the intensity of partisan feeling at each end of the spectrum hints at the possibility (though not, to be sure, the probability) of a sequence composed of nationalization - denationalization - renationalization - redenationalization, such a spectacle seems somehow less far-fetched on the Dark Continent, given the situational factors associated with privatization campaigns.

Latin America, to complete this cursory overview, looks to be intermediate between the European and African cases, but even within this regional arena there is much diversity in the impetus behind the privatization and deregulation programs. To be exact, some routine conversions of public enterprises to mixed enterprises, sales of public enterprises to private investors, and divestments of government shareholdings in mixed enterprises took place years ago, as, for instance, in the case of the Paz del Rio steel mill in Colombia. Quite different, however, is the more concerted effort at destatization that has appeared since the early 1970s, at least as a talking point, on the policy agendas of Chile, Argentina, Uruguay, Brazil, Peru, Venezuela, Jamaica, Mexico, Ecuador, Costa Rica, and perhaps the Dominican Republic.

No argument is being put forward that these constitute a close-knit family of cases. Though the policy affinities are suggestive, there are also some rather obvious differences among them, particularly in respect of the context of state shrinking. In both Peru and Chile, for example, an interest in privatization surfaced in the aftermath of periods--the Velasco and Allende administrations, respectively--in which a huge, and ultimately indigestible, share of the nation's economic enterprise had been dumped rather abruptly on weak public-sector management systems that proved incapable of absorbing them smoothly and effectively. Stretching the point further, it could be contended that something of the sort occurred in Mexico during the administrations of Echeverria and Lopez Portillo, when the Mexican bureaucracy, much like a gigantic ziggurat, went crashing down the path of statism--confiscating part of the value of bank deposits and imposing exchange controls, nationalizing the country's financial intermediaries, and spawning a plethora of new state firms. Yet here the similarities end.

The expansion of the Peruvian state came after an interval of minimal interventionism and was managed by a center-left reform-minded military. Privatization, starting with the state's shedding its fishing fleet, likewise began under a military government, that of Morales Bermudez, and continued somewhat desultorily under the successor civilian administration of Belaunde. Throughout, the political environment remained remarkably sedate, considering the magnitude of the Velasco reforms. In Chile, the public sector prior to the frenzy of Allendista expropriations had already grown to a moderately substantial size. When the impulse to privatization came, it was in the wake of the widespread political disorder and administrative breakdowns of the closing months of Allende's rule, not to mention the severe political repression that followed. In Mexico, the pre-Echeverria parastatal sector packed even greater weight than Chile's, having evolved over a similar period of time, but the heady brew that inspired the rampant growth of parastatals and other controls in the decade following 1972 was not ideology. Instead, the tequila that sustained such intoxicating visions of state-led industrialization was concocted of windfall profits from oil and deep draughts from the fountain of foreign loans. And unlike the turbulent political changes of Chile or the calmer political transitions in Peru, the Mexican political structure remained essentially unshaken throughout, even into the cautious privatization program instituted by President de la Madrid.

Beyond these three cases the intercountry differences are magnified still more. In Costa Rica, where one out of every three or four workers is employed by the government and where recurrent balance of payments problems came about because the central bank lacked the control necessary to restrain expenditures and imports by state agencies, privatization of sorts has been embraced by both major parties. With assistance from USAID and as part of a debt service package approved by the IMF, the Costa Rican Development Corporation (CODESA), an umbrella organization operating some eighteen government businesses, agreed to refrain from further investments and to auction off its existing holdings, which were, for the most part, originally intended for the private sector anyhow. AID and central government funds are to be employed in refinancing CODESA's debts at the time of sale. In contrast, reorganization of the sprawling parastatal and public sectors of Brazil, even though they account for a smaller portion of total employment, involves a multitude of actors and interests, with financial dimensions surpassing the entire Costa Rican GNP.

Forms of State Shrinking

As one would expect from the foregoing, the programs to redefine the role of the state and redimension its activities have been fully as pluriform and as multiply generated as the interventionism that preceded them. Both state shrinking and privatization, therefore, are essentially portmanteau terms to cover a variety of processes, structures, and contexts. A few definitions, sorted out from the rich variety of country experiences, should stand us in good stead at this point.

Deregulation or _debureaucratization_ will refer to a reduction in indirect intervention through the abolition or simplification of controls and regulations. Implying, as it does, a primary reliance on general or nonselective monetary powers and fiscal policies to manage aggregate variables rather than measures that influence resource allocation within the parameters of aggregate demand and supply, deregulation-debureaucratization involves a devolution of decision making to the market and to nonstate or private economic actors, including cooperatives and various not-for-profit entities whose operations are nevertheless constrained by market relations. Included, therefore, are cutbacks in public expenditures of all sorts, whether capital outlays or current expenditures for the purchase of goods and services. The simplification of administrative procedures to reduce bureaucratic red tape--as in the various export promotion programs that have been undertaken--constitutes yet another form.

Examples of deregulation abound in contemporary Latin America, notwithstanding the region's historic attachment to interventionism: the phasing out of price controls; the removal of rental and interest-rate ceilings; the removal of foreign exchange controls and fixed and overvalued exchange rates; a shift from import quotas to tariffs and the lowering of these to more uniform levels; the relaxation of government regulations on postreform agricultural firms, as in Peru and Chile; reduction in the use of qualitative or selective credit controls; and modification of severance pay and other obligations embodied in labor legislation. Contraction of the deficit of the nonfinancial public sector in relation to GNP follows as part of an overall objective that can be summarized as "getting prices right" in a more open economy and minimizing "crowding out." Much of the pervasiveness of these measures stems, of course, from the fact that they are part of the standard policy package in the stand-by arrangements that have been negotiated by many countries with the IMF and the structural adjustment loans that are being made by the World Bank.

Fiscal retrenchment is partly implied by deregulation-debureaucratization as, presumably, such policies make it possible to reduce subsidies and the costly and often overstaffed administrative apparatus of the state. More substantial cutbacks in government spending, however, are likely to come, if they materialize at all, from pruning the area of social administration and associated transfer payments, from reducing military expenditures, from lowered interest charges on the public debt, and from cutting the deficits of public enterprises. In point of fact, the latter two seem to be the more realistic areas in which to hope for action, and since the interest rate level is essentially a matter for monetary policy (and the fiscal impact thereon), it is the last that will primarily concern us here. This, in turn, leads us squarely into the issue of privatization.

Outright privatization or privatization proper covers the cases in which publicly owned and publicly managed assets are sold or otherwise transferred to private investors and management. (In Latin American usage, denationalization is reserved for the cases in which the latter are foreign.) Aimed at tapping the technological, managerial, and marketing resources of private firms, including their cost-consciousness, this measure can also be understood as a means of stretching public funds further by mobilizing private savings for projects already in operation.[10] Included under the rubric of privatization proper are also the multiplying instances in which the state divests its shares in mixed enterprises.

By and large, outright privatization is what many people have in mind whenever the term "privatization" is used, but, as we shall see, this is too restrictive if results rather than form are what matters. Even so, ambiguity is not altogether absent from all cases of outright privatization. What, for instance, is one to make of the Mexican government's decision to dispose of its interest in two automotive companies, Renault de Mexico and VAM, the latter the local assembler of American Motors Corporation vehicles? The buyer in both instances was Renault, which is, of course, a French parastatal--and a major shareholder of American Motors to boot.

In a fair number of cases, <u>semiprivatization</u> accomplishes most, if not all, of that which is hoped for in privatization proper, for in it private firms are invited to share in the ownership and management of the undertaking. The use of management contracts to place public assets under private management is another version of semiprivatization. The important thing is decisional control, the aim being to introduce greater business discipline into the state's portfolio of industrial and other holdings and partially withdrawing state financial resources for other uses, presumably those with lower social opportunity costs. Semiprivatization in the management contract form has also been employed as a convenient, perhaps necessary, transitional device to rehabilitate state companies and prepare them for outright privatization.

Whether or not this last step is taken, however, most of the advantages of privatization proper can be tapped by this alternative, as Brazil, for instance, has demonstrated so effectively in its <u>tri-pe</u> policy of combining Brazilian public and private capital with foreign capital and management-engineering-scientific expertise. Designed to "safeguard" national interests, semiprivatization can also be thought of as a way to help pave the way for local business to enter technically more complex fields. At the same time, it almost necessarily delegates state control to private management, for unless the terms of association match private preferences, the private funds and organizational contributions would not be forthcoming. This negotiation of operating terms consistent with private-sector preferences is, for example, illustrated by the huge new collieries that have been opened up in Colombia by Esso Inter-America in collaboration with the Colombian government. With the natural resources owned by the latter and the former's technological and organizational assets, including its international marketing networks, the project is the kind of joint venture (foreign, domestic) mixed (public, private) enterprise that almost perfectly typifies the rationale of semiprivatization.

<u>Simulated privatization</u>, in a sense, was partly anticipated a good many years ago when public enterprises were first set up as decentralized autonomous entities in order to exempt them from various limitations in the scheme of public administration. They did not, in most cases, operate as commercial undertakings, but at least their governmental character was diluted. Under simulated privatization, though, matters are taken further and the working rules by which parastatal firms operate are drawn up so as to conform their operations to market-derived performance criteria, even though the

state remains the sole owner. Occasionally used, like semiprivatization, to prepare the way for privatization proper, more often simulated privatization appears principally to be intended to raise the efficiency and productivity of resource organizations that are to remain indefinitely in the hands of the state.

If the latter, why, then, include public enterprise strengthening as a version of privatization? There are at least two grounds for so doing. First, this reorientation of parastatals tends not only to subject them to closer governmental insight and accountability but also heightens the salience of commercial objectives over the social-political objectives for which public enterprises were not uncommonly instituted in the first place. Second, the movement to compel parastatal companies to observe more scrupulously the canons of economic efficiency has often, but by no means always, been derived from IMF-approved stabilization programs that aim at curbing economic indiscipline, negligence, and managerial complacency and resource misallocations in general. As deficit-ridden public enterprises add substantially to the public sector borrowing requirement and, in Latin America at least, have borrowed heavily abroad and thereby contributed to the external debt problem, the recent IMF/World Bank adjustment programs have necessarily singled the parastatal sector out for special attention. Thus, in this as in the other versions of privatization, a healthy respect for the allocative functions of the market is of the essence.

Partial or peripheral privatization may be said to occur under two sets of circumstances. The first is when a public enterprise is shorn of its monopoly position in certain functions or when some of its operations are abandoned. During 1978 and 1979, for example, a Peruvian state company named ENCI was relieved of its import monopolies for certain manufacturing inputs and also dropped its much criticized role in cotton marketing. (To the extent that simulated privatization enforces profitability as a performance criterion, one may expect to see more of this voluntary relinquishing of unprofitable or less-profitable lines of business.)

The second variant is often called contracting out, which is the assignment, through competitive bidding, of some auxiliary enterprise operations to private contractors: refuse collection, meal service, building construction and management, janitorial and laundry services, livery services, and so on. Inasmuch as this form of partial privatization takes place within the boundaries of parastatal operations, it tends to be less visible than the others. It may nonetheless be one of the most effective means available of nurturing small- and medium-scale entrepreneurship and nudging resource management to higher levels of efficiency.[11] Where the contracting out is on a sufficiently large scale, it can, given the relative stability of the public customer's demand, also serve as a useful way of contributing a supply of investment-grade securities to strengthen fledgling capital markets.

Illustrations of this last form of privatization are legion, particularly at the municipal level. Among the national-level cases, the resort to oil field service and drilling contracts by nationalized oil companies is one of the most well known examples. The Venezuelan Agricultural Marketing Corporation's handing over, in 1981, to local farmer and community groups responsibility for operating warehouses and wholesale markets is another case in point.

Sources of the Privatization Impetus

Doubtess political and ideological preference are sometimes present in these state-shrinking episodes (as in the Chilean monetarism of Pinochet), but to see this policy experiment as primarily ideology-driven would be a mistake for at least two reasons. First, a turn toward privatization clearly transcends the rather limited region of the world in which laissez-faire ideology has ever had much appeal to begin with, and there is no plausible evidence that the people of other lands have on any considerable scale experienced a road-to-Damascus conversion to the new faith, however evangelical the proponents of privatization may at times sound. But it is not just for this reason that we may dismiss ideological and political-preference explanations as too contrived and simplistic.

Second, it is the policy, not the ideology, that offers novelty, the ideology having been around in its essential form since the time of Hume and Smith. True, later elements of theoretical embroidery have been added by such as Hayek, Mises, and Friedman but it is not at all clear that these modern free-market advocates have in any respect improved upon the classical presentation of the ideology as such. If ideological appeal has a role in the explication of what has come to pass, it is as part of a research question about what circumstances may have contributed to the newfound attractiveness of state-shrinking policy preferences and ideologies. Attention is, in other words, more fruitfully directed to situations, circumstances, and structures--to the objective basis of policy formation. Several sets of factors appear to have played a role in this contemporary policy inflection, the relative weight of each varying from country to country, and perhaps, from time to time as well.

One set of conditions has to do with scale. The steady rise in the costs of civil administration (on account of increased social complexity), of welfare expenditure commitments (for demographic as well as political reasons), and, in the less-developed countries, the growth of expenditures on infrastructures and other development-related fixed investment in industry have led to a situation of fiscal overload, particularly in view of the typically weak tax systems of the Third World. Further, because of rapid population growth and urbanization, as well as rising per capita incomes, Third World governments have been faced with a rapid growth of state responsibilities in the area of social administration. While the parastatal sector was relatively small, its deficits could be absorbed without undue difficulty. Not so when the number and scale of public enterprises both increase and run head on into other growing claims on a public exchequer that normally tends to be strapped for funds in any case.

Put to the test, it has tended to be more feasible on a variety of counts to eliminate some subsidies to the privileged and to put the state's industrial, commercial, and financial enterprises on a paying basis (or to shift them to the private sector) than to curtail other categories of public expenditure. Especially has this been so where the IMF and other foreign financial institutions have been keeping a sharp eye on the public sector borrowing requirement as part of conditionality agreements, but whether the main barometer is the external debt burden, as in developing nations, or the rate of domestic inflation, as in the advanced industrial countries, there has been growing recognition of the need for austerity to restore health to the fiscal structure and the economy as a whole.

As a corollary, the greater the size of the public and parastatal sectors, the greater their potential impact on such matters as the claims on loanable funds ("crowding out"), the deflection of resources from productive uses, aggregate savings and capital formation rates, and productivity levels. Again, matters that could be overlooked on a small scale have developed consequential implications when associated with the size the public and parastatal sectors have attained today.

Scale very probably figures in still another way in the calculus of privatization, for with scale has generally come increasing complexity and considerable difficulties of administrative coordination (in lieu of the coordination automatically provided by the market), hence the growing problems in policy harmonization and performance monitoring. On the one hand, this growth has heightened the risk of suboptimization and internal contradiction among multiple goals and brought enhanced possibilities for goal displacement, goal substitution, and a gradual loss of coherence in the manifold operations of government. On the other, the ever more densely layered bureaucracy has raised troubling questions about accountability, not least in countries in which administrative oversight from the executive is lax, legislative oversight weak to nonexistent, and citizen oversight outside the pale of the prevailing civic traditions.

Even in the advanced industrial societies, the very complexity of the bureaucratic structure and of the issues with which it deals tends to mitigate the effectiveness of these supervisory functions, enhancing the possibilities for information and issue management amidst the interplay of bureaucratic politics and clientelism. In all cases, as has become painfully clear, whenever governments take an increasing hand in the economy, they provide powerful incentives for individuals and groups to invest more in the political process to affect the distribution of benefits and costs. From this insight comes both the growing general acceptance of the advantages of destatization and, as we shall see, no small part of the opposition thereto--to say nothing of the erosion of public confidence in the effectiveness of social engineering.

In one further respect, the appropriateness of state shrinking appears to be a function of scale. Insofar as nationalization has played a Fabian role, that of socializing "the commanding heights of the economy" in order to place in the hands of the state the chief levers of economic control, in many if not in most countries the public and parastatal sectors have already attained sufficient size for this objective. Both local private and multinational interests have, in a sense, been tamed and domesticated by the countervailing power of government. Since the law of diminishing returns would seem to apply as much to the problem of economic control as to other relations, the very growth of the state apparatus in the past has tended to obviate any social need for further extensions of it in the future.

In several respects, it may be posited that destatization policies are also a function of time (the age of the parastatal sector), especially in the less-developed countries. The first way this is so harks back to the original logic of a part of the interventionary program, namely, its role as a development catalyst. In the so-called NICs (newly industrialized countries), the years of heavy investment in infrastructure and social overhead capital are now beginning to come to fruition.[12] So, too, with the arduous process of building up an experienced industrial labor force. Public enterprise also assumed the risks of initiation, the heavy start-up costs, and the deferred profitability of building ahead of demand in fields where investment tended to be lumpy. By now, therefore, the business environment has become generally more hospitable in an economic sense: less fraught with risks and uncertainty and far richer in externalities such as a more plentiful supply of technical personnel, more reliable economic information systems, and experienced workers and entrepreneurs. Along the way, a maturing private-sector management has accumulated substantial organizational and production experience--and all the learning by doing that derives therefrom. With its greater maturity has come a greater capacity to assume the duties once performed, <u>faute de mieux</u>, by state entrepreneurs in capital raising, risk management, strategic planning, international marketing, and so on. All this has provided the private sector in a number of countries with capabilities only dreamt of two or three decades ago, while growing ties with foreign business have likely worked to strengthen this self-confidence. As the almost unprecedented criticisms of statism (or "statization") in Brazil and Mexico during the 1970s indicated, the private sector had gained enough strength that it could begin more realistically to view itself as an option to state entrepreneurship in a spreading array of investment fields.

In a more general way, longevity has, in addition, tended to favor the professionalization of public enterprise management the world over, not only through learning-by-doing in the buildup of microeconomic managerial experience but also through the development of external and internal information systems serving the parastatal sector.[13] Further, though horror stories still abound (e.g., the Argentine YPF, or the Turkish agricultural input distributor who handled transport and inventory so badly that inefficiences were estimated at $50 million), the professionalization of parastatal management has been strengthened decisively as the NICs have moved increasingly into what Hirschman has called process-centered industries, i.e., industries in which management capacity is more sharply defined by objective criteria of performance than it is in product-centered industries.[14] That this is the case comes from the fact that in process-centered industries, petrochemicals being an extreme example, a limited number of key technical processes set narrow limits on the range of choices open to management and labor, hence their more technologically constrained behavior.

Further, the advance of the state's industrial effort in the developing economies has led of late into more complex branches of manufacturing, branches in which foreign collaboration and provision of intricately sophisticated technologies are often essential. This collaboration has, correspondingly, obliged the state to operate its newest industrial promotions in such a way as to be compatible with the overseas suppliers of advanced organizational and material technologies--which is to say, with much closer regard for economic efficiency. Concurrently, of course, the increasing complexity of the state-operated industrial undertakings has invited reconsideration of the convenience of falling back on the market as the prime coordinating agency in substitution for increasingly cumbersome administrative coordination mechanisms.

Ties between government-owned enterprises and multinational corporations, in turn, point to another structural factor favoring privatization (in one or another of its forms): to wit, the increasing internationalization of economic processes generally and of public enterprises in particular as they conform to the evolving rules of the game. Along with developments in the GATT and other measures for trade liberalization, as well as in the evolution of the several regional integration schemes, the emerging international divison of labor that is exemplified in the global production systems being developed by multinational corporations will almost certainly add to the pressure for privatization and state shrinking.

Partly this reflects shifting sectoral priorities as derived from recent economic experience, especially the greater appreciation nowadays of the importance of export promotion and diversification. Inevitably such a shift implies if not a contraction of the state at least a change in the character of its intervention so as to reconcile domestic price structures with international price alignments and to make more room for market signals in management decisions about resource allocation. It may well be, as Mazzolini hints, that private firms, being more flexible and adaptable, enjoy a comparative advantage over public enterprises in dealing in competitive international markets.[15] To the extent, then, that export expansion rises in priority on the policy agenda, a greater reliance on, or at least cooperation with, private companies is implied. With their well-functioning international distribution and financing networks and their administrative control systems, the MNCs' new linkages among industrial production operations in different parts of the world seem, in other words, to make for a greater complementarity between the objectives of such corporations and the current export development goals of the LDCs, particularly the more advanced ones. Since this latter category includes most of Latin America, it seems probable, therefore, that the movement of industrial production to that region, unless thwarted by protectionist measures in the industrially advanced countries, will provide an additional push for the privatization trend: by widening the interface between state enterprises and private enterprises in both complementary and competitive relationships and by intensifying the competitive pressure generally in the business operating environments of LDCs and NICs.

Given this structural trend, public enterprises will almost necessarily, in an increasing number of instances, be compelled to emulate the market-based operating mode of private concerns in their home markets. Still more is this the case as public enterprises themselves venture overseas, as they have done on a growing scale, into the open competition of export markets and foreign operations.[16] Much has been made of the rivalry this foreign expansion represents for private MNCs, such as in the public enterprise's greater ability to accept a lower return on capital while expanding its market share, but the flip side of the coin is no less significant. Alone, or in the increasingly popular joint ventures with foreign firms, state-owned companies will be drawn more and more into following the working rules of the market sector. Pricing retaliation by large MNCs, the invocation of GATT-approved antidumping measures, and GATT sanctions against discriminatory government procurement all tend to work in that direction. Above all, the MNCs sometimes have a key bargaining chip in being able, should defensive strategy call for it, to withhold the transfer of advanced technology. By the same token, to minimize frictions in their overseas locations, public enterprises will also be constrained to play down or even discard the political objectives that sometimes surrounded their establishment and to step carefully around such legal ambiguities as their ability to invoke the doctrine of sovereign immunity (as Pemex did in dealing with the international consequences of an oil spill) in order to secure extra protection (and, therefore, competitive advantage).

More limited in effect, outside the European Economic Community, is the impact of regional integration, a modest revival of which appears to be under way after some years in which the whole effort grew frayed. Public enterprises, including multinational public enterprises, have played a small but not entirely negligible role in this revival and seem destined to contribute a bit more in the years ahead. Since, however, the taxpayers of the home countries of such firms are likely to resist operating them at a sizable deficit, thus subsidizing consumers in other regional markets, and since the intra-regional customers are, ultimately, not likely to favor paying "taxes" to other governments in the form of unacceptably high prices on parastatal products, the move into regional markets will constitute yet another factor, albeit a minor one, in conforming the operations of such firms more closely to market criteria.[17]

The gradual opening of the world's economic systems--or re-opening in the case of those that went through an import-substitution phase of industrialization--should move micro-economic organization closer to the market pattern in other important respects. During the 1970s private-sector lending and investments moved far ahead of funding from governments and international institutions in relative importance, and once the present financial crisis has subsided this is likely to continue to be the case.[18] Though bankers today may have their doubts, the greater resort of parastatals to foreign borrowing during the 1970s very probably abetted the professionalization of management by requiring that the projects submitted for external financing be, at least ostensibly, bankable. Even more shaping up of their operations along commercially viable lines is prerequisite to the parastatals' successful participation in international equity capital markets, another interesting--and, from the perspective of privatization, promising--development of recent years. One can already note, in the publicity surrounding some of the recent capital-raising efforts of European parastatals, a tendency to remark the presence of government equity participation almost as incidental information--and in any case secondary to the demonstrated quality of management. Furthermore, considering the unhappy experience most commercial banks have had with foreign lending in recent years, equity capital transfers are almost certainly going to weigh more heavily than loan capital transfers to many countries in the years just ahead--another circumstantial factor favoring the privatization movement.

Internationalization of the world economy has brought in its train one final development that bears on privatization, especially in the context of less-developed and newly industrialized countries. With the global spread of the operations of investment banking houses, management consulting firms, accounting firms, and law firms, there has been a tremendous accumulation of experience and familiarity with all aspects of the special problems of foreign operating environments, including the valuation of assets, the handling of acquisitions and mergers, and such like. In effect, then, there has been a substantial increase in the institutional capacity and expertise to handle exactly the sorts of legal and organizational conversions that tend to be associated with privatization--a significant reduction, as it were, in the transaction costs connected with this policy option. One will not quite yet find at the corner bookdealer's a how-to kit for would-be privatizers, but there are now firms specializing in managing the process and the handbooks some have issued are perhaps the next-best thing to the self-help approach.

One final structural change merits mention insofar as we are concerned with privatization in LDCs and NICs. This is the change in sectoral priorities in development programs that has recognized, in the first place, the importance of agricultural renovation and, in the second, the role of smaller and medium-sized firms in generating employment--this latter in addition to their performance capabilities in specialized subcontracting. Together with the already-noted renewed emphasis on export promotion, these new policy imperatives imply a more pragmatic recourse to the flexibility and adaptability of private, market-sensitive firms than to large, parastatal operations that, with few exceptions (the Kenya Tea Authority being one), have seldom proven particularly adept in agrarian modernization, small-business development, and export diversification.

In short, much has been made, particularly by strident nationalists, of the nefarious effects of IMF conditionality agreements and the World Bank's structural adjustment loans, and some have gone so far as to allege complicity between these institutions, the GATT, and multinational corporations in a campaign to roll back the frontiers of the state. On balance, however, it seems more reasonable to conclude that though the standard corrective measures incorporated into stabilization programs--realistic pricing (including capital and foreign exchange), deficit reduction, increased transparency in external trade controls, and the like--do help tilt development policy in a direction more compatible with privatization (as broadly construed), the main impetus to these policies comes not from external pressures, nor even from conjunctural political dynamics, much less from ideological conversion. Rather, as the very pervasiveness of the policy suggests, state shrinking responds, *au fond*, to much deeper structural changes that have been working themselves out in the world's economies over the past two decades or so.

The collaborators in this research project have endeavored to map out the dimensions of this redirection of policy as these are reflected in the policy experiences of several countries in different parts of the world. They have also tried to indicate the stress lines that inevitably develop whenever such reorientation is attempted. Like many of the world's children, privatization has not always been fortunate in the parents it has got. This, too, will be recognized in the pages following. Whether this fact discredits privatization any more than inept (or worse) parents invalidate the general relationship of parenthood remains, of course, to be seen.

Notes

1. Although this volume, inevitably, touches on the operations of parastatals or public enterprises, we have held to the necessary minimum the direct references to the now voluminous literature on that subject. Readers wishing to probe the topic further are fortunate that there is now available a superlative bibliography: Alfred H. Saulniers, comp., _Public Enterprise: An International Bibliography_ (Austin: Office for Public Sector Studies, Institute of Latin American Studies, University of Texas, 1985). A supplement is also available.

2. Disenchantment with the more exuberant claims of social engineering has been reflected in a legion of recent books dealing with U.S. experience, one of the most controversial being Charles A. Murray's _Losing Ground: American Social Policy_ (New York: Basic Books, 1984). One of the best critical assessments of the social reform efforts in the Third World has been made of the ambitious Peruvian programs. See Richard Webb, _Government Policy and the Distribution of Income in Peru, 1963-1973_ (Cambridge: Harvard University Press, 1977). For Peru's southern neighbor, see the excellent study of precoup Chile by Alejandro Foxley, Eduardo Aninat, and J. P. Arellano, _Redistributive Effects of Government Programs: The Chilean Case_ (Oxford: Pergamon Press, 1979). Of great help, too, for understanding the limitations of social programs in Latin America have been the work, published in a number of places, by James Malloy and Carmelo Mesa-Lago on social security systems.

3. Criticism of a different stripe has issued from the Left, but the net result is that what is called "state capitalism" has lost credibility from that political vantage point as well. See James Petras, "State Capitalism and the Third World," _Development and Change_ 8 (1977): 1-17, for a cogent presentation of this sort of critique.

4. T. C. Smith, _Political Change and Industrial Development in Japan: Government Enterprise, 1868-1880_ (Stanford: Stanford University Press, 1955).

5. Much has been written about these Eastern European departures from Soviet orthodoxy, but two convenient recent assessments are Peter T. Knight, _Financial Discipline and Structural Adjustment in Yugoslavia_, World Bank Staff Working Papers #705 (Washington, D.C.,1984); and Patrick de Fontenay et al, _Hungary: An Economic Survey_, IMF Occasional Paper #15 (Washington, D.C.,1982).

6. Among the many works examining the poor performance are Robert Bacon and Walter Eltis, _Britain's Economic Problem: Too Few Producers_ (London: Macmillan, 1976); and Richard E. Eaves and Lawrence B. Krause, _Britain's Economic Performance_ (Washington, D.C.: The Brookings Institution, 1980).

7. Marquis W. Childs, Sweden: The Middle Way on Trial (New Haven: Yale University Press, 1980), details well the conditions--a sluggish economy, faltering productivity, inflation, a loss of competitiveness in international markets, and a crushing tax burden--that brought the more private sector-oriented coalition to power for 1976-1982. See also Erik Lundberg, "The Rise and Fall of the Swedish Model," Journal of Economic Literature 23, no. 1 (March 1985): 1-36, for additional insights into the devitalization of welfare interventionism.

8. Across the Pacific, another Commonwealth country, Canada, has also gone a long way down the privatization road. Much of the Canadian experience has been lucidly reported in T. M. Ohashi and T. P. Roth, Privatization: Theory and Practice (Vancouver: The Fraser Institute, 1980).

9. An insightful review of one of the better parastatal systems is found in N. Raphaeli, Jacques Roumani, and A. C. Mackellar, Public Sector Management in Botswana, World Bank Staff Working Papers #709 (Washington, D.C.: December 1984).

10. In certain instances--e.g., in the second Belaunde administration in Peru--an element of restitution was involved, though not necessarily directly. Expropriated newspapers and television stations were sold back to the private sector, but not in all cases were the new owners the same as the old.

11. As ancient as taxfarming, contracting out has also been favored as a way of increasing employment. See, for instance, International Labour Office, Employment, Incomes, and Equality: A Strategy for Increasing Productive Employment in Kenya (Geneva: ILO, 1972). See also Keith Hart, "Small-Scale Entrepreneurs in Ghana and Development Planning," Journal of Development Studies 6, no.4 (July 1970): 104-120.

12. In this, the catalytic role envisaged for such state corporations as CORFO, NAFINSA, and the BNDE in handling the start-up problems of industry resembles the experience of Japan many decades earlier.

13. This has, naturally, taken place first in the industrially advanced countries, a development spotted almost twenty years ago by William S. Rukeyeser in "Creeping Capitalism in Government Corporations," Fortune 77, no. 4 (15 Sept. 1968): 124-127 & ff.

14. A. D. Hirschman, The Strategy of Economic Development (New Haven: Yale University Press, 1958, 1967).

15. Renato Mazzolini, Government Controlled Enterprise (New York: Wiley, 1979).

16. Douglas F. Lamont, Foreign State Enterprises: A Threat to American Business (New York: Basic Books, 1979), looks primarily at the other side of this interaction but the picture is essentially the same. See R. Joseph Monsen and K. D. Walters, Nationalized Companies: A Threat to American Business (New York: McGraw-Hill, 1983), for a reworking of the same theme. Airbus Industrie has enjoyed outstanding success, for example, in a highly competitive field.

17. William Glade, "El papel de las empresas del sector público en la integración de la estuctura industrial latino americano," Revista de la Integración 8, no. 19/2 (1975): 7-54.

18. This shift in the relative importance of supplier sources in funding has, in all likelihood, served to reverse the pro-statist bias of lending in the 1950s and 1960s, as observed in Louis Mark, Jr., "The Favored Status of the State Entrepreneur in Economic Development Programs," Economic Development and Cultural Change 7, no. 4 (1959): 422-430.

Chapter 2

The Problem of Public Enterprise in Developing Countries: Is Privatization the Solution?

John F. Coburn and Lawrence H. Wortzel

Introduction

Just twenty-five years ago, there were very few state-owned enterprises (SOEs) in either the industrialized or the developing countries of the non-Communist and Socialist worlds. In recent years, however, the state has come to play an increasing role in business ownership. Although this trend was pronounced in many countries of Western Europe, it has been most notable in the developing nations of Asia, Africa, Latin America, and the Middle East.

Table 1 illustrates the number of state companies in selected developing countries and the major position state ownership occupies in their national economies. In Venezuela, for example, 7 of the 10 largest companies are numbered among some four hundred state-owned enterprises. In Brazil, the 10 largest commercial enterprises are SOEs; these companies represent 5 percent of GDP, account for 70 percent of total government investment, employ 1.4 million persons, and are responsible for half of Brazil's $90 billion foreign debt.[1] Egypt's SOEs account for about 80 percent of that country's total industrial output, and Turkey's 150 state-owned companies control an estimated 47 percent of Turkish industry.[2]

Researchers who have studied the growth of SOEs have concluded that the motives for building a state-owned sector have been based primarily on economic policy rather than on political ideology.[3] For example, many SOEs were established to invest in areas that were important to the country's development but were either too costly or too risky for the local private sector to enter or "off limits" to foreign capital for reasons of national interest. Typical of these cases were government investments in steel, mining and minerals processing, petrochemicals, and other "basic industries." In some instances, however, investments were made in high-technology areas, as in the case of Embraer, Brazil's state aircraft company.

A second motive for creating SOEs was to maintain government control over industries thought to be best run as monopolies. State-owned telecommunications, electric power, and commodity-trading companies are common examples.

Rescuing failing private companies to preserve employment and essential services constitutes a third major reason for state intervention in economic enterprises. The Jamaican government's takeover of much of the sugar and hotel industry during the economically troubled 1970s illustrates this phenomenon.

Finally, many state-owned enterprises have come into being through the nationalization of foreign-owned enterprises. This has been particularly prevalent in the mining, telecommunications, and petroleum industries.

The creation of an SOE has, in certain instances, solved the problems it was created to handle. Korea and Brazil, for example, have developed efficient steel industries that are competitive on a worldwide basis. Brazil's Embraer has developed efficient aircraft that are not only in service in Brazil but also in use by airlines in the United States and elsewhere. But these are the exception rather than the rule. Unfortunately, many SOEs seem to have created more problems than they have solved. The World Bank, in its 1983 World Development Report, concludes that the problem with SOEs is economic inefficiency, leading to a financial burden that echoes throughout the economy.[4] Increasingly, the call is for "privatization," the argument being that subjecting the SOE to the discipline of the marketplace will, per se, make it more efficient.

So much has been written recently about privatization of public enterprise that one could easily view it as the solution to the general problem of state-owned enterprise throughout the world. To be sure, privatization is taking place. The privatization initiatives currently under way in Britain and, to a lesser extent, West Germany, are well documented. In the developing world, significant public enterprise divestment has occurred in Chile, and initial privatization steps have been taken in (among others) Panama, Brazil, Jamaica, Sri Lanka, Pakistan, Bangladesh, and Senegal. In addition, plans for privatization exist in a number of countries (e.g., Venezuela, Peru, and Malaysia), although actual divestments have yet to occur.

Against this backdrop several important questions emerge: How successful has privatization been to date, and how extensive will it be in the developing world over the next few years? To what extent will Britain's privatization program be replicated elsewhere? And to what extent will privatization provide a lasting cure for the ills of public enterprise?

In principle, privatization is a highly desirable objective and should be vigorously pursued wherever possible. In practice, however, given economic and political realities in most of the developing world, extensive privatization is unlikely to take place over the next few years. Because of the immense state sector in many developing nations, and because of the economic and political difficulties associated with divestiture, it is likely that--even in the most successful pursuit of privatization--a large number of companies will remain under state control. This will be especially true for the largest enterprises, which often represent the greatest financial deficits and which in many instances dominate the most crucial sectors of the economy.

This means that in most of the developing world, privatization--however desirable--simply will not take place to an extent sufficient to provide a solution to the problem of state enterprises. For this reason, it would be a mistake to view privatization as a panacea.

Instead it should be seen as one of a number of strategic actions that, when taken together, would result in the overall reform and improvement of state enterprise. Privatization will have to be pursued selectively, but, in the interim, enthusiasm for privatization must not divert the attention of government leaders and international development policymakers from the equally important task of instituting the necessary structural, policy, and management reforms within existing state companies to ensure that, as soon as possible, they are made to operate with a reasonable degree of efficiency, productivity, and financial gain.

In this chapter we briefly review some of the financial, economic, and operational difficulties experienced by most SOEs and then examine the privatization record to date, focusing on impediments to privatization. Based on this examination, we identify the characteristics of SOEs that make them appropriate candidates for privatization and suggest strategies for carrying this out. Finally, recommendations are offered for achieving more efficient management for those SOEs that, for whatever reason, are likely to remain in state hands.

The "Problem" of State Enterprise

Much has been written in recent years about the varied problems of state enterprises: operating deficits, low productivity, heavy dependence on domestic and foreign credit, poor quality of goods and services, corruption, and suboptimal resource utilization. These ills are by no means universal; efficient and profitable state-owned companies do exist, even in the developing world. Singapore Airlines, Petroleo Brasileiro, the National Commercial Bank of Jamaica, and Korean Steel are notable successes. Unfortunately, these companies form a minority, and the evidence suggests that, on balance, the financial burden of most state enterprises far outweighs whatever social and political benefits they provide.

The burden of poorly performing state enterprises rests on the shoulders of all nations, but most heavily in the developing world, which can least afford it. It is one thing to have an inefficient state sector in the United Kingdom, Germany, or Sweden, where a strong private sector exists and where both consumers and producers have a reasonable degree of choice among domestic and imported goods and services. But in the developing world, state enterprises often substitute for the private sector and in many instances are the only source of the products or services they represent. In some countries, such as Mexico, Egypt, Tanzania, and Indonesia, the public-enterprise sector virtually overwhelms the economy because of the high proportion of GNP, national investment, public borrowing, and employment that it represents. In these countries, when public enterprises are inefficient and costly, the impact is usually felt nationwide.

Much has been written about the causes of poor performance in state enterprise: unclear (and often conflicting) objectives; the imposition of political (and often uneconomic) activities; the control of management process (input) rather than performance (output); the confusing lines of authority and responsibility between SOEs and their supervisory entities; overstaffing for social ends; and many others that need no elaboration here.

Privatization: The Solution?

Given the plethora of problems besetting state enterprise during a time of world recession, international debt crisis, and increasing economic and fiscal conservatism, the privatization of state enterprise is being proposed with increasing frequency as the only lasting solution to the state enterprise dilemma.[5] Despite the publicity in favor of privatization during the past few years, however, the record to date has been modest at best. Table 2 summarizes privatization trends in major developing nations with market economies and sizable state sectors. The values assigned each country are based on our assessment of each country's "net" record in recent years. Actual and professed privatization minus any nationalization of enterprise that may have occurred during this period:

Net Privatization Formula

Actual Privatization + Professed Privatization - Nationalization = Net Privatization

As this table suggests, the record on a worldwide scale is meager. The most successful efforts to privatize have taken place in just a few countries, but even in these countries, a large number of public enterprises still remain. For example:

-- Chile, the first country since Japan in the 1800s to undertake large-scale privatization, has reversed the expropriation (as opposed to selling shares) of 259 companies and has sold off other companies worth $400 million. Despite this very major effort, 66 companies still remain in government hands; these companies account for 18 percent of GNP and have an asset value more than ten times that of the privatized companies.[6]

-- In the past three years, Jamaica has sold three small companies--an airline food service company, and two agricultural companies--and has leased bus company routes and several sugar mills to private operators.

-- In 1982 Brazil sold ten relatively small SOEs and is said to be planning to sell some thirty-six more, yet hundreds of companies remain under government control.

-- Bangladesh and Pakistan have sold off a variety of small rice, flour, cotton, and jute mills, but in each of these countries the major "infrastructural" government companies remain unsold.

In the rest of the developing world, privatization has consisted more of rhetoric than of action. For example, Venezuela, Peru, and Argentina have all vowed for several years to privatize many of their SOEs, but none has yet taken any visible action to this end.

Barriers to Privatization in Developing Nations

Why has the privatization track record not been more impressive, particularly in the developing world, where the problem is most acute? The answer lies in three factors that seem to represent major obstacles to any large-scale privatization effort in developing nations: (1) financial barriers; (2) political barriers; and (3) the lack of a clear plan.

1. Financial barriers: In addition to the sheer number of state-owned enterprises, the market value of these enterprises in most countries far exceeds the availability of private capital to pay for them.

   Capital availability is a problem, even in the industrialized countries. Consider, for example, the case of Great Britain, a country with sophisticated capital markets and a solidly established private sector. To date, the sale of slightly more than half of the government's share in four companies (Britoil, British Aerospace, Cable and Wireless, and the Port Authority), together with complete divestiture of Amersham International, have soaked up some $3.25 billion in private sector capital.[7] Full divestiture of British Airways would require another $1.2 billion.[8] The sale of 51 percent of British Telecom will require private investment capital of $6 billion--a sum more than five times the largest public equity offering ever made in the United States ($1.2 billion by AT&T in 1983). This sum is also 25 percent greater than the value of all public issues in Great Britain last year.[9] Needless to say, adding companies like British Leyland, Rolls-Royce, British Airways, and others to this list within the next few years will place a substantial burden on local capital markets. In fact, as much as a quarter of the shares of British Telecom will have to be offered in the United States, and this divestment may have to be spread over several years to lessen its impact on capital markets.

   If the partial privatization of ten state enterprises in Britain will tax the country's private capital markets to the extent described above, imagine how difficult it would be to execute the sale of large SOEs in countries in the developing world. What sources of domestic private capital could possibly buy out the majority portion of large SOEs in countries like Bolivia, Pakistan, Peru, Turkey, Tanzania, Egypt, or Bangladesh? In Jamaica, where would local private capital come from to buy the government's share of Air Jamaica, the Public Service Company, or the bauxite companies? Even in more developed countries such as Portugal, Venezuela, Argentina, Brazil, and Mexico, where could enough private capital be found to make significant inroads in their hundreds of SOEs, some of which are among their largest enterprises and, in some cases (like PEMEX, Petrobras, and PDVSA), rank among the one hundred largest companies in the world.

The impact of privatization, in at least some instances, will not be limited to the capital required to execute the sale of the enterprise. In some cases, a sizable injection of capital may have to be made to get the company into an operating position to be sold. Britain has managed this successfully with British Airways, Jaguar, and Rolls-Royce. In other cases, SOEs may need to expand to meet demand for their products and services, and, once privatized, these firms may be regular customers of the local capital markets or financial institutions.

Moreover, even if sufficient capital can be found, there is likely to be a large opportunity cost attached to using the capital for privatization. Using capital in this way diverts it from investments that might have considerably greater impact on the country's economic growth. The propensity of business executives to choose the least risky of a group of alternative investments is well known. Given a choice between buying an existing SOE and starting a new enterprise, they are likely to opt for the existing enterprise, particularly if it is being offered at a discounted price, as in Britain and Chile.

To be sure, some of the financial burden could be eased by selling all or part of the SOE to foreign investors. In many cases, however, doing so would compromise one of the major reasons for forming the state enterprise in the first place: to keep what were considered key industries and activities under national control. In these instances, foreign capital might be politically unacceptable.

2. Political barriers: Even if large-scale privatization were financially possible, there is little reason to believe that such a program would be politically feasible in many countries. This is especially true for most of the developing countries, where private-sector ownership of large enterprises is discouraged in many sectors, and where the concentration of economic wealth in a few private hands (whether foreign or domestic) is a politically sensitive issue.

   Table 3, which depicts ownership patterns in key sectors of the economies in nine of the largest Latin American countries and Jamaica, illustrates the degree of state control in sectors that are considered to be of "strategic national importance" or "national sensitivity." As it happens, these sectors contain many of the largest companies, which frequently are entities using enormous amounts of domestic and foreign debt and producing sizable economic losses. Unfortunately, these are also the companies that, for political reasons, are the most difficult to privatize.

   In the case of Venezuela, for example (table 4), state enterprises dominate most of the key productive sectors of the economy. Despite the promises and plans of the new Lusinchi government to launch a large-scale privatization program, it is difficult to see how any of the companies listed in table 4, with the possible exception of Aeropostal airline, could withstand the political backlash that a privatization effort would undoubtedly create. In fact, the net trend may be toward government ownership in Venezuela and not in the opposite direction. A new coal mining company is currently being formed (CarboZulia), a new state-owned bauxite company has recently been established (Bauxiven), and there is talk of a second large-scale steel mill company (SiderZulia). There is also debate in leftist political circles about nationalizing the only remaining private electric company, Electricidad de Caracas.

3. Lack of planning: The third obstacle to privatization programs is the absence of planning and structure for such programs once they are announced. Among the most crucial aspects of this are (a) the absence of clearly established criteria for determining which enterprises are to be privatized, and in what order; (b) the lack of clear "rules of the game" as to what form of privatization to pursue in different situations (divestment, leasing, or management contracts); (c) the lack of clearly established procedures specifying the mechanics of the privatization process; (d) the absence of a clearly established organizational entity within the government for handling the privatization program; and most important, (e) the lack of clearly established goals as to the overall scope, timing, and results of the program. Moreover, because the president or prime minister usually plays an active role in the program's decision making on a day-to-day basis (rather than limiting involvement to policy-making and delegating the detailed implementation to others), the program often becomes highly politicized, and the speed of implementation is drastically reduced as a result.

Therefore, regardless of how desirable privatization may be in principle, in practice there are some important barriers to carrying it out, which must be recognized and overcome. In particular, governments must spend enough time to plan their privatization efforts in advance, and they must be careful in choosing only the best candidates for privatization to ensure success during the early stages of the privatization "learning curve."

Deciding When to Privatize: The "Zero-Base SOE" Model

The decisions surrounding privatization in any country and in any industry depend on many different economic and political variables, and therefore vary from one set of circumstances to another. To say, for example, that, in general, textile mills, hotels, or cement companies should belong to the private sector might be appropriate for Indonesia, Peru, or Venezuela, but might be inappropriate or unrealistic in Tanzania or Mexico. Moreover, the choices depend on the existing mix of enterprises in the country as well as on other national characteristics.

One approach is to adopt a "zero-base" model for determining national industrial ownership. In zero-base budgeting, one begins with a budget of zero, and every expenditure must be carefully justified by organizational unit and by function. In applying a zero-base model to its state-owned enterprises, the nation would begin with the assumption that all industry should be private (e.g., zero state enterprise) unless certain conditions exist making private ownership either undesirable or infeasible. The conditions for exempting an enterprise from private ownership would be carefully spelled out for each country, depending on its own political, social, and economic interests. Under this model, the entire state-enterprise sector would be subjected to this "zero-base SOE test" every few years. In this way, each SOE's existence would have to be justified periodically in terms of the specific benefits it provides against the costs incurred. Those enterprises no longer meeting this criterion would be excluded from the nation's "SOE budget" and would, therefore, become candidates for privatization.

A periodic examination is recommended because economic and political environments change over time. For example, state ownership of steel or electric power companies are usually called for at early stages in a country's economic development. As the country grows, however, such firms may well become capable of conversion to viable private enterprises that provide necessary goods or services without subsidization. Similarly, SOEs created to provide employment become less necessary as alternative employment opportunities open up. Finally, as a country matures politically, its government may be able to substitute regulatory control for direct control and still achieve the desired social and economic results. Even if the periodic zero-base SOE test does not lead to privatization, the recurring process may lead to better SOE performance because of the inevitable questions it will raise about SOE goals, management, and operating methods.

Criteria for including certain enterprises or sectors in the "national SOE budget" under the zero-base approach might include the following:

-- if there is sufficient domestic private capital, or if there is a high opportunity cost of local capital for privatization, coupled with politically or economically unacceptable use of foreign capital

-- if it is impossible to obtain a reasonable sale price for the private offering

-- if social benefits provided by the enterprise are important, and if under private control the enterprise would be likely to pursue a strategy resulting in the elimination of its principal social benefits (e.g., raise prices, eliminate workers, reduce or eliminate service, disinvest in high priority regions)

-- if regulatory control cannot be substituted for ownership control

-- if privatization were to result in an unacceptable concentration of ownership in the hands of oligarchic groups.

Applying the above criteria to politically moderate, middle-income, market economy countries (such as Colombia, Venezuela, Portugal, Mexico, Argentina, Sri Lanka, Korea, or the Ivory Coast), the following industries would probably not qualify for inclusion, and would therefore be candidates for privatization, under the "zero-base" model: hotels, textile mills, sugar mills, food processing companies, commercial banks, cement companies, and small manufacturing companies.

Once the industries or companies to be privatized have been chosen within a given political and economic setting, two further decisions must be made. First, priorities must be set among the candidates because it is likely that there will be more candidates than the economy can handle at any one time. Priorities should be based on some criterion of expected gains in economic efficiency in comparison to the capital required to purchase the enterprise. One way to do this would be to construct *pro forma* financial statements covering some relevant time horizon under the alternative of both public and private ownership. Where appropriate, a comparison could also be made of the relative social benefits anticipated under each mode of ownership. The enterprises could then be ranked according to the magnitude of the benefits to be gained from privatization.

To minimize strain on capital markets, private investors can be encouraged to use debt rather than equity capital in buying SOEs--in a sense applying the concept of the leveraged buyout to the sale of state enterprise. Since there are not likely to be lending institutions equipped to handle such transactions, a development bank would have to lend private investors the funds to buy the SOE, and the loan would be repaid out of earnings. The leveraged-buyout alternative should be limited, however, to those situations in which the investors in the firm will also be its managers.

Alternatives to 100 Percent Divestment

Privatization can be achieved by various routes: full or partial divestment, leasing to private interests, and management contracts are among the most common. Whereas divestment is generally the preferred form of privatizing state enterprise, it is not possible in cases where the state is not willing or able to sell land or transfer title to mineral rights or transportation routes. In Jamaica, for instance, the Jamaica Omnibus Service was "privatized" by leasing routes to private operators, and the major sugar estates are being removed from national control through the use of management contracts with private operators.

When there are more divestment candidates than the country's capital markets can handle, an alternative to consider is partial privatization--selling some portion of state shares either to the general public, to one or more specific groups or individuals, or to the SOE employees themselves. If, after the sale, the government is willing to limit its role to that of investor and to leave the management to the private-sector partners, a partial sale may accomplish as much as 100 percent divestment.

Another possibility is to establish joint ventures with foreign capital. Such arrangements can be advantageous when managerial or technical expertise is required to make the enterprise more efficient. This alternative is also appropriate when the foreign partner can assist in arranging export opportunities by providing market access or marketing expertise. Examples of successful joint ventures of this type include the government of Colombia and Exxon in coal mining, the Venezuelan government and a consortium of Japanese and North American investors in aluminum, and the government of Liberia and Bethlehem Steel in iron ore mining.

What to Do until (or instead of) Privatization

Although partial privatization, joint ventures, leveraged buyouts, and other techniques may speed the privatization process, there will still be some SOEs that must remain under state ownership either permanently or for a time. Whereas privatization is an important element in solving the problem of state enterprise, it cannot be viewed as the only answer. In some circumstances, privatization may not be feasible from a financial or political vantage point. In other circumstances, it may be feasible but may take many years to effect. In either event, most countries will probably have to live with the majority of their SOEs for some time. It is therefore worthwhile to make efforts to improve the performance of the SOEs that will remain.

What can be done in lieu of privatization to improve the performance of state enterprises? To be sure, much as been published over the past decade about reforming state enterprise. Much of this focuses on clarifying objectives, improving the relationship between enterprises and their sponsoring ministries, establishing elaborate schemes for measuring the cost of social objectives, establishing formal performance contracts between the enterprise and the government, and developing shadow-pricing mechanisms that allow the enterprise's true economic performance to be measured.[10] Most of these measures have been tested, but for the most part, they have been difficult to implement as permanent or even temporary solutions.

There may be some simpler and more practical short-term actions governments and state-owned enterprises might adopt. Taken together, they could have an important long-term impact on the SOEs. These actions would also benefit the privatization effort inasmuch as strengthening an SOE's financial condition will greatly facilitate the sale of its shares to a risk-averse private sector. Such actions would also result in a stronger enterprise--one more capable of sustaining itself when the time for privatization comes. Some of these short-term actions include the following:

1. Minimizing management turnover. The cost of management turnover in any organization is enormous. Unfortunately, rapid management turnover is endemic within the state-enterprise sector of most developing nations. Conversely, it is no coincidence that some of the most efficient and profitable SOEs in the world are those that have enjoyed senior management continuity. Petroleos de Venezuela, Renault, Embraer, and Singapore Airlines are examples. In France, the case of Elf Aquitaine is illustrative. After

building this state-owned petrochemical giant into one of France's most profitable companies, Elf's president, Albin Chalandon, was replaced in 1982 by the new Socialist government for what were largely political motives. Since then, Elf's profits have declined 40 percent, and the company faces a crisis of mounting long-term debt, refining losses, and declining cash flow.

To avoid such unnecessary disruption, SOE chief executives should be allowed at the minimum a three- to five-year renewable term of office. In addition, the chief executive's term should not coincide with terms of those in public office. Most important, SOE chief executives should be appointed by the SOE Board of Directors, rather than by the political ministry, as is frequently the case. Finally, contracts should be drawn up between the board and the chief executive that specify the terms and conditions of dismissal--based on specific performance indicators rather than on vague, subjective, political grounds.

2. Conducting formal annual audits. Just as private sector shareholders expect periodic audits of the company's financial and management practices, so should public enterprise stakeholders expect audits of their companies.[11] Even if the overseeing government ministry does not require it, SOE managers and Boards of Directors themselves should take the initiative to conduct such audits as a way of enhancing managerial self-discipline and preventing the kind of scandalous behavior that has been too often exhibited by SOE management--even in such prestigious companies as PEMEX in Mexico and Pertamina in Indonesia. Independent audits are relatively inexpensive to perform, and in most capital cities there are several domestic and international auditing firms to choose from. From the government's standpoint, audits have the benefit of forcing the company to produce an annual set of consistent financial statements that, if done for all SOEs, greatly facilitates the ministry's job of evaluating performance, approving budgets, and reviewing major expansion proposals on a consistent basis. Conducting audits will also assist the eventual privatization program. In Jamaica, one of the major obstacles to the current privatization effort is the fact that many state enterprises have not been audited for several years and therefore lack reliable financial statements on which to base a corporate valuation.

3. Offering management bonuses. Because SOEs are part of the government, SOE salaries are tempered by the government wage scale, even though the enterprise may be autonomous and fall outside the civil service system. Relatively low management salaries are probably an unavoidable fact of life for these entities. Unfortunately, low salaries may make it impossible for the SOE to attract the good management it needs. This problem is most acute in the developing countries, where management talent is in short supply, anyway.

The use of incentive bonuses may be a way to attract and retain better management. Because many SOEs exist (at least in principle) as profit-making entities, applying a portion of the company's profits to pay management bonuses would seem perfectly appropriate and would help to bridge the perennial gap between SOE and private-sector compensation. Even in cases where SOEs are not profitable because of artificially low prices or government-imposed social costs, management should be allowed to earn a bonus for having achieved or surpassed certain agreed-upon performance targets (such as increasing productivity, developing new markets, enhancing sales). To implement this notion, companies could develop special formulas to accumulate a corporate-wide management bonus pool during the year, to be paid out to key executives at year-end, based on specific, predetermined criteria for management performance. The formal yearly audit could be used to develop the required data.

4. Permitting greater control and autonomy to SOE managers. The literature on state-owned enterprises often depicts SOE managers as helpless pawns of the political system, their hands tied by the many restrictions, contradictions, and political vagaries imposed on them. This may be the case in many situations; however, SOE managers probably have more power and control than they believe they have. They might gain the autonomy that everyone agrees they need simply by taking more calculated risks--by sticking their necks out more in defense of the enterprise and its basic productive objectives. The case of Petroleo Brasileiro (Petrobras) is exemplary. This company has had such strong leadership for so many years that today it is virtually a ministate unto itself.[12] In the case of Ferrominera, the large Venezuelan iron ore company, strong and persistent management has taken many risks in terms of reducing employment and cutting costs. Today the company has stemmed what was a very severe seven-year decline in profitability, despite the continued depression in world iron ore prices. The Turkish state tobacco enterprise provides another example of a dramatic turnaround resulting from strong and independent management. Of course, there are risks associated with independence, and too much autonomy can lead to dismissal, as in the case of Elf's Chalandron. But if governments want real managers to run their SOEs, this is the risk they and their SOE managers will have to take.

Of course, there are numerous other reform measures that could and should be taken to improve SOE effectiveness, including the introduction of competition, the expanded use of SOE-multinational joint ventures (SOEs gain management and technology while multinationals gain markets and raw materials), and the professionalization and depoliticization of SOE boards. If these and other relatively simple measures are adopted, the 1980s could see major SOE improvement throughout the world.

Conclusion

On balance, privatization--however desirable--may not offer the long-awaited solution to the problem of state enterprise, particularly in the developing world, where the problem is most acute and where privatization is most urgently needed. Therefore, while pursuing privatization, government leaders and international development policymakers are encouraged not to lose sight of the possibilities for reforming state enterprises if they are to remain in government hands. Some relatively simple and immediate actions can be taken as initial steps in this process. Taking these steps could even lead to a new paradox: SOEs that would be attractive to private-sector investors but that are too profitable for the government to sell.

Table 1

Size and Importance of State-Enterprise Sector in Selected Developing Countries

Country	Approximate Number of SOEs	Indication of National Economic Importance
Mexico	600 with full or partial government ownership	Over 10% of GDP
Brazil	500 with full government ownership; 200-300 more with partial government ownership	About 5% of GDP
Venezuela	400 with full or partial government ownership	Over 25% of GDP
Peru	150 companies with full or partial government ownership	About 20% of GDP; over 50% of national investment
Argentina	300 companies with full or partial government ownership	N/A
Jamaica	Between 75-100 companies with majority government ownership	N/A
Turkey	150 companies, mostly with full government ownership	N/A
Egypt	N/A	Over 60% of manufacturing value-added
Tanzania	400 companies with full government ownership	About 15% of GDP and nearly 40% of manufacturing value-added
Sri Lanka	125 companies with full or partial government ownership	N/A
Pakistan	175 companies	N/A
Korea	N/A	Nearly 10% of GDP and about 28% of national investment
India	200 companies with full government ownership	Over 10% of GDP

Sources: World Bank; _New York Times_; _Wall Street Journal_; _The Economist_; and other journals.
Note: N/A = no information available.

Table 2

Privatization Trends in Major SOE Countries

Europe		Latin America		Other	
U.K.	++	Chile	++	Senegal	++
W. Germany	+	Brazil	+	Bangladesh	+
Portugal	0	Jamaica	+	Pakistan	+
Italy	0	Panama	+	Sri Lanka	+
Austria	0	Venezuela	0	Indonesia	0
Sweden	0	Peru	0	India	0
Norway	0	Colombia	0	Malaysia	0
France	-	Argentina	0	Korea	0
Spain	-	Ecuador	0	Egypt	0
		Costa Rica	0	Nigeria	0
		Bolivia	-		
		Mexico	-		
		Guyana	-		
		Nicaragua	-		
		Trinidad	-		

Key:

++ Privatization program solidly in place with visible results.

\+ Announced government policy or program to privatize major portions of state sector, but tangible results not yet visible.

0 No observable trend toward either private or public ownership.

\- Net decrease in private-sector role over past few years; net increase in government ownership.

Notes

1. *New York Times* (17 July 1983).

2. *Wall Street Journal* (17 February 1984).

3. See, for example, Yair Aharoni, *Markets, Planning and Development*; Renato Mazzolini, "Government Controlled Enterprises: What's the Difference?" *Columbia Journal of World Business* (Summer 1980), pp. 28-39; Raymond Vernon, "The International Aspects of State-Owned Enterprises," *Journal of International Business Studies* (Winter 1979), pp. 7-14.

4. World Bank, *World Development Report, 1983* (New York: Oxford University Press, 1983).

5. The term "privatization" is used to refer collectively to all of the various means of decreasing state control of business enterprise: full or partial divestment; leasing to private operators; the use of management contracts with private managers; and so forth.

6. Mary M. Shirley, *Managing State-Owned Enterprises*, World Bank Staff Working Paper no. 577 (1983), p. 59.

7. *Fortune* (31 October 1983).

8. *Wall Street Journal* (13 December 1983).

9. Ibid.

10. Many of these remedies are discussed in *World Development Report, 1983*.

11. See Yair Aharoni, "Performance Evaluation of State-Owned Enterprises: A Process Perspective," *Management Science* 27, no. 11 (November 1981): 1340-1347, for a lucid discussion of performance measurement in SOEs.

12. *Wall Street Journal* (17 November 1983).

Other sources:

Kempe R. Hope, "Improving Public Enterprise Management in Developing Countries," *Journal of General Management* 743 (Spring 1982): 72-85.

Leroy P. Jones and Edward S. Mason. "Role of Economic Factors in Determining the Size and Structure of the Public Enterprise Sector in Less-Developed Countries with Mixed Economies," in *Public Enterprise in Less-Developed Countries*, ed. Leroy P. Jones, pp. 17-47 (Cambridge: At the University Press, 1982).

Chapter 3

Privatization: Ideology and Praxis

Horacio Boneo

Introduction

"Something is rotten in the state of Denmark" are the words of Marcellus in Hamlet (1:4). "And surely it has to do with its excessive size" would probably have been Horatio's answer if the scene were set today. There is an increasing sense of malaise with regard to the growing size of public bureaucracies, a malaise that is not limited to neoconservative regimes suddenly in charge of mixed economies with large public sectors. Even countries avowedly on the road to socialism are attempting solutions that assign an increasing role to the private sector. One of the focal points of the controversy appears to be related to the seemingly unstoppable growth of the state's involvement in the production of private goods through public enterprises.[1]

That public enterprises are increasingly becoming problematic is something beyond discussion in many developing countries. They are operating in areas entirely unrelated to any logical conception of public policy; they are confronting large losses; there are blatant examples of inefficiency; and the list goes on. Some criticisms are just part of the rhetorics of opposition, but quite a few are real enough to constitute a source of preoccupation for governments.

The solutions to these problems depend very much on the kind of diagnosis that is made of the basic causes of the present situation. One line of argument maintains that in the last fifty years we have had, under different guises, all sorts of "creeping socialism."[2] The real option is a complete overhaul of the system with a hegemonic new ideology based on free markets leading the way and reversing the trends. If a "statist" ideology has resulted in the incorporation into the public sector of a large number of enterprises, a new "free market" ideology will result in privatizations and divestiture, if there is a strong enough will behind the specific efforts.

Obstacles to privatization found in past attempts are fabled. If an enterprise is offered for sale through a public bid and the government does not receive offers, this means simply that the enterprise's price is zero or negative, but governments have not had the political courage to give away the enterprises or even subsidize their purchase. This position seems to be a sort of application to today's situation of the economic theory of natural liberty. Conservatives are happy to quote Adam Smith's famous dictum, "The sovereign . . . seldom maintains any but unproductive laborers, at the expense of the capital of the people, which maintains none but productive,"[3] or Say's Golden Maxim that the very best of all plans of government finance is to spend very little. Still, the essence of the ideological arguments is related to the freedom to choose and to the market as an essential part of a system of natural liberty. But in developing countries the freedom of choice seems to have rather small ideological appeal to people below the poverty line, and the functioning of markets has raised far too many empirical doubts.

The argument in this chapter runs along different lines. I argue that most of the growth of the public-enterprise sector is a consequence of structural characteristics as well as of short-run problems of the developing societies, and that quite frequently state intervention is not the product of "statist ideologies" but rather is an instrument of last resort. I further argue that the same--or similar--problems leading to the growth of the public-enterprise sector make it difficult to "shrink" it through the massive sale of public enterprises. There are, nevertheless, alternative solutions that are possible if we accept the idea that "privatization" refers not only to ownership, but also to the way in which the production units are managed and relate to central government. This, of course, does not imply that the sale of public enterprises is to be avoided; rather, my argument is that such sales have a small place in a viable policy of "privatization."

The next section deals with the argument that the public-enterprise sector is the consequence of "creeping socialism" by briefly reviewing the ways in which that sector has come into being. I shall then discuss other arguments that have been advanced in relation to the sale of private enterprises and the validity of those arguments in the Latin American context. The fourth section is centered on the kind of obstacles that are usually confronted in the sale attempts. I then turn my attention to some privatization alternatives and conclude with a discussion of some necessary changes in society that might be required to reverse the present and <u>continuing</u> trend.

The Changing Patterns of Public-Enterprise Growth

It would be quite difficult to understand the problems that we face today in relation both to the operation of public enterprises and to the attempts to transfer some of them to the private sector without a brief reference to the ways in which the public-enterprise sector has evolved. Although this brief (and incomplete) review will be made with reference to the Latin American context, some parallels can probably be found with other regions.

There seem to be two clearly differentiated patterns of growth. In some countries we can find spectacular growth in a very short period following a revolutionary change and usually--but not always--related to ideology. The outstanding case is of course Cuba, but we can also mention the Dominican Republic after the fall of Trujillo and Nicaragua after Somoza, where the properties of the dictators and their cliques were expropriated. Chile under Allende, Peru under Velasco, Jamaica under Manley, and Guyana throughout the independence period are also cases of extremely rapid growth of the public-enterprise sector.

The reasons for the expansion are quite easy to detect, but it should be emphasized that in almost all cases the expansion outran the original intentions of the revolutionary regimes. Chile is a good example of this phenomenon. The Unidad Popular government intended to nationalize only a limited--though large--number of enterprises in a few, well-defined fields. Its program intended to nationalize only 91 enterprises, but the actual number of enterprises that fell into the government's hands was much larger: firms abandoned by owners, bankrupt firms, plants occupied by workers, increased that number more than threefold. By June 1972, 264 enterprises were taken over but only 36 of these were included on the original list.[4]

The problems introduced by these cases of rapid growth are clear: expansion outruns the management capabilities of the government, a phenomenon that also seems prevalent in some African situations.[5] This situation might be tolerated for a while, but sooner or later pressures for improving the situation--partly through the sale or conversion to cooperatives of some enterprises--might emerge, in spite of the ideological characteristics of the government.

Nevertheless, the other kind of public-enterprise growth is much more relevant to the argument here. In some of the large Latin American countries--Argentina, Brazil, Mexico--we find a different evolution: long-term growth at a slower but steady pace, which does not seem to be too related to the periodic changes in government ideology. I shall not attempt detailed reconstruction, but it is worthwhile to point out five causes of growth that seem to explain most of the present size and scope of the sector.

First, there is a heavy concentration of state ownership in the public-utilities sector. In most cases, these utilities were built by foreign capital in the late years of the nineteenth and the beginning of the twentieth centuries, under rather favorable terms. A very tense relationship evolved between state and foreign enterprises, which usually resulted in the interruption of new investment and even of adequate maintenance for long periods. When the utilities were finally nationalized, the state normally found obsolete and extremely undercapitalized firms.[6] This still seems to be the main source of problems in many enterprises, particularly the railways.

A second area of heavy concentration of public ownership is the financial sector. Although public banks are found in the early years of independence, the sector grew primarily as a consequence of government attempts to develop and consolidate a national industrial sector during the Second World War and its aftermath. In some cases the banks attempted to develop a more effective capital market by purchasing shares and participations in some promoted enterprises--CORFO in Chile being one of the pioneering cases. Even this kind of policy, which only attempted to develop the <u>private</u> sector and a much-needed capital market, was criticized as "statism." In Argentina the noncontrolling shareholdings in 382 enterprises that were in the hands of the National Development Bank and the National Savings Bank (Caja Nacional de Ahorro Postal) were listed as public enterprises and their sale as one of the main achievements of the Martinez de Hoz privatization policy.[7] Within the group of public banks, we find examples of very effective competitive behavior and of blatant inefficiency. Unfortunately, it is very difficult to make an overall evaluation, since the banking sector is rarely discussed in the literature on public enterprises.

A third field of concentration of public ownership is the exploitation of nonrenewable natural resources. In Argentina and Brazil it was decided from the beginning that some resources were to be developed by the state. In most of the other countries, foreign enterprises, which were nationalized throughout about the last five decades (beginning with the conflictive nationalization of the oil industry in Mexico in the late thirties to the recent peaceful purchases of oil and iron ore industries in Venezuela), were in charge of initial exploitations. The prevailing force here was nationalism, which can be found within conservative, middle-of-the-road, and socialist ideologies.[8] Here again governments usually found problems, ranging from wide fluctuations in prices in world markets to the need in some cases of advanced technologies, quite difficult to manage.

Gap-filling another cause of growth and a strong motivation in most African and Asian countries, exists to a lesser degree in Latin America, and its appearance is much more recent. The initial impetus for industrialization came from import-substitution of consumer goods produced by private industry. This early phase was soon exhausted and resulted in heavy pressures on the balance of payments. The governments attempted to overcome this pressure through the production of intermediate goods. In most cases initial efforts, which usually failed, included a role for the national private sector. Therefore inexperienced governments became involved in the production of steel, heavy chemicals, paper, and the like.[9] Their performance is certainly not heartening. Many of the new plants were located in the wrong places or with inadequate technologies, were small by international standards, and soon became obsolete. Costs overruns and construction delays were the norm. The present inefficiency of many of these enterprises is a consequence of very early mistakes; governments today would probably not repeat these errors, but they are forced to live with the consequences of past mistakes.

The last cause of growth is a relatively recent development: the increasing role of the state in the rescue of sick units.[10] This area deserves more than passing comment, for it is at the root of the problems with privatization. It is the consequence of the structural weaknesses of the private national industry so carefully nurtured by the states in the early fifties. The problem that private national industry experienced can be related to the absence of a capital market and to the general weakness of financial institutions.

In the Argentine case, which is rather typical, we find two periods in which large numbers of productive units came into government hands. During the sixties, most of the financing required by enterprises facing difficulties was provided--one way or the other--by the government. Part of it took the form of official bank loans, and the rest was arrears in the payment of taxes and social security contributions. A law (no. 17507 of 1967) was passed in an attempt to consolidate and restructure such debts. But even under very favorable conditions many enterprises were not able to fulfill the terms of the agreements and were taken over by the government. The second period, ten years later, resulted directly from reforms of the financial system. The main feature of the 1977 reform was the deregulation of interest rates (formerly fixed by the Central Bank) coupled with a 100 percent government-backed guarantee of deposits. Quite a few private banking institutions expanded rapidly on the basis of very high interest rates for deposits. After a while, some large banks went bankrupt, and the Central Bank, as warrantor of the deposits, became burdened with all sort of assets. In this way the government became the owner of small industries, weekend houses, cinemas, and the like, which are common and easy targets of criticism of the role of the state.

My first point in this long, incomplete, and slightly biased history is a suggestion that the present overexpansion and problems facing the productive activities of the state are not the consequence of some sort of "creeping socialism" whose solution is to be found in a change of ideology. As a matter of fact, a large part of this slow and constant growth of the public-enterprise sector occurred, at least in Argentina and Brazil, under rather conservative regimes. The expansion of the state seems to be much more related to both structural weaknesses of society and short-run crises, which are also at the root of the problems faced today by privatization efforts.

My second point is that many of the efficiency problems are not directly related to management inadequacies in today's public enterprises. The problems of the railways started well before their nationalization; wrong investment decisions in the past affect today's results; and the "sickness" of rescued units obviously existed prior to their incorporation into the state.

Nonideological Arguments for the Sale of Public Enterprises

Although a large part of the discussion on privatization is conducted in ideological terms, a number of arguments that run along different, nonideological lines have been advanced in relation to the sale of public enterprises. The first point usually raised is that the state is per se an extremely inefficient entrepreneur, and the allocation of resources would improve significantly if public enterprises were transferred to private hands. Such inefficiency is proved by a sort of casual empiricism involving examples that can be found in all areas of management: inadequate selection of top personnel; bad investment decisions; widespread overstaffing; low salaries for managers combined with salaries above market levels for workers.

The second argument relates to the increasing importance of the funding requirements of public enterprises within fiscal deficits. The sale of public enterprises would contribute to a reduction in fiscal deficits in two ways: first, by reducing the drain of public-enterprise deficits on the Treasury; and, second, by providing revenue from the sale.

The third refers to the burden on public management that a growing number of public enterprises introduces. On the one hand, there is an increasing need of managers for enterprises entering the state domain, since in most cases it is difficult or inconvenient to maintain the old management. On the other hand, the larger and more heterogeneous the public-enterprise sector, the greater will be the burden on top government officials, whose scarce time is occupied, one way or the other, with the problems of public enterprises. The last argument is related to the share of public enterprises in the total fiscal deficit. If, as I mentioned in the second section, some of the public enterprises are heavily undercapitalized, to place their operation on a sounder footing would require important amounts of additional capital, and this might be impossible, given the difficult situation of the government's budget. But if the enterprises were sold, the new private owners would inject the additional capital that might be necessary to convert the enterprise into a profitable operation.

The validity of these arguments depends on the context in which they are made. Let us begin with the point that public enterprises are more inefficient than private, and that their privatization would significantly improve the allocation of resources. In more technical terms we might say that in the theoretical neoclassical firm, owner and manager coincide, and the cost of the relations between a "principal" and an "agent" (unavoidable in the case of public enterprises) is eliminated. But, given the usual structure of modern private enterprise, these costs are rarely avoided even there, although they might be much smaller than in the public sector. The argument can thus be posed in a different way. If public enterprises are clearly more inefficient than the private ones in a given setting, there are two possible solutions to the problem: one, of course, is privatization; the other is an improvement both in the relations between public enterprises and central government and in the internal management of the enterprises so as to make their efficiency equivalent to that of comparable private enterprises. There is considerable empirical evidence that the last course of action is possible. On the one hand, we have throughout the world a sufficient number of examples of public enterprises whose management standards are equivalent to or even better than those found in the private sector. There are, of course, some obvious European examples, but even within Latin America a sufficient number of highly efficient public enterprises can be pointed out, for example PETROBRAS (Petroleos Brasileiros), and the CVRD (Companhia Vale do Rio Doce).

I must add that the basic assumption that private management is always better than public management seems to be a bit exaggerated. There is very little doubt that the management of a first-rate transnational is probably better than that in a typical Latin American public enterprise. But it is equally evident that the management of the T.V.A. or of Renault is probably better than that of a typical Latin American <u>private</u> enterprise. For the argument to be true, one has to look at the average management capabilities of potential buyers. And, in fact, the purchase of a public enterprise can be very good business for a local private enterpreneur, even if the allocation of resources or the productive efficiency of the firm does not improve.[11]

The second argument--the incidence of public enterprises in budget deficits--is usually quite evident, but must be qualified. First, the public-enterprises deficit might not be exclusively a result of management inefficiency, but simply of a pricing policy that is determined by the central government. For instance, during the Martinez de Hoz period in Argentina, public-enterprise prices were used as an anti-inflationary tool, and, as a consequence, average prices were reduced over 50 percent in real terms. During the same period, the physical productivity of the enterprises increased substantially.[12] Second, the deficit of public enterprises is usually concentrated in a few big losers or related to very large investments that cannot be financed out of internal savings. Table 1 gives the percentage composition of Treasury contributions to the main public enterprises in Argentina for the 1965 to 1980 period. As can be seen, Treasury contributions were concentrated in two big and permanent losers: the railways, and the Post Office. Most of the other contributions, like those corresponding to the electrical companies in the 1973 to 1977 period, correspond to the construction of large generating plants. Even if all public enterprises--with the exception of the railways and the Post Office--were sold, the Treasury burden would not change substantially. And, of course, big losers are not usually the blue chips that private entrepreneurs are willing to buy. The situation seems to be similar in some other countries. In Peru, for instance, according to a World Bank mission, "the losses largely reflect the performance of only five companies: AEROPERU, PEPESCA, PESCAPERU, Moraveco and Cementos Yura."[13]

There is another complaint that runs along similar lines: the "crowding-out" argument. Precisely in order to avoid the pressures on the Treasury, the public enterprises have been pressed in the last few years to obtain funds in the financial markets. It is argued that their requirements produced interest rates higher than those that would otherwise have prevailed, thereby displacing productive investment alternatives in the private sector. The argument that the funds released by the withdrawal of public enterprises from financial markets would go to investment alternatives made possible by the lower interest rates is certainly a little naive in a country where speculation outruns production as the main concern of wealth holders. One might argue that the funds thus released might as well go to the purchase of foreign assets (increases in liquidity and decreases in interest rates correlate quite well with the black market price of the dollar) or, eventually, to conspicuous consumption. It should be added that, if the public enterprises were privatized, they would continue requiring funds in the financial market at a similar or even higher rate than when they were in the public sector.

The third argument refers to the burden that a large and heterogeneous group of public enterprises introduces to public management, both at firm and at central government levels. This is a very valid argument, although probably more so in an African than in a Latin American context. Nevertheless, some caveats should be introduced. If there is a definite shortage of managerial skills in relation to the needs of the economy (as happened in many countries after independence or after drastic changes in government with the consequent flight of managerial personnel), the problem is common to both the public and the private sectors. If the problem is exclusively limited to the public sector, the reason is usually to be found in the remuneration and recruitment policies of that sector, and improvements in those policies will help considerably in the solution of the problem at enterprise level. In the case of the burden on central government officials who deal with public enterprises, the solution can be found in restructuring the relationships between central government and public enterprises in the direction of a greater operational autonomy for the latter. As in some of the other cases, privatization is not the only solution possible.

The last argument is entirely valid, but it remains to be seen whether the private purchasers of public enterprises are able to inject new capital after the financial requirements of the purchase itself are met. This would usually be a problem in countries with very undeveloped capital markets and in which the private purchasers have to rely on their own financial means for both the purchase and the addition of new equity.[14]

In conclusion, one might say that the standard arguments advanced in favor of privatization are only partially valid and that it is possible to find, in most cases, alternative solutions to the problems, solutions that do not require the sale of the enterprise. This does not imply that privatization is a solution to be avoided. As a matter of fact, it is probably a very good solution in a large number of cases. But before analyzing the place of privatization in the reshaping of the state, it is necessary to discuss the practical obstacles that are usually found in relation to privatization attempts.

Obstacles to and Problems of Public Enterprise Sale

It is quite obvious that privatization is a difficult task. Even under the most extreme examples of neoconservative regimes, the performance of privatizers is far from brilliant. In Argentina, during the five-year administration of Martinez de Hoz (March 1976-March 1981), with a stable economic team ideologically committed to reducing the size of the production activities of the state, with full support from the military establishment,[15] and without any meaningful opposition from organized labor or political parties, the public-enterprise sector increased its size considerably. Even if we disregard the entrants in the sector, performance in privatizing the units that were already in the public sector in March 1981 is astonishingly poor.[16] The strong Pinochet regime, in which the influence of the Chicago and Virginia schools was intense, privatized a large number of small and medium enterprises, but the largest newcomer of the Frei and Allende years--the Copper Corporation, CODELCO--remained in the public sector.[17] Even Mrs. Thatcher, whose conservative purity cannot be doubted, has a slightly disappointing record. According to David Heald and David Steel, the average yearly income from privatization was 441 million pounds during the last four years, slightly less than the cost of maintaining the garrison in the Malvinas.[18] Unless we assume that the ideological discourse is strictly pour la gallerie, there must be considerable obstacles to and problems in the process.

We might begin with strictly technical problems, of which the worst seems to be the valuation of the assets to be sold. How much is a complex, functioning public enterprise worth? In an inflationary context were the values included in the accounting statements meaningless? The present value of the future flow of earnings is rarely applicable. In the case of losing enterprises, the results will be a negative figure. In the more typical case, future earnings will depend on both the savings to be obtained through reorganization and the new capital injections, which cannot be estimated by the seller. The valuation of assets and liabilities tends to be a very difficult task in large, complex enterprises.

A few examples that go beyond the quite obvious difficulties in the valuation of physical assets can be mentioned. Let us suppose that the enterprise has long-term contracts partially fulfilled. How much is this worth? Of course, they can have a negative value if the forecasted income from the contracts is less than the cost of their fulfillment. The price of an airline (like Austral in Argentina) depends directly on whether or not the sale of assets includes the rights to certain routes. The valuation of liabilities is similarly difficult and will depend on the number and tenure of the workers whom the new owners intend to fire. Most of the enterprises for sale have huge debts with the social security system and other organizations, and the valuation of those debts depends on the negotiation of the rates of adjustment for inflation to be used, surcharges for delayed payment and the like.[19] In other words, both the seller and the potential buyers have only a very approximate idea of the real worth of any enterprise.

A second problem relates to the impact of the introduction of risk into the determination of the final sale price. The price that the potential purchaser is willing to pay will include discounts related to the risks involved in the operation. There are at least two types of risk that should be accounted for: the technical risk involved in the valuation of the net worth of the enterprise, and the political risk involved in the operation. The larger the enterprise, the greater its complexity, and the more scarce and unreliable the data on which valuations are based, the greater will be the discount factor applied by the potential buyer. With regard to the second of these risks, there will usually be groups within society that can potentially reach power and that will be very much opposed to the sale. If there are possible scenarios that include renationalization without adequate compensation or some type of aggressive measures toward the privatized enterprise, this risk will also be incorporated. Again, the larger the enterprise and the more crucial the field of its operation, the larger will be the risk factor. It should be added that normally this kind of risk will increase if the buyer is a foreign enterprise. Therefore, it can be assumed that the sale price will be much lower than the "real worth" of the enterprise and some transfer of wealth from the government to the buyer will occur.[20] Since this transfer will be made to either some already rather rich national entrepreneur or to a foreign enterprise, the opponents of the operation will have some sound arguments, and the political risk will be enhanced in a sort of vicious circle. The low sale price resulting from the introduction of risk will also affect the attitude of the government officials directly involved in the sale. Privatizing might be an overall policy enthusiastically endorsed by the government as a conceptual whole, but the specific operations will be the responsibility of individual officials, who might be accused at a later stage of "giving away" the enterprise. In many instances they will refuse a sale at a too low price, or require endorsement from the higher levels, which will experience the same misgivings with the added problem of a subordinate opinion that the sale price is below the "real worth" of the enterprise.

The third problem is related to the nonexistence or inadequacy of capital markets in developing countries. Even in a developed country, the privatization of large public enterprises is not an easy task. The sale is not new investment, that is, the creation of new production goods. It is, rather, a transfer of secondary assets, which requires an adjustment in the private sector's wealth portfolio--an exchange of cash and other assets for equity--which might be quite difficult to obtain. In the developing countries, the kind of stable financial market in which the bulk of long-term financial assets are held by contractual savings institutions, insurance companies, or pension funds simply does not exist. Even in a rather sophisticated economy like Argentina's, transactions of existing shares in the stock exchange amount to daily figures between US$1 or 2 million, and the absorption of issues of new shares is negligible. Therefore, the kind of ideal process in which the shares of large public enterprises are sold gradually to a broad base and, at a later stage, management control is transferred to the new shareholders is not feasible. In the typical case, both ownership and management have to be transferred in a single operation to individual buyers. These buyers, except in the case of very small enterprises, are either foreign enterprises or members of the very few wealthy industrial groups, which might not be interested in some enterprises at almost any price. When the situation is such that there are only a few potential buyers, the transaction might bring some important economic and social costs: first, the purchase of existing public enterprises might have a "crowding-out" effect on new investment; second, it might increase the concentration in certain industries, and monopolies--whether public or private--have never been praised for their positive effect on resource allocation; third, when the sale of public enterprises is made to financial groups--as seems to have been partly the case in Chile--there might also be unwanted inefficiencies. A large portion of the available credit of these financial groups might go to the purchased enterprises, regardless of more efficient alternatives. Furthermore, if--as happened in Argentina and Chile--there is a major financial crisis, the "privatized" enterprises in the hands of bankrupt banks will probably go back to the government.

Fourth, since most of the potential purchasers are already wealthy groups, the distribution of income will worsen.[21]

The pressures for and against privatization deserve a special comment. In almost all countries there seems to be a wide gap between the ideological debate and policy statements concerning privatization and the specific discussion and practical implementation of specific cases. During certain periods, if one limits oneself to the content analysis of policy statements or interviews with policymakers, it would not come as a surprise to find the policy administered by the Pinkerton Detective Agency. Even during so-called statist governments, the argument for maintaining enterprises in the public sector refers mostly to a few important cases in the fields of banking, public utilities, nonrenewable resources, or production for defense.

There are very few politicians who would not agree with the two following propositions, if made at the conceptual level: (1) that the state has overexpanded, and there is not a single valid reason for its production activities in a large number of fields; (2) that a large number of public enterprises should be privatized. But the situation is completely reversed at the level of implementation, with the obvious exception of the very small enterprises. In specific cases there are always groups interested in maintaining the enterprise under government control. Some of these groups are quite obvious: the present management, which, most probably will be replaced if a change of ownership occurs; workers, who usually find governments more pliable opponents in salary negotiations and in relation to tenure; suppliers, who might have found rather comfortable _modus vivendi_ with the public enterprise. In many cases, public enterprises are monopolies that do not practice discriminatory pricing, even where it is feasible and convenient. For instance, the attempts in Argentina to break the reinsurance-business monopoly in the hands of the state were strongly opposed by the small insurance companies, which were charged the same rates as large insurers. A privatization of the reinsurance business would have resulted in special rates to large operators and put out of business a large number of small firms. Furthermore, the political opposition, even if it agrees in principle with privatization, will use specific cases not as examples that a policy it supports is implemented, but as examples of bad implementation, of public enterprises whose privatization is more urgent than the ones chosen by the government, of low sale prices (the government is giving away national assets), of corruption in the operation, and the like. In other words, it seems that each specific case of privatization implies important short-run political costs to the government in charge and benefits that have all the wrong characteristics from the point of view of politicians; that is, they are direct, and therefore cannot be easily captured by the government; they exist only after an accumulation of cases have been implemented; and even the indirect effects are only felt in the long run.

There seems to be, though, a sort of threshold effect. If the number and inadequacy of public enterprises is below certain limits, the "micro" effects of interest-group opposition will tend to predominate. But if the number becomes too large and the inefficiency of the sector too widespread, the situation might reverse. The more dramatic cases are those professedly socialist countries that have nevertheless introduced policies of privatizing part of the public sector and fostering the growth of the private sector.

To these few examples I might have added a number of additional ones. In the case of the takeover of sick units, there are usually court controversies that must be solved before the first privatization steps can be undertaken. In many countries there are laws and statutes that have to be changed to make the sale of public assets feasible. But my intention was simply too show that privatization is not an easy game and that the difficulties that are found are not related to the ideological standing of the governments, but mostly to structural problems that are quite similar, in spite of country and regime differences.

Privatization Alternatives

The sale of public enterprises is not the only possible way of "privatizing" public production. There are some alternatives that, although difficult, do offer greater chances of implementation. The most obvious is what might be called the "privatization of management," in the sense of redressing the balance between "public" and "enterprise" elements, a balance that seems to be, in many cases, biased toward the first element. I shall not attempt here to discuss this problem extensively, but I should point out that the early literature (and practice) on public enterprises put excessive stress on the *use* of public enterprises as a policy tool. The more profound the changes that governments attempted to introduce in society, and the more undeveloped the economy, the stronger was the emphasis on this role as instrument. Little attention was paid to alternative tools, or to the costs in terms of managerial efficiency of these measures, thus leading to what might be called the *abuse* of public enterprise as a policy instrument. Public enterprises were used for regional development, frequently resulting in the most inadequate locations. Their prices were used as an instrument for fighting inflation or for the redistribution of income. Attempts to use public enterprises as a tool for solving employment problems resulted in overburdened cadres, and managerial positions were often filled with little regard for the specific technical requirements of the jobs.[22] We find scores of situations in which production, regulation, and policy functions are mixed in a haphazard way within an enterprise. Empirical analyses of the functioning of public enterprise systems in many countries are full of horror stories of this type. But the results of these past mistakes are now so evident that the trend is reversing:

> The storm and controversy over the relevance of public enterprises in the modern world, the gigantic battles between the proponents of *laissez-faire* and the apostles of socialism is now rather subdued. The question is no longer asked whether public enterprises are necessary or desirable. Public enterprises exist and are growing in the scope and coverage of their activities. Even the classic strongholds of *laissez-faire* societies have admitted public enterprises into the most important areas of

> national life. In the world of developing countries with their terrifying problems of poverty, malnutrition, illiteracy, disease and incredibly low standards of living, there is a burning desire to do something to rectify the burdens of history and in this task public enterprises are playing a most significant role.
>
> But even the most ardent protagonists of public enterprises, and I frankly count myself in this group, must pause to ask a fundamental question: Is it adequate merely to create public enterprises? The fact remains, and only the blind will ignore it, that the world of public enterprises is passing through a stage of grave trauma. There is a sense of malaise, a seeming lack of motivation, huge underutilised capacities, inflated inventories, bureaucratization of procedures, and looming over all, losses of colossal magnitudes. The public enterprises are in the red. . . .
>
> The time has come, I believe, for those who are responsible for policy formulation, for monitoring and supervising, and for managing public enterprises, to take a good hard look at these stark issues.[23]

After all, one of the main arguments for selling an enterprise to the private sector is the assumption that the new owners--on the basis of their profit-maximization behavior--will introduce the measures that are needed to solve these "stark issues." If sale is not feasible, the same task can be assigned to the present owners. I am not, of course, arguing that the improvement of the efficiency of public enterprises, the restructuring of their relationship with the central government, and the formation of adequate managerial cadres are easy tasks. But they are possible, and there are enough examples of good public management to prove my assertion. As a matter of fact, cases of improvement in management are easier to find than fortunate experiences of large-scale sales of public enterprises to the private sector.[24]

Another alternative to the sale of "whole" enterprises is what has been called "peripheric" privatization: the sale of parts of the enterprise while maintaining the core under public ownership. If an oil enterprise cannot be sold, it might still be possible to sell the ships that transport the product and buy transportation services on the open market. The principal merit of this alternative is that, by diminishing the size of the assets to be sold, many of the limitations that apply to large-scale sales are not operative. It might be added that if the markets in which the peripheric sale is realized are very competitive, prices in the open market might be lower than the cost to the enterprise of maintaining production under its own control.[25]

There are also some liabilities under this alternative. The peripheric sale might increase the monopolistic power of some existing private enterprise--indeed, this might have been the very reason why the public enterprise chose to undertake "peripheric" production. In other cases, the result will be a bilateral monopoly between a public enterprise and a private supplier, and it is difficult to imagine a situation with a greater potential for corruption. Last, but not least, privatization through peripheric sales might be, in many cases, antagonistic to privatization through improvement in the management, as discussed above. There is usually a very direct relation, in both public and private enterprises, between efficiency and growth. The experience in cases of adequate public management suggests that their first concern is, of course, improving the efficiency of existing operations. But as soon as progress is made there, the management will start looking for profitable alternatives for expansion. The more promising candidates will usually be opportunities for vertical or horizontal integration--the opposite of peripheric privatization.[26] The most effective examples of this type of privatization can usually be found in the sale of assets that are not related to the main production process; for instance, railways usually have large tracts of land included within the initial concessions. Further examples of unproductive assets can probably be found in almost all public enterprises.

The third alternative, which I believe promising, is privatization through partnerships, both national and multinational, with the private sector. This solution might be difficult to attain in relation to existing assets, but it is a good strategy for future expansions that, otherwise, would be entirely undertaken by the public sector. Brazil has advanced considerably along this road, although the experience is too new for a complete evaluation.

This alternative probably could not be used in all fields in which the state acts, for a number of preconditions seem to have to be fulfilled for a successful outcome. First, there must be some sort of balance in the contributions of the partners--whether they are constituted of capital funds, technology, or political legitimacy. Second, the technical and dialectical abilities that are required in the partnership negotiation must be evenly distributed between the potential partners. Third, to have a true joint venture neither partner should receive benefits from the jointly owned enterprise other than a share in the net earnings of that enterprise (or such external benefits should be made part of the initial negotiation). Such conditions are difficult to obtain, and, in many cases, this hybrid solution might be quite unstable.[27] Nevertheless, it seems to be a promising road.

In this section I have dealt with some alternative measures through which it might be possible to obtain some degree of "privatization" of existing public-enterprise sectors. This is only part of the issue. The present trends--an overall world recession, the weakness of national private sectors, the large indebtedness of some Third World countries--point toward an expanding public sector acting as an instrument of last resort in the rescue of sick units. In the last section I shall turn my attention to some changes that must be introduced at a more general level to compensate for this alarming trend.

Some Necessary Reforms at Other Levels

The issues discussed in the previous sections relate to the problems created by the overexpansion of the state in the productive field, the difficulties experienced in the attempts to sell public enterprises, and the need for alternative "privatization" measures. But there is an even worse issue, hinted at in the concluding paragraph of the last section: things can deteriorate in the future, through increased state intervention in the rescue of sick units.

From the conservative point of view, sick enterprises are not a problem, but rather a slightly sad aspect of the ecological balance of the market. After all, one of the main advantages of the market system is its disciplinary role: the fear of bankruptcy is one of the main pressures toward efficiency in an enterprise. Furthermore, we do not live in a static world. Technological improvements and changes in consumer preferences result not only in bankruptcies, but even in the disappearance of whole sectors: automobiles replaced horse carriages; verbal and visual communications outpace written ones; air transportation is rapidly substituting for alternative carriers.

Even accepting this reasoning, there are many cases in which viable enterprises become sick and their recovery appears to be good and necessary from the point of view of society's welfare.[28] Often this particular situation is caused by bad management or when otherwise healthy enterprises run into financial problems. In industrialized countries, both cases are usually solved by civil society without need for government intervention. Replacement of management, when owners and managers are different--a widespread situation in large enterprises--is a rather simple solution to the problem. A functioning long-term capital market and specialized brokers take care of most of the situations arising mainly from financial constraints.

But the conditions in developing countries are rather different; ownership and management usually coincide, and long-term capital markets are nonexistent (or governmental). The situation is worsened because bankruptcy laws are outdated, and the legal proceedings might take several years. In the end, the enterprise has physically disappeared, and the only ones to receive whatever money can be recovered are the lawyers and accountants who have been involved in the proceedings. Both facts tend to explain why governments tend to act as instruments of last resort and also why this solution might be "economically" better than bankruptcy proceedings.

It seems obvious that strong steps should be taken to solve these root problems. Adequate bankruptcy laws seem to be a necessary and not too difficult first step. The creation of a long-term capital market is a long-run task and will require--once again--strong government involvement. But, if successful, many of today's difficulties regarding the sale of public enterprises will disappear.

The second level of reform refers to government itself. One possibility has already been discussed: the "privatization" of public-enterprise management will require considerable changes in central government. But there are other reforms to be undertaken. It should be remembered that public production is an alternative to public regulation of private production and that frequently the reason for choosing the first option is the perceived weakness of the government as regulator. This must be corrected. Some of the overall changes discussed in the previous paragraph--particularly the building-up of a long-term capital market--will take a long time. In the meanwhile, governments will be called on more than once to rescue sick units. This will require developing the ability--and the institutions--needed for three crucial tasks: (a) selecting--if possible--the right cases for intervention; (b) developing the capability of healing the sick firms;[29] and (c) devising mechanisms for selling at least the medium-sized enterprise in a more effective and efficient way. In other words, an efficient public-enterprise system will also require an efficient government.

Conclusions

The purely ideological arguments regarding privatization do not help very much in the search for solutions to the kind of problems that have been discussed throughout this chapter. Problems are minimized and ignored, even if actual privatization experiences show, time after time, their importance. An ideology is nothing but a structured and interpretative system of beliefs that, to be transformed into changes, must go through the sieve of social reality. "Populist" governments are frequently accused of demagoguery when the sum of their promises exceeds available resources. The promises can be morally accepted, but the demagoguery is to be found in their lack of realism. But in this sense, there is also demagoguery in neoconservatism: it is easy to privatize in public speeches or in postulated programs; the difficult thing is to do it within the government. Realism is as necessary in the introduction of societal changes as it is in the allocation of economic resources.

The shrinking and reshaping of the state is a challenging task that goes far beyond the few issues discussed in this chapter. I have not underlined problems and obstacles with the defeatist intention of accepting the state and its public enterprises in their present, most inadequate, shape. I have done it out of the conviction that it is possible to confront such problems and devise viable strategies for change only if we find the root of the problems and if we understand the logic and resources of the actors involved.

Table 1

Treasury Contribution to Public Enterprises, 1965-1980

(Percentages)

Year	Railways	Post Office	Electrical Sector	Others	Total
1966	69.3	11.6	6.9	12.2	100.0
1968	76.5	5.9	1.6	16.0	100.0
1970	60.3	18.4	1.5	19.8	100.0
1972	52.1	20.6	3.7	23.6	100.0
1974	45.8	22.0	16.3	15.9	100.0
1976	47.7	7.0	31.7	13.9	100.3
1978	65.1	30.4	0.3	4.2	100.0
1980	65.8	28.7	-	5.5	100.0

Source: SIGEP

Notes

Horacio Boneo is senior researcher at the Centro de Estudios sobre Estado y Sociedad (CEDES) and the Consejo Nacional de Investigaciones Cientificas y Tecnicas (CONICET), Buenos Aires, Argentina. The research here reported was assisted by a grant awarded by the Joint Committee on Latin American Studies of the Social Science Research Council and the American Council of Learned Societies.

1. There is less discussion on the role of the state in the production of <u>public</u> goods, although the private production and the "marketization" of such goods have been suggested as possible ways of privatizing economies. Some significant attempts in this direction were made in the case of Chile, under the more direct influence of the Chicago and Virginia schools.

2. The main exponent of this line of thought in Argentina, Ing. Alsogaray and his Union of the Democratic Center (UCD), go as far as to suggest that the recent economic policy conducted by Martinez de Hoz (March 1976-March 1981) under the military dictatorship cannot be considered as a case of liberalism.

3. This, as usual, is a rather partial reading of Smith's work. He used the term "unproductive" simply in the sense of not useful for capital formation. In Book 5 of <u>The Wealth of Nations</u>, he suggests that the sovereign must provide for "certain public works and certain public institutions, which it can never be in the interest of any individual, or small number of individuals, to erect and maintain, because the profit would never repay the expense to any individual or small number of individuals, though it may frequently do much more than repay it to a great society."

4. Kenneth N. Nieser, "Ideology, Regime Types and Decisions in Public Enterprises: A Comparison of the Allende and Pinochet Regimes in Chile," manuscript (December 1983).

5. See the chapter by V. V. Ramanadham in this volume.

6. A large number of these foreign firms were British. Immediately after the war, some Latin American countries, like Argentina, found themselves with very large amounts of unconvertible pounds sterling, which were used for the purchase of public utilities. And in some cases the Latin American governments attempted to form mixed enterprises with the foreign owners, which did not succeed.

7. In terms of absolute numbers, these operations are quite impressive, but in terms of value, they probably represent less than one-tenth of what was paid for just one of the private enterprises nationalized during the period, the Compañia Italo-Argentina de Electricidad.

8. One factor that should be mentioned is the "richness" of certain public-sector industries arising as a consequence of sudden changes in export prices. After the oil price increases of 1973 and 1979, the oil countries found themselves in possession of large amounts of foreign exchange. It was difficult to spend these funds internally without resulting inflation. To use those funds to subsidize private investment would have introduced serious inequalities. The purchase of the foreign enterprises that were exploiting nonrenewable natural resources appeared an easy way out.

9. In some of these new fields there was no interest on the part of foreign producers.

10. Such rescues are a very typical and old source of public-sector growth in Western Europe, beginning with the banking crisis in Italy and the creation of the Instituto per la Ricostruzione Industriale (IRI) in the late twenties.

11. An obvious case is the consolidation of a monopolistic situation through the purchase of a previously competitive public enterprise.

12. If prices are not raised, the problem will remain and private enterprise will require subsidies. If the deficit can be attributed almost exclusively to political underpricing, solving the problem does not require privatization.

13. World Bank, Peru: The Management and Sale of State-owned Enterprises, Report No. 4088-PE (Washington: The World Bank, 27 August 1982).

14. The usual down payment in the case of privatization is about 10 percent of the price. Quite frequently, purchasers hope to finance subsequent payments out of earnings and depreciation allowances. Sometimes, even the money for the down payment is raised in the short-term financial markets. It is probably hopeless to expect that this kind of purchaser will make additional investments. As a matter of fact, what usually happens is that privatized enterprises fail to make the scheduled payments to the government.

15. See Andrés Fontana's chapter in this volume.

16. Jorge Schuarzer, "La expansión económica del estado subsidiario," Tesis y Ensayos CISEA (Buenos Aires, 1983).

17. It should be added that the trend has been reversed, and that the financial crises of the early eighties have resulted in a considerable increase of the state participation.

18. See their chapter in this volume.

19. These problems were solved by selling the enterprises without liabilities and without personnel. This can, however, lead to a negative price if the liabilities absorbed by the government are greater than the sale price of the assets.

20. It has been argued that the "real" price is nothing but the sale price: whatever the "market" is willing to pay. This would be true in the cases of competitive markets, full knowledge, and a normal economic situation, which usually is not the case.

21. World Bank, Peru.

22. It should be added that the trade-offs between production efficiency and social objectives that were used as a justification of the decision were quite biased. Plants in the wrong places did very little for regional development, and the cost in terms of efficiency of that little was awesome. Similarly, underpricing rarely solved inflation problems.

23. Praxy Fernandes, "Public Enterprises and the Bottom Line," in Financial Profitability and Losses in Public Enterprises of Developing Countries, ed. Zia V. Ahmed, p.43 (Ljubljana: ICPE, 1982).

24. The privatization policies of some state governments in western Canada are frequently mentioned as success stories. But they seem to be rather special cases, which cannot be replicated easily in a poor, developing country.

25. This, of course, is not always the case. There are reports of cases in which the new prices were much higher than under direct administration.

26. This is the way in which parts of the Brazilian public enterprise sector have been recently expanded.

27. See V. V. Ramanadham, ed., Joint Ventures and Public Enterprises in Developing Countries (Ljubljana: ICPE, 1980).

28. This might be sound economic reasoning, but frequently is not politically feasible. Governments do not worry about the "death" of sick units--after all, as Sir Edward Coke pointed out four centuries ago, they have no soul. But they do worry about the consequence of their death: the unemployment created, the missed production, the financial consequences. And frequently they are forced to act, even when the disappearance of the enterprise is the best outcome.

29. Nothing could be worse than the present situation in which the sick units continue in a short of vegetative life under the umbrella of the government (and the Treasury).

Part II

COUNTRY EXPERIENCES IN LATIN AMERICA AND THE CARIBBEAN

Chapter 4

Armed Forces and Neoconservative Ideology: State Shrinking in Argentina, 1976-1981

Andrés Fontana

Introduction

In this chapter I deal with two aspects of the process of privatization and redimensioning of the state carried out in Argentina during the Martinez de Hoz years.[1] The reflections I present here belong to an ongoing research project; they are, for that reason, strictly preliminary. Moreover, they constitute a group of ideas to be confronted with empirical data; they are not the result of careful empirical analysis. For that reason, most of my assertions are of the "black-and-white" type in that they lack both flexibility and satisfactory reference to concrete situations.

The first aspect of the theme I deal with relates to the location and meaning of the state-size issue within the framework of the neoconservative initiative displayed in Argentina since March 1976. The privatization plan and other public policies aimed at redimensioning the Argentine state did not arise from a sole concern with the exaggerated expansion of public expenditure and the low levels of efficiency in the public sector. They rose from a more general concern with the governability of Argentine society and as part of an attempt to redefine the terms of the process of power formation. In the following section I deal with the state-size issue in relation to the diagnosis of the Argentine crisis formulated by the neoconservative team (hereafter, NCT) headed by Minister Martinez de Hoz.[2]

The second aspect of the theme regards the relationship between the NCT and the military corporation (hereafter, MC) as members of the political regime. Most of the attempts to characterize the type of authoritarianism imposed in Argentina in 1976 have emphasized the convergence of the NCT's diagnosis of the crisis with the MC's concerns and perceptions with respect to the Argentine political reality of the mid-seventies. The symbiosis of neoconservative ideas with those belonging to the MC--the latter strongly influenced by the national-security doctrine--rapidly became a nonquestioned assumption of the analyses on the period. Thus the economic program of Martinez de Hoz--including those policies oriented to the reduction of state size and intervention--was regarded as the plan or project of the armed forces. Governmental propaganda and, particularly, Martínez de Hoz's speeches, encouraged this belief. In turn, the identification of the Martínez de Hoz project with the armed forces took for granted a high degree of political homogeneity among the military.

On the basis of those premises it would be reasonable to assume that the major obstacles to privatization and state-redimensioning policies were not political but administrative, legal, technical, and financial. Nevertheless, interviews with public officials (civil and military) of the period have suggested that the relationship between the NCT and the MC "inside the state" was rather conflictive; they also showed that the political homogeneity of the armed forces was mainly centered around the war against "terrorism and subversion" but did not embrace other political and economic matters; and finally, these interviews have indicated that such aspects of the inner dynamics of the military regime constituted one of the major obstacles to the success of neoconservative initiatives regarding the state-size issue. That is the argument I develop in the third section of the paper.

The Neoconservative Diagnosis of the Crisis and the State-Size Issue

Neoconservative Diagnosis and State Interventionism

The literature on the new military authoritarianism has emphasized the political and ideological affinity of the military and neoconservative groups. Certainly, the convergence of those political actors was a crucial factor in determining the character assumed by the military regimes established in the Southern Cone during the 1970s. The articulation of military power in conjunction with neoconservative technocrats did not merely produce the adoption of a certain economic orientation; it transcended that field and generated policies aimed at transforming the relationship between state and society, the social structure, and even the patterns of individual behavior in daily life.

Those policies were structured at the political-discourse level on the basis of a diagnosis of the crisis provided by the neoconvervative technocrats. They did not explain the crisis of the mid-seventies only on the basis of recent and current events, but from a historical perspective; the crisis was a result of the historical cycle started in the 1930s with state intervention to support industrial development. Thus it was necessary to design and carry out a group of policies that, supposedly, would bring this historical cycle to its end. This "curative treatment"--to use the authoritarian metaphor--could only be enforced with the political support of the armed forces. Acting as a corporation with its own interests and hierarchical structure, the Argentine armed forces "occupied" the state and assumed direct responsibility in political and administrative matters.[3]

The rationale for the neoconservative diagnosis was the connection between state intervention, strengthening of labor, and of business corporative organizations and crisis. These were regarded as aspects of the same process insofar as the strengthening of corporative organizations--and the crisis itself--determined increasing state intervention. According to the neoconservative diagnosis, that process started in the 1930s but was consolidated as a historical trend only in the following decade, with the emergence of Peronism. Since then it has not been reversed, in spite of recurrent changes in the political regime and different attempts to cope with the crisis. Actually, those attempts only deepened the crisis. For the neoconservatives, the reason was that the major determinant of the crisis--namely, a relationship between state intervention and corporative power that tends to distort the "natural order of society"--had not been affected but rather revitalized by all the past administrations, including the military ones. Only a deep political operation aimed at disarticulating that disruptive relationship between state and corporative power could resolve the chronic crisis.

The diagnosis rested on a model of social organization in which individual transactions in a free market constitute the basic network of social relations. This market ideally is free from restrictions imposed by the state and from distortions produced by the power of corporative organizations. According to the model, market mechanisms are not only a warranty for the freedom of individual consumers and producers, for private initiative and for the fairness of transactions, but also the only way to achieve social efficiency in the production and allocation of goods and services. Therefore, the state ought to restrain itself and play a subsidiary role.

In contrast with that model, the mid-seventies' crisis was thought to be a result of many years of growing state intervention, uncontrollable corporative power and recurrent use of collective action as a means of defending sectorial interests. Thus the neoconservative account of the crisis went beyond the economic field to indicate its political nature. In general terms, the argument was that state intervention to promote industrialization--namely, income redistribution by political decisions, high levels of protection from foreign competition, and the participation of the state as entrepreneur--had generated an inefficient industrial bourgeoisie unable to meet international standards and an overexpanded public sector, the source of increasing fiscal deficit. Simultaneously, the state favored the strengthening of labor unions, which were usually successful in obtaining wage increases by means of political pressure. The industrial bourgeoisie was, in turn, able to compensate for the growth of labor costs by raising prices, with almost no constraints, since it was free from foreign competition. This advantageous situation too was rooted in political power.

On that basis, the neoconservative diagnosis produced a convincing explanation for the outstanding aspects of the crisis, namely, the outrageous inflation rates, the wild struggle for income distribution, the uncontrollable power of unions, the overexpansion of the public sector, and the anarchy of the state apparatus. Even subversion and terrorism were linked in the neoconservative diagnosis to the social indiscipline produced by a model of industrialization that violates the "natural laws of the economy." A working-class organized on the basis of a powerful corporative structure used to attaining the improvement of its living standards by means of collective action and state intervention; of an inefficient bourgeoisie, protected by the state and relatively weak compared to the working class; of a highly politicized society, not only because of the mobilizing capacity of its working class but also because of a long tradition of state intervention in the resolution of social conflicts. All this constituted, according to the neoconservative diagnosis, the appropriate grounds for the emergence of subversion "in all its forms."

The State-Size Issue

It was in the framework of the aforementioned interpretation of the Argentine crisis that the neoconservatives raised the state-size issue. Although the neoconservative onslaught mainly referred to the public sector's inefficiency and the inflationary consequences of the growing fiscal deficit, the attack on the state was motivated by a broader political concern.[4] In their political discourse appeared the reasons and consequences of a state that was physically overexpanded and politically weak, a state that was permeated by sectorial interests and not clearly differentiated from a highly statized society, a state that was incapable of ordering itself as much as it was unable to control society.

It is true that the solutions for the economic crisis proposed by the NCT implied repression of the working class, particularly trade union leaders. If the economic program was to be successful, their mobilizing capacity had to be neutralized steadily. The neoconservative solution for the chronic character of the crisis, however, required a deeper operation than the use of repression and the subordination of working-class interests: it was necessary to dismantle the peculiar interconnection between corporative interests and the state. Politics was not to be perceived any longer as an effective means for defending sectorial interests. In this perspective, the disarticulation of the political determinants of the crisis was a precondition for the solution of the deep problems of the economy.

For the neoconservatives the physical expansion of the state was the institutional expression of a power relationship between the state and sectorial interests.[5] That relationship was a threat to order and the possibility of ruling society. From that perspective, the solution of the Argentine crisis called for the dismantling of a bureaucratic structure that had encouraged--and, in turn, was the result of--the formation of a parasitical bourgeoisie and the rise of collective demands in the political arena. Only a small state could discourage expectations and punish inefficiency. Consequently, the first role the NCT established for the state was to discipline and order itself. Second, insofar as the crisis was perceived as the crisis of the welfare state and the crisis of "artificial development," the state was supposed to dismantle or get rid of all those organizations--both productive and administrative--inherited from the long tradition of interventionism.

It was on that basis that the idea of a small, governable state came about. In addition, the small and efficient state was adequate to allow governance by a social group that would not establish political alliances with those who had benefited from populist and developmentalist policies. That group, principally linked to agroexport and finance interests, could not attain political power within the framework of Argentine democratic institutions. However, the neoconservative discourse, centered on governability concerns and the caos-order dichotomy, established a suitable connection between the interests represented by the NCT and the interests and concerns of the MC. That was the basis of the convergence of neoconservative ideas and military power. The neoconservative political discourse, however, was mainly a diagnosis of the crisis, but not a political project or a concrete proposal for structuring a new type of society. Therefore, the political alliance with the military was based on ideological affinities and political agreements with respect to the diagnosis and immediate solution of the crisis but did not presuppose a solid sharing of views with respect to how Argentine society should look, beyond the matter of social discipline and political order. In other words, although the military accepted the neoconservative diagnosis of the crisis, there was no reason to assume that it would support any proposal based on the diagnosis.

Military Corporation and Neoconservative Technocracy: Convergence and Discord

The Political Alliance

The lack of a political discourse for civil society was a major factor in the armed forces' decision to ally itself with neoconservative technocrats. The political discourse of the armed forces, strongly influenced by the national security doctrine and thus centered on the fight against subversion, was only appropriate for the internal solidarity of the military.[6] However, the alliance with neoconservative technocrats provided the armed forces with a coherent proposal for the ruling of society under a crisis situation. At the same time, the emphasis on discipline and order, at the core of the neoconservative diagnosis, entwined the national-security issues that preoccupied the military.

Joining the efforts of the armed forces to "eradicate subversion," the neoconservative proposal promised to transform the old morphology of Argentine society, which was responsible for the recurrent rise of Peronism and working-class protest after every military coup. If subversion was actually to be eradicated, said the neoconservatives, it was necessary to implement a set of policies capable of transforming the corporative structure of the working-class organization and ideology and replace them with a new framework for social identity.[7] A similar treatment was to be accorded the industrial bourgeoisie. Both objectives would be achieved by imposing the disciplining logic of market mechanisms.[8]

It was no longer a matter of reestablishing the "normal patterns" of capital accumulation, with the expectation of gaining consensus once the crisis was over, social peace was achieved, and economic growth was again at work. Recent history had proved that to be an illusion. Rather than expecting to satisfy--even in the long run--the social actors' demands, it was necessary to discipline and transform them according to a new set of social rules.

The neoconservative technocrats thus became a crucial factor in the configuration of the military regime by providing the political discourse for civil society. Martinez de Hoz rapidly became a central figure of the military government. Most of the proposed changes in the morphology of society were to be produced by means of the economic policy designed by the NCT.

The performance of the NCT, however, faced important restrictions due to certain differences between its ideology and the MC political viewpoints and interests, the present of the MC in the state, and the lack of political homogeneity among the armed forces. On the one hand, the ideological convergence was significant but only partial. On the other hand, that convergence was not the major reason for the alliance of the armed forces with neoconservative technocrats. That alliance was mainly due to the fact that the neoconservative technocrats represented the economic interests and political viewpoints of the most powerful social groups--particularly those linked to international finances and agroexport business. The ideological convergence was thus subordinate to a political alliance. Similarly, ideology was subordinate to politics in that the neoconservative dictates had often to be adapted to national-security considerations because political power remained in the MC.

The military established, simultaneously, two parallel alliances with different timing and objectives. There was an alliance among the three branches of the armed forces--as a military corporation--which was exclusive with respect to the NCT and the regime's social support. The core of this alliance was the war against subversion. This brought about the so-called brotherhood of blood among the military and minimized their political disagreements. The objectives and temporal horizon of this alliance, however, transcended the war against subversion and aimed at the continuity and strengthening of the MC's political power. The rationale of this alliance was the control of the state apparatus by the MC and the subordination of the dynamics of civil society, and of the state itself, to the decisional logic of the military.[9]

The other alliance that constituted the military regime included the neoconservative Right. The objectives of this alliance concerned the disciplining and restructuring of civil society and the recomposition of the state's finances and public bureaucracy. The military did not consider this alliance crucial in the political field, as it was subsidiary to the MC's internal pact. In addition, the military imposed implicit deadlines on the NCT, linked to the achievement of certain results regarding the economy, public finances, and even the improvement of social conditions. In consequence, although the NCT enjoyed a high level of autonomy in policymaking, it did not share political power with the military.[10]

The armed forces adopted neoconservative political discourse but did not become neoconservative itself. Although lacking a structured discourse for civil society, the military did have its own viewpoints with respect to a large number of issues--principally, with respect to the roles of the state and the social and political conditions for national security. Those viewpoints, however, were not universal among the armed forces. The Argentine military had a long tradition of internal political disagreements.[11]

The military's own views and its political heterogeneity constituted a major source of restrictions on the performance of the NCT. The latter, in turn, displayed its policies to the extent possible--always reminding the public that it was "the armed forces' program"--and tried to expand its political space within the regime to secure the viability of its initiatives as well as its own stability as an economic team.

The Military Corporation and the Neoconservative Political Project

The limitations and ambiguities of the relationship between the MC and the NCT described here diverge with the widespread belief in the identification of the armed forces with a neoconservative project. The interviews I have carried out so far have suggested that in 1976 there was nothing that could be properly called a political project. At that time, rather than assessing alternative political proposals, the military chose--from among several candidates--an individual (Martinez de Hoz) with certain personal characteristics and a set of ideas regarding the nature of the crisis.

For the military it was important to find somebody able to respond adequately to the urgency of the country's situation. The armed forces' decision to appoint Martinez de Hoz was mainly influenced by his ability to propose relatively simple solutions for the immediate problems of the economy and state finances and to make proposals in language accessible to the military. Of course, the availability of international contacts that would guarantee the normalization of the balance of payments situation as well as the MC's access to generous financial resources was also a major factor determining the armed forces' decision. However, the capacity for providing such contacts was not exclusive to Martinez de Hoz.

In addition, the group that joined Martinez de Hoz in 1976 did not have an elaborate governmental plan. They belonged to Argentina's conservative Right, either because of social background or ideological affinity, but they were not what could be regarded as a group of "ideologists" belonging to that sociopolitical sector. What they had produced through the years, however, was an interpretation of the political and economic dynamics of the country, from which they were able to infer a set of "solutions" for the crisis.

Those solutions implied important changes with regard to the roles of the state and the political weight of labor and business corporative organizations. They also implied the subordination of economic-growth objectives to the achievement of social discipline and political order. Such solutions, however, did not embrace important aspects of social structure. They lacked, for example, a proposal for the relationship between capital and labor, or for the reorganization of the social security system.[12] It was much more a plan for what they meant to "eliminate" than for what they proposed to establish. That was made evident by the large number of "provisional" decisions that remained provisional.

Further evidence of the rather pragmatic approach of the NCT was its behavior with respect to the bourgeoisis. After the rapid subordination of working-class interests, the NCT observed that the major obstacle to the success of its economic program--which was aimed at controlling inflation--was the unresponsiveness of the entrepreneurs. The economic program presented in April 1976 by Martinez de Hoz was not monetarist; it was severe and meant to introduce discipline into the economy, with the collaboration of the business community. Only when it became clear that the bourgeoisie was unwilling to adapt itself to the program's patterns did the NCT start to resort to monetarist formulae.[13]

It was throughout this process of increasing hardening of the NCT's attitude toward the bourgeoisie that a neoconservative program actually took shape. It never reached a level of elaboration and systematization comparable to Chile's, however.[14] This was due to three major factors. First, the Argentine armed forces imposed a number of restrictions that limited the autonomy of the NCT, thus hindering in advance those initiatives to introduce deeper transformations in society. Second, the presence of the MC in the state institutional system--in contrast with the unipersonal government of Pinochet--made political bargaining with the military power extremely difficult. Third, the Argentine military regime did not achieve those results during the first years in power that allowed the Chilean regime to reach a high degree of institutionalization and facilitated the design and implementation of a broad program of socioeconomic reforms in connection with the interests of a dominant social block.

Military Constraints on Neoconservative Policies

The restrictions imposed by the military on the NCT did not refer only to privatizing and state-redimensioning policies. Adolfo Canitrot, for example, points out that the Argentine armed forces vetoed any policy that meant high levels of unemployment. According to him, this attitude was not only due to national-security reasons, but was also related to the armed forces' ideology, according to which the working class is to be kept in a subordinate position, but also is to be protected by the state.[15]

Similarly, the way many military regarded the working-class corporative organizations differed from the neoconservative perspective. Some of the militiary never stopped regarding the trade union leaders as potential members of a political alliance, and also as a guarantee against the spread of Marxism within the working class. From that perspective, trade unionism continued to play a significant role in the national-security problem, which did not have any point of reference in the neoconservative proposals.

Nevertheless, it was with respect to state-shrinking policies that the major disagreements between the MC and the NCT took place. A major problem the NCT faced in that field was the suspicion of military groups of what they called an "irresponsible dismantling" of the state, and also of what they perceived as a probable denationalization of enterprises and resources that belonged to the state or were under its control.

That attitude was not necessarily linked to the availability of strategic inputs for national defense. In many cases it was based only on political suspicion and nationalist postures in front of the NCT's international connections. Such political issues as the negotiations around the privatization of INDER (National Institute for Reinsurance) or the suspension of state guarantees for banking transactions showed the power of the nationalist agrumentation of military sectors. In both cases they affirmed that the policies the NCT defended meant that reinsurance and banking activities would finally fall into foreign hands.

Although most of the conflicts between the MC and the NCT were not made public, interviews have shown that several military groups were against the neoconservative attempts to reduce the size of the state. In several cases, military public officials argued that public expenditure or efficiency reasons were too narrow a perspective from which to assess public enterprises that created employment and helped to develop frontier areas. Similarly, they asserted that the NCT could not decide that the price of a state-owned enterprise was "zero" because at a certain point in time there was no demand for it in the market.

To protect "the interests of the nation" may or may not have been the true concern of the military with regard to each particular case. Members of the NCT have argued that those military who opposed their policies were related to vested interests, which would be affected by either privatizations or the suppression of state intervention. Nevertheless, what seems important to note is that, whatever the true motivation of the military, its opposition to NCT policies was successful, as the nationalist argument as well as those arguments related to the defense of the state patrimony usually found acceptance within the MC.

The NCT had to gain the political confidence and support of the military leaders gradually to expand its political space within the regime. It made important progress in that respect but was never completely successful. The changes introduced in the economic program in 1978 and the negotiations around the continuity of the NCT in 1980 were perhaps the most significant examples in that respect.[16]

Another factor that conspired against privatizing initiatives over and over again was the interference of private interests. Detached from society, the military regime was not susceptible to the influence of aggregated demands of any social sector and elusive with respect to political suggestions even when they came from its own allies. Nothing indicated, however, that the permeability of the state with regard to individual private interests disappeared or decreased significantly. On the contrary, the subordination of legal procedures to a somewhat patrimonialist management by the state probably facilitated the proliferation of arrangements between private interest and top-level public officials (either civil or military).

In general terms, it would be difficult to establish whether civil or military public officials were more susceptible to private influence. Nevertheless, with respect to privatizing initiatives it was the military public officials who most frequently hindered those decisions or projects that would affect individual private interests. On the other hand, in those instances where the private interests were linked to a "rapid and efficient privatization," the NCT was the appropriate contact.

The Feudalization of the State

Beyond the problems caused by ideological disagreements, political restrictions, and private-interest interferences, a major obstacle to state-shrinking initiatives was the feudalization of the state. On the basis of what was called the "power scheme," the armed forces decided in 1976 to share both the political responsibility for the government and the direct control of the state. Acting as a corporation with its own interests and hierarchical structure, the armed forces occupied the state and divided its institutional, administrative, and productive apparatuses into three equal shares.

Each of the armed forces regarded the area under its control as a private patrimony to be managed at its own discretion, excluding any other power. In turn, most of the top-level public offices--namely, ministries, province and city governments, autarchical public agencies, state enterprises, and the like--were headed by military officers, either active or retired. As members of the MC, irrespective of their position as public officials, the military were responsive to the line of command that linked them to their commander in chief. All this caused a fragmentation of the state into three independent jurisdictions, the juxtaposition of a military hierarchy on the traditional civil service structure, and a centralization of the final decision-making power at the top of each of the armed forces.

The feudalization of the state constituted a major obstacle to the implementation of those initiatives aimed at privatizing or dismantling public agencies and enterprises. The military did not always oppose such initiatives. In many instances it actively participated in the state-shrinking process the NCT proposed. However, the general trend was that the military heading a public agency or enterprise to be privatized or dismantled "accepted the philosophy" but interfered with the specific decision affecting its territory in the state field. The opposition could be open or silent. Sometimes it questioned partial aspects of the privatizing proposal, for example, price-setting procedures; other times it criticized the whole initiative. In any case, whenever there was military resistance to state-shrinking initiatives, it was very difficult to neutralize its power and carry out the project.[17]

The neoconservative public officials did not have any choice but to accept the rules of the game set up by the MC. They bargained with the military at all levels and frequently resorted to their influence at the top of the armed forces' hierarchy to neutralize the resistance they faced in the lower strata. That was a losing game for the NCT,

Final Comment

The preliminary interpretation of the Argentine case presented here emphasizes the relationship between political power and state-shrinking initiatives. It argues that the lack of political and ideological affinity between the MC and the NCT was a major obstacle to the successful implementation of the state-shrinking program forwarded by the latter.

Although the presence of the military as a corporation in the state gave rise to an unusual power structure, the consequences of that power structure in relation to the success of state-shrinking initiatives is still meaningful in general terms. The relationship between political power and the implementation of those initiatives in the Argentine case was mediated by the lack of ideological affinity between the MC and the NCT. This seems to show that the success of state-shrinking projects is directly linked to the ideological commitment of those who control political power.

In that respect, the state-size issue cannot be advocated on the sole basis of efficiency reasons because it is not possible to discuss the problem of state size without referring it to the roles of the state, and therefore to a political project or model of society. Even the most technocratic governments--as are the military ones--do not have "efficiency" as a basic motivation. They always have a certain notion of what type of society should be developed. Insofar as the state-size issue is not related to that problem, it cannot achieve the ideological and political weight needed for a successful display of state-shrinking initiatives.

Notes

1. José A. Martínez de Hoz was minister of economics of the military regime between March 1976 and March 1981.

2. Most of the literature on the Martínez de Hoz period refers to his political orientation or ideology as "liberal" or "neo-liberal." The literature, however, takes into account principally his sympathy for market ideology and preference for monetarist solutions for economic problems. I have chosen the term "neoconservative" to emphasize the political aspects of his proposal. Those political aspects stress the need for social discipline and refer the economic crisis to the process of power formation--more specifically to the relationship between labor and business corporative organizations and the state (see Norbert Lechner, "El proyecto neoconservador y la democracia," Flacso working papers, Santiago de Chile, March 1981).

3. In March 1976 the Argentine military adopted a threefold institutional design to commit the military corporation as a whole to the governmental process and, by that means, to ensure its political support of the regime. Thus the three branches of the armed forces participated equally in the political responsibility for the government and the direct control of the state administrative and productive apparatus.

4. See John K. Galbraith, "The Conservative Onslaught," *New York Review of Books* (22 January 1981), pp. 30-36.

5. See Emilio de Ipola and Liliana De Riz, "Un juego de cartas políticas: Intelectuales y discurso político en la Argentina actual," in *América Latina: Ideología y cultura*, ed. Francisco Rojas Aravena, San José, Costa Rica: Ediciones Flacso, 1982; Manuel Antonio Garreton, "Evolución política y problemas de la transición a la democracia en el régimen militar chileno," Flacso working paper no. 148, Santiago de Chile, June 1982; and Norbert Lechner, "El proyecto neoconservador."

6. See Manuel A. Garreton, "De la seguridad nacional a la nueva institucionalidad. Notas sobre la trayectoria ideológica del nuevo estado autoritario," *Revista Mejicana de Sociología* 40, no. 4 (1978): 1259-1282.

7. See Oscar Landi, "Crisis y lenguajes políticos," *Estudios Cedes* 4, no. 4 (1982).

8. Adolfo Canitrot, "La disciplina como objetivo de la política economica. Un ensayo sobre el programa económico del gobierno argentino desde 1976," *Estudios Cedes* 2, no. 6 (1979).

9. Oscar Landi, "Conjeturas políticas sobre la Argentina post-Malvinas" (Paper presented at the World Congress of the International Political Science Association. Rio de Janeiro, 1982); and Andrés Fontana, "Fuerzas armadas, partidos políticos y transición a la democracia en Argentina" (in press).

10. Jorge Schwarzer, "Martínez de Hoz: la lógica política de la política económica," Ensayos y Tesis Cisea, no. 4 (March 1983).

11. A good account of this can be found in Robert A. Potash, El ejército y la política en la Argentina, 11th ed. (Buenos Aires: Editorial Sudamericana, 1982); and Alain Rouquie, Poder militar y sociedad política en la Argentina (Buenos Aires: Emece, 1983).

12. See, for example, the reform carried out in Chile: Jose Pablo Arellano, "Elementos para un analisis de la reforma provisional," Notas Tecnicas Cieplan, no. 34 (1981).

13. Adolfo Canitrot, "Orden social y monetarismo," Estudios Cedes 4, no. 7 (1983).

14. Alejandro Foxley, "Experimentos neoliberales en América Latina," Estudios Cieplan 7 (March 1982); Tomas Moulian and Pilar Vergara, "Estado, ideología y políticas económicas en Chile: 1973-1978," Estudios Cieplan 3 (June 1980); and Pilar Vergara, "Las transformaciones de las funciones económicas del estado en Chile bajo el régimen militar," Estudios Cieplan 5 (July 1981).

15. Adolfo Canitrot, "Teoría y práctica del liberalismo. Política antiinflacionaria y apertura económica en la Argentina, 1976-1981," Estudios Cedes 3, no. 10 (1980).

16. In 1978 Martínez de Hoz had to give up on an anti-inflationary program because of military pressures. In general terms the argument against the program was based on a concern with high levels of unemployment. In 1980 the MC decided that the NCT would be replaced in March 1981, at the end of Videla's administration. The basis of the attacks on Martínez de Hoz was that his economic program had deindustrialized the country.

17. In the field research I am carrying out I classify the cases of privatization into four groups: 1) Those that are not susceptible to privatization because of technical or financial reasons, irrespective of the potential support or disagreement of the armed forces. 2) Those that do not conflict with military interests and do not present technical or financial problems with being privatized. 3) Those that conflict with certain military interests but about which there is not complete agreement with regard to privatization among the military. 4) Those that conflict with military interests and that the three branches of the armed forces consider unfit for privatization.

Chapter 5

State Enterprise and Modes of Privatization: A Critical View Based on Brazilian Examples

Sérgio Henrique Abranches

Introduction

The problems most capitalist countries faced in the 1970s have produced a generalized distrust of postwar economic-policy models, all of them based in varing degrees on state intervention in the market. The most radical critiques--on the liberal side--have associated state intervention with oppression and located in the free operation of market forces the necessary condition for freedom. But the complex web of social and economic interests makes the objective utilization of concepts such as freedom, oppression, costs, and benefits very difficult if not altogether impossible. These are not unambiguous concepts to be straightforwardly applied according to some general, objective laws everybody would agree on. Societies are historical entities that follow specific patterns of development. The nature and scope of state intervention will vary substantially with the political definition of the ways through which social needs are going to be provided for. Social or collective needs are not simply an aggregate of individual needs or preferences, but politically, socially, and culturally articulated demands that may have a different rationality and obey rules of calculation different from those each individual would apply to determine his or her own costs and benefits. Answers to what state intervention means in terms of social costs and benefits and what should be its limits are political, and therefore variable. There may be some general principles that would bear on all general solutions, but any specific solution must be qualified by the specificities of each socioeconomic situation.

In Latin America the relationship between state intervention and political freedom has been neither linear nor invariant. In Chile and for some time in Argentina, liberal policies were implemented under very repressive political regimes. In Brazil liberal policies were very illiberally implemented by the first military government in a context of increasing political authoritarianism. Afterwards, more interventionist policies were implemented under an already very repressive political order. Recently there have been some attempts at economic liberalization in a context of political transition.

The fact that both "interventionist" and "liberal" economic policies have been associated with authoritarian rule show at the very least that there is no necessary relation between either laissez faire and political freedom or state intervention and political oppression. Both may coexist with authoritarian and democratic regimes. It may be hypothesized, though, on the basis of the postwar record, that the most perverse forms of these two economic orientations with the greater social costs are more likely to emerge under authoritarian rule.

The controversial and ideological nature of the issues involved call for a clarification of the concepts and points of view, which may then become the guideline for analysis.

Privatization and Bureaucratization: A Conceptual Scheme

The unprecedented growth and extension of the economic functions and power of the state have been accompanied by the increasing politicization of social and economic activities that became subjected to several forms of public scrutiny and political control. These mechanisms of public control have proved themselves to be flawed and incomplete, though necessary. Several activities that were thought to be essentially private have acquired such proportions and collective implications that they had to be submitted to some mode of regulation or control. Regulation and control have been historically associated to state intervention, but this is a contingent, not a necessary, association. There are suitable forms of selfregulation and public, political control of social and economic activities other than state/bureaucratic intervention.

The social and political rights of citizenship have also been very much enlarged in these decades in most liberal-democratic societies. But the actual fulfillment of these rights became increasingly dependent on the decisive mediation of public and private organizations of all sorts: unions, political parties, government agencies, private corporations. Organizational mediation also means regulation: the means and ways of fulfilling citizens' rights are determined by these organizations. Organizational mediation became the main, if not the sole, means for the translation of individual and collective claims over rights and needs into the actual provision of goods and services. It should be stressed that this increasing organizational density has taken place in both the private and public spheres. Mediation is jointly performed by private and public organizations. Markets are controlled through organizational means and the crucial linkages between collective demands; market controllers and state agents are made possible through several organizational interactions.

The relationships between the extension of the sphere of political control over social and economic affairs, the enlarged scope of organization, and the growth of state intervention are historical and contingent, not necessary or structural. They developed together in the twentieth century in many places, but they are quite different and relatively autonomous processes. Under authoritarian statism, for instance, the power and functions of the state are greatly expanded, organizational density increases in both the private and public spheres, but political control through citizen participation is severely curtailed. Moreover, the state comes to monopolistically control the critical axes of organizational mediation.

Processes that have been contingently associated in specific circumstances should be analytically separated. State intervention, for instance, is not the same thing as collective/public control. Quite the contrary: to be legitimate and democratic, state action has to be subjected to adequate public scrutiny. The sphere of public control, that is, the polis, cannot be mistakenly reduced to the sphere of government, nor should the state bureaucracy be seen as the only--or even the proper--instrument for public control of economic and social relationships.

Public control requires publicity and unrestricted citizenship, and therefore the democratization of the whole organizational network for the fulfillment of the collective needs of society as well as of citizens' social, economic, and political rights. The organization network includes private organizations, market arrangements, and any action that may have relevant collective outcomes.[1] Its democratization is an ongoing process, rather than a final state to be reached after some defined goals have been achieved.

On more than one occasion, state intervention has been impervious to public scrutiny. This is precisely the case with regard to authoritarian statism. However, in any situation characterized by the absence of political control, the state's actions have often lost sight of the original goals they were devised to achieve or the social needs they were to provide for. The failure of existing political arrangements to create the appropriate conditions for public control have largely contributed to the deformation of legitimate state actions of regulation or provision of goods and services. There are several empirical examples of state intervention--either through regulation or production--that proved quite necessary or unavoidable in the political, social, and economic circumstances at the time. The creation and development of Italy's IRI (Institute for Industrial Reconstruction), Brazil's oil monopoly (Petrobras) and its mining corporation, the CVRD, and some of the British nationalizations seem to fit this category. There are also many situations in which the market would not be able to provide for a given need or achieve a specific collective goal. State enterprises are, then, legitimately created to fill strategic gaps in the industrial structure private enterprise can or should not occupy.

Direct productive activities of the state have also resulted from the political determination to prevent the denationalization of a strategic economic sector or as an alternative to heavy imports; both possibilities represent an undesirable dependency on foreign factors that might become a critical hindrance in a country's development path. In these cases state control of production comes as a choice of agent, but the economic activity itself may be performed within the market, even if under suboptimal conditions.

There are, however, situations in which state control occurs because the conditions of production would not allow the activity to remain within the rules set by the market. In such cases state production becomes a means of maintaining the provision of goods and services at prices that would not allow an enterprise to remain in the market. This may happen either as support for viable profitable private production of other goods or services or to ensure the provision of necessary goods and services the market is permanently or temporarily unable to provide through private production. There may even be cases in which the state is called on to produce goods and services as use values rather than exchange values, that is, as social utilities rather than marketable goods. As some Marxist authors note, to maintain market conditions in general, the state may be forced to paralyze the operation of the market sectorially. In other words, the state would establish production under a decommodified form to ensure the maintenance of the commodity form as the general, dominant form of production.

Regulation may also be used to decommodify or recommodify production according to the needs of the economy and society. Recommodification is a very common process, which takes place when economic sectors or enterprises that were decommodified as a result of adverse market conditions, technical obsolescence, "savage competition," or any other factor, may either be the object of specific regulations or provisionally statized to make commodity production viable again. Put differently, there are occasions in which state intervention becomes ngcessary to restore the rule of the market because a portion of either labor power or capital has been thrown out of the market (the commodity form). In this sense the state creates the conditions that will allow the market to prevail.

Such state intervention may also take the form of provision of goods and services that although directed to fulfill popular demands, also contribute to the improvement of the general conditions for the operation of private enterprise in the market. Free public education is a case in point, as it provides the means for both labor and capital to enter into productive relations under normal market rules.[2]

Decommodification or production outside the market can also be a part of social policy itself, providing use values to the people independently from the market or the accumulation process. House construction by tenants with materials given by the state is an example.

In any case, state intervention will be the result of political choices made under specified rules of decision that may be more or less democratic. Likewise, actual outcomes may be either negative or positive, to the few or to the many, depending on how and why a specific intervention was implemented.

Direct productive activities of the state--both within and outside the market--represent the control of means of production by the state apparatus. Control may be the result of explicit choices concerning the mode through which the economy or sectors of the economy are going to be developed, by whom, at what pace and level of risk. These are critical decisions that help to shape a country's pattern of development. Usually, the economic space of private enterprise is clearly secured and the limits of state action delimited. But state control can also be an unexpected--and sometimes undesirable--outcome of either state or private action or of both.

Rescue operations to save private undertakings from total bankruptcy are a common source of unintended or undesired "statization" of productive assets. The takeover of productive or commercial assets of defaulted enterprises by state-run banks is another way the state comes to the control of economic undertakings.

The difference between the assumption of state control of production due to planned development-policy decisions and the fortuitous "statization" of private concerns may be crucial at times, especially when one is to evaluate the scope of privatization measures. The implications and political, social, and economic meaning of the privatization of a state oil monopoly are of a totally different nature from those associated with the privatization of a bankrupted paper mill than ended up controlled by a government development bank.

In this sense there are at least four different and relevant kinds of privatization:

(1) Privatization of capital control--the transfer of productive capacity from state to private control, which may be accomplished through a regular commercial operation, as when a state enterprise is sold to private parties, through a subsidized transfer, or through a unilateral transfer. Joint ventures between state and private enterprises may also lead to at least a partial privatization of control. The expansion of private participation in a sector previously monopolistically controlled by the state would also lead to partial or relative privatization of control. Control here would refer to the sector as a whole rather than to a particular enterprise. The enterprises under state control would remain so, but private capital would take care of expansion of productive capacity through new enterprises.

(2) Privatization of the provision of goods and services that are a mandatory state responsibility due to their social nature. An example would be the provision of health care by private hospitals paid with public funds.[3]

(3) Privatization of the logic of operation of state enterprises, that is, the management of state-controlled productive units according to the rules of the market. Entrepreneurial decisions would become totally or largely independent of extramarket considerations such as social welfare, "the public interest," and social costs. Likewise, there could be a "publicization" of private undertakings, as opposed to "statization," when they are forced, through regulation or other form of pressure, to follow extramarket rules of operation, even if "publicization" would require some form of state assistance, but not control.

(4) The privatization of the outcomes of state intervention, that is, a particular group's privileged appropriation of outcomes of state action. This leads to the biased distribution of public resources in favor of a particular segment, to the detriment of more broadly beneficial applications. It usually entails the transformation of rights into privileges and legitimate benefits into clientelistic

favors. There are forms of subsidy and provision of external economies and social benefits that might fall into this category, depending on price policies and patterns of product or resource allocation.

As far as policies aimed at establishing the limits of state action are concerned, these differences are critical. They would determine in some cases the "publicization" rather than the privatization of certain activities, whereas in others they would lead to a sharp reduction of state intervention. For the purposes of this paper, however, I shall be concerned basically with privatization of control.

Privatization policies have been devised for several reasons, some quite legitimate, others not always so. Demands for selective privatization or selective deregulation on behalf of a specific social sector may be opposed for very sound political and social reasons. This applies mainly to entrepreneurial demands for deregulation and fiscal relief while supporting the maintenance of regulation in the field of labor relations. In Brazil, for instance, several entrepreneurial sectors joined a noisy campaign against "statization" of the economy, but did not support the unions' demands for relaxation of governmental control over their activities and the elimination of repressive strike legislation.

Another common illegitimate justification for privatization is based on an a priori definition of state enterprises as necessarily inefficient. This is a very controversial question. There is empirical evidence to support both sides. On the one hand there are state enterprises that have an economic record that would pass any efficiency test based on market criteria. On the other hand, there are state enterprises that would never be able to reach efficiency levels based on market criteria, especially the criterion of profitability. But if one uses criteria more appropriate to the public sector, criteria that give more weight to other components of performance, these enterprises would not be negatively evaluated. Moreover, under certain conditions economic efficiency in some sectors may not be attainable at all, although the maintenance of the activity is considered socially necessary. It is, therefore, totally justifiable for social and economic reasons that they remain under state control as a condition for their viability.

These are political questions that cannot be answered on a priori basis; they deserve careful consideration and are not amenable to exclusively technical solutions. Moreover, they should not be a matter of dogma and orthodoxy.

There are more solid grounds for privatization policies, among them the devolution of control over activities that can be easily left to private enterprises, especially when these operations mean an increase of spending that might either be eliminated to reduce public deficits or be allocated to other activities of greater overall utility. Privatization may also be a necessary measure from the point of view of the rationality of capitalist production itself.

Obviously, it could still be criticized by those who oppose the entirely different grounds.

Another justification for explicit privatization or reduction of state intervention may be the necessarily temporary and exceptional character "rescue operations" ought to assume. In many cases, there is no justification whatsoever for the state to permanently control enterprises that were absorbed for very fortuitous reasons. In terms of public interest there would be better ways to spend the money. For the private sector there are strong reasons why rescue by the state should be considered a last resort and its temporariness mandatory. It may become either an unacceptable privilege or a case of state encroachment into traditionally private controlled markets. In any event, this kind of intervention is contradictory to market or capitalist rationality first, because it might entail an undesirable protection against the selective mechanisms that are supposed to operate under the capitalist principle of competition; second, because it would represent an unnecessary reduction of the prevalence of the commodity principle and a real instance of "statization" of a segment of the productive structure.

If the commodity principle is to be the dominant one, the division of the market between the state and the private sector will never be totally stable. There are several instances in which state control could revert to the private sector once they have reached a point at which the commodity principle is perfectly viable, unless there are stronger reasons to maintain state control, such as the decision to prevent denationalization or to maintain price, wage, or employment policies outside market-determined criteria. Circumstantial increases in the number of enterprises controlled by the state for several reasons, some of them mentioned here, may reach a point at which the financial, political, and managerial costs become unbearable not only for their inflationary effects, but also for their pressures on the budget and personnel requirements, not to mention the extreme possibility of unmanageability of the state apparatus due to its size and complexity. In these cases, selective privatization and "destatization," together with measures aimed at reducing the size of the state, may become socially necessary. As there are legitimate reasons for state control, there are legitimate grounds for privatization. When privatization is advisable, but there is no interest on the part of private parties and state control is not socially justifiable, the rational choice would be liquidation. Again, the criterion for decision is political. The greater the publicity of the decision-making process, the more likely that the collective interest will be preserved.

It should be stressed that the adequacy of particular policy instruments and general forms of intervention will vary not only with variations in space or time in the economic structure but also with changes in the balance of political forces. Political representation--as a means of political control--also has distinct effects on the efficacy of intervention.[4]

Sometimes state control is mistaken for bureaucratization, especially when one is stressing inefficiency and deviation from market standards. This is clearly a misconception of both. The notion of bureaucratization may designate different processes, in the same way privatization and statization do.

Bureaucratization may be a result of greater organizational density, an outgrowth of organization. The latter requires adherence to some formal procedures, institutionalized routines, hierarchy, cadres, rules of action. These will constitute the bureaucratic face of organizational intermediation that might or might not lead to bureaucratic encroachment on citizens' rights.

Bureaucratization is sometimes used to name technobureaucratic control over the decision-making process.[5] Major decisions are made through this form of "closed politics," beyond the reach of the mechanisms of political and public control. State technobureaucratic agents, usually associated with specific social groups, assume the monopolistic or oligopolistic control of policy formation, and constitute bureaucratic power jurisdictions. The proliferation of such jurisdictions leads to the fragmentation of the state apparatus in a context of power centralization. The contradiction is only apparent, for the result is the constitution of a few strong power centers within the state, a complex network of intra- and interbureaucratic alliances that encapsulate the policy process and shield it from popular control. Those admitted into these jurisdictions gain control over critical resources and enjoy a wide spectrum of privileges and benefits.

There are costs associated with this form of bureaucratization, even for those private circles that belong to a state bureaucratic jurisdiction. First, centralization of the decision-making process together with its closed nature give sovereign power to the state technobureaucracy. Private partners in this "corridors-of-power game" face the risk of sudden shifts in policy orientation as the interbureaucratic correlation of forces changes. Issue-oriented changes in the relative power distribution among jurisdictions are very likely, even if the broader state power structure and the core hierarchy of jurisdictions remain unchanged.

Second, the advantages a particular group or cluster of interests may obtain, as a part of a state bureaucratic jurisdiction may not be transferable to individuals: therefore, what have been collective benefits and privileges may become heavy individual costs for a particular entrepreneur seeking to obtain state resources for his own business. The contradiction between the collective interests of an economic sector and the particular interests of any single entrepreneur may turn what seemed a profitable arrangement into a dreadful political trap. In other words, the distance between sectorial class interests and particular entrepreneurial interests may progressively undermine the basis for the formation of collective identities in the private sector and their support for authoritarian bureaucratic arrangements that might in principle be favorable to them. The lack of circulation of information among competing state bureaucratic jurisdictions often leads to erratic and contradictory decisions on the same policy issue.[6] There are also social costs associated with the exclusiveness and narrowness of the interest served by this bureaucratization of the policy process. Circumstantially, state bureaucratic jurisdictions would make decisions on behalf of broader social interests excluded from their network. Even then, however, they are likely to have some highly undesirable externalities. The most perverse form of this type of bureaucratization is to be found in authoritarian regimes, where this mode of managing the state apparatus and control of the policy process becomes dominant. But to a lesser degree it happens quite often everywhere and should be the object of explicit corrective action to prevent the stiffening of the democratic process.

A third meaning of bureaucratization refers to the excessive growth of governmental bureaucracy. Excess size turns the state into a ponderous structure that tends to decrease efficiency and manageability and rising costs. Costs become far greater than benefits and the structure begins to expend more on its own maintenance than on the achievement of its goals.

Finally, bureaucratization also means red tape, formalism, diffidence, and rigid hierarchy. This form of bureaucratization leads to inefficiency, rising costs, and paralysis.

As a preventive move against overbureaucratization as an outcome of greater organizational density, "debureaucratization" becomes an important element of the permanent process of democratization of the organizational structure of society. When it aims at countering the tendency toward technobureaucratic control of the decision-making process associated with the growth of state intervention and the technical requirements of planning, it is a part of the permanent process of democratization of the decision-making process. When the targets are the more perverse forms of encapsulation, "debureaucratization" becomes an element of the more encompassing processes of liberalization and democratization of the whole political order. It then aims at changing both the regime and the management of the state structure, that is, the rules that regulate politics and policy as collective actions as well as the power coalition that supports them.

Debureaucratization would also be a part of programs of administrative reform, rationalization of the state machinery, implementation of cost-effective procedures, technological modernization, and organizational change, all of them designed to correct distortions caused by the excess growth of state bureaucracies. Finally, it could also be thought of as the elimination of red tape, "bureaucratism," formalism, as the simplification of procedures and methods and improvement of the population's access to the government delivery systems. It can be very effective in reducing operational as well as social costs, as the distortions it attempts to eliminate are conducive to privilege and corruption, selective mechanisms that negatively affect the chances of the weaker segments of society to benefit from public services.

The Brazilian State Sector

Demands for privatization in Brazil are usually based on arguments about the excessive growth of the state productive apparatus. The empirical evidence to support this propostion is often biased and tends to overestimate the presence of state enterprises in the economy. On the other hand, a large part of the numerical growth of state enterprises has resulted from a misuse of legislation: many bureaucratic agencies were transformed into enterprises to enjoy budgetary, financial, and operational autonomy and to avoid the more restrictive regulation on expenditures, wages, and personnel policy imposed on the so-called agencies of direct administration, that is, the government bureaucracy. Besides the negative organizational and financial effects of this artificial creation of enterprises, the proliferation of unproductive "enterprises" has produced a gigantic, uncontrollable, and decentralized budget and made the so-called indirect administration almost unmanageable. In 1979 the government created a special secretariat in the Planning Ministry to control the expense budget of these agencies (i.e., enterprises and agencies organized as enterprises, autonomous agencies, and foundations). It now controls 485 enterprises, which had investment expenditures in 1982 on the order of three billion dollars, gross revenues of about thirty-five billion and employed 1.5 million persons.[7] However, only about half of them are real enterprises. These accounted for 87 percent of investment, 27 percent of revenues, and 41 percent of employment. Productive state enterprises have had quite a record of growth in the last twenty years, as the economy itself developed at a very accelerated pace. This was also a period of accelerated industrialization: industrial growth during the 1955-1968 period was on average 7.8 percent. Between 1968 and 1982 gross fixed-capital formation had an average rate of growth of 7.9 percent, and GNP increased an average of 7.8 percent. Gross fixed-capital formation in the state productive sector began to grow faster in the late 1960s and has in fact been one, but not the only, factor for the impressive growth of productive capacity in Brazil. Between 1965 and 1969, its participation in capital formation actually declined from 9.2 percent to 4.4 percent. In 1973 it already represented 10.5 percent of gross fixed-capital formation. This was the peak year of the expansion cycle that began in 1968, after which most sectors showed declining rates of investment. The leading sector in the period of growth, the automobile industry, for instance, had already doubled capacity.

But investments in the state productive sector continued to grow, for obvious reasons: they are highly indivisible, huge blocks of long-term investment that take several years to be completed.[8] Estimates of gross capital formation in the downturn are still provisional, but it seems that it was either negative or very low, about 1 percent on average, from 1977 to 1982. From 1977 to 1980 it was 6.43 percent, and state enterprises grew an average 29 percent. Their participation increased from 20 percent in 1977 to a high of 41.8 percent in 1979, then decreased to 35.3 percent in 1980.

During the peak years capital-accumulation rates were very high throughout the economy. As a matter of fact, all industrial enterprises--and most particularly the leading firms--presented impressive capital accumulation and investment rates.[9] In the state productive sector, rates remained high after deceleration: capital-accumulation rates jumped from .50 to 1.30 from 1977 to 1980 and investment rates from .37 to .61. The net value of production of the state productive sector rose in this period an average 12 percent and its fixed investment 38 percent.

In the favorable environment of a booming economy from 1968 to 1974, state enterprises displayed a rather marketlike behavior that could be interpreted as at least a partial privatization of their logic of operation. In this sense, there may have been occasions in which they entered into interest conflict with private businesses either because of their competition or because of a more aggressive managerial or entrepreneurial strategy. Some started to diversify and integrate their activities, thus sometimes entering into sections of the economic space previously reserved to private enterprise, or crossing the limits defined by their "statutory" goals.

But these modes of growth, which could be seen as an increase in "statization," were marginal. The growth of state enterprises took place mainly at the core of the state productive sector, that is, in oil, mining, petrochemicals, electric power, and steel production. Growth of productive capacity within these activities was really portentous. With recession, as state productive investment was maintained for a period, it is quite probable that the relative participation of the state productive sector in the industrial structure has increased, but through real capacity increases from within, rather than as a result of state takeover of new economic spaces outside the boundaries of its traditional jurisdiction.

Many state enterprises enjoyed a high level of entrepreneurial autonomy and were able to perform under conditions very similar to those of private ventures. Their price policies, market strategies, and behavior were clearly within market standards. Some were even able to raise markups and transfer some unexpected costs--mostly financial--to prices. Markups did not grow as much in the state productive sector as in the private sector, especially in the segments controlled by large foreign enterprises.[10] They did improve, though, even after downturn (18 percent from 1979 to 1980). In the petrochemical sector, markups increased about 33 percent and the CVRD's (the mining company) by 35 percent.

This growth record has created some important advantages. First it helped to prevent a steeper decline in employment and income. Second, it contributed to an amelioration of the situation of the domestic capital-goods sector, which was badly hit by the downturn. Although the entrepreneurs in the sector are among those who complain most against state enterprises, the latter represents 60 percent of their markets. Their complaints are directed toward the instability of government orders, heavy cuts in investment, and bureaucratic encapsulation of the decision-making process. But it is clear that if the state enterprises had not resisted governmental attempts to cut their investment drastically, the domestic capital-goods industry would have collapsed.

The privatization of the market strategies of the enterprises during their growth cycle does not seem to have had more social costs than benefits. On the contrary, the balance seems favorable, at least from what can be inferred from the available evidence.

The privatization of the logic of state enterprises began to show a perverse side after 1980, mainly as a result of government policy and in some cases mismanagement of the enterprises themselves. Increasing inflation, foreign indebtedness, and public deficits led the government to impose heavy expenditure cuts on all agencies, including state enterprises. Unable, however, to account adequately for the whole state budget, the economic authorities failed to devise appropriate selective criteria for the distribution of cuts. Therefore, general figures were imposed, to be negotiated step by step, case by case. This gave rise to savage competition among state agents and between them and private groups. Those with greater power resources were favored by this peculiar form of budget management. The lack of positive selectivity leads to power-based selectivity, thus producing negative distributive effects: state enterprises with fewer power resources, but either more needy of financial help or operating in a more socially sensitive sector would be bypassed in favor of the more powerful but were also more likely to suffer less from larger cuts; the state's social services would lose dear resources to the state productive sector, thereby increasing the social costs of the adjustment policy; the private sector would have to fight state and government agencies trying to get a share of funds destined for private enterprises, and so on. All this redistributive struggle takes place in a policy environment that lacks any priority criteria whatsoever and that is totally determined by the daily management of mounting problems without any long- or middle-term strategy.

The problems of the state enterprises became almost unsolvable after the government decided to use the enterprises as an instrument for the procurement of foreign currency. They were almost forced to go into foreign financial markets to get the resources they were demanding from the Treasury or to reactivate investment projects that were postponed because of the unfavorable international economic environment or because they required better technical and economic formulation. The outcome was an uncontrollable, gigantic, and inept indebtedness of little productive impact, aggravated by two relatively large devaluations of the cruzeiro. The debt is thus almost unserviceable and certainly unpayable under the present terms and the existing economic conditions. Obviously, state enterprises could count on the complicity of creditors and foreign partners in this pointless endeavor.

The pricing policies of state enterprises became extremely cost sensitive, adding fuel to inflation and increasing the social costs of the crisis. Pressed by the economic authorities on one side, skyrocketing financial costs on the other, plagued by managerial jeopardy and having to face mounting complaints from the private sector, state enterprises for the first time began to lay off workers, to impose lower wages, and to cut social and fringe benefits. They have in fact become a new source of social costs: they are getting government resources that should be allocated to the social-expenditure budget; they became a powerful partner in the pressure network for more stringent wage control; and they are now contributing to, rather working against, unemployment.

The solution to these distortions does not seem to be privatization of control, but rather a new economic policy. Problems arose from bad economic policy, rather than from direct state productive activities as such.

Brazilian Examples of Modes of Privatization of Control

The most important cases of privatization in Brazil illustrate several possible forms of reduction of direct state control over productive activities: association, either through service contracts, market sharing, or joint ventures; devolution, the transfer of productive enterprises to the private sector; and liquidation, discontinuation of operation of enterprises under state control that are not considered to provide goods or services within the scope of the social priorities and that the private sector is not able or willing to absorb. The reasons that led to privatization have varied widely. In some cases privatization has been an answer to pressing adverse "conjunctures." In others it was conceived as part of a strategy to control new markets. In still others privatization came up as a part of sectorial development programs, as an explicit policy of association between private (domestic and foreign) capital and the state. Finally, privatization has been one of the main goals of a program of "debureaucratization" and "destatization," which contemplated both transfers and liquidation, as well as the rationalization of the state productive sector, aiming at reducing its size and complexity and eliminating redundancy, overlapping, and fragmentation. All these moves have had mixed results. Some are still in progress, and previous definitions may change with changing political and economic circumstances. Some have utterly failed, and others have had no noticeable result so far.

I shall briefly discuss four examples of different modes of privatization in Brazil, their context, outcomes, and implications. The first is the government's decision to authorize service contracts between the state oil monopoly and foreign oil companies for exploration in Brazil. The second is the decision to establish a modern petrochemical industry, through a tripartite participation scheme that joined together state, multinational corporations, and domestic private groups. The third is the association between the state mining corporation--the CVRD--and a number of foreign parties in mining and industrial ventures. Finally is the "debureaucratization" and "destatization" program.

"Statization," and therefore privatization, became an important issue in Brazil at the end of the 1960s and beginning of the 1970s, especially with the first measures of political liberalization, which created the conditions for more open discussion of government policy and permitted a freer circulation of ideas and demands through the press. Active sections of the entrepreneurial class together with some of the major newspapers, liberal intellectuals, and politicians launched a noisy campaign against "statism," asking for rigid control of state growth, deregulation, debureaucratization and privatization of several state enterprises. The campaign also exposed what seemed to be unacceptable advantages and privileges granted to the managers of state enterprises (some participants even talked about the constitution of a Brazilian nomenklatura). The demands for debureaucratization of the decision-making process were clearly the most relevant as far as the private sector was concerned: they meant a return to the sector's capacity for directly influencing policy formation, through sectorial representation. Participation in the policy process, decentralization of decisions, and deregulation seem to have been the main targets of the heavy public attack on statism. As we shall see, privatization of capital control at the core of the state productive sector is very unlikely and could be politically and economically unacceptable.

Since the 1950s the traditional pattern of economic decision-making in Brazil has been characterized by the direct participation of representatives of the private sector in collegial sectorial policy and planning agencies. At the beginning, they were informal groups with great decision-making power and composed of representatives of the major state economic agencies and the private sector. They were progressivley bureaucratized after 1964, but private representation continued. In the 1970s, however, private representation was excluded from almost all policy councils and agencies, the most important exception being the National Monetary Council.[11]

Loss of participation and regulation without representation seem to have been the major components of entrepreneurial dissatisfaction. There were also those who opposed state intervention for strong ideological reasons and as a matter of principle. And there were those who joined the campaign for more immediate and pragmatic reasons, such as obtaining government assistance and favors.

The campaign had its biases. There was a clear exaggeration in the private sector's complaints of "suffocation" of free enterprise by state enterprises. As I pointed out before, state enterprises, although growing in size, weight, technological and economic capacity, have remained mostly within the boundaries of the traditionally state-controlled section of the productive structure. Domestic private capital would be unable to develop on its own and even foreign capital would not be interested in developing under the conditions and at the pace required by the country's pattern and stage of industrialization. Therefore, if acceptable, privatization would have entailed internationalization and denationalization and even then might have failed to serve the country's collective interests. Privatization at the core was opposed by the nationalist-statist military groups, the nationalist sections of the private sector, and the major oppositions groups.

"Suffocation" was an unpleasant reality as far as the political environment in general, and the policy-making process in particular, were concerned and did affect all of civil society, not only the entrepreneurial class. All social forces were suffering from the rarified atmosphere of technobureaucratic, authoritarian decision-making. And there clearly were groups that suffered much more than the entrepreneurs, because they were victimized by other components of authoritarian rule, such as police repression, censorship, severe restrictions on union activity, and socioeconomic exclusion. The controls imposed on the working class were relaxed only after 1974. Wages were kept at unnecessarily low levels during the whole boom period--to the point that several enterprises began privately and informally to negotiate wage increases higher than those authorized by the government. Several workers, union leaders, and political militants literally died of suffocation in the regime's prisons.

The fact that many entrepreneurs were eager to join the "antistatization" campaign but denied support to workers' demands for freer union activity and the end of repressive strike regulation has contributed to the weakening of the campaign's political force and legitimacy. Only after the entrepreneurial leadership realized that their demands were legitimate only within the broader scope of a movement toward democracy were the credibility and legitimacy of their claims more generally ascertained.

The genuine and true claims of the entrepreneurial sector reverberated in public opinion. Every citizen had something to complain about with regard to excessive state intervention, regulation and bureaucratization of all sorts. The political situation was more favorable: liberalization, even though enforced from the top, oxygenated the political realm and stimulated the debate on the course the country should take in the future. The deteriorating economic situation seemed to support private claims of public inefficiency and increased discontent and helped to sustain the campaign against statism.

Statism came to be more correctly understood as a perverse mode of intervention, characterized by bureaucratic encapsulation, excessively minute regulation of every private affair, and centralization of power and bureaucratization. There was growing agreement that the extent and modes of state intervention should be revised through more democratic forms of decision making.

Results have been meager so far: centralization increased as the economic crisis worsened; deregulation did take place as an attempt to curb inflation; government price controls were relaxed; actual control of union activity was liberalized, but the relevant legislation remains authoritarian and repressive.

Privatization through Service Contracts

Petrobras has always been one of the dearest targets of antistatist manifestations. It is by far the largest Brazilian enterprise. An object of military concern and control since the beginning, it has always been powerful and a symbol of national development. The oil monopoly was decided in the 1950s in the context of an impressive mass mobilization around nationalist and developmentalist issues. Highly legitimate and supported by strong forces it appeared as the national champion against foreign cartels. But it was created at a moment in which the exploration and development of domestic oil resources was neither urgent nor economically rewarding, unless reserves were easy to find and explore. Petrobras's priorities were, then, directed in other directions, such as transportation, refining, and distribution. Whether its policies were right or not is still a matter of controversy. There is an unending and yet rather obscure dispute on the enterprise's exploration strategy and its evaluation of the country's oil potential. On the other hand, it is true that it has postponed for too long a revision of its priorities in favor of greater investment in exploration and that its record in this area is less than satisfactory. Petrobras was not prepared to accelerate exploration and production in the short run by the time of the oil crisis. It had, however, enough productive capacity to meet the country's demands for crude refining. Although the country was unable to become self-sufficient in the provision of crude oil, it was able, by means of Petrobras's rapid expansion of refining capacity, to completely substitute domestic production of diesel and gasoline for imports. Refining has been the monopoly area in which Petrobras has achieved its best results. Since the oil crisis it has also been quite successful in increasing the energy efficiency of its refineries.

Both exploration and refining have remained more than an occasional interest for private parties. Foreign oil companies not only saw their hopes of entering exploration and production frustrated by the creation of the oil monopoly, but they also faced the nationalization of refinfing and (most of all) had to accept Petrobras's participation in commercial distribution. Domestic groups hoped to enter the immensely profitable oil market through association with foreign groups, association with Petrobras, or privatization of some segments of Petrobras's activities. The "majors" have always tried to make clear to government authorities their interest in the domestic oil market. They would be willing to enter exploration and production by any means, from concession of areas to service contracts with a risk clause.

The oil crisis caught Brazil in bad shape: a major importer after two decades of accelerated industrialization, the country had just begun to establish the petrochemical industry; oil reserves actually being explored represented less than one third of need; the economy was already showing signs of deceleration of growth; the balance of trade showed some inflexibility on the import side, making it difficult to redefine imports in the short run to account for the sharp increase in the import bill due to the new oil prices. As the whole industrialization effort was made in terms of import substitution, short-run cuts in imports would necessarily have a recessive impact.

It was in this politicoeconomic context that the government began to study the idea of some relaxation of the oil monopoly.[12] In the press interest groups were proposing outright privatization, arguing that Petrobras had been inept in managing the legal monopoly and deserved the major blame for the country's energy crisis. The inefficiency of the state as an entrepreneur was again and again used as an argument against the state oil company, with specially emphasis on its performance in exploration.

It seemed, however, that the campaign for the privatization of Petrobras was doomed to fail. After all, recently inaugurated general-president Ernesto Geisel was the CEO of Petrobras when he was selected as the fourth president after the establishment of the authoritarian military regime. He was also known to be important within the nationalistic section of the military. After intense pressure and open conflict in Congress and in the press, the president decided to adopt service contracts with the major foreign firms for exploration and development of oil fields and announced his decision in a coast-to-coast television speech. Contracts were to have a risk clause that established that there would be no repayment of lost investments, and areas for exploration were to be defined and clearly demarcated by Petrobras, which would also continue as the holder of the oil monopoly. Therefore, after a given period, it should assume control of the fields.

The decision was justified on the basis of the country's balance-of-payments problems and the need for a major exploration effort to substantially reduce the country's oil imports. It was hoped that the influx of capital and technology would rapidly produce the desired results, as the successive increases in fuel prices had not discouraged consumption; the previous five years of growth had had as their chief leader the automobile industry; the Garoupa field, Petrobras's latest discovery and the most important in years, proved to be smaller than expected; and the balance of payments showed signs of going out of control.

Justifications notwithstanding, the decision faced widespread opposition. Nationalist sectors in the state bureaucracy, the MDB (the opposition party), Congress, and the military feared that service contracts would constitute the first step toward the elimination of the oil monopoly and total denationalization of the sector, besides constituting a hard blow to the country's sovereignty.

The most effective opposition came from inside Petrobras. Its powerful technostructure had every reason to dislike the decision. First, it constituted public recognition of the enterprise's failure, and Petrobras was very proud of its achievements. Petrobras technicians were always prepared to show that the decision to invest in activities other than exploration was rational and justified. Besides, they argued, nobody could have foreseen the extent of the 1974 oil-price hike. They also considered any relaxation of the legal monopoly a danger and distrusted the multinational oil corporations that proposed service contracts. The technostructure endeavored to restrict the scope of the contracts and even to work against their effectiveness. There were some delays in implementing the contracts, access to geological and technical information on the selected exploration areas was denied to private firms, and the first areas selected were potentially high risk. Again, Petrobras technicians found their actions justified. Delays were not intended: the demarcation and selection of the areas was a difficult and delicate operation. Access to information was against company rules; it cost Petrobras money and time to gather the information and foreign enterprises might gain access to information on other areas and on Petrobras's own plans. And areas for service contracts ought to be in the high-risk sections, otherwise the contracts were not justified at all.[13]

The decision had a high political cost and a negative impact on the government's legitimacy. Petrobras was also hurt, especially insofar its prestige and morale were concerned. The benefits were almost null. Since then, the country has doubled its oil-production capacity, but exclusively through Petrobras's own intensification of exploration, new discoveries, and diminution of the time between discovery and production. Those who hoped that foreign capital and technology would represent the solution for Brazilian oil problems proved to be wrong. Under existing conditions their contribution was not that relevant. Those who feared that the service contracts would endanger the oil monopoly were also wrong. The slight weakening of control that might have resulted from them was not enough to create a real risk to the legal monopoly. Those, on the other hand, who were expecting a share in the oil market and a share of the high profits it yielded were also frustrated. Perhaps the major positive effect of the affair was a change in Petrobras's internal correlation of forces: the sectors of its technostructure linked to exploration and production were strengthened and thus enabled to enforce a new entrepreneurial strategy that is now paying off through a considerable increase of reserves and production. Brazil is, today, the third largest Latin American oil producer, after only Venezuela and Mexico. Output has reach 500,000 barrels a day.

Privatization through Joint Ventures

The production of basic and intermediate petrochemical products represents a case in which privatization was achieved with relatively better results. In the 1960s the Brazilian market for petrochemicals was characterized by Petrobras's refining monopoly on the one hand and foreign-controlled production of final goods on the other. There was an important empty space in between represented by the production of basic and intermediate petrochemicals. By the mid-1960s the area had become perhaps one of the major opportunities for large-scale import substituting industrial production, as well as an important missing link in the integration of the country's industrial structure. Private investment was disencouraged for mostly political reasons, although financial and technological difficulties also served as an obstacle to investment decisions in the sector. Political risk was thought to be high because some sectors of the state apparatus considered the activities involved as a natural extension of the legal monopoly. There were, however, some private parties willing to take the risk. Besides, right after the military takeover in 1964, several official statements confirmed the government's commitment to private enterprise, some concerning the petrochemical and mining sectors explicitly, as reassurance that nationalistic and interventionist plans of the previous administration were not going to be implemented.

A private domestic group started to look for foreign partners to join a project for construction of a naphtha cracker to produce ethylene. At the same time, the group tried to convince Petrobras to join them. Union Carbide, on the other hand, proposed to start producing ethylene through a naphtha cracker of its own. Petroquimica Uniao was eventually set up in the mid-1960s as a joint venture of foreign and domestic private capital and the state, represented by Petroquisa, Petrobras's sectorial petrochemical holding. At first results were not very encouraging. Union Carbide's project failed for technological reasons. The other project was completed in 1972, after several delays, cost overruns, and technical problems. But the original private group had to leave the venture for financial reasons, and Petroquisa took over in 1974. Private participation was reduced to a very small share.

The statization of the petrochemical plant, together with the refinery that was its original base, was an incidental but timely move: the country's industrial situation was different; the market for basic and intermediate petrochemicals was increasing at a fast pace; and the demand for growing imports turned it into an area of special interest for import-substituting investment. It had already been for some time an issue on the planning agenda of several state agencies--especially Petrobras and the National Development Bank--that were studying the best alternative formats for the sector as well as the most promising technical options.

In November 1964 an "informal study group" was created within the National Development Bank (BNDE) to examine the question and define some guidelines: the projects best fitted to provide for the requirements of the national economy should be implemented as a whole investment package, as sectorial investment programs to have a decisive impact on the rhythm of development.[14] It was a time of huge projects of accelerated industrial growth. The idea was to develop the petrochemical sector through an association between Petrobras and the BNDE. There was not much room for private participation. Petrobras would be in charge of the managerial and technical aspects of the program, and the BNDE would take care of the heavy financial support required. The program was organized into eighteen integrated projects for the production of basic, intermediate, and final petrochemical goods. Aside from the private initiatives mentioned above, which might have contributed to a revision of these original plans, there was strong inside opposition to the statist nature of the whole conception. The planning minister decided to involve private interests in the discussion of the petrochemical project, thus paving the way for the "destatization" or privatization of the Brazilian petrochemical program.

From the first moves in 1964 to the establishment of a new petrochemical complex in the mid-1970s, a complex process of alliances, pressures, and counterpressures, almost totally within the state itself, but with the active participation of some important private groups, took place. The final decision was clearly a compromise. The petrochemical pole would not be in Sao Paulo, but in the northeast--Bahia--and its development would be implemented through a tripartite association of private Brazilian groups, foreign enterprises, and Petrobras, through Petroquisa. The state would control the basic raw-materials unit of the pole and might not participate in some minor, peripheral ventures.

This solution illustrates a successful movement toward partial privatization of what could have been a totally state-controlled program. It was also adopted for the establishment of yet another petrochemical complex, in the southern state of Rio Grande do Sul. At the present time there are signs, mainly in the press, of mounting pressure for a redefinition of the formula with a reduction of state participation through transfer of Petroquisa's control of some ventures to private parties and the adoption of the "tripartite" formula in the control of the raw-material units in the two new poles. The Petroquimica Uniao was included among the enterprises to be privatized under the "destatization" program.

Privatization in the petrochemical sector came as a reaction to plans for state control. There was in fact no transfer of control, but a sort of preemption by the private sector that acquired beforehand, that is, before plans began to be implemented, the right to participate in a new market that was to be totally controlled by the state. This shift was made viable by a series of moves and countermoves involving several state bureaucratic jurisdictions.

In the mining sector there was no legal monopoly, but the state enterprise, Vale do Rio Doce, controlled about 80 percent of the market. It is one of the oldest state ventures in Brazil, created in 1942 as the result of the nationalization of British-controlled iron ore deposits in the state of Minas Gerais.[15] The CVRD was able, through very efficient investment and commercial strategies, to grow very fast in the 1950s. A highly aggressive commercial policy and good management led the company to dominate the market. Its powerful position within the state apparatus was turned into actual control of the formulation of the country's mineral policy. In the 1960s its managers decided to begin an ambitious expansion program, stimulated by its excellent financial situation and booming exports. The program would be centered on diversification.

The CVRD's expansion plans contemplated private--and foreign--participation in its new ventures from their inception. There were several reasons to diversify as well as to find private partners. Among the most important were to reduce the risk of huge investments in a single activity dependent on the behavior of foreign markets; to use the CVRD's technical and commercial expertise in mining, handling, and transport of ore, oil, and grain to increase Brazilian exports and to attract new foreign capital investment to the country; and to secure new foreign markets for its own products. The CVRD's expansion plans covered three different groups of activities. First were what could be considered its core activities: mining, transport, and commercialization of iron ore. It controls most of the market in these activities and could use its market power to enter into association with other enterprises at the same time as it prevented damaging denationalization. The CVRD thus established joint ventures with U. S. Steel and Kawasaki Steel. In both cases, the contracts commit the foreign partners to buying a portion of production for their own steel plants. In the area of sea transport, it also established new ventures in association with a Japanese group, the Nippon Brasil Bulk Carriers. Afterwards the CVRD would face problems in maintaining association in iron ore activities due to the world steel crisis. U. S. Steel got out, and Kawasaki Steel renegotiated the level of its participation and the volume and timing of both investments and ore orders.

The second group of activities comprises metallurgy and the production of pellet feed. The CVRD created three new enterprises in association with foreign enterprises: one with Japanese groups; another with the Italian IRI subsidiary, FINSIDER; and the third with the Spanish state enterprise, INI. All partners are committed to buy a part of production.

The third group comprises activities that are totally outside the company's traditional market jurisdiction: mainly nonferrous metallurgy and paper production. The latter comes as a result of the CVRD's exploration of its hugh forests, also in association with Japanese groups. The former constitutes the only sector in which the CVRD has tried to enter into association with private domestic groups. It has established a joint venture with private Brazilian groups and seven foreign consumers to explore important bauxite reserves. All the ventures are now facing financial and technical problems, the latter basically due to a lack of know-how on the part of the involved parties.

In the late 1970s the CVRD started to face, for the first time since the 1940s, financial and managerial problems. Its expansion plans were jeopardized. Some ventures were abandoned in the planning stage, others delayed. Its growing weaknesses enabled private partners to renegotiate association agreements, to change both market commitments and their control of the decision-making process. Moreover, what seemed a secure process of relative privatization of economic ventures that would have been state controlled, in fact entailed the risk of denationalization.

It is clear that the decision to allow denationalization of control in the mining sector to take place is a political one and will not depend on the CVRD's financial health. Besides, the company is now in much better shape, as international prices of and demand for ore have improved again. Privatization in the mining sector led to the enlargement of the space open in it to foreign capital, but it was implemented as a deliberate policy by a state enterprise prepared to use its entrepreneurial and power resources to maintain control over the sector as a whole and to prevent denationalization. It was a risky move, and the new administration has already revised original plans in order to avoid additional complications. The association with private domestic groups has also faced some problems, but may serve as an initial experiment for future ventures in a sector that will sooner or later be the object of an integrated development plan.

The huge complex of productive and mining activities to be established in Carajas opens new space for the association of state enterprise and private domestic groups.

<u>Debureaucratization and Destatization</u>

The cases analyzed so far illustrate instances of privatization that came about in one way or another through the initiative of a state enterprises that already controlled a sector of economic activity. The "destatization" program is the most important example of privatization as an explicit government policy. Its political origins are clearly in the antistatization campaign. It legitimated the notion that something should and could be done to decrease the size of the state and to transfer some enterprises under its control to the private sector.

In the mid-1970s some measures were already implemented as an answer to entrepreneurial reaction against "statism." The most important was perhaps the change in the orientation of the BNDE. Although the BNDE has always been the main financial source for the domestic private sector, the bulk of its financing was directed to the state productive sector, first to support huge projects for electric-power production, later to implement the steel program. After 1975 its president joined the private sector in criticizing excessive statism and even sent President Geisel a list of enterprises to be privatized with the help and support of the bank, a move he considered to be consistent with the bank's role in Brazil's economy.

The list was not used, but the idea of privatization remained. During the debate around the succession of President Geisel it came again to the fore. Appointed general-president Figueiredo promised to adopt specific measures against statization. After his inauguration, in July 1979, he instituted the National Debureaucratization Program, to be coordinated by former planning minister Helio Beltrao, for some time in the private sector and a permanent preacher against "statism," bureaucratization and centralization. The program's main objective (its secretary general even gained cabinet status) was to "reverse the historical trend of the Brazilian Administration towards unnecessary growth, excessive centralization of the decision-making process in government, abundant regulation and, consequently, widespread inefficiency."[16] Its major success was its "Citizen's Project," which aimed at the elimination of simplification of a long list of documents and procedures in order to ease the access of citizens to public services. The project enjoys some degree of popularity and a measure of achievement. Although it has not been able to do too much at the core of the state, especially in terms of the debureaucratization and decentralization of decision making, the program introduced several measures of decentralization and simplification at the periphery.

Destatization was also an important goal of the National Debureaucratization Program. The minister proposed a project that was approved by the president, but he failed to maintain total control over its implementation. In 1981, the president signed a decree creating regulations for the transfer, transformation, and discontinuation of state enterprises. The process would be jointly controlled by three ministers: Planning, Debureaucratization, and Finance. They should present together for presidential consideration a list of state enterprises that could (a) be transferred to the private sector, through sales of stock; (b) could be discontinued and their activities absorbed by government agencies in the "direct" administration (the case of enterprises created to enjoy autonomy and to avoid control, but which have no productive activity); (c) be liquidated; or (d) be transferred to state or local governments. Capital control could be transferred in the cases of (a) private enterprises that came under the control of the state due to default in their financial or fiscal obligations; (b) enterprises created by the state that could be privatized because there already were private domestic groups in the market able to assume adequate control over their activities; or (c) subsidiaries of state enterprises that were not essential for the achievement of their parent company's goals, although the latter should continue under state control.

The core of the state productive sector was explicitly excluded, as control could not be transferred when enterprises performed activities in the interest of national security; were entitled with a legal state monopoly; when control was established for the provision of social or strategic economic goods necessary for the welfare of society or to support accumulation in the private sector, only viable under state control; when enterprises were created to enforce national (domestic) control over sectorial development or to prevent denationalization of basic sectors of the economy.[17]

The program aimed at selective privatization. As the planning minister once said, "Destatization means to diminish the activity of the state in areas in which it is not essential, when the state is only competing with private enterprises, having no contribution to development. What is really intended is to concentrate the action of the state on these activities in which it is really essential and a necessary support for the the market economy itself."[18] Minister Beltrao said that the program should be concerned only with the unnecessary growth of the state, that statization would be characterized by the unnecessary growth of the state apparatus, by a growth of the state as opposed to private enterprise.[19]

The three ministers constituted a tripartite Special Commission, presided over by the representative of the planning minister, to implement the decree. The commission listed over one hundred enterprises that should be privatized, representing about 5.8 percent of the state productive sector's net income in 1982. Most of the enterprises represented no relevant productive asset at all. Some, however, would represent more controversial cases of privatization: five in the steel sector; one in the petrochemical sector; and two mechanical industries. In some of these cases intrastate pressure has prevented privatization so far. The enterprises belong to powerful state bureaucratic jurisdictions, and their employees oppose privatization. In other cases, privatization has been prevented by the economic crisis: private groups are in no condition to mobilize huge sums of money, and the state is not willing just to give its enterprises away. About thirty enterprises were "destatized"; ten were transferred to the private sector; seven were merged into others; ten are being discontinued; and two were explicitly forbidden to compete with private enterprises.[20]

The most promising aspect of the program was rationalization through discontinuation, mergers, and change of organization format within the bureaucracy itself, a reduction of size and expense without transfers to the private sector. But the Planning and Finance ministries were more interested, for political and pragmatic reasons, in speeding up transfers as a way of gaining popularity and legitimacy in the context of a grave crisis of credibility of the economic and monetary authorities. Thus, the program lacked political support from within, was narrowed in scope to fit short-term political interests, and has achieved very little so far.

In spite of its meager results, the destatization program contained some important ideas that together with administrative reform and serious debureaucratization--in all categories--could substantially improve the operation of the state apparatus, reduce unnecessary expenditures, and increase efficiency. Debureaucratization could serve as a means of democratizing the state and establishing greater public control over its activities. Certainly the programs here analyzed lacked the necessary political resources and a broader strategy that could lead to a political movement of reform of the state apparatus from within, strengthened by public support. They were short-circuited by pragmatism and, in some cases, such as "destatization," by a search for fast results and visibility and by short-sightedness.

Decisions concerning the state apparatus, either to statize or to privatize, are essentially political and dependent on actual circumstances. There may be some general rules, principles, and ideas to guide any coherent set of policies aiming at a better utilization of state resources for the public good. But they cannot be applied in an orthodox manner nor evaluated with no regard for the specifics of each case. There are no valid criteria to be applied a priori in the evaluation of state activities nor indisputable principles about the goodness or evil of state intervention. State activities are not good or bad in themselves. It depends on the actual political, social, and economic conditions that create them and on their actual implementation. In both the decision to establish a state activity and its implementation public control through democratic political instruments may make quite a difference.

Notes

1. I have developed these notions theoretically in "Neither Citizens nor Freeman: The Political Predicament of Subjects of Liberal Democratic Orders," Helen Kellogg Institute for International Studies, University of Notre Dame, mimeo, October 1983.

2. See, for instance, Claus Offe, "Theses on the Theory of the State," New German Critique, no. 6 (Fall 1975):62-74.

3. Sergio Henrique Abranches, "The Politics of Welfare Development in Latin America," Iuperj, Serie Estudos, no. 8 (1983).

4. Bob Jessop, "Recent Theories of the Capitalist State," Cambridge Journal of Economics, 1 (1977):105-138.

5. I have analyzed this process in "The Divided Leviathan: State and Economic Policy Formation in Authoritarian Brazil," (PhD diss., Cornell University, 1978).

6. See ibid. for Brazilian examples.

7. Data from the Secretariat for the Control of State Enterprises (SEST). For more details, see my "The State Productive Sector and the Crisis" (paper presented at Berkeley/Stanford conference on Opportunities and Constraints in Peripheral Industrial Society: The Case of Brazil, January 1984).

8. Ibid.

9. Maria da Conceicao Tavares et al., "Estrutura Industrial e Empresas Lideres," Finep, mimeo, 1978.

10. Ibid.

11. See Abranches, "The Divided Leviathan." For analysis of the agencies, see idem and Olavo Brasil de Lima Jr. eds., As Origens da Crise--Estado e Politica Economica no Brasil, forthcoming.

12. For an engage and more journalistic account, see Fausto Cupertino, Os Contratos de Risco e a Petrobras (Rio de Janeiro: Civilizacao Brasileira, 1976). Getulio Carvalho provides a more academic account, which favors the service contracts: Petrobras--Do Monopolio aos Contratos de Risco (Rio de Janeiro: FGV, 1980).

13. From interviews.

14. For details, see Peter Evans, Dependent Development: The Alliance of Multinational, State and Local Capital in Brazil (Princeton: Princeton University Press, 1979); and Luciano Martins, "A Expansao do Estado no Brasil: Seus Problemas e seus Atores" (Rio de Janeiro: Finep, 1976), mimeo.

15. Sergio Henrique Abranches and Sulamis Dain, "A Empresa Estatal no Brasil: Padroes Estruturais e Estrategias de Acao" (Rio de Janeiro: Finep, 1978), mimeo, provides the details.

16. Quoted from Joao Geraldo Piquet Carneiro, secretary general of the Debureaucratization Program, "Three Years of Debureaucratization" (Brasilia: National Debureaucratization Program, 1982).

17. For a study of the debureaucratization program, see Elisa Reis and Joao Batista Oliveira, "Debureaucratization, Political Loyalty and Social Justice: Reflections on a Current Brazilian Experience" (paper presented to the first International Conference on Comparative Historical and Critical Analysis of Bureaucracy, Zurich, October 1982). See also Decree No. 86215, (15 July 1981).

18. Antonio Delfim Neto, in Secretaria de Planejamento da Presidencia da Republica, "Desestatizacao: Textos e Legislacao" (Brasilia, 1982), p. 7.

19. Helio Beltrao, in ibid., p. 11.

20. See Secretaria de Planejamento da Presidencia da Republica, "Desestatizacao"; and Carneiro, "Three Years," for the data.

Chapter 6

Economic Privatization: Lessons from the Chilean Experience

Jorge Marshall R.

Introduction

One of the most salient features of the neoconservative program applied in Chile after 1973 has been privatization in almost all spheres of economic life. This phenomenon changed a long trend in Chile's economy of almost steady growth in the functional scope of the public sector in the areas of regulation, economic development, and production of goods and services.

This chapter analyzes this privatization process and tries to answer four questions: Why is this process taking place in the Chilean economy? What is the duration and extent of privatization in Chile? What lessons can we learn from this experience? What are the prospects for privatization?

It is important to bear in mind at the outset that privatization is only one of the ways to shrink the scope of state involvement in economic affairs. In the Chilean case, privatization is associated with a complete program of deregulation of domestic markets, including the financial sector, and liberalization of international trade and financial relations. Also, these structural changes are taking place at the same time as one of the strictest stabilization plans in the economic history of the country is being applied. Most of the privatization was carried out during the deep recession of 1974-1976. This plan influenced the outcome of privatization, so a brief review of it is necessary background for the analysis.

Why Privatization? A Historical Perspective

In the early twentieth century Chile was an examplar of economic freedom. It was an active participant in the international division of labor, exporting between 30 percent and 40 percent of GDP and importing a similar amount of capital and consumption goods. Trade was a buoyant activity, and even today one can see the vestiges of those years in the decayed luxury of old merchant houses in Valparaiso and Santiago.

Agriculture, industry, and some services benefited from the exporting activity. The government, which financed almost 90 percent of its budget through taxes on trade, was often tempted to extend its operations into the production sphere, but free-market ideas dominated and managed to keep it out of most of the country's economic life.

This stage of Chile's economic history, known as the "nitrate expansion era," came to a halt in 1914. That year three factors marked a shift in the economic development of the country. First, difficulties caused by the war in the international transportation system and in external markets reduced the demand for Chilean exports; this affected not only the exporting sector but also those that heavily depended on export performance. Second, 1914 was the beginning of a long period of crisis in the international economic system, which lasted until the late 1940s. From the point of view of developing countries, the main characteristic of this period was a reduction in the role of trade as an engine for domestic growth. Third, when the war was launched in 1914, there was already a synthetic substitute for nitrate, the staple that had accounted for more than two thirds of Chile's exports.

Because of the continual fluctuations in international markets, by the middle of the teens the most orthodox ideas, which had dominated economic affairs in the second half of the nineteenth century, had already lost much of their influence. Although in the late nineteenth century there had been some attempts at instituting nationalistic policies, mainly under the Balmaceda administration (1886-1891), these ideas did not become dominant in economic spheres until after 1914. An important step in this direction was the publication in 1912 of Encina's path-breaking "Nuestra inferioridad economica," which alleged that the precarious industrial development of the economy was partly a consequence of free-trade policies and of the mineral-exporting character of the Chilean economy. The twentieth century would see increasing nationalism in economic policy. Nationalism was dominant in the 1920s, and undisputed after the Great Depression.

After World War I, the old generation of economists, educated in classical orthodoxy, was displaced by a new generation with less trust in orthodox policy prescriptions. Among the latter were C. Keller, D. Martner, P. Ramirez, and G. Subercaseaux. The influence of this group can be seen in the increasing protection of domestic industry and the greater extent of state participation in economic affairs between 1915 and 1930.

During this period the main role of the state was to devise indirect policies to stimulate or protect domestic activities. The basic tools were import tariffs and cheap credit for domestic producers.[1]

One of the main effects of the Great Depression, at the level of economic ideas, was to generate increasing support for unorthodox postulates for economic policy. These postulates were more active state participation in the economic sphere, diversification of domestic activities, regulation of trade relations, and closer attention to employment problems.

Different authors (Ellsworth 1945; Hirschman 1963; and Keller 1936) agree that government actions played a key role in Chile's recovery from the Depression.[2] Three measures implemented in the early 1930s were first, isolation from the external crisis through an additional increase in trade barriers and devaluation of the exchange rate; second, the devising of a special program to stimulate construction; and third, the organization of employment programs, like the one in gold-washing mines, which sought to employ former nitrate workers.

A new step in government involvement in the economic sphere was carried out in the late 1930s and early 1940s, when external markets failed to supply many intermediate and capital goods that the domestic economy and the industrialization process needed. Thus, through the newly organized economic agency, CORFO (Corporacion de Fomento), the state coordinated the supply of scarce products (Baltra 1965).

Between 1915 and 1945 almost all of the roles the state had assumed were in the sphere of regulation. Productive activities were still the exclusive preserve of the private sector. In the late 1940s this arrangement would change as the state undertook some major investment in the industrial sector. In a few years a significant network of public enterprises was created. These investments were concentrated in energy production, oil extraction and refining, steel production, industrialization of sugar beet production, and other mining and manufacturing projects (Mamalakis 1976).

But despite the expansion of public investment, the industrialization process did not have the same results before and after 1945. As is indicated in table 1, the rate of growth of GDP in the 1934 to 1946 period was 3.6 percent per year. In the 1946 to 1958 period the average growth rate was 2.4 percent. Some recovery was experienced in the 1958 to 1971 period, with an average rate of 4.8 percent, but again this was lower than expected when the inward industrialization policies were implemented, and also lower than the average performance of other Latin American countries.[3]

The 1945 to 1970 period was one of relatively slow economic growth and increasing dissatisfaction with the organization of the economy. As we have seen, in creating that organization the government had an important role. Apart from its intromission in productive activities, beginning in the late 1940s (the postwar period) the government significantly expanded its regulatory role. At times, this regulation was pushed more by emergency circumstances than by a delineated plan.[4]

Perhaps the clearest example of this process is the case of trade policies. During the postwar period the high levels of industrial protection were altered only by the periodic tightening of trade restrictions. After 1950 international trade was controlled by the Consejo de Comercio Exterior (CCE). This agency was in charge of export and import policies, and at any time it could ban imports or exports. It also had to prepare the annual foreign-exchange budget, a practice that had started in 1947. The budget contained the list of all goods whose import would be permitted in that year, the import quota, and the exchange rate applicable to each item. The rate was to be taken from a multiple exchange-rate system.

But there were problems. Usually the annual budget was not ready until after the first quarter, and it was frequently changed during the year. Thus, the time frame for producers to formulate production and investment plans was extremely short and uncertain. This environment tended to favor speculative operations rather than productive activities. (Ffrench-Davis 1973: 68-69; Johnson 1967).

In a mid-1950s study on the nature of Chile's economic problems, N. Kaldor pointed out that the main obstacle to accelerated development was the lack of an appropriate institutional arrangement for the continued resolution of conflicts. According to Kaldor,

> In a competitive or quasi-competitive capitalist society, conflicts are resolved through the impersonal mechanism of the market. In a socialist state or in a planned economy, they are resolved through the fiat of the authorities --perhaps with greater justice, but at the cost of having to exert a great deal of power and compulsion. The difficulties in countries like Chile arise from the fact that Governments, under the influence of varying political pressures, have been ready to renounce the use of the impersonal market as an arbiter without erecting any effective alternative instrument for harmonising or compromising between particular interests and the general social interest. The Chilean Governments have long ago lost any innate inhibitions against State interference in economic life, and pursued a policy of intervention with a multiplicity of detailed and complicated controls--such as quantitative import regulations, multiple exchange rates, credit controls, discriminatory tax concessions and so on--without any clear overall view of either the basic objectives which these instruments were intended to serve, or of any overall attempt to assess their efficacy in relation to such objectives. (1980:234-235)

This view has been reiterated by conservative and nonconservative authors. According to Ffrench-Davis, one of the latter, in the early 1950s Chile's external trade was characterized by a complicated network of import quotas, extreme instability in government decisions, continuous capital gains, and corruption (1973:24). And, in a critical analysis of this period, Pinto (1962:124) pointed out the lack of clear goals in economic policy. According to Pinto, this phenomenon generated a "real battery of arbitrary schemes, occasional measures and legislation." Thus, one could go over a long list of authors who point to institutional deficiencies in the Chilean economic system.

Several of the institutional problems and state expansion itself should not be considered as independent of social development in a democratic society. In this sense many state policies reflected the nature of social and economic conflicts in Chile.

Although there were several attempts from the postwar years until 1970 to reform the economic system, the state remained a central piece in the economy, and there was little change in the relationship between the private and public sectors. By 1970 the hypothesis that poor economic performance and high inflation were a consequence of excess government intervention had regained an important position in the economic debate. The experience in the next three years would increase the plausibility of this hypothesis.

In 1970 a radical program of economic transformation was implemented. The main tool for economic change was the expansion of state control over economic affairs. Under political pressure the government went far beyond what it had planned for the expansion of state control of productive and distributive activities in the economy. On the other hand, beginning in 1972 the economy showed clear stagnation and highly repressed inflation symptoms. Even though the advocates of laissez faire could not show a direct causal link between these developments and the state's expansion, the simultaneity of these two phenomena strengthened the belief that intervention leads to economic difficulties.

The rest of the story, to the state's retreat from the economy after the 1973 coup, belongs more properly to the political sphere.

Privatization in Practice

Each of the programs applied to Chile's economy in the 1960s and 1970s had its own underlying analysis of the causes of the apparent failure of the inward industrialization process. It is not my purpose to survey those analyses, but only to concentrate on the one that led to the recent privatization process: the neoconservative experiment.

According to the neoconservative diagnosis, the root of Chile's economic problems (slow economic growth, persistent inflation, chronic balance of payments crises) was government interventionism and protectionism. What is particular to this analysis is that it sees the problem as lying not in the *type* of protection or the *form* of government intervention, but in protection and intervention themselves. In this sense, a free market is associated not only with economic efficiency, but also with social progress and development. Thus, the ultimate objective in this program is to reduce the state's role to a minimum.

Because protectionism and interventionism were characteristic of several decades of Chile's economic development, the neoconservative program took the form of a major restructuring of the economic system. This restructuring considered both the private and the public sectors. With regard to the private sector, reform was twofold. First, the progressive retreat of the public sector from economic affairs led to an expansion of the private sector. As we shall see, the main mechanism of this expansion was a liberalized financial market. Second, the liberalization of the economy, and particularly the reduction of protection from foreign competition, led to an internal restructuring in the private sector. In this process some activities expanded while others contracted.

In the public sector, the reform process followed a simpler rule. Except in the area of defense, there was continual reduction of the size of government. In general, this process took two forms: the first was deregulation or liberalization of economic activities; the second was a reduction in the amount of economic resources channeled through the public sector and the transfer of resources to the private sector. The main aspect of this process was privatization.

The deregulation process applied in Chile after 1973 had three aspects. The first, and one of the first economic measures of the military government in late 1973, was the liberalization of goods markets. After 1973 the prices of only a few products were still controlled, and even these were soon incorporated into the general system of free-floating prices.

The second part of the deregulation process concerned the financial system. The timing of this deregulation was arranged to permit the privatization of banks, enterprises, and other public assets. Thus, the basic steps toward financial deregulation preceded privatization.

In May of 1974 the interest rate for nonbanking financial institutions was deregulated. Since at that time the commercial banking system and the mortgage credit institutions were in government hands, this measure created the first financial base for the private sector. This differential treatment led to an accelerated transfer of financial deposits from these state-controlled institutions to the new financial corporations that could pay higher interest rates.

The privatization of commercial banks took place mainly during 1975. After that they were also deregulated, and the private financial sector entered an accelerated growth period.

The percentage of savings in public and private institutions at the end of each year is presented in table 2. The figures for 1969 and 1970 serve comparative purposes. Note that at the end of 1974 the banking system, still under government control, accounted for an unusually small percentage of total savings, whereas private institutions had increased their share.

When the privatization of the banking system was completed at the end of 1975, the deregulation of international financial movement was initiated (Ffrench-Davis and Arellano 1981). At that time the high differential between domestic and international interest rates meant large profits for those who enjoyed the limited access to foreign credit (Zahler 1980).

The third component of the deregulation package was the reduction of tariff protection. In five years the average tariff rate was reduced from over 100 percent to a uniform 10 percent, and all non-tariff restriction on trade was eliminated. Capital movements and foreign investment were also deregulated. The former was an important factor in the large private debt accumulated in this period.

Government intervention was further reduced by the contraction of public expenditure. Table 3 shows this expenditure as a share of GDP[5]. Total expenditure fell from levels around 40 percent in 1970 and 1974 to 30 percent in 1979. This gives us a rough measure of the extent to which the public sector has shrunk. With respect to the composition of public expenditure, the evolution has not been the same in all sectors. From the figures in table 3 it can be seen that general administration (which includes defense and police) has increased in importance; social services have been reduced somewhat, and economic activities have been the most affected by the reduction of the size of government expenditure.

The reduction in the amount of resources controlled by the public sector affects more than public expenditure; it also affects employment in the public sector, public enterprises, services from public institutions, land owned by the public sector, and so on. I shall analyze this process from the point of view of the privatization of public assets and other resources. For this purpose I shall distinguish among three types of privatization: outright, partial, and simulated.

Outright Privatization

In this category I include the transfer of public assets, by sale or otherwise, to private-sector ownership and management. In the Chilean experience the main assets transferred were manufacturing enterprises, commercial banks, and agricultural land.

In 1973, at the beginning of the neoconservative program, the state had almost absolute control of the financial system. Between 1970 and 1973 the government had acquired a significant share in most commercial banks. Thus, the first step in the privatization process was to transfer the nineteen banks to the private sector. This was done mainly in 1974 and 1975. By 1977 there were still four banks in government hands, but by 1980 only one remained. Naturally, those that took longer to transfer were the more financially troubled ones.

With respect to the manufacturing sector, in 1973 the state had ownership participation in 229 enterprises and had taken over the management of another 259. As in the case of commercial banks, this large number of firms in the public sector was the result of Allende's administration. Before Allende (in 1970), the state participated in only forty-six enterprises.[6] The transfer of enterprises followed soon after the privatization of the banking system. In general they were sold with a relatively small initial payment and the rest due within a period of six to eight years and a real interest rate of around 10 percent. The interest rate has to be compared with the average real interest rate of 30 percent to 50 percent prevailing at that moment in the already-liberalized financial market.

In 1978, after some time had passed since the transfer of both commercial banks and manufacturing enterprises, it was possible to measure selling conditions. It happened that privatization had occurred under extremely advantageous conditions for the new owners. Foxley (1983a) and Vergara (1981) have estimated an undervaluation of public enterprises and banks of between 25 percent and 40 percent. See table 5. The low sale price in relation to the value of assets three years later was influenced by the recessive economic conditions at the time of privatization, mainly between 1975 and 1976, the worst years after the shock treatment applied to stop inflation. Thus, because of the recession, most assets appeared to be unprofitable, so their selling prices were lower than under normal economic conditions.[7]

In agriculture privatization affected the land expropriated during the agrarian reform (1964 to 1973). As can be observed in table 6, almost 30 percent of the total area expropriated between 1964 and 1973 was transferred back to former owners. Of the area assigned to the beneficiaries of the reform, however, by 1978 almost 40 percent had been sold or leased to third parties. This phenomenon, as we shall see, is closely related to the reduction of credit and technical assistance from public institutions.

Apart from these transfers of large-scale assets and resources to the private sector, outright privatization also affected many other assets of lesser value. This was the case with machinery, tractors, trucks, buildings, and other assets that were part of public institutions' or enterprises' investment plans. The reduction of public expenditure came at the expense of a significant contraction of public investment.[8] Unfortunately, the total value of the assets transferred to the private sector has not been determined, but the figures already given show the general trend of this process.

Partial Privatization

The privatization process in Chile affected not only state-owned assets, but also some of the functions that public enterprises or institutions had had. For me, partial privatization is the combination of retention of public ownership of enterprises or institutions and a divesting of some of their functions to the private sector. In principle, partial privatization can be explicit or implicit. In the former case there is legislation or a contract that sets the conditions of privatization and limits what the private institution can do. An example of this type of privatization is the transfer of pension funds from public to private administration. Implicit privatization is characterized by the simple abandonment of some public function under the assumption that the private sector will take up that function as a spontaneous reaction to the government's move. An example of this case is the reduction in several credit or assistance programs oriented to productive activities.

In Chile's neoconservative program, explicit partial privatization was concentrated in the social services: health, social security, and housing. With respect to health, since 1974 there have been numerous attempts to transfer the supply of health services to the private sector. In general, the reforms introduced have been less significant than those initially proposed (Raczynski 1982) and have consisted mainly of the transfer of management functions in some public units and the creation of private institutions to compete with the public system.

The first of these reforms started in 1975 with the transfer of small units to private management, which were to maintain the "non-profit-seeking" character of the public sector. This type of privatization has been extended to other units, including the most modern hospital in the country (ibid.). Although there is no complete evaluation of this experience available, there are signs suggesting increasing efficiency in the supply of health services. But there have also been complaints about "voluntary" payments that private managers have required from beneficiaries.

The other aspect of health privatization is the creation of private institutions that may receive the compulsory contribution made by wage earners to the health system. These institutions must provide a service at least as good as that of the public institutions. Since the compulsory contribution is a fixed percentage of taxable income, and the services provided by the health system are based on need without regard to income differential, privatization is advantageous to workers with higher incomes, whose contribution to the public system had exceeded the benefits received. The public system loses, under these conditions, part of its financial support (Arellano and Saez 1981).

With regard to social security, a similar scheme has been followed. Pensions have been transferred from the pay-as-you-go system administered by public institutions to a private funding system. Private companies dedicated exclusively to this activity are supposed to compete in the administration of these pension funds and may collect commissions for their services.

One of the most important effects of social security reform is not the transfer of the administration of the pension system, but the transfer of the power to decide where a massive accumulation of financial funds is to be invested. Thus, the reform redistributes control of national capital toward the private sector. In two years the private system had accumulated a level equivalent to 7 percent of all financial assets; and in a medium-run projection of the accumulation of financial resources in private hands, Arellano (1983a) estimates that this level could reach around 8 percent of GDP in five years, more than 20 percent in ten years, and around 60 percent in twenty years.

In housing, privatization has been less drastic. The new system of subsidies for low-income groups gives a more prominent role to private real-estate enterprises, and the financing of housing has been made more dependent on the private capital market. An important characteristic of housing policy has been its instability. Several types of subsidies and organizations to allocate resources in this sector have been attempted with relatively little success with regard to either the efficiency of subsidies or the volume of new constructions (ibid.).

Another area of explicit partial privatization is found in public enterprises. Some functions, like maintenance of equipment or less-important procedures were transferred to private enterprises. As I shall discuss in the next section, government instruction with regard to privatization usually went farther than the actions actually taken by public managers. This makes it difficult to evaluate the exact extent to which minor functions have been transferred to the private sector, although the reduction in employment in the major public enterprises that have remained in the public sector might serve as an approximate indicator of this type of privatization. As can be seen in table 7, from 59.5 thousand workers in 1974, before the privatization process at this level had started, in 1979 the same enterprises had only 35.5 thousand persons, that is, 40 percent less employment in five years.[9]

An important phenomenon in the Chilean partial privatization experience was the simple elimination or contraction of some programs that public institutions or enterprises had been responsible for in the past. The main examples are found in agriculture, where different credit and technical assistance programs have been curtailed (see table 8).

Simulated Privatization

This third category in the privatization process corresponds to the imposition of market performance criteria on public enterprises. At the beginning of Chile's neoconservative program one of the main macroeconomic problems was the large deficit in public enterprises. In 1973 total Central Bank credit extended to the public network of enterprises was around 15 percent of GDP. The new military government imposed a strict policy of self-financing, reducing all types of contributions or subsidies to public enterprises (in the first years of the new administration the profit motive was the management rule of public enterprises). When the deficit was eliminated in most enterprises, government directives aimed at obtaining positive short-run profits. In part this was possible because of the lack of investment or medium-term development plans for these enterprises.

One of the difficulties of large-scale privatization operations has been that the boundaries of this process have been determined in the political sphere; there have been no specific criteria regulating the extent of privatization. Consequently there has been no clear policy with regard to public enterprises. Thus, the only way to evaluate their economic performance is through their ability to generate a surplus.

Problems in the Privatization Process

In Chile's experience privatization has not been smooth. In fact, this has been one of the most debated issues in the neoconservative program. Privatization has not only affected local interest groups associated with the sector in which the transfer is being made, but it has also, since it is a large-scale operation, contributed to the delineation of the basic features of the new economic system the neoconservative program tried to erect. In this sense more general interest groups and classes are also affected. On the other hand, there have been several macroeconomic consequences of the privatization process, depending on the economic conditions in which the program was implemented.

In this section I shall analyze these problems and consider three types of problem: those originating in the interaction of conflicting interests with respect to privatization; those resulting from the effects of the economy's market structure on the outcome of privatization; and those resulting from the effect of large-scale privatization on income distribution, employment, and the level of activity. The magnitude of these effects seems to depend on the characteristics of the economy at the time of privatization and on the speed at which the process is implemented.

Local Interests and Privatization

The privatization process involves multiple interest groups. These range from specific interest centering around one enterprise or institution, to general political or ideological alliances with respect to the whole process. In the case of enterprises, there are private captialists, workers, downstream buyers, upstream suppliers, bankers, and so on. These groups may form coalitions to express their position in the privatization process. In the case of some services, like health, interest groups are even more important because of professional associations that take part in the process.

Thus, one problem with privatization is the harmonization of interests among different coalitions, or simply the resolution of conflicts between groups. To analyze this problem one could relate privatization to the so-called economic theory of public actions (Stigler 1971; Posner 1974), according to which interest groups, organized around specific issues, are key factors explaining public actions and policies. For example, if in some sector the groups in favor of privatization are more influential than the groups against privatization, this theory would expect privatization to take place regardless of the findings of technical economic analysis. On the other hand, the more influential the groups opposed to privatization, the more difficult implementing privatization will be.

This approach, which Kalt and Zupan have recently criticized in their analysis of the regulatory process (1982), is even less appropriate to Chile's privatization experience because the latter has been inserted in a more general program of social and economic transformations that this theory does not consider. But this does not mean that local interests are totally indifferent to the privatization outcome. On the contrary, interest groups may affect the process in several ways. This influence could be significant when there are strong coalitions with specific interests in the outcome of privatization.

Raczynski (1982) has shown how the privatization of health services had to face a continual debate between the medical association and the government. This might have been one of the reasons for the long period between the first proposition of privatization in 1974 and the effective measures in that direction in 1980.

Another case of the importance of interest groups is found in the transfer of some functions of public enterprises. Public managers tend to see this operation as a threat to their power. This creates a conflict between managers and government officials who want accelerated privatization. Thus, there are usually more plans for transferring functions than there are concrete actions to put those plans into effect. Alternatively, when seen as unavoidable, privatization could benefit those managers who participate in both sides of the transfer. (Along these lines, domestic interest groups have also influenced several privatization policies.) Even though they have little influence over the final outcome, unions and other worker organizations have tended to oppose the privatization process on the grounds of possible threat to their jobs and benefits.

Although local interest groups are important to a complete analysis of the privatization process, in the Chilean case they have not played a central role. The privatization debate has been a more global political phenomenon. In that sphere privatization was welcomed by the business community and looked at askance by most worker organizations.

Planning Privatization

An important feature of less-developed economies is the existence of imperfect markets. Naturally, this situation is not exclusive to these economies, but in them it has a more relevant role in the behavior of the economic system. In this context, market imperfection means that oligopolistic structure is a common characteristic in the industrial sector. It also implies the existence of family and commercial conglomerates in the most important economic activities, the lack of a private or public system of economic information, a heterogeneous financial market in which there is credit discrimination, differential access to foreign goods and capital markets, and so on. All these elements should be taken into account when any government considers a privatization plan. The outcome of privatization in terms of efficiency, income distribution, and employment depends on these market characteristics. Then, since apart from privatization the economic authority may have other economic targets, the privatization process should be complemented by additional measures if those targets are to be reached.

In the Chilean experience, although there might have been other targets than mere privatization, they were not discussed when specific policies were designed. This was one of the main causes of the concentration that followed each of the privatization steps.

In the first stages of privatization, when commercial banks and most enterprises were transferred, access to information and credit was crucial. At that time (1974 to 1976), the domestic economy was in a deep recession with extremely high interest rates. Thus the access to foreign credit that domestic conglomerates had, as well as their close monitoring of the information around the privatization process determined the outcome of privatization: concentration.

In 1978 domestic conglomerates controlled 66 percent of credit external to the banking system and 60 percent of domestic credit from the financial system. In that year, an analysis of the 250 principal enterprises found that only 5 conglomerates controlled 90 enterprises with a capital value of 53 percent of all enterprises in the survey (Dahse 1979).

A similar pattern of privatization with concentration appears in the transfer of pension funds. As mentioned, this transfer could lead in ten years to an accumulation of financial assets of around 20 percent of GDP. In May of 1981 there were eleven private institutions involved in the administration of pension funds. Of these, nine had been organized by major economic conglomerates. The stockholders of these nine enterprises directly controlled more than 46 percent of the capital and reserves of the entire domestic financial system, and about 60 percent of the circulating liabilities (Arellano 1983a). Thus, a few conglomerates, which dominate the financial market, have organized the pension-administration societies and attracted the majority of the social security contribution of workers.

The increased efficiency the transfer was supposed to generate has not materialized because of market concentration. Price petition among conglomerates has not occurred, which has led to an increase in the cost of services. In the social security reform, specifically, there has not been the expected reduction in administrative costs; on the contrary, the fees charged by private firms are higher than those charged by public institutions. The main reason is that the new system has faced vigorous noncompetition in prices, which has raised marketing and advertising costs. The latter represented 40 percent of operational outlays in 1982 (Arellano 1983b).

To summarize, the outcome of privatization depends to a great extent on the structural characteristics of the economy. In the Chilean case these characteristics were not taken into account when the process was designed, which led to a simultaneous process of privatization and concentration. The latter could have been avoided through a planned transfer process.

Timing of Privatization

When privatization is a large-scale operation, as in Chile, its effects go beyond the specific sector or market in which the process takes place. These external effects depend on the state of the economy at the moment of privatization. Thus, for example, implicit partial privatization can hardly succeed in recessive conditions: the reduction of public programs may not necessarily generate a demand for similar services in the private sector.[10] This, in turn, has several consequences in terms of economic activity, employment, investment.

On the other hand, the privatization process might be gradual or concentrated in a short period, but in each case it will have different effects on other macroeconomic variables. Perhaps the most important of these effects is on investment. The privatization of public enterprises represents a reduction in the public-sector demand for capital. If there is not an equivalent, offsetting movement by the private sector, the final effect would be a reduction of investment.[11]

The ability of the private sector to increase its demand for capital is closely determined by the situation of the economy and the speed of the adjustment toward a new "desired" stock of capital. Thus, to avoid reductions in investment, the privatization of physical capital not only should be gradual, but also must be done under normal economic conditions.

In the Chilean experience, most of the enterprises were transferred while the economy was in recession, and in a relatively short period of time. Thus, privatization did not contribute to a rapid recovery. In this context, the low selling price of public assets (reported in table 5) might be explained as a measure to encourage private demand for that capital and reduce the "crowding out" of new private investment.[12]

On the other hand, within the private sector privatization could generate an excess demand for financial credit. The latter is needed to complete the transfer operation from the public sector. In part this excess demand was covered by external credit, but in the domestic market there was also an increase in interest rates, with concomitant adverse effects on economic activity.

In the case of implicit partial privatization, when several public programs of investment credit or technical assistance are reduced during a recession and in a very short period, it is difficult for the private sector to take over these activities in the short-run, so investment and economic activity would be affected.

Another avoidable effect of privatization is an increase in unemployment. The retreat of the government from some activities in the hope that the private sector will fill the gap can reduce or stop employment growth in the public sector. Between 1974 and 1979 the number of workers in public institutions was reduced by 100,000. This represents around 3 percent of the labor force. In this period the average unemployment rate was over 15 percent (Marshall and Romaguera 1981).

In conclusion, privatization may lead to several outcomes, depending on the policies and the timing of the process. In general, it should be a gradual process that takes place under normal economic conditions. Privatization and regulation are not independent phenomena: to avoid undesirable results, regulation may be needed during the privatization process.

Neoconservative Crisis and Prospect for Privatization

From the point of view of the neoconservative program, the privatization process together with the deregulation of economic activity were the centerpieces of a new stage of economic development in Chile. Without state interference and in an open environment, it was thought, the economy would enter a period of rapid and stable growth.

For some time in the late 1970s there were many people who thought that the neoconservative dream would come true and that the country would experience a period of unprecedented growth. But in the early 1980s the dream took a very different direction. After five years of recovery and growth (1976 to 1980), with decreasing inflation and with an improving situation in the balance of payments, the government began to face increasing economic difficulties. As can be seen in table 9, total GDP fell 14.3 percent in 1982 and 2.0 percent in 1983. Total unemployment in 1982 and 1983 was around 30 percent.[13]

Doubtless there are short-run causes of the recent economic crisis, particularly the overvaluation of domestic currency, the deterioration of the terms of trade, and the increase in the interest rate in international financial markets. But the magnitude of the 1982-1983 recession cannot be explained if the structural characteristics of the economy are not considered.

The rapid process of privatization and concentration had made the economic system extremely vulnerable to any type of financial difficulty. The economic logic of the conglomerates emphasized financial speculation over real accumulation and technological progress, and their answer to the first stagnation symptoms helped to aggravate the recession (Foxley 1983b).

On the other hand, one of the main consequences of the new recession was the bankruptcy of several conglomerates, among them the two biggest. The bankruptcies resulted from failure to pay the large domestic and external debt that these conglomerates had accumulated during expansion. Since the state has now guaranteed most of the external debt, the economic difficulties have been, in part, transferred to the state.

At the end of 1981 the Banking Commission took over the management of two banks and six other financial institutions. Both banks were part of economic conglomerates. During 1982 there were attempts to resolve the financial crisis, but toward the end of the year the situation got worse. At the beginning of 1983 the management of another five banks was taken over, three banks were liquidated, and two others were kept under government supervision. These ten corporations represented around half of the total capital in the financial system.

The emergency aid that the Central Bank gave to the ailing financial system between May 1982 and March 1983 is equivalent to more than 15 percent of 1982 GDP (Arellano 1983b). However, the control of banks meant immediate control of productive firms that were unable to repay the large debt contracted in the recovery and growth years.

The experiences of the 1981-1984 recession have affected the credibility of the neoconservative program. There is almost general agreement that the excesses of that program influenced the magnitude of the crisis. Thus, the economic prospects for privatization indicate a partial reversal of the tendencies that have operated since 1973.

There are four main lessons from the failure of the neoconservative program, which should be applied to the organization of the economic system. First, privatization and deregulation are not independent processes. Goals having to do with one of them might require some action with regard to the other. Privatization will usually change the structure of market competition and then it may create the need for economic regulation. After privatization more and not less regulation may be required.

In the Chilean experience this phenomenon was particularly important in the financial sector, in which the private market grew at an unprecedented pace between 1976 and 1981. Since at the same time as privatization there was almost complete deregulation, the private market did not play the role it should have. It has become clear since the crisis that speculation was a common practice in the financial market, with adverse effects on economic activity.

Second, privatization and concentration is an extremely dangerous combination. The objectives and behavioral logic of economic conglomerates do not necessarily coincide with those of the economy as a whole. In this sense, the efficient maintenance of an economic organization based on the private sector needs to defend itself from excessive economic concentration.

An important decision that could limit financial conglomerate power will be the one concerning those commercial banks that have been intervened because of financial failure.

Third, rather than an ideological objective, privatization should be conceived as a tool to organize the economic system, and, like other tools, it needs to be evaluated in terms of efficiency. This evaluation should reopen several avenues for public intervention in Chile.

With respect to this point I have in mind actions like a more active role for public enterprises, especially in investment; public programs oriented to small producers with less access to technology and credit in the private market; and control of investment funds, including financial resources in pension funds.

The final lesson of the recent Chilean experience is that between total privatization and complete state control of productive assets there are several alternatives, involving public and private efforts. This type of joint venture may also include the organization of or support for self-managed and cooperative enterprises.

Table 1

Growth of GDP and Manufacturing
(Percentage)

Period	Rate of Change GDP	Manufacturing
1913 - 1929	2.7	5.2
1929 - 1934	-0.8	0.4
1934 - 1946	3.6	7.4
1946 - 1958	2.4	3.3
1958 - 1971	4.8	5.4

Sources: Mamalakis (1978), Muñoz (1968), and Reynolds (1965).

Table 2

Amount of Savings, Year End
(Percentage)

Sector	Savings							
	1969	1970	1974	1975	1976	1977	1978	1979
Public	46.7	49.3	30.0	29.7	33.6	31.4	28.7	31.8
Mixed	40.5	39.5	62.5	56.2	36.1	17.8	7.8	3.5
Private	12.8	11.1	7.5	14.1	30.3	50.9	63.5	64.7
--Banks	12.8	11.1	1.7	11.3	26.9	42.0	54.7	54.0
--Other	--	--	5.8	2.8	3.4	8.9	8.8	10.7
Total	100.0	100.0	100.0	100.0	100.0	100.0	100.0	100.0

Source: Banco Central, <u>Boletín Mensual</u>, in Foxley (1983a).
Note: Totals may not add to 100 because of rounding.

Table 3

Public Expenditure in Relation to GDP
(Percentage)

Year	Total Expenditure [a]	General Administration [b]	Social Services	Economic Activities
1969	36.3	4.6	19.7	9.4
1970	40.6	5.7	21.7	10.8
1974	39.6	8.2	17.6	10.2
1975	38.8	8.2	18.3	6.4
1976	33.7	7.2	15.9	5.0
1977	32.4	7.0	17.4	4.5
1978	31.8	6.5	16.0	5.7
1979	30.3	6.1	15.6	5.0

Source: Marshall (1981a)
[a] Includes service of public debt
[b] Includes defense and police

Table 4

Number of Public Enterprises

Type of Enterprise	Number 1970	1973	1977	1980
State participation in ownership				
--Enterprises	46	229	45	23
--Banks	--	19	4	1
Intervened enterprises	--	259	21	--
Total	46	507	70	24

Source: Foxley (1983a), and Vergara (1981)

Table 5

Valuation of State Enterprises, 1978
(Sale Value/Value of Assets)

Evaluator	Valuation of Banks (%)	Valuation of Public Enterprises (%)	Total (%)
Foxley (1983a)			
--low discount	--	--	67.8
--high discount	--	--	72.8
Vergara (1981)			
--low discount	69.5	76.8	73.7
--high discount	62.7	63.2	63.0

Table 6

Results of Agrarian Reform, 1979

Disposition of Expropriated Land	Hectares	Percentage of All Expropriated Land
Restored to former owners	2,965,640	29.8
Area assigned to peasants [a]	3,521,141	35.3
Other transfers [b]	1,639,772	16.5
To be assigned or transferred	1,839,315	18.4
Total expropriated (1964-1973)	9,965,868	100.0

Source: Universidad de Chile, in Foxley (1983a)
[a] Part transferred to third parties
[b] Transferred to other public or private institutions

Table 7

Employment in Public Enterprises

Year	Number of Workers (thousands)
1964	49.6
1970	55.8
1974	59.5
1978	35.9
1979	35.5

Source: Marshall and Romaguera (1981).

Table 8

Public Development Programs

Year	Credit Assistance (millions of 1978 pesos)	Employment in Development Programs (thousands of workers)
1969	3,006.5	--
1970	3,414.8	44.3
1974	746.0	69.5
1975	359.1	--
1976	484.5	--
1977	812.1	--
1978	1,022.7	34.4
1979	1,488.4	32.0

Sources: Marshall (1981b), and Marshall and Romaguera (1981).
Note: 1978 exchange rate=$1/32 pesos.
A dash signifies no information.

Table 9

Growth of GDP and Employment
(Percentages)

Year	GDP Growth	Employment Growth	Total Unemployment Rate
1974	1.0	-3.6	9.2
1975	-12.9	-4.0	16.5
1976	3.5	-1.0	20.2
1977	9.9	3.0	18.6
1978	8.2	4.0	17.9
1979	8.3	6.0	17.3
1980	7.5	5.0	17.2
1981	5.3	4.1	15.6
1982	-14.3	-9.1	27.0
1983 (est.)	- 2.0	--	32.0

Source: Banco Central and ODEPLAN, in Meller and Solimano (1983).
Note: Dash signifies no information.

Notes

Helpful comments and suggestions from H. Fruling, S. Helper, A. Jadresic, S. Weintraub, and the participants in the ILAS-CEDES conference on state shrinking, Austin, Texas, March 1984, are gratefully acknowledged.

1. The first social security institutions were also created between 1915 and 1930.

2. For a complete analysis of the effect of the Great Depression in Chile, see Ellsworth (1945).

3. In the 1946 to 1970 period the average growth rate in Latin America was around 5.5 percent, whereas the Chilean average was 3.7 percent.

4. During the postwar period there were several positive effects of the public sector's economic role. In several respects development in this period was due to the state's contribution, but here I shall emphasize the negative aspects of that role.

5. This definition of the public sector does not include public enterprises.

6. The post-Allende public enterprises are almost all large enterprises, with more than one hundred workers each. The number of manufacturing enterprises with more than one hundred workers is around six hundred for the whole country.

7. This situation occurred because of both imperfect financial markets and short time frames in asset pricing due to high uncertainty in a period of drastic economic reforms.

8. Public investment fell from 10 percent of GDP in 1974 to 4 percent in 1979 (see Marshall 1981a).

9. Part of this reduction may also be attributed to simulated privatization.

10. This happens not only because the price in the private market exceeds the one charged by the public sector, but also because private investment takes time to adjust to the new demand.

11. That is, private investable funds are being used to finance current fiscal budget.

12. Around 1970 private investment represented around 6 percent of GDP. Between 1974 and 1976 this investment was only around 3.5 percent of GDP. Naturally, the recession in those years is the main explanation for this difference.

13. Open unemployment has oscillated between 15 percent and 20 percent. To this figure one needs to add workers on welfare to get total unemployment.

References

Arellano, J. P. 1983a. "Social Policies and Income Redistribution in Chile." Ph.D. dissertation, Harvard University.

-----. 1983b. "El financiamiento del desarrollo." In Foxley et al. Reconstrucción económica para la democracia, by A. Foxley et al., pp. 189-236. Santiago: Editorial Aconcagua.

-----, and R. Saez. 1981. "Reforma de la previsión y financiamiento de la salud." Mimeo. CIEPLAN.

Baltra, A. 1965. "Desarrollo general de la economía." In Geografía económica de Chile, pp. 435-452. Santiago: CORFO.

Dahse, F. 1979. Mapa de la extrema riqueza. Santiago: Editorial Aconcagua.

Ellsworth, P. T. 1945. Chile: An Economy in Transition. New York: Macmillan.

Ffrench-Davis, R. 1973. Políticas económicas en Chile: 1952-1970. Santiago: Ediciones Nueva Universidad.

-----, and J. P. Arellano. 1981. "Apertura financiera externa: La experiencia Chilena en 1973-1980." Colección Estudios CIEPLAN, no. 5: 5-52.

Foxley, A. 1983a. Neo-Conservative Experiments in Latin America. Berkeley & Los Angeles: University of California Press.

-----. 1983b. "Despues del monetarismo." In Reconstrucción económica para la democracia, by A. Foxley et al., pp. 15-94. Santiago: Editorial Aconcagua.

Hirschman, A. O. 1963. Journey toward Progress. New York: Twentieth Century Fund.

Johnson, L. 1967. "Problems of Import Substitution." Economic Development and Cultural Change (January): 202-216.

Kaldor, N. 1980. Essays on Economic Policy II. New York: Holmes & Meier.

Kalt, J. P., and M. A. Zupan. 1982. "The Politics and Economics of Senate Voting on Coal Strip Mining Policy: Inadequacies in the Economic Theory of Regulation." Kennedy School Discussion Paper, Harvard University.

Keller, C. 1936. "Aspecto de nuestro problema social." Estudios (Santiago) no. 38: 9-20.

Mamalakis, M. 1976. _The Growth and Structure of the Chilean Economy_. New Haven, Conn.: Yale University Press.

-----. 1978. _Historical Statistics of Chile_. Westport, Conn.: Greenwood.

Marshall, J. 1981a. "El gasto público en Chile: 1969-1979." _Colección Estudios CIEPLAN_, no. 5.

-----. 1981b. "El gasto público en Chile: 1969-1979. Metodología y resultados." _Notas Tecnicas CIEPLAN_, no. 33.

-----, and P. Romaguera. 1981. "La evolución del empleo público en Chile, 1970-1978." _Notas Técnicas CIEPLAN_, no. 26.

Meller, P., and A. Solimano. 1983. "Desempleo en Chile: Interpretación y politicas economicas alternativas." In _Reconstruccion económica para la democracia_, by A. Foxley et al., pp. 149-188. Santiago: Editorial Aconcagua.

Muñoz, O. 1968. _Crecimiento industrial en Chile, 1914-1965_. Santiago: Instituto de Economía, Universidad de Chile.

Pinto, A. 1962. _Chile: Un caso de desarrollo frustrado_. Santiago: Editorial Universitaria.

Posner, R. A. 1974. "Theories of Economic Regulation." _Bell Journal of Economics and Management Science_. (Autumn): 335-358.

Raczynski, D. 1982. "Reformas al sector salud: Diálogos y debates." _Colección Estudios CIEPLAN_, no. 10: 5-44.

Reynolds, C. W. 1965. "Development Problems of an Export Economy." In _Essays on the Chilean Economy_, by M. Mamalakis and C. W. Reynolds, pp. 203-357. Economic Growth Center, New Haven, Conn.: Yale University.

Stigler, G. J. 1971. "The Theory of Economic Regulation." _Bell Journal of Economics and Management Sciences_ (Spring): 3-21.

Vergara, P. 1981. "Las transformaciones de las funciones económicas del estado bajo el régimen militar en Chile." _Colección de Estudios CIEPLAN_, no. 5: 117-154.

Zahler, R. 1980. "Repercusiones monetarias y reales de la apertura de la economía Chilena, 1975-1978." _Revista de la CEPAL_ (Santiago) (April): 137-163.

Chapter 7

Peru: An Insider's View

Felipe Ortiz de Zevallos M.

The Historical Process

In 1948 a right-wing *caudillo*-type military government established a liberal framework for the Peruvian economy. During the 1950s, public expenditures totaled only 8 percent of GNP and were directed toward infrastructure, health, and education. Sectorial development banks were among the few state-owned enterprises (SOEs) that deserved that name.

A combination of external and internal factors brought about an economic crisis by the end of the decade. Liberal policies lost ground to an approach favoring greater state intervention. In 1959 the Law for Industrial Promotion was enacted with a clear orientation toward import substitution. The Central Office for Plans and Programs and the high-level Commission for Housing and Agrarian Reform were also established to deal with the economic and social problems caused by increasing urban migration and population growth. Public expenditures, however, remained low in comparison to other Latin American countries: only 11 percent of GNP by 1960.

A one-year institutional military government in 1962 called for greater state participation in the process of economic development. The National Planning Institute was created and the military introduced the concept that national security involved not only defense matters but also development issues.

During Pres. Fernando Belaunde's democratic first government (1963 to 1968), state intervention increased. The Agrarian Reform Law was enacted and the Banco de la Nacion created, tariffs were raised, and credit as well as the price of basic goods and services were subsidized. An ambitious program of public projects in infrastructure and housing was carried out. The state payroll increased significantly. Public-sector deficits caused by these as well as other populist measures, fueled inflation and forced a radical tax reform in the late sixties.

However, the participation of SOEs in the economy remained very much the same through the decade. Aside from the Empresa Petrolera Fiscal (later PETROPERU), which developed a minor participation in oil refining, and some public services and century-old monopolistic "*estancos*" for coca, salt, alcohol, and tobacco, state ownership in the manufacturing sector was restricted mainly to the navy shipyard, the steel mill at Chimbote, a fertilizer plant at Cusco, and two small factories--a cement and a food-dehydrating plant--in Arequipa. Peruvian shipbuilding tradition dates from the nineteenth century. The steel mill, later incorporated as SIDERPERU, was built in the late 1950s as part of a TVA-style regional development program for the

Santa Valley. The industrial facilities in the two southern cities were built under reconstruction and development programs after severe earthquakes affected those cities during the 1950s.

A revolutionary military government came into power in 1968. During its first phase (1968 to 1975), under Gen. Juan Velasco, it attempted a radical transformation of Peruvian society and economy and sought the elimination of local oligarchies and foreign dependence. Extreme nationalism and radical social and economic reforms characterized Velasco's tenure. Highly protectionist trade policies discouraged competition and domestic productivity. Stagnation in primary production resulted in trade deficits. The historical trend of state intervention was reinforced to include the expropriation of foreign and local interests in basic sectors and industries, as well as the establishment of new SOEs and monopolies. Thus, during the early seventies, oil and mining activities carried out by foreign groups--International Petroleum Co. (Standard Oil NJ), Cerro de Pasco Co., and Marcona Mining Co.--were taken over. Also included were Grace's paper complex, the entire fishing industry, all of the national press, part of the banking and insurance sectors, and some other manufacturing industries such as chemicals and cement.

The military government, however, lacked a clear philosophy regarding SOEs. Their growth was, according to Alfred Saulniers, the "result of the attempt to meet a few vaguely-identified, imprecise objectives in an uncertain time horizon and within an unknown constraint field."[1] Since the Constitution of 1933 lacked norms for public entities and the Civil Code of 1936 referred their regulation to special legislation, a comprehensive normative law to endow SOEs with both a coherent legal and administrative structure as well as a level of responsible autonomy for their operation should have been a logical prerequisite in a process that, according to one of its civilian ideologists, shifted Peru "from an oligarchic state to state capitalism."[2]

However, if this is an <u>ex post facto</u>, theoretical definition of what Velasco's government attempted to accomplish, it was definitely not that clear <u>ex ante</u>. The first phase's rhetorical goal was a noncapitalist, non-Communist, third way to achieve a "social democracy with full participation," in which an ill-defined social property sector, neither private nor public, would predominate. State ownership was to be only a transitional stage to such a nirvana. This partly explains the inability of the military government (which passed so many laws that attempted to regulate almost every specific aspect of economic activity) to pass a general normative law for state entrepreneurial activity, even though a draft had circulated in various government agencies since 1971.

Therefore, SOEs expanded very significantly (from 18 in 1968--or 40, if other converted government offices are taken into account--to the 174 high given by the first census, in 1977), and the process was carried out under the very unusual approach that state ownership was not to be permanent but only an intermediate stage before reaching the vaguely conceived goal of social property.

Great disorder was the obvious result. The expansion of enterprises with state participation was largely uncoordinated and unplanned; their operation often lacked clear objectives. Efficiency lost importance as performance criteria and no clear alternative social values were developed for this third-way system, a system that lacked both capitalist incentives and Communist discipline. Many enterprises were established as appendages to ministries and had no real autonomy; their everyday operational decisions were affected by political interference, especially in sensitive areas like pricing policy.

The liquidity abundance in international financial markets made it feasible and, of course, more politically convenient, to charge less than real prices for goods and services provided by SOEs and to borrow from abroad to cover subsidies and losses. It also made it possible to start new projects and ventures with little capital and high debt ratios. During the 1970s, of the total investment cost of the many ambitious programs carried out by Peruvian SOEs, only one eighth was financed with the firms' own funds, and even a significant part of the capital transfers from the central government was financed by the state through borrowing.

By 1975 the resources and managerial capacity of the Peruvian state had been stretched beyond their limits. As a result of the above-mentioned expropriations (which also gave title to shares of other, often unrelated, companies that were held by the intervened firms), of the transformation of several government offices into enterprises, of the takeover of a wide variety of failing companies, and of the creation of new ventures, especially in trading, finance, communications, and mining, the size of the Peruvian state, as measured by total public expenditures, was twice what it had been only seven years before (see table 1). The government paid little attention to serious warnings regarding the significance of this transformation, coming even from sympathetic foreign analysts. As Shane Hunt of Boston University affirmed in 1974, "In the next decade, the Peruvian economy will prosper or atrophy according to the effectiveness with which the new public enterprises are managed."[3] Unfortunately, he was a prophet.

Some analysts believe that the expropriation of the national press in 1974, which raised significant political opposition, and the takeover of Marcona's iron deposits, more the result of ill-tempered abruptness than a rational decision, were crucial in leading to the replacement in August 1975 of Gen. Velasco as chief of the revolution. Gen. Francisco Morales Bermudez, more a pragmatic technocrat than an emotional leader, then became president of the military government, thus initiating its second phase.

By that time, however, the Peruvian economy was already in deep trouble. Partially due to inadequate state intervention and controls, national production was running short of global demand, imports exceeded exports, local savings reached a record low, and taxes did not match up with increasing public expenditures. All of these gaps, added up, led to a chronic shortage of foreign exchange and, upon the saturation of external-debt possibilities, to unchecked inflation rates.

The main objective of the military government's second phase was the "consolidation of structural reforms." Since it was widely believed that the state had grown much too quickly, 1975 may be identified as the turning point in reference to the trend of state-intervention policies predominant through the sixties and early seventies.

Prior to August 1975, there was only one case of attempted rationalization through divestment. In the first semester of 1974, PESCAPERU received specific authorization to transfer the assets and reassign the equipment of the fishing companies nationalized in mid-1972. The company was to keep proceeds from the sales and capitalize them.

The second phase, however, did not provide a rational and overall alternative strategy for dealing with SOEs or with mounting economic problems and a truncated political process that had lost its way in the search for a better society. What to do with a failing and increasingly oppressive revolution was the main discussion topic among the military. A silent but deep political struggle originated a set of confusing and contradictory short-sighted decisions regarding economic policy. Slowly but firmly, however, ideologists and radicals were replaced and the social-property sector was, in military terms, "disactivated."

In October 1975 the Council of Ministers established the Multisectorial Commission to examine the basic problems regarding SOE operations and formulate policy recommendations for their solution.[4] Its final report analyzed the wide latitude of legal forms for SOEs and the consequent variation in the degree of central government control. The commission recommended a reduction of the number of permissible forms and a centralization of all state shareholding activities in the Corporacion Financiera de Desarrollo (COFIDE), as the holding company. The commission also suggested the enactment of new legislation to restore the greatly circumscribed autonomy of SOEs in labor matters such as hiring and firing, setting wages and salaries, and deciding on promotions. The budgetary process was, in the commission's opinion, "creating rigidities and delays."[5] Transfers from the firms to the central government in the form of taxes and mandatory profit remittances were criticized for not taking into account that profits do not necessarily mean cash liquidity. It was claimed that some firms had to borrow to transfer registered but not cashable profits to the central government.

The commission accused the comptroller general's control system, essentially legalistic in nature and based on the examination of the firms' procedures, of "asphyxiating, immobilizing and crushing SOEs." Controls were applied with such a counterproductive excess of zeal as to be characterized as "abuse of authority, absolutist and omnimodal power (causing) a rupture of management and institutional authority."[6]

The recommendations of this commission--composed mostly of high-level bureaucrats--were not followed, but a new Multisectorial Commission--which included prominent representatives of the private sector--was appointed in November 1976 with the objective of proposing norms for improving the efficiency of SOEs and drafting a normative law for them. This second commission, which worked all though 1977, criticized the lack of both distinct and specific objectives as well as clear-cut pricing strategies for SOEs. It also recommended that some SOEs be divested to the private sector. The system of control also came in for its share of criticism. The commission counseled an end to political interference in management decisions, and longer terms for boards of directors, thereby freeing them from continual and politically motivated turnovers. Suspension of the rules providing for payment of anticipated profits to the Treasury was also recommended.

The solutions proposed to the problems described by both commissions would have been considered self-evident by any experienced observer of the entrepreneurial activity of the Peruvian state. Their recommendations, however, were set aside. Because it was a long-term issue, very few in the government were willing then, as they are now, to expose themselves to political criticism in a transitional period by seriously addressing a complex topic from which little benefit could be derived in the short run. The system, therefore, has continued very much the same.

By 1978 political vagaries regarding crucial economic issues crashed against hard and urgent realities. The Peruvian economy was flat broke. It lacked sufficient foreign exchange for its external payments, and inflation was running to three digits. A harsh IMF-supported program which reduced very significantly average wages and domestic consumption, was implemented.

In the area of public divestment, the government modified the bylaws of the Stock Exchange Regulatory Commission in order to offer to private national interests some shares of stock it owned. Some months later a law followed that permitted ministers to propose "the suppression, merger, or restricting" of any decentralized agency, including SOEs, as well as "the total or partial sale of shares of public enterprises, or those in which the government has a holding," as long as the activities did not correspond to tax-related or reserved activities.[7]

Several companies and shares were proposed for sale in the ninety days allotted to the ministers under the law, but no interested buyers appeared, partly because of the depressed conditions of the economy, partly because the offer involved the establishment of new commissions to value the firms and to set up the mechanisms for the disposal of shares. Also, the income generated by the sale of stocks held by a public enterprise was to be transferred to the Treasury and matched by a corresponding transfer to the company of ten-year government bonds paying only 10 percent interest with a two-year, no-interest grace period. With inflation running over 70 percent a year, this mechanism was very unattractive to SOE managers and boards eager to defend the asset value of their companies' portfolios.

When no takers appeared, the main effort during the last stage of the Morales Bermudez administration concentrated on improving the financial solvency of SOEs through a process of mergers, debt capitalizations, and building up of equities. Paramonga, the former Grace paper complex, was forced to merge with several other paper factories and was later saddled with an unfinished and unwanted newsprint mill developed by INDUPERU to use locally available bagasse as input. The government assumed PEPESCA and AEROPERU debts. Unpaid subsidies to PESCAPERU and PETROPERU were canceled. Capitalization of taxes and profits was also permitted for a series of other companies. An agreement was reached with the former national owners of cement plants, who had refused to accept any payments from the government and were fighting the expropriation in the judiciary. An amiable compromise emerged in the form of twenty-year concessions for mixed enterprises in which the former owners would eventually regain control, but in which the state would retain possession of 49 percent of the companies' stock.

Parallel to this process, the military government decided on a gradual return to civilian rule and called general elections for a new constitutional convention (_asamblea constituyente_). The resulting constitution was a compromise between the social-democratic, French-style "_diriguisme_" philosophy of the old and predominant Aprista party and the modern pro-free market attitude of the Popular Christian Party (PPC). Accion Popular, Fernando Belaunde's party, decided not to participate in a political gambit that eventually proved very successful.

The new constitution calls for a mixed social-market economy in which private initiative, as well as free trade and freedom of the press, are guaranteed. Several of its articles deal with the responsibility of the state as planner and entrepreneur. Article 113, for instance, assigns state entrepreneurial activities "the goals of promoting the nation's economy, providing public services, and achieving development objectives." The law may also reserve for the state, according to Article 114, certain productions or services for "social" or "national security" interests.

President Belaunde won the 1980 national elections by a surprising 47 percent. His electoral platform called for the continued operation of SOEs in infrastructure and banking sectors, but also for the infusion of private capital into SOEs concerned with other production activities. On his inauguration day, the new government decided to reprivatize media enterprises, allowing the former owners to reduce the number of administrative personnel and compensating them for the effects of the expropriation.

Pres. Belaunde, more a charismatic and visionary politician than a realistic administrator, has basically concentrated his efforts on reestablishing liberty and expanding public expenditures through a series of housing and highway projects. An architect by profession, he is more concerned with the development of these projects than with choosing among alternatives for critical economic issues or deciding who should do what and how. With a liberal style, however, he wields autocratic control over the leaders of his party, among whom he prefers those who were his university students. Since he gets bored easily with legal, economic, or financial technicalities, during the first half of his term (until December 1982), he relied on President of the Council of Ministers and Minister of Economy, Finance, and Commerce Sen. Manuel Ulloa for most decision making on economic policy. (Ulloa, a successful international broker with significant diplomatic talents, had been his minister in 1968.) The first appointed cabinet included two representatives of the PPC and two independent figures: Alfonso Grados--a self-proclaimed social democrat--and Pedro Pablo Kuczynski. The latter, one of the very few in the new government with proven managerial experience, was to serve as minister of energy and mines and control the largest SOEs.

Belaunde's inauguration speech and Ulloa's first report to Congress a month later called for the establishment of a neoliberal model in which private enterprises would undertake economic growth, a free market would provide the incentives for expansion and efficiency, and the state would refrain from undue interference in the market. They both, however, lacked explicit and specific policy guidelines regarding critical issues--like functionality, objectives, information, control, pricing, financing, and divesting--for current state entrepreneurial activities. It should be noted that they, as well as many of their party colleagues, were forced out of Peru for more than a decade and were therefore not fully aware of the current significance of SOEs. Ulloa's report included some of the other ministers' working drafts. Kuczynski completed and published his own report in September 1980, with a specific chapter on SOEs in the energy and mines sectors.[8]

What Kuczynski quickly looked for and obtained was the conversion of his sector's public corporations into state-owned enterprises under private law. This shortcut for increasing their flexibility--a kind of "privatization of management"--was to be, according to the minister himself, only a palliative until a more stable and inclusive legal and administrative framework was designed to deal with the common problems of all enterprises with state participation. He also drafted a new petroleum law and tax incentives to make expanded oil exploration and exploitation activities more attractive to foreign investors under contract from PETROPERU and obtained congressional approval for them. Also, in accordance with the constitution, MINPECO's monopoly in the marketing of mineral production was restricted to state-owned mining companies.

What was definitely clear in the new government attitude toward SOEs was a feeling that they should try to operate very much as private firms, compete in the market, and generate profits. The liquidation of unprofitable enterprises was sometimes announced, not on the basis of public versus private-sector relations, but for fiscal purposes. Thus, Article 96 of the Budget Law for 1981 read, "Public enterprises should self-finance their operating expenses. Otherwise, the executive should fuse them with other enterprises or liquidate them to maintain a balanced budget." In fact, very few were fused or liquidated. The government's imprecise attitude in the early eighties regarding SIDERPERU, for instance, was a clear demonstration that it lacked a specific program regarding what to do with each SOE. At a time of worldwide dumping prices for steel, import tariffs were reduced, thereby provoking huge losses for the state-owned plant and significant gains for many private importers. An obvious by-product of such an open-door trade policy should have been the liquidation of SIDERPERU, since, with its current manufacturing equipment, the firm has been completely unable to compete with larger and more modern installations abroad. However, this decision has not been taken because of political pressure. As a result, SOEs' losses and debts have accumulated unnecessarily.

During May 1981, with strong World Bank backing and significant support from the U. S. government, a consultative group meeting for Peru was held in Paris. In it, the government submitted a 1981-1985 public-investment program that totaled U.S. $11.5 billion, an annual average of 8.3 percent of projected GDP over the five-year period. Ulloa's speech at the meeting and the one he gave to the Senate before leaving for Paris were not fully precise regarding the role of SOEs. "We have rejected the past strategy of exaggerated state control . . . ," he said, while calling for "a concentrated effort to strengthen the ministries and public enterprises by improving their organization, modernizing administrative procedures, and paying competitive salaries to attract the necessary skilled staff."

By then, a new Multisectorial Commission for the Evaluation and Reorganization of Public Enterprises was established. According to Brian Branch, who assisted the commission as part of fieldwork for his M.A. thesis on the subject, it faced serious difficulties in fulfilling it duties: a lack of familiarity with state entrepreneurial activities; the resistance of various government entities directly involved with public firms; and, again, the absence of higher-level political support.[9]

In June 1981, in compliance with extraordinary powers given by Congress for the reorganization of public entities, the executive issued a set of new laws, including Decree-Law 206, Law of the System of Financial Support and Promotion of Entrepreneurial Development, and Decree-Law 216, Law of the Entrepreneurial Activity of the State. Decree-Law 206 created CONADE (Corporacion Nacional de Desarrollo), an enterprise under public law, to direct and orient state intervention in entrepreneurial activities. Decree-Law 216 was the first coherent legal effort to discriminate among the different modalities of SOE: enterprises under public law, state enterprises under private law, mixed enterprises, and shareholdings of the state. It was also the first attempt to regulate organization, function, economic and financial status, labor laws, methods of evaluation, and relations with the various levels of the central government. Decree-Law 216, however, does not define what an SOE is or should be, or what its specific areas for appropriate state intervention are, whether exclusive or not. It thereby grants wide latitude for the sale or retention of current state holdings. Although it improved the legal structure significantly, Decree-Law 216 was not sufficient to establish clear policy guidelines for the future operation of SOEs.

By mid-1981 a conflict had emerged among those in government who thought that first priority should be given to a drastic privatization of SOEs, whatever the political and economic costs, and those who believed that divestment should be only one aspect of an orderly rationalization process that should concentrate first on improving overall efficiency. Those who think that a "new order" is not needed and that the responsible "entrepreneurial autonomy" for which they stand will limit control and further privatization have continually opposed CONADE and Decree-Law 216. This conflict brought about Tulio de Andrea's resignation as chairman of CONADE in November 1981.

During December, an ill-conceived draft of a law that would authorize the executive to divest state shareholdings completely in a given list of enterprises was discussed in Congress and tabled until the next session. The fate of SOEs began to be discussed in an increasingly emotional environment; the topic became a highly sensitive political issue.

In an attempt to cool things down, the government called on me, as an independent figure, to replace Andrea. Before I was formally appointed in January 1982, Ulloa gave a television address in which for the first time he discussed extensively the entrepreneurial role of the state. Considering that the search for a national consensus on the role of the state had been an explicit objective in the Accion Popular party's political platform for the 1980 elections, Ulloa called for a public debate that would result in a law authorizing the executive to carry out a rationalization process.[10]

One month later, I, as chairman of CONADE, gave a speech suggesting the restriction of state intervention, not necessarily through SOEs, to five typical cases: "collective goods or services; natural monopolies or those resulting from small markets; products with inefficient markets due to scarcity of information, lack of resource mobility, or high transaction costs; those activities with significant externalities; and those that fulfill a national strategic objective."[11] In accordance with CONADE's proposal, state ownership was to be considered only if other forms of intervention--such as a special normative framework, or specific taxes or subsidies--were not suitable or were less convenient.

At the same time, the Ministry of Economy, Finance, and Commerce and the Central Bank were negotiating with the IMF the first-year goals for an extended fund facility, which was to last until 1984. The economy was not in good health: large deficits were recorded in the balance of payments and public-sector accounts during 1981; reduced exports combined with higher imports, and growing interest and dividend payments abroad resulted in a current account deficit equal to 8.1 percent of GDP; lower government revenues from exports and income taxes, together with a high level of government spending and investment, contributed to a public-sector deficit of 8.3 percent of GDP. The 1982 goal for the public-sector deficit in the IMF agreement--4.0 percent of GDP--was widely considered to be unrealistic, taking into consideration the ambitious World Bank-supported public-investment program being implemented and the projected unusual losses of state-owned mining companies caused by uncharacteristically low metal prices. Unlike the more neutral World Bank attitude, the IMF staff appeared to firmly support privatization.

During 1982 CONADE and a Senate commission worked out a draft of a bill that included a conceptual normative framework defining the scope and limits of state intervention in entrepreneurial activities and a classification of the enterprises currently falling within the state's sphere in one, more than one, or none of the five categories. A procedure was established for the divestment of those that fail to be classified as subject to state intervention. The Senate, however, mainly because of the reluctance of the ruling party to decide on a normative issue with no political short-term benefits, repeatedly postponed discussion of the bill.

In the meantime, the ridigity of public expenditures and of the SOEs' investment programs became obvious. After neglecting or tabling the discussion of the problem as a whole while there were external funds available to finance any cash shortages, the Treasury and Central Bank officers became increasingly upset by a fixed structure, responsible for half the total public-sector financial requirements, over which they had little control. Accustomed to working with short-term deficits that could be window-dressed by nominally raising taxes or slashing expenditures, they were very unsympathetic toward CONADE's long-term approach of establishing a general framework for improving overall efficiency. Some even thought that abruptly selling state shareholdings might quickly and magically raise cash to fulfill the impossible and short-sighted IMF goals. The political implications or even the actual feasibility of raising immediate cash in a weakened domestic capital market were not analyzed to any great extent.

Kuczynski resigned in July 1982. He included a section about SOEs in his concluding report: "It is not only the divestment of SOEs that should be discussed, which for the larger ones is not only an impossible objective, in view of scarce private national savings, but an undesirable one, taking into consideration power and wealth distribution. What is currently missing is an all-inclusive definition of policy regarding the operation of SOEs."[12]

By the second semester of 1982, the economic situation had worsened (table 2). Short-term foreign credit had to be raised significantly to cover a public-sector deficit that had soared to 8.8 percent of GNP. This financial loophole was also used to avoid an open violation of the IMF agreement. Sen. Ulloa resigned as president of the Council of Ministers by year end. Before resigning, however, he (surprisingly) submitted to Congress the draft of a bill including a proposal for the liquidation of CONADE, his own eighteen-month-old creation. Congress rejected it. Yet, before leaving office, he enacted the CONADE-drafted rulings of Decree-Law 216. During 1982 CONADE's affiliated firms--COFIDE and Inversiones COFIDE S.A.--proceeded with the liquidation of some of the small companies under their supervision that were failing.

Vice-Pres. Fernando Schwalb, a corporate lawyer who was Peruvian ambassador to the United States, was nominated to replace Ulloa.

Schwalb selected Foreign Affairs as his ministry and brought in Carlos Rodriguez Pastor, an orthodox banker formerly with the Wells Fargo Bank in California, as minister of economy, finance, and commerce. The new president of the Council of Ministers' report to Congress included a section on SOEs in which he insisted on the prompt approval of CONADE's draft bill.[13]

The new minister of economy, finance, and commerce, however, had little time for anything but the external debt arrangements. Upon my resignation as chairman of CONADE, its vice-president, Manuel Velarde --a lawyer, partisan, and old friend of the president--was nominated to replace me. He was able, with Sen. Ulloa's support, to have the draft bill approved by the Senate. The new law still has to be reviewed by the Chamber of Deputies. Velarde also managed to stop a new attempt by the Ministry of Economy, Finance, and Commerce to replace CONADE as the institution in charge of monitoring state entrepreneurial activities.

For the Peruvian economy, 1983 was a disastrous year. GDP fell by 12 percent, partly because of natural disasters: unusual floods in the north and severe droughts in the south. External debt payments had to be postponed. The operations of two failing private banks were taken over by state-owned banks. The public-sector deficit rose to 12 percent of GDP. The inflation rate was 125 percent for the year, and the exchange rate was depreciated by 130 percent. The IMF program goals collapsed when faced with such a harsh reality.

With a tenacity worthy of a more comprehensive cause, Rodriguez Pastor reached an agreement with the IMF for a new one-year standby program oriented toward a reduction of public-sector financial requirements to, again, 3.8 percent of GDP in 1984. The program calls for adequate price increases for SOE products, a reduction in their investment programs and some forms of privatization (that is, less state interference in both the financial markets and the trade of basic foodstuffs), a reduction in the size of PESCAPERU, and the partial divestment of the Tintaya mining project.

This program, because of its recessionary effects, has been strongly opposed even from within the government. National elections are to be held in March 1985, and the results of the November 1983 municipal elections were considered a defeat for the government parties: the Aprista party won 34 percent of the vote and the United Left won the Lima mayoralty.

Current Situation and Perspectives

Classification of SOEs

According to Decree-Law 216 (June 1981), there are four forms for the participation of the Peruvian state in the property of enterprises:

(1) Enterprises under public law--created by law to develop activities that correspond to the state, to which their enterprises' capital must belong directly and exclusively.

Their liquid assets are considered public funds and their management is subject to the general budget regulations. Their fixed assets can be bought or sold only through public bid. State sovereignty attributions can be transferred to these enterprises. Currently, there are fifteen enterprises of this nature.

(2) State enterprises under private law--fully owned directly or through holdings by the state. Currently, there are sixty-three of these enterprises.

(3) Mixed enterprises--private corporations in which the state participates in association with third parties. The state must have, directly or indirectly, a 51 percent share, or more than 20 percent of the stock and veto power over all major decisions of the shareholder's board. Currently, there are forty-nine of these corporations.

(4) Enterprises with state shareholdings--private corporations in which the state has an indirect minor participation and the rights and obligations of any other stockholder. Currently, there are twenty-three of these corporations.

The most recent list of all these enterprises is included as Appendix A. The total number, 150, is not large by Latin American standards; however, in some other countries, a considerable number of local and municipal bodies are considered enterprises. The wide diversity of the Peruvian parastatal sector is also atypical.

<u>The Significance of SOEs to the Economy</u>

The 150 SOEs play a major role in the Peruvian economy. They are responsible for an estimated 15 percent to 20 percent of GDP. The state wholly owns the four largest production complexes in Peru: PETROPERU (oil), CENTROMIN (mining), SIDERPERU (steel), and Paramonga (paper). SOEs account for over half of all public investment and employ about 125,000 persons.

Enterprises with state participation dominate certain sectors of the economy. They control all production of electric power, gas, water, fertilizer, iron, rail transportation, and telecommunications and dominate the steel and fish-processing industries, as well as the production of paper and, to a lesser extent, that of cement. PETRO-PERU purchases all oil produced locally by foreign companies and controls domestic sales and exports. State-owned mines produce 25 percent of copper output and 40 percent to 50 percent of zinc, silver, and lead.

SOEs also control much of Peru's commerce. Until recently, mineral exports were a monopoly of MINPECO, and similar trading enterprises import, or purchase domestically and sell, such basic foodstuffs as rice, wheat, corn, sugar, coffee, vegetable oil, and milk products. In 1980, for example, about 70 percent of all exports and 35 percent of consumer and raw-material imports passed through the hands of SOEs. Total sales for the fifteen largest SOEs add up to approximately 15 percent of gross national sales.

Similarly, state banks prevail in Peru's financial sector. In

1980 state-owned financial institutions were responsible for three fourths of all loans and two thirds of all sight and savings deposits. State financial institutions do virtually all medium- and long-term lending in Peru.

Administrative Structure

There is no coherent system for administering the shares of SOEs. Many are held directly by a ministry, which means the minister appoints the state representatives to the shareholders' board and instructs them to appoint the corresponding members of the board of directors. The remaining shares are held indirectly by other enterprises, whose shares may also be owned by others or, at the end of the chain, by the ministries. More than one public entity may hold the shares of a given company. With some exceptions, the enterprises run directly by a ministry have had far less authority than those run indirectly. However, there is also little managerial experience regarding the interlinkage of an enterprise with its parent holding company.

Assessment of SOE Performance

The 1981 Multisectorial Commission, judging from the data available for ninety-seven SOEs, found that as a whole these companies earned a profit that amounted to a 4 percent return on equity in 1980. A mission of the World Bank made a more in-depth assessment of a smaller sample (twenty firms), all but one wholly state-owned and chosen to represent some of the most important enterprises with state participation.[14] The sample included thirteen companies producing cement, paper, steel, petroleum, copper and other minerals, fish products, and tractors, and seven service enterprises providing electricity, port services, telecommunications, air and water transport, water and sewerage, and marketing services.

According to the World Bank report, the firms reviewed fall into two main categories: (a) companies, often nationalized, that were allowed to operate with considerable autonomy under private law and enjoyed continuity of management; and (b) companies, often state-created, that were subject to extensive government interference in their structure and daily operations and that had a high turnover of managers.

The performance of the twenty SOEs in the sample was below that of the average Peruvian private firm. The 1980 return on assets of the sample, for instance, was 0.4 percent compared to 10.1 percent for a sample of private manufacturing companies. Measures like subsidized prices and costly government intervention sacrificed profits. In addition, the monopoly position of most of these firms, plus a lack of incentive to maximize profits, contributed to lower operating efficiency than in private companies.

In general, the more autonomous firms earned higher profits--6 percent return on assets in 1980--and had a lower debt and greater liquidity than the others. At the same time, their production was expanding more slowly, probably reflecting the fact that their investment decisions were more attuned to market and financial constraints. Their debt/equity and liquidity ratios were also more in line with those of private firms in Peru.

Legal Framework

In spite of Decree-Law 216, the legal framework for SOEs remains very confusing. Many state enterprises under private law have their own legislation, which in some cases strictly limits their autonomy. The powers of the directors and shareholders' boards may also vary from company to company.

Although general budget regulations should be restricted in principle to enterprises under public law, they normally refer indiscriminately to all SOEs. For instance, a very recent regulation (DS N 612-83-EFC) forces those enterprises with a majority of stateholding participation to ask specific authorization from the central government for the following: to start new investment projects; to hire more personnel or increase wages; to buy or rent new office space or vehicles; and to raise, during the current year, the 1983 level of expenditure on gasoline, advertising, and overtime.

However, this same decree, with such a strong tendency toward checking procedures and not results, pays lip service to Decree-Laws 206 and 216 and instructs CONADE to present a proposal in 120 days regarding how SOE operations should be reorganized and carried out. Hence, there is a constant conflict between those supporting entrepreneurial autonomy and those who prefer to treat SOEs like appendages to the central government and subject to all budget regulations. Therefore, little progress has been made regarding the elimination of legal duplication and the appropriate simplification of the legal framework of the SOE.

Current Problems

The three main current problem areas for SOEs in Peru have to do with their function, efficiency, and solvency.

Function

Most problems would disappear if public opinion and elected politicians would accept the premise that an SOE, as a profit-making unit, belongs to the state but is not a part of national government. An enterprise should be a deliberate creation for the rational accomplishment of specific goals through time. Since the transformation of inputs into outputs implies a technological process, such transformation requires a formal organization and a stable hierarchy for the decision-making process to achieve, by the efficient assignment of scare resources to alternative ends, a microeconomic optimization.

Why do politicians accept more easily the autonomy of, say, a public library, a museum, or a university, but it is so hard for them to keep their hands off the operation of an SOE? The answer is obvious: it is hard for them to surrender power. In Peru several state enterprises under private law grew as appendages to ministries:

therefore, every time a new minister was appointed, he expected to nominate a new board. The president must approve all appointments, and also authorizes every trip abroad by any employee, even of some of the mixed enterprises. According to the World Bank report, a director of one SOE claimed to have accumulated thirty-three government questionnaires during a six-month period in 1978, which were still unanswered by 1980, although he is required by law to answer them. It is easy to see that SOEs are overadministered and undermanaged.

Efficiency

Most SOEs lack a clearly defined mission and a short list of simple, understandable, and attainable objectives. Therefore, their operations are similar to that of a soccer team on a field with no goals. It is not surprising, then, that they act not for maximizing results, but for minimizing efforts. Until now, no system has been fully developed in Peru to establish reasonable and consistent objectives for SOEs or to monitor their performance and evaluate their products. Ministers, instead of determining policies and overall objectives, prefer to impose decisions on everyday operations.

Decree-Law 216 attempts to create a more effective system of control. Plans for state business activities are to be approved by the CIAEF (Interministerial Commission for Economic and Financial Affairs) after CONADE recommendation. It is also CONADE's responsibility to exercise _ex post facto_ control of SOEs by monitoring and evaluating their performance without interfering in normal operations. The comptroller general should continue to exercise control with regard to legality and veracity, but in an _ex post facto_ manner through annual external audits and investigations. External auditors selected by the comptroller are not at present of adequate caliber for the job, however.

The information required for a new management by objectives (MBO) system, however, is seldom available, and few SOEs have detailed cost-accounting data. A high rate of turnover of top- and mid-level managers, due mainly to insufficient salaries, is a major limitation on improving overall efficiency with regard to the development of MBO.

Solvency

Since they were created with a high debt/equity ratio and more often than not they have not been allowed to charge real prices for the goods and services they provide (not to mention the inefficiency their poor functioning causes), most Peruvian SOEs are severely undercapitalized. This is obviously a serious and urgent problem for a country currently strapped for cash.

Divestment Possibilities

The CONADE-drafted Divestment Law pending approval in the Chamber of Deputies pursues several goals: the reinforcement of Decree-Law 216 by defining the different mechanisms and systems of control for the different types of SOE; the classification of the goods and services that could be subject to state intervention in their production; the enforcement of the requirements for establishing a new enterprise with a majority of state-holding participation; and the definition of the requirements for divesting, totally or partially, any state majority shareholdings in corporations of private law, as well as a definition of the possible means--public bid, stock exchange offerings, private offerings--for such a process. Finally, it details which specific SOEs are subject to full or partial divestment (see Appendix A) and establishes tax regulations that will facilitate the fusion, transfer, or transformation of such enterprises.

A search for rationality, flexibility, and gradualism was the main criterion for the drafting of the Divestment Law. It confirms Decree-Law 216 by saying that enterprises under public law can be created only by law. At the same time, it establishes that state shareholdings in enterprises in which the state has only a minor participation can be transferred with no formal authorization. It also defines five categories of goods and services that could be susceptible to state intervention in their production: (1) collective goods or public services; (2) monopolies; (3) finance and insurance; (4) basic needs related with nutrition and health; (5) strategic activities. It also establishes that in each case the formation of an SOE should be compared with other forms of intervention. This comparison must also be reviewed periodically.

CONADE's gross estimate of the sale value of shares and enterprises subject to divestment is US $200 million, about 1 percent of GNP. The World Bank report on the subject discusses market and political constraints, some economic and social costs, and a recommended selling strategy for a divestment process of this nature.[15]

Private consultants hired by CONADE came up with rather similar conclusions and proposed leasing as an attractive alternative when total divestment appears to be a complicated process.

Trends in National Opinion

The positions of the major political parties regarding SOEs were not very different during their confrontation before the 1980 elections. According to Accion Popular, the government party,

> it is necessary to define and specify, within the context of current realities and limitations, that the state has overexpanded and that it is necessary to define a set of priorities for its areas of intervention. . . . The government plan proposes the divestment of some enterprises to the private sector, especially through a diffused shareholding . . . . The ministries' lack of orientation toward normative functions, which should be the essence of government, has caused those functions to be replaced by an increasing orientation toward the direct production of goods and services.[16]

The Popular Christian party (also a partner in government) feels that "public enterprises have grown in a disorderly and accelerated way. . . . [It is necessary] to affirm the subsidiary role of the state as director and promoter and to review its entrepreneurial activity in the context of its real possibilities."[17]

The major opposition force, the Aprista party, finds that "state entrepreneurial activities demand new legislation oriented toward the reduction of the current number of enterprises to the strictly needed, the submission of their performance to criteria of efficiency and results, and the simplification of their wide diversity of operational frameworks."[18]

In a survey administered during 1980 by the Universidad del Pacifico, Accion Popular was presented with a sample list of SOEs and asked to propose an ownership structure for each of them.[19] From the list of twenty-four, Accion Popular's explicit position was to keep thirteen wholly owned by the state and partially divest the remaining eleven to local investors, thereby establishing mixed enterprises with variable levels of state participation (see table 3).

During the Senate discussion of the divestment bill, the Aprista party proposed different wording for the classification of enterprises subject to state intervention--that is, natural resources, defense, essential public services, basic infrastructure, large transportation and communication systems, and finance and insurance--and opposed the divestment of some enterprises (indicated in Appendix A) as suitable for such a process. The Aprista proposal also asked for congressional authorization each time an enterprise was to be divested or liquidated.

It could be said that there are currently three positions in the Peruvian political arena regarding the fate of SOEs. First, there are those--a minority sector in Accion Popular, a larger share of the PPC, academic followers of the neoliberal and monetarist schools, the daily newspaper _La Prensa_, some local entrepreneurs--who favor a drastic privatization process. On the other extreme, there are those in the leftist parties, including a faction of the Aprista party, who consider an expanded state a convenient government objective. Since there are financial constraints on such a development at the present time, these last groups may consider it more practical to advocate a tactical consolidation of the current situation.

A pragmatic rationalization stands in the middle, supported in principle by various leaders of all three major parties, the World Bank, the armed forces, several representatives of local entrepreneurs, and those who, not knowing much about the subject, avoid extreme positions in principle.

Agenda for a Pragmatic Rationalization

This middle-ground position, in my opinion, should basically include the following:

(1) The completion of a coherent legal framework through the Chamber of Deputies' approval of the Divestment Law, the replacement of an abundant set of specific regulations with a short number of general rules, including those related to the general budget, and a precise definition of the appropriate criteria for the relationship between the SOEs and the comptrollet general's office.

(2) The establishment of a few holding companies as enterprises under public law--for example, commercial banking, investment financing, oil, fishing, mining, water and sewerage, electrical power, communications, civil infrastructure, defense, and industries and services--and grouping all current SOEs under their control.

(3) The approval by the president of members of the board of directors for these holding companies and their collective naming by the CIAEF at the suggestion of the board of CONADE. Every two years, one third of the board members of each enterprise should be replaced. The boards of these holding companies should be free to choose their managers and the board members of their affiliated firms.

(4) The gradual divestiture of the enterprise mentioned in Appendix A and the reduction of personnel and unnecessary fixed assets in overcrowded SOEs.

(5) The implementation of a management by objectives system similar to the one suggested by the World Bank report (see figures 1 and 2).[20]

(6) The improvement of the solvency of SOEs through capitalization of debts and a rational review of investment programs, taking into consideration current financial restraints.

(7) The design of a long-term career in administration of SOEs and the founding of an association of managers of SOEs.

Projections

In the next eighteen months, during the remaining term of the current administration, some progress may be forthcoming regarding the agenda I have outlined here, especially regarding the approval of the Divestment Law and its rulings, the design of the holding-company administration structure, the reduction of personnel, and the divestiture or liquidation of minor participations and enterprises. However, I expect no significant change, due to the proximity of the general elections.

The new government will probably be composed of either the Aprista party by itself, or in combination with minor participation by independents or small political groups; or of a coalition of all forces to the right of the APRA. In both cases, the pragmatic rationalization approach will probably be followed with minor variations.

It is very probable that shift toward a drastic privatization attitude or a great expansion of the state will be considered by Peruvian authorities before 1990.

Table 1

Size of the Peruvian State

	1955	1960	1967	1970	1975
AGGREGATE VALUE (% OF GDP)					
Central government	7.3	8.0	8.9	8.1	11.5
SOEs and others	0.5	0.8	1.7	3.3	9.9
Total	7.8	8.8	10.6	11.4	21.4
FIXED INVESTMENT (% OF GDP)					
Central government	3.4	1.2	2.4	2.6	2.8
SOEs and others	0.5	1.1	1.6	1.9	6.0
Total	3.9	2.3	4.0	4.5	8.8
PERCENTAGE OF GROSS CAPITAL FORMATION	21	14	27	36	51
EMPLOYMENT (000)					
Central government	140	168	251	289	354
SOEs and others	8	11	19	43	100*
Total	148	179	270	332	454
PERCENTAGE OF NON-AGRICULTURAL EMPLOYMENT	10	9	14	15	18

Source: E.V.K. FitzGerald, _The Political Economy of Peru_, 1956-1978 (Cambridge: At the University Press).

* I have corrected FitzGerald's estimate.

Table 2

Public Sector Statistics, 1976-1983
(Percentage of GNP)

Sector	1976-78	1979	1980	1981	1982
Central government	6.3	0.6	2.8	4.9	4.0
Income	14.9	18.0	20.5	17.9	18.0
Expenses	21.2	18.6	23.3	22.8	22.0
Rest of public sector	2.7	0.9	3.6	3.4	4.8
Public sector deficit	9.0	1.5	6.4	8.3	8.8
Public investment	6.7	5.5	7.3	8.1	10.3
Central government	2.6	3.0	3.6	4.1	3.7
Rest of public sector	4.1	2.5	3.7	4.0	6.6

Source: Banco Central del Peru, official bulletin.

Table 3

Accion Popular Survey Response, 1980

SOE	Should Remain State-owned	Should Become a Mixed Enterprise with Local Private Partners	% of Proposed State Participation
AEROPERU		X	40
Banco Continental	X		
Banco Internacional	X		
Banco Popular	X		
CENTROMIN	X		
CPV	X		
COFIDE	X		
ELECTROPERU		X	40
EMADI	X		
ENAFER	X		
ENCI (EPSA)		X	40
ENTEL		X	49
EPPA PERU		X	40
EPSEP	X		
ESAL	X		
HIERRO PERU		X	40
INDUPERU		X	50
MINERO PERU		X	50
MINPECO		X	50
PARAMONGA		X	30
PESCA PERU		X	30
PETROPERU	X		
SIDERPERU	X		
SIMA	X		

Source: Peru 1980: Elecciones y planes de gobierno CIUP (Lima: Universidad del Pacifíco, 1980).

Appendix

Peruvian SOEs

	Assets (U.S. $Millions)	Equity (U.S. $Millions)	1982 Income (U.S. $Millions)	No. of Workers	Parent Entity	Principal Activity and Comments
Enterprises under Public Law						
1. Corporación Nacional de Desarrollo (CONADE)	150	150	--	--	MEFC	Main entrepreneurial holding in charge of monitoring non-financial SOEs' performance
2. Banco de la Nación	1,320	100	415	6,820	MEFC	Main financial agent of the state
3. Banco Agrario del Perú	445	135	215	3,485	MEFC	Agricultural development bank

Notes: The quality of the information in this appendix is suitable only for the purpose of obtaining a general overview of Peru's SOEs. Information obtained regarding number of workers comes from companies. Dash means fewer than 50.

N.A. means not available

N.S. means not significant for the purposes of this study

[a] includes FONAVI, a special fund for housing projects

[b] 1981 figure

[c] means subject to partial divestment, according to the new law

[d] means subject to total divestment, according to the new law

Parent entities:
- MEFC Ministry of Economy, Finance, and Commerce
- MEM Ministry of Energy and Mines
- MA Ministry of Agriculture
- MH Ministry of Housing
- MTC Ministry of Transport and Communications
- MITI Ministry of Industry, Tourism, and Integration
- MP Ministry of Fishing
- MG Ministry of War
- MM Ministry of Navy
- M Ar Ministry of Air Force
- INCS National Institute of Social Communication

Appendix--continued

	Assets (U.S. $Millions)	Equity (U.S.$Millions)	1982 Income (U.S. $Millions)	No. of Workers	Parent Entity	Principal Activity and Comments
4. Banco Industrial del Perú	525	45	115	1,665	MEFC	Industrial development bank
5. Banco Minero del Perú	270	20	70	1,300	MEFC	Mining development bank
6. Banco de la Vivienda del Perú	395	230 [a]	120	775	MEFC	Housing development bank
7. Banco de Desarrollo Amazónico	N.A.	N.A.	--	N.A.	MEFC	Amazon development bank, still at the preoperational level
8. Servicio Nacional de Abastecimiento de Agua Potable y Alcantarillado (SENAPA)	5	5	--	1,800	MH	Water & sewage supply, national level. Assets & equity figures are nominal
9. Servicio de Agua Potable y Alcantarillado de Lima (SEDAPAL)	155	115	45	3,300	SENAPA	Water & sewage, Lima
10. Servicio de Agua Potable y Alcantarillado de Arequipa (SEDAPAR)	15	15	5	480	SENAPA	Water & sewage, Arequipa
11. Servicio de Agua Potable y Alcantarillado de Trujillo (SEDAPAT)	5	5	5	330	SENAPA	Water & sewage, Trujillo
12. Empresa Nacional de Comercialización de Insumos (ENCI)	55	15	100	N.A.	MA	Food & fertilizer marketing
13. Empresa Nacional de Edificaciones (ENACE)	10	--	10	1,100	MH	Public housing projects

14. Industrias Militares del Perú (INDUMIL)	45	10	15	1,500	MG	Military equipment
15. Empresa Pública de Certificaciones Pesqueras del Perú (CERPER)	--	--	5	380	MP	Sanitary & quality control office for fish products; organized as an SOE
Enterprises under Private Law						
1. Empresa Pública de Electricidad del Perú S.A. (ELECTROPERU)	1,615	810	150	6,300	MEM	Electricity supply, national level
2. Petróleos del Perú S.A. (PETROPERU)	1,200	215	1,445	8,700	MEH	Oil extraction, refining & marketing
3. Petróleos Transoceánica S.A. [c]	140	35	75	300	PETROPERU	Shipping subsidiary
4. Servicios Petroleros S.A. (SERPETRO)	N.A.	N.A.	N.A.	N.A.	PETROPERU	Drilling & exploration subsidiary
5. Empresa Minera del Perú S.A. (MINERO PERU)	520	195	170	3,500	MEM	Mining & mineral refining
6. Empresa Minera del Centro del Perú S.A. (CENTROMIN PERU) [c]	570	145	450	17,100	MINEROPERU	Mining & mineral refining
7. CENTROMIN PERU Inc. Lmtd. S.A. [c]	--	--	--	--	CENTROMIN PERU	Subsidiary
8. Empresa Minera del Hierro del Perú S.A. (HIERRO PERU) [c]	145	95	125	3,600	MEM	Iron
9. Agencia Naviera San Nicolás S.A. [c]	5	--	20	--	HIERROPERU	Shipping agent subsidiary
10. Empresa Minera Especial Tintaya S.A. (TINTAYA) [c]	65	30	--	190	MINEROPERU/ CENTROMIN/ Inversiones COFIDE	Copper mining project

Appendix--*continued*

	Assets (U.S. $Millions)	Equity (U.S. $Millions)	1982 Ircome (U.S. $Millions)	No. of Workers	Parent Entity	Principal Activity and Comments
11. Minero Perú Comercial S.A. (MINPECO) [c]	360	(35)	860	600	MEM	Metal trading. Negative equity due to losses. A recent capitalization has restored lost equity
12. MINPECO USA INC.	N.A.	N.A.	N.A.	--	MINPECO	Subsidiary
13. MINPECO UK Ltd.	N.A.	N.A.	N.A.	--	MINPECO	Subsidiary
14. Corporación Financiera de Desarrollo S.A. (COFIDE)	805	125	125	660	CONADE	Long-term & development financing
15. Inversiones COFIDE S.A.	160	65	--	--	CONADE	Recently formed holding enterprise
16. Empresa Siderúrgica del Perú S.A. (SIDERPERU)	315	170	175	5,000	Inversiones COFIDE	Steel
17. Sociedad Paramonga Ltda S.A. [c]	190	105	125	3,700	Inversiones COFIDE	Pulp & paper
18. La Papelera Peruana S.A. [d]	5	--	5	280	Inversiones COFIDE	Paper products, managed by Paramonga
19. Compañia Celulósica y Papelera del Norte S.A. [d]	--	--	5	190	Inversiones COFIDE	Paper products, managed by Paramonga
20. Cemento Yura S.A. [c]	55	30	15	350	Inversiones COFIDE	Cement
21. Cemento Sur S.A. [c]	5	5	5	170	Inversiones COFIDE	Cement

22.	Empresa para el Desarrollo y Explotación de la Palma Aceitera (EMDEPALMA) [c]	25	10	5	1,000	ENCI/ Inversiones COFIDE	Palm oil project
23.	Empresa Promotora del Carbón (PROCARBON) [c]	--	--	--	--	MINERO/CENTRO-MIN ELECTRO/I. COFIDE	Institution for development of coal, organized as SOE
24.	Empresa Promotora Bayovar S.A. (PROBAYOVAR) [c]	5	5	--	--	MINERO/ENCI I. COFIDE	Phosphates mine project
25.	Empresa de Transporte Aéreo del Perú S.A. (AEROPERU) [c]	45	10	80	1,800	Inversiones COFIDE	Airline
26.	Artesanías del Perú S.A. [c]	--	--	--	100	Inversiones COFIDE	Handicraft promotion & marketing
27.	Compresoras Andinas S.A. (COMPASA) [d]	--	--	--	--	Inversiones COFIDE	Compressors
28.	Química del Pacífico S.A. (QUIMPAC) [d]	25	15	15	280	Inversiones COFIDE	Salt & caustic soda
29.	Fertilizantes Sintéticos S.A. (FERTISA) [d]	10	10	10	450	Inversiones COFIDE	Fertilizers
30.	Empresa Nacional Pesquera S.A. (PESCA PERU) [c]	200	25	205	6,000	MP	Fishing - fishmeal processing. Number of workers recently reduced to 1,200
31.	Empresa Peruana de Servicios Pesqueros S.A. (EPSEP) [c]	10	5	5	1,050	MP	Fish marketing
32.	Empresa Nacional de Telecomunicaciones del Perú S.A. (ENTEL PERU) [c]	230	95	130	6,800	MTC	Telecommunications service, national level

Appendix--continued

		Assets (U.S. $Millions)	Equity (U.S. $Millions)	1982 Income (U.S. $Millions)	No. of Workers	Parent Entity	Principal Activity and Comments
33.	Servicios Industriales de la Marina S.A. (SIMA PERU)	100	30	50	5,200	MM	Shipyard
34.	Industria Aeronáutica del Perú S.A. (INDAER PERU) [c]	--	--	--	--	M Ar	Not yet in operation; currently developing a plane assembly plant
35.	Empresa Nacional de Puertos S.A. (ENAPU)	185	140	90	4,200	MTC	Port services, national level
36.	Compañía Peruana de Vapores S.A. (CPV) [c]	125	60	110 [b]	1,800	MTC	Shipping
37.	Corporación Peruana de Aeropuertos y Aviación Comercial S.A. (CORPAC)	85	65	40	3,100	MTC	Airport services, national level
38.	Empresa Nacional de Transporte Urbano del Perú S.A. (ENATRUPERU) [c]	20	15	5	2,600	MTC	Bus service, Lima
39.	Empresa Nacional de Ferrocarriles S.A. (ENAFER PERU) [c]	115	80	40	6,100	MTC	Railroad service, national level
40.	Empresa Nacional de Turismo S.A. (ENTUR PERU)	25	20	10	N.A.	MITI	Hotels, national level
41.	Empresa Nacional del Tabaco S.A. (ENATA) [d]	5	5	5	310	MITI	Tobacco
42.	Empresa de la Sal S.A. (EMSAL) [c]	10	5	15	600	MITI	Salt
43.	Empresa del Alcohol Industrial S.A. [d]	--	--	--	60	MITI	Denatured alcohol

45. Empresa Estatal Industrial Cachimayo S.A. (INCA) [c]	15	5	5	260	MITI	Fertilizers
46. Empresa Comercializadora del Arroz S.A. (ECASA)	200	5	180	1,200	ENCI	Rice marketing
47. Empresa de Comercialización de Productos Pecuarios S.A. (EMCOPESA) [c]	5	--	5	130	MA	Meat processing & marketing
48. Empresa de Mercados Mayoristas S.A. (EMMSA) [c]	--	--	--	170	MA	Wholesale marketing
49. Empresa Ganadera Amazonas S.A. (EGASA) [c]	5	5	5	460	ENCI	Livestock
50. Tiendas Afiliadas S.A. [d]						
51. Administración y Gerencia S.A. [d]	10 [b]	--	50 [b]	500 [b]	MA	Retail marketing in Lima; currently in liquidation
52. Supermercados S.A. [d]						
53. Compañía de Negociaciones Mobiliarias e Inmobiliarias S.A. (CONEMINSA) [d]	10 [b]	10 [b]	--	--	Banco de la Nación	Real estate subsidiary
54. Inversiones Inmobiliarias El Dorado S.A. [d]	--	--	--	--	Banco de la Nación	Real estate subsidiary
55. Banco de Materiales	N.A.	N.A.	N.A.	N.A.	MH	Financing for low-income, self-constructed housing
56. Empresa de Cine, Radio y Televisión Peruana S.A. (RTP) [c]	10	5	5	650	INCS	Radio & television
57. Empresa Peruana de Servicios Editoriales S.A. (EDITORA PERU) [c]	5	--	10	560	INCS	Publishing
58. Agencia Peruana de Noticias y Publicidad S.A. (ANDINA) [c]	--	--	--	170	INCS	News & advertising agency

Appendix--*continued*

	Assets (U.S. $Millions)	Equity (U.S. $Millions)	1982 Income (U.S. $Millions)	No. of Workers	Parent Entity	Principal Activity and Comments
59. Compañia Minera San Juan de Lucanas S.A. [d]	10 [b]	5 [b]	--	N.A.	Banco Minero del Perú	Small mine taken over by bank
60. Compañia Minera Condestable S.A. [d]	--	--	5	240	MINERO PERU	Copper mine
61. Propiedad Minas Justa S.A. [d]	--	--	--	--	HIERROPERU	Not operating
62. Agencia Portuaria San Juan, S.A. [d]	--	--	--	--	HIERROPERU	Not operating
63. Servicios Transmar S.A. [d]	--	--	--	--	HIERROPERU	Not operating
Mixed Enterprises						
1. Banco Continental	470	30	130	2,855	Nación/COFIDE (+90%)	Commercial banking
2. Banco Nor Perú (CONTINORTE) [c]	70	5	30	415	Continental (+90%)	Subsidiary
3. Banco de los Andes [c]	40	--	15	470	Continental (+90%)	Subsidiary
4. Financiera San Pedro S.A. [c]	75	5	40	--	Continental (99%)	Investment financing
5. Almacenera Continental S.A. [d]	--	--	--	N.A.	Continental (100%)	Warehouse subsidiary
6. CONTIDATA S.A. [d]	--	--	--	N.A.	Continental (100%)	Real estate subsidiary
7. Conturismo S.A. [d]	N.A.	N.A.	--	--	Continental (100%)	Real estate subsidiary

9.	Banco Popular del Perú	450	20	155	3,500	Nación (+95%)	Commercial banking
10.	Compañía de Fomento e Inversiones S.A. (PERUINVEST) [c]	60	5	25	120	Popular (+85%)	Investment financing
11.	Compañía Orrantia S.A. [d]	N.A.	N.A.	--	--	Popular (+90%)	Real estate subsidiary
12.	Almacenes Generales de Depósito S.A. (KOLKANDINA) [d]	--	--	--	--	Popular (+90%)	Warehouse subsidiary
13.	Compañía de Transportes Especializados S.A. (CITESA) [d]	--	--	--	--	Popular (+90%)	Transportation subsidiary
14.	Distribuidora de Materiales S.A. [d]	--	--	--	--	Popular (+90%)	Transportation subsidiary
15.	Compañía de Inversiones Populares S.A. [d]	N.A.	N.A.	--	--	Popular (100%)	Real estate subsidiary
16.	Empresa de Comercialización de Servicios de Cómputo S.A. (COMPUTO) [d]	--	--	--	N.A.	Popular (100%)	Data-processing subsidiary
17.	Negocios de Distribución S.A. (NEDISA) [d]	--	--	--	--	Popular (+90%)	Retail subsidiary
18.	Compañía de Transportes Locales S.A. [d]	--	--	--	--	Popular (+90%)	Transportation subsidiary
19.	Banco Internacional del Perú (INTERBANC)	265	15	95	2,335	Nación (+95%)	Commercial banking
20.	Financiera Peruana S.A. (INTERFIP) [c]	30	--	15	50	Internacional (+95%)	Investment financing

Appendix--<u>continued</u>

	Assets (U.S. $Millions)	Equity (U.S. $Millions)	1982 Income (U.S. $Millions)	No. of Workers	Parent Entity	Principal Activity and Comments
21. Internacional de Inmuebles S.A. [d]	N.A.	N.A.	--	--	Internacional (100%)	Real estate subsidiary
22. Empresa de Servicios Internacionales S.A. (INTERSEV) [d]	--	--	--	N.A.	Internacional (100%)	
23. Banco Central Hipotecario del Perú [c]	345	10	220	1,480	MEFC/5 state banks (70%)	Mortgage financing
24. Banco Peruano de los Constructores (BANPECO) [c]	65	10	25	345	Hipotecario (50%) Popular (7%)	Construction development bank
25. Popular y Porvenir, Compañía de Seguros S.A. [c]	115	20	100	690	Nación (+90%)	Insurance
26. Reaseguradora Peruana S.A. [c]	160	10	260	170	Nación (+90%)	Reinsurance
27. ELECTROLIMA S.A. [c]	375	200	205	3,200	ELECTROPERU (55%) I. COFIDE (9%)	Electricity supply, Lima
28. Sociedad Eléctrica de Arequipa Ltda. S.A. (SEAL) [c]	25 [b]	15 [b]	15 [b]	N.A.	ELECTROPERU (84%) MEM (15%)	Electricity supply, Arequipa
29. Compañía de Servicios Eléctricos Ltda. S.A. (COSERELEC) [c]	10	5	5	N.A.	ELECTROPERU (48%) MEM (N.A.)	Electricity supply, Chiclayo & Ica

30.	Energía Hidroeléctrica Andina S.A. (HIDROANDINA) [c]	60 [b]	50 [b]	15 [b]	N.A.	ELECTROPERU (94%)	Electric supply to ELECTROLIMA
31.	Empresa de Energía de Chimbote S.A. [c]	10	10	5	80	MEM (95%) ELECTROPERU (4%)	Electricity supply, Chimbote
32.	Empresa de Energía de Piura S.A. [c]	20	20	10	240	MEM (66%) ELECTROPERU (33%)	Electricity supply, Piura
33.	Sociedad Industrial de Huancayo S.A. [c]	5	5	--	90	MEM (71%) ELECTROPERU (26%)	Electricity supply, Huancayo
34.	Compañía Peruana de Teléfonos S.A. (CPT) [c]	175 [b]	130 [b]	45 [b]	3,900	MTC (17%)	Telephone service, Lima
35.	Fábrica de Equipos de Telefonía S.A. (FETSA) [d]	--	--	--	80	INDUMIL (40%)	Telephones & equipment
36.	Cementos Lima S.A. [c]	65	40	70	530	I. COFIDE (49%)	Cement
37.	Cemento Andino S.A. [c]	30	20	30	450	I. COFIDE (49%)	Cement
38.	Cemento Norte Pacasmayo S.A. [c]	55	30	30	450	I. COFIDE (49%)	Cement
39.	Mina Aguila S.A. [d]	25	5	--	400	I. COFIDE (40%)	Mining project

Appendix--continued

	Assets (U.S. $Millions)	Equity (U.S. $Millions)	1982 Income (U.S. $Millions)	No. of Workers	Parent Entity	Principal Activity and Comments
40. Motores Diesel Andinos S.A. (MODASA) [d]	20	10	15	350	I. COFIDE (52%)	Diesel motors
41. MORAVECO S.A. [d]	15	--	--	1,200	I. COFIDE (51%) Banco Industrial (43%)	Car frames & electrical appliances
42. Manufacturas Nylon S.A. (MANYLSA) [d]	20 [b]	5 [b]	10 [b]	N.A.	Banco Industrial (97%)	Nylon fibers
43. Compañía Peruana de Gas S.A. (SOLGAS) [d]	10	5	15 [b]	360	PETROPERU (85%)	Domestic gas marketing
44. Empresa Minera Los Montes S.A. [d]	15	--	5	170	CENTROMIN PERU (99%)	Copper mine
45. Reactivos Nacionales S.A. (RENASA) [d]	5	--	5	110	CENTROMIN PERU (93%)	Mineral refining reactives
46. Consultores Mineros Metalúrgicos S.A. (COMMSA) [d]	--	--	5	40	CENTROMIN PERU (99%)	Consulting engineering
47. Industrias Navales S.A. [d]	--	--	--	--	PESCAPERU (84%)	Small shipyard
48. Representación y Gestión Empresarial (REGSA) [d]	--	--	--	--	PESCAPERU (69%)	Consulting & management services
49. Compañía Pesquera Estrella del Perú S.A. (COPES) [d]	15	--	20	490	EPSEP (51%)	Canned fish

Enterprises with State Shareholdings

1.	Bayer Industrial S.A.	75	15	50	690	I. COFIDE (14%) B. Industrial (14%)	Acrylic fibers & chemicals
2.	Compañía de Minas Buenaventura S.A.	50 [b]	20 [b]	40 [b]	N.A.	CENTROMIN PERU (19%)	Mining
3.	Industria Maderera del Oriente S.A. (IMOSA)	--	--	5	380	I. COFIDE (17%)	Plywood
4.	Forestal Amazonas S.A. (FASA)	--	--	--	80	I. COFIDE (17%) IMOSA (70%)	Sawed wood
5.	Aceros del Sur S.A. (ADESUR)	5	--	5	40	I. COFIDE (10%)	Steel products
6.	Fundición Andina del Perú S.A. (FUNAPER)	--	--	--	240	I. COFIDE (7%)	Metal products
7.	Nuevas Inversiones S.A. (NISA)	--	--	--	--	I. COFIDE (5%)	Cement holding
8.	Sindicato de Inversiones y Administración S.A. (SIA)	--	--	5	--	I. COFIDE (4%)	Management services & cement holding
9.	SOGEWIESE Leasing S.A.	N.A.	N.A.	N.A.	--	COFIDE (10%)	Leasing
10.	Banco Arabe Latinoamericano (ARLABANK)	N.S.	N.S.	N.S.	N.S.	B. Nación (5%)	Multinational banking

Appendix--continued

	Assets (U.S. $Millions)	Equity (U.S. $Millions)	1982 Income (U.S. $Millions)	No. of Workers	Parent Entity	Principal Activity and Comments
11. Banco Eurolatinoamericano (EULABANK)	N.S.	N.S.	N.S.	N.S.	B. Nación (2%)	Multinational banking
12. Banco Exterior de los Andes y España (EXTEBANDES)	N.S.	N.S.	N.S.	N.S.	B. Nación (10%)	Multinational banking
13. Banco Latinoamericano de Exportaciones (BLADEX)	N.S.	N.S.	N.S.	N.S.	B. Nación (2%)	Multinational export financing
14. Helicoidales y Tubos Compañía Anónima (HELITUBCA)	10	10	--	--	I. COFIDE (25%)	Steel pipes
15. Radio Panamericana S.A.	N.A.	N.A.	N.A.	N.A.	ENTEL (12%)	Radio station
16. Productos de Alambre y Denerivados S.A. (PROLANSA)	5	5	10	440	I. COFIDE (14%)	Wire
17. Refractarios Peruanos S.A. (REPSA)	10 [b]	5 [b]	10 [b]	N.A.	CENTROMIN PERU (10%)	Refractory bricks
18. Compañía Minera Magistral S.A.	5	--	5	N.A.	CENTROMIN PERU (20%)	Mining
19. Barrenas Sandvick Andina S.A.	5	--	5	N.A.	Buenaventura (7%)	Mining equipment
20. Industrial Textil Piura S.A.	N.S.	N.S.	N.S.	N.S.	B. Popular (-5%)	Textiles

21.	Fabricantes Técnicos Asociados S.A. (FTA)	N.S.	N.S.	N.S.	N.S.	B. Popular (-5%)	Records
22.	Lima Caucho S.A.	N.S.	N.S.	N.S.	N.S.	B. Popular (-5%)	Rubber products
23.	Compañía Peruana de Seguros de Crédito a la Exportación (SECREX)	N.S.	N.S.	N.S.	N.S.	B. Popular (-5%)	Export credit insurance

Figure 1

Peru: Management by Objectives System for State-Owned Enterprises

CIAKF	Ministries	CONADE	ICSA	Enterprises
-Provide central coordination	-Provide sectoral expertise	-Coordinate management of publicly owned enterprises.	-Manage State's portfolio of companies. -Act as secretariat to CONADE. -Monitor enterprises, act as clearinghouse for information. -Provide technical assistance, troubleshooting.	-Do strategic and operational planning on basic objectives. -Implement plans.

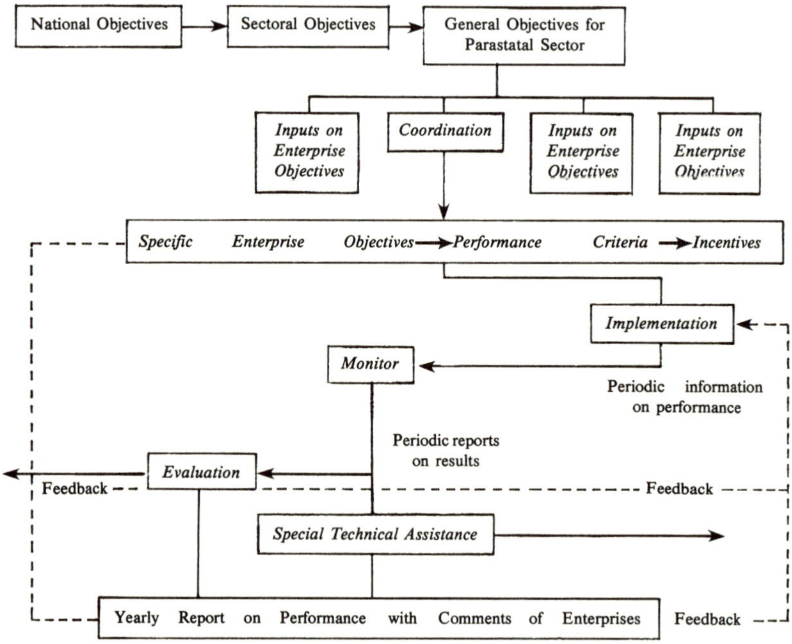

Source: "Peru: The Management and Sale of State-owned Enterprises," Report no. 4088-PE (World Bank, 27 August 1982).

Figure 2

Peru: Hypothetical Example of a Management by Objectives System for a State-Owned Power Company

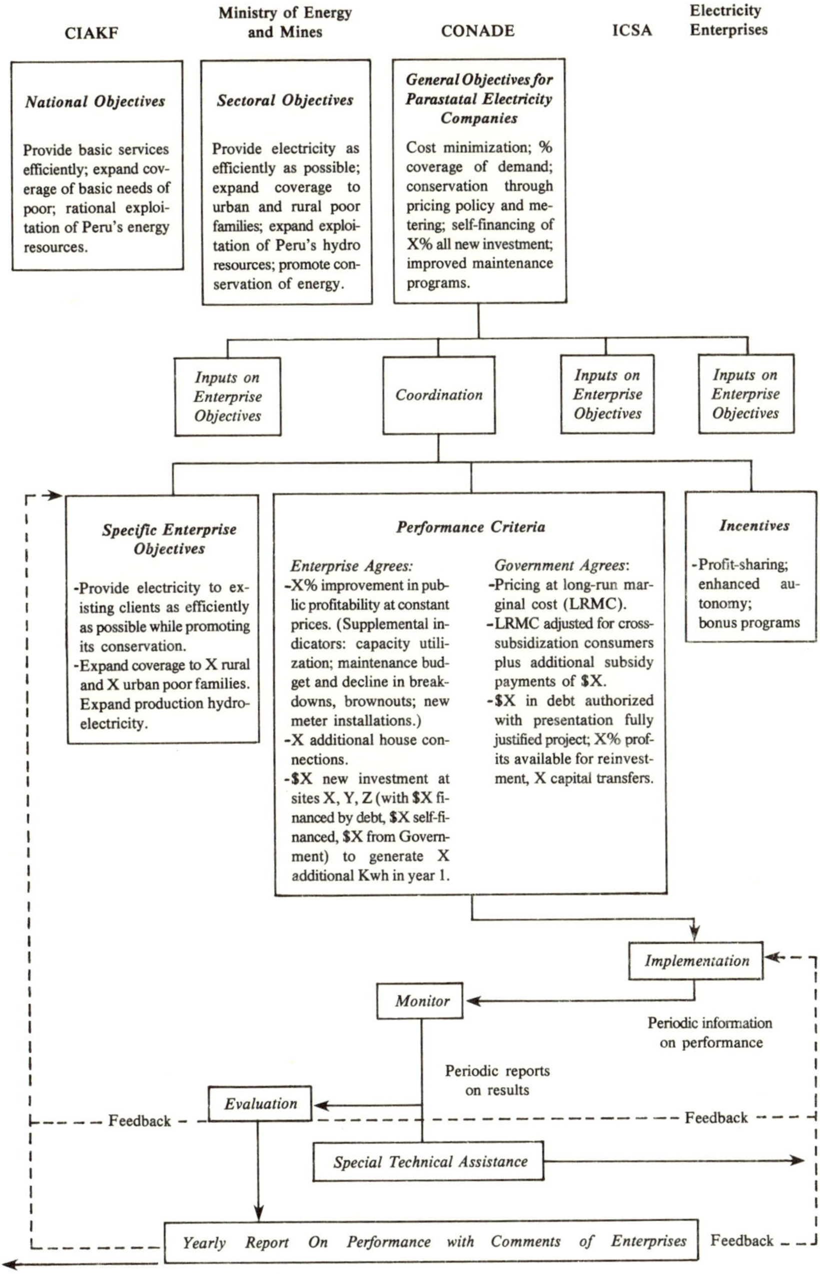

Source: Same as figure 1.

Notes

1. Unpublished.

2. Francisco Guerra García, *Del estado oligarca al capitalismo del estado* (Lima: Ediciones CEDEP, 1983).

3. "Direct Foreign Investment in Peru: New Rules for an Old Game," in *The Peruvian Experiment*, ed. Abraham F. Lowenthal (Princeton, N.J.: Princeton University Press, 1975), p. 348.

4. The following discussion is taken from unpublished material by Alfred Saulniers.

5. *Informe final de la Comisión Multisectorial de Empresas del Estado* (Lima, 1976).

6. Ibid.

7. Decree-Law 22264, Article 26.

8. *Lineamientos preliminares de política en el sector de energia y minas, 1980-1985* (Lima, September 1980).

9. "Public Enterprises in Peru: The Perspectives for Reform," Technical Papers series, no. 37 (Austin: Institute of Latin American Studies, 1982).

10. "Mensaje a la nación del presidente del Consejo de Ministros y Ministro de Economía, Finanzas y Comercio, Doctor Manuel Ulloa Elías" (Lima: República del Perú, January 1982).

11. "The Entrepreneurial Role of the Peruvian State," Intercampus, Universidad del Pacifico, February 1982.

12. "Memoria de energía y minas, 1980-1982," by Pedro-Pablo Kuczynski Godard (Lima: Ministerio de Energía y Minas, August 1982).

13. "Mensaje a la nación del presidente del Consejo de Ministros y Ministro de Relaciones Exteriores, Doctor Fernando Schwalb L.A." (Lima: República del Perú, February 1983).

14. "Peru: The Management and Sale of State-owned Enterprises," Report no. 4088-PE (World Bank, 27 August 1982).

15. Ibid.

16. "Propuesta de lineamientos del Plan de Gobierno de Acción Popular, 1980-1985 (Lima, 1979).

17. "Plan de gobierno" (Lima, 1980).

18. "Bases del Plan de Gobierno del Partido Aprista Peruano" (Lima, 1979).

19. "Perú 1980: Elecciones y planes de gobierno" (Lima: Centro de Investigación de la Universidad del Pacífico, 1980).

20. See note 14.

Chapter 8

The Context of Venezuelan Privatization

Mauricio García de Araújo

What I shall try to do herein is to give a series of comments on the question of state growth and state shrinking in Venezuela and on the development of state-owned enterprises. To this end, I shall begin with a very brief summary of the origin of the problem in Venezuela, as it leads into the present situation, and describe the current conflict over state shrinking and privatization. This will provide at least some basis for an assessment of the prospects for privatization in the next five years.

I think that it is fair to say, with regard to the origins of the problem in Venezuela, that, as Horacio Boneo has pointed out elsewhere in this volume, Venezuela constitutes one of the cases where public enterprises just seem to grow and grow all the time, independently of who is in power, be it dictatorship or democracy, and within the democratic context, independently of which political party is in power. Be it the Social Christians or the Social Democrats, the parastatal sector has expanded. The same holds true, for that matter, whether the economy is growing or not. If we look back, we can trace the beginning of state-owned enterprises in Venezuela to the early 1920s. Their growth has been more or less constant since the early 1940s, although it did accelerate after 1974 (up to around 1979). This seems to confirm, therefore, the validity of the interpretation that the growth of state-owned enterprises in Venezuela has not been a consequence of ideological motivations so much as of, first, structural economic needs in the country, and, second, the fact that the oil revenues in Venezuela have flowed through the state. The latter circumstance has been, I would agree, decisive. The state, in other words, has seen its economic role enhanced by oil wealth, as well as by a general political attitude that has favored the use of oil revenues to diversify the economy, to promote growth, to satisfy social needs--in essence, to use oil as an instrument for national development. Most have probably heard of the dictum that became an objective of Venezuelan economic policy in the late thirties and early forties: sowing the petroleum. By this is meant the use of oil revenues to diversify the economy and make it less dependent on petroleum before these revenues should run out. In this sense, sowing the oil has become both an objective and a challenge for Venezuelans ever since.

The increase in special state-owned enterprises, which took place after 1974, was, for example, a direct consequence of the quadrupling of oil prices. The fact that oil revenues tripled in one year, that the foreign exchange inflow quadrupled in a like period, and that the level of international reserves at the Central Bank quintupled in two years after 1973 meant more economic power for the state. The government decided to use that power in no uncertain terms; therefore, beginning in 1975, it embarked on an exceedingly ambitious development program with the objective of further diversifying the economic base of the country. This, as noted, had been tried before, but now the strategy involved improving the export potential of the economy along with actively promoting economic development. Unfortunately, however, petroleum revenues did not grow from 1974 to 1979. In fact, they actually decreased after 1975. This meant that to finance the very ambitious program that had been initiated in 1975, the government was forced to borrow abroad more and more each year. Later, of course, oil prices again increased significantly, doubling in 1979. Yet the trend toward external borrowing was not reversed. Indeed, it fostered a lack of fiscal discipline. Because of this breakdown in financial discipline, in turn, the need for external borrowing grew to the extent that external debt has today become one of the most significant problems in Venezuela.

What, then, are the dimensions of the public sector in Venezuela? I would briefly summarize it in the terms of several parameters. First of all, the public sector as a percentage of GDP in current prices grew from 12 percent in 1973 to 45 percent in 1981. But to my way of thinking, there is an even more meaningful figure if one adds up all the expenditures of the consolidated public sector, that is to say, the central government, the state-owned enterprises, the decentralized agencies, and the regional governments. Taken all together, the total expenditures of the public sector in Venezuela have grown eight times in the last ten years. The total expenditure, equivalent to about 40 percent of GDP in 1972, has grown to the equivalent of 72 percent of GDP in 1982. In terms of annual gross fixed investment, the public sector accounted for about 30 percent of annual gross fixed investment in the early 1970s. In 1982 it accounted for 60 percent of the total. In terms of employment, the number of people employed by the public sector grew from about three hundred thousand in the early 1970s to about one million in the early 1980s. In the neighborhood of 23 percent of the labor force of the country is now employed by the public sector. In addition, the entrepreneurial character of the Venezuelan public sector has grown significantly. Today, and for the past few years, it has resembled a gigantic conglomerate, involved in everything, but with a management structure and organization that do little for the bottom line: profit.

As I have said in the past, in Venezuela the visible hand of the state is present everywhere and has a direct impact on almost every aspect of economic life. It is, nevertheless, not a very steady hand, for the decentralized public administration must also be taken into account, specifically in terms of what it means for the coherence of policy guidance. For various reasons, there has for some years been a trend toward the decentralization of public expenditures. In consequence, today roughly 79 percent of the total consolidated expenditure of the public sector is accounted for by the decentralized sector, including the decentralized public administration. Indeed, 63 percent of the consolidated expenditures of the public sector is accounted for by the state-owned enterprises alone. So free-wheeling has this system been that the decentralized public agencies and companies account for 61 percent of the total external debt of the public sector. As this suggests, practically all the state-owned enterprises operate in the red, running up losses that account for about two-thirds of the fiscal deficit of the consolidated public sector. This is so in spite of the fact that public enterprises operate in a fair number of fields in which one could reasonably expect to find opportunities for profitable business. For example, state-owned enterprises totally dominate the fields of petroleum, petrochemicals, iron ore, steel, aluminum, and public utilities. Almost 100 percent of shipping, 100 percent of airlines in international traffic, and 50 percent of the airlines in national traffic, are state companies. Some 46 percent of the deposits of commercial banks are in the hands of banks that are owned by the state, though it must be acknowledged that most of the banks that have been taken over by the state have been nationalized because of failures of the private administrators who directed them before.

Thus, the growth of the state-owned enterprise system in Venezuela has been a consequence of oil revenues flowing into the hands of the state and of a conscious position to use state capitalism to promote economic diversification and economic growth in the country. It is important to note that, with the exceptions to be noted shortly, there has not been any significant political disagreement over this objective. On the contrary, there has been a general consensus on the objectives of this state capitalism as a means of dealing with structural economic needs. The Venezuelan constitution, in fact, establishes that all basic industries must be owned by the state. Past efforts to change or in some way adapt the system of state capitalism have been geared more than anything else toward improving the efficiency of the system and toward changing the legal framework in which the system has operated. Take, for example, two of the efforts that were made in the past, namely, the public administration commission that operated from 1969 to 1974, and the commission for the reform of public administration (1974 to 1979). Neither of these efforts was really aimed at privatization. The first was undertaken to deal with defects in the legal structure in the system of adscription (the system whereby each state-owned enterprise is adscribed to a particular ministry for regulation and supervision) and, from 1974 to 1979, to emphasize accountability, feedback, and control.

As has been remarked, privatization has, despite the general consensus on state capitalism, been used as a campaign issue in the last three elections, mostly by the opposition party. In the last four elections, the government has changed hands from one party to the other. Not a single government has been reelected since 1968 in Venezuela. Nevertheless, for all the campaign discussion, very little has actually been done about privatization up to this time. This is so, moreover, even though the private sector, breaking with the prevailing consensus, has traditionally criticized the model of state capitalism, the inefficiency of state-owned enterprises, and the operating losses of most of these enterprises. Above all, it has consistently criticized the radical change in the balance of power between the state and the private sector that has taken place in Venezuela in recent years. What can we say, then, about the likelihood of privatization of state shrinking?

Elections were held in Venezuela in December 1983, and a new government just took office in February of 1984. This new government was elected with 57 percent of the popular vote and a clear majority of both houses in Congress. It has, therefore, a clear mandate in the political sense, and mostly this mandate has to do with dealing with the economic crisis that Venezuela had been experiencing in the past few years, one of the worst economic crises in its contemporary history. We have had no growth in real terms for five years, and worse yet, the last GDP was down by about 3 percent to 4 percent in real terms. The crisis in our balance of payments has been underscored by dropping oil prices and a consequent reduction in oil revenues. Aggravating the situation has been a lack of confidence and capital flight, which in 1982, together with the drop in oil prices, meant a loss of about eight billion dollars in external assets in one year. Not surprisingly, an adverse change of this magnitude led the government to impose exchange controls in early 1983. At the same time, we have been faced, as mentioned earlier, with a very acute problem of external indebtedness, the total external debt of Venezuela having reached about thirty-four billion dollars. About twenty-seven billion dollars of this is owed by the public sector, about seven billion dollars by the private sector. I say "about" because, as there were no exchange controls in Venezuela traditionally, there was no need to register private debts; hence, private debts are only now in the process of being registered with the exchange control office and the final tally is not yet complete. We do not, therefore, have a final estimate, but it should be in the neighborhood of seven billion dollars as a reference figure.

The main problem concerning the public debt has been the inadequate maturity profile of the total external debt of the twenty-seven billion dollars; 52 percent was due in 1983 and an additional 12 percent comes due in 1984. This means that 64 percent of the total debt of the public sector is due in less than two years. Now 69 percent of the total debt, as mentioned before, was contracted by the centralized agencies, and fully 76 percent of the debt of the centralized agencies is due in the first two years. Most of the companies that contracted this debt, however, do not have the cash flow to repay the debt on the original maturity. There is no need to go into the reason why this debt was contracted on such a short term; the whole exercise indicates that there were basic flaws in the way that the debt was contracted on the part of the borrower, as of the lender. Whatever, the fact that Venezuela had such easy access to commercial bank lending sources, in an era of rising interest rates made the loan spread associated with short-term loans attractive to the managers and treasurers of the state-owned enterprises. Because the banks very aggressively competed with each other in lending money to companies of the Venezuelan private sector and because there was no adequate supervision, debt management was very poor or inefficient. Now the country has to face up to the fact that these conditions meant that an excessive accumulation of short-term debt took place, one that cannot be serviced adequately and that has had to be stretched out over a longer period of time. When one adds this to the balance-of-payments problem, there comes about a classic example of a liquidity squeeze, one that called for a rescheduling over a longer period.

On account of the foregoing, the climate today is ripe for a new look at the role of the state in economic affairs. Central to this task is a reexamination of the functioning of state-owned enterprises and of the problems they face. So conspicuous have these problems become that over the past two to three years, we have seen a significant increase in the amount of criticism levied against state-owned enterprises and, for that matter, against the inefficiencies of the state-capitalism model. Obviously, the most commonly made comments refer to the excessive losses of state-owned enterprises and to their excessive level of foreign debt--to the burden that these enterprises have come to represent. The budgetary failure of these enterprises translates into a huge amount of money, which could, with a more prudent policy, have been invested in real growth for the country. The important aspect of this new criticism is that, for the first time in many years, it has not been made only by people in the private sector but also by leaders of both major political parties; hence, there is a new consciousness of the magnitude of the problem and of the need to do something about it in the near future. For the first time in twenty years, Venezuela is today facing sharp fiscal and foreign exchange constraints, and, over the next few years, the possibility of public sector growth will continue to be constrained, especially if, as seems likely, there is further weakening in the world petroleum market. Thus, the opportunity is present now for a fresh look at all of these problems, and for the first time in decades conditions open up the possibility for new decisions.

Under the circumstances, what are the prospects for privatization in the next five years? To assay an answer, we must be very realistic in looking at these prospects, leaving aside how each of us individually feels about it. Personally, I should very much like to see many of these companies turned over to the private sector, but, quite frankly, I do not think it is likely to happen, in spite of the conditions I have described. Let me give some of the reasons why, using the classification that David Heald employs in his chapter: basic industry; strategic entities; and nonbasic, nonstrategic, decentralized agencies. The basic industries are oil, petrochemicals, iron ore, steel, aluminum, and hydroelectricity. By constitutional law, these are reserved to the state. Therefore, the state will maintain full ownership of all of these industries unless the law is changed, and change in the constitution of Venezuela, as in many Latin American countries, would be extremely difficult. It could, practically speaking, only be done under extreme circumstances. Therefore, independently of the fiscal and foreign exchange constraints, it is quite unlikely that privatization will be in any way attempted in the basic-industry field. What we are rather more likely to see here is a twofold development. The first is joint ventures, which already exist in some areas of basic industries in Venezuela, most prominently in aluminum and petrochemicals. More particularly, it is probable that there will be a move toward joint venturing in some of the secondary areas of basic industries: the downstream operations and activities. The second probable development is what William Glade has called "simulated privatization": the imposition of market-performance criteria on public enterprises. There is, in fact, simply no way to avoid a move toward improvement of the quality of management and control in these enterprises. With regard to the strategic entities, of which the financial entities are the most prominent, I think that it is likewise very unlikely that we shall see outright sale, though we may see efforts to improve their management. Finally, for the nonbasic, nonstrategic industry, there may well be some efforts at divestment through outright sale, or possibly leasing or contracting out of the administration of these enterprises. To put the problem in perspective, though, we need to keep in mind that these enterprises are generally small. Thus, they will not much change the larger problem. Neither the losses nor the overall size of the state will be significantly changed by the sale of these enterprises. The new government will probably advertise its intention to divest itself of some of these manufacturing enterprises, but the practical outcome will be conditioned by constraints imposed by the recession: the scarcity of financial resources and foreign exchange. At the very least, these factors will slow down the actual implementation of any privatization moves.

To conclude, I should like to make two brief comments about the "fiduciary" system that has developed in Venezuela, a system in which labor unions, technocratic groups, political parties, and even business interests have come to share power with the state and state-owned enterprises. Any attempt to divert or to reform state-owned enterprises will thus have to be negotiated between the state and the representatives of all these fiduciary groups. Considering how recent is any regular, sustained experience with elected regimes in Venezuela, preservation of the social compact among all these groups has to be an overriding national priority. Although this structural feature of Venezuelan political organization will hinder broad-side privatization, it will probably not be an obstacle to divestment in the case of the smaller manufacturing enterprises that might be sold to investors. As for the means of privatization, the terms and guarantees for payment, including the period for payment, may well be influenced by political considerations. To put it forthrightly, the party in power may favor selling these enterprises not to the traditional entrepreneurs but to new investors, especially to small- or medium-sized entrepreneurs with political connections or political influence in the party. I think that this is likely to happen because, independently of who is in power, the government would try to use divestment to foster the diversification of entrepreneurial groups in Venezuela. Of course, such a policy might lead to problems later on. Some of these groups of investors, for example, may not have the financial wherewithal to buy the companies and to put in the additional capital that in most cases would be needed. Most of these state companies have had losses and are now undercapitalized. Thus, we could conceivably see a boomerang effect later on in the process of privatization. Finally, and this brings me to my last comment, I share the view that the problem that we are really addressing in Venezuela is that of a redirection of the economic role of the state. Given that both major political parties share the conviction that the state should promote development, the question becomes how to make that effort more efficient, less costly, and more manageable. Hence, the fundamental challenge in Venezuela involves privatization in its broader sense: not so much outright sale as improvement of management policy and management control to make the state more efficient than it has been. This may sound as if I am not very optimistic about the prospects for privatization, but I think it is a more realistic view. The party now in power, Acción Democrática (AD), has proven itself to be very pragmatic. Just as it was a champion of state capitalism in the early sixties and mid-seventies, if economic and financial considerations suggest now a strong need for a change, AD might well undertake to make that change, provided it finds adequate backing from the private sector. Consequently, the private sector has a singularly important role to play, if there is going to be any significant privatization in Venezuela during this decade. This will involve it not only in sharing the role of the state but, more than anything else, also in helping to improve management.

Chapter 9

State Shrinkage: The Jamaican Experience

Peter J. Kennedy, Jr.

Introduction

In its 1983 _World Development Report_, the World Bank notes a "new realism" that is compelling governments to reexamine their role in the process of economic development. Increasingly, the bank observes, governments are rejecting interventionism and relying on private initiative and market forces to determine the most efficient means of allocating scarce goods. Although this perceived trend has taken on any number of forms in varying political and economic settings, it is generally marked by the curtailment of indirect intervention in economic affairs (for example, deregulation) and, in some caes, the divestment of public- or state-owned enterprises.[1]

In the developing world, few leaders have been associated with this "new realism" as closely as Edward Seaga, who took over as prime minister of Jamaica in late 1980. Seaga inherited a critically debilitated economy, which had failed to register any real growth during the seven preceding years. His recovery program was an ambitious one, involving massive infusions of private and multilateral capital and the reorientation of economic policy away from import substitution and toward export-oriented growth. Crucial to the Seaga strategy was the deregulation of the economy and the transfer of state enterprises to the private sector.

This chapter is a study of the first three years of the Seaga government's privatization efforts. My primary focus is the government's divestment program: its logic, scope, and the political and economic environment that has shaped its character. I shall analyze examples of successful divestment, as well as the numerous and complex obstacles that have impeded the Jamaican government's efforts to date. I shall also investigate a curious incident of "reverse divestment" and consider examples of "simulated privatization," by which the government, short of actual divestment, has imposed more demanding performance and efficiency standards on public-enterprise management. Finally, I shall consider the broader issues of state shrinkage in the contemporary Jamaican context.

In terms of organization, the first section of this work charts the historical growth of the state sector in Jamaica. It focuses on the rise of state ownership and government intervention under the Michael Manley government (1972 to 1980). The second section describes the nature of the privatization undertaken by the Seaga government. Micro case studies of key divestment targets are contained in the third section. The fourth part considers evidence of simulated privatization and various efforts to attenuate government involvement in business and economic affairs. The fifth part deals with the interaction of forces either promoting or hindering the process of state shrinkage. Final thoughts on the outlook for divestment, deregulation, and state shrinkage in Jamaica are contained in the concluding section.

The Jamaican government's efforts to trim back the public sector are still operational. Any conclusions suggested in this study are therefore tentative. Nevertheless, the unfolding of events during the first three years of the Seaga government provides important material for analysis. The parameters of policy are clear--and they are unlikely to be significantly altered by near-term events.

The limitations of a research endeavor such as this should be apparent. Government officials still holding office are understandably reluctant to offer the type of information that would allow one to make critical distinctions between real and apparent problems in policy and its implementation. In Jamaica, at least, state intervention is an extremely delicate political issue. Government officials, as well as various stakeholder groups, are constrained in their on-record comments. It may well require a change in regimes before current officeholders reveal the full extent of the difficulties encountered in "going private." With that said, I shall attempt in the following pages to integrate the less-public thoughts of Jamaican leaders and other stakeholders to whom I have had access in the course of preparing this study.

Background: Statism in Jamaica

From colonial times up to the mid-1970s, Jamaican governments rarely intervened directly in economic affairs. Even with the birth of the socialist Peoples' National party (PNP), which held power between 1955 and 1962, Jamaica's government promoted policies supportive of private capital formation. Indeed, the scope of public-sector activity was carefully circumscribed so as not to interfere with the entrepreneurial pursuits of private, especially local, capital. State support took the form of tax incentives, protectionist trade policies, export marketing assistance, and price supports for agricultural products. Public enterprise was rare and largely confined to rail transportation, agricultural trading, and, later, air transport and food processing.[2]

Spurred by massive investment in the bauxite and tourism sectors, the Jamaican economy expanded rapidly in the period leading up to and following independence in 1962. IMF statistics indicate that Jamaica's real gross domestic product grew on the average of 6.2 percent per year between 1960 and 1972. During that period, per capita GDP measured in real terms grew by 49.4 percent.[3]

Although unquestionably rapid, Jamaica's economic growth during this period was uneven. The twin pillars of bauxite and tourism continued to expand throughout the 1960s, but without creating significant links with the rest of the island economy. Perhaps the most serious consequence of this was the growth in unemployment, which jumped from about 13 percent in 1960 to 25 percent in 1971.[4]

Widening income disparity was another side effect of Jamaica's pattern of development. The expansion of the bauxite sector during the 1950s and 1960s produced a new class of labor elites who were well paid and well represented by the big trade unions. At the same time, however, the plight of the lower 40 percent of the work force worsened considerably. By one estimate, between 1958 and 1970 the share of the bottom 40 percent of the population's total earned income declined from 7.2 percent to 5.4 percent.

By the early 1970s, the issues of joblessness and income disparity had come to dominate the national political scene. The Jamaica Labour party (JLP), which had governed since independence, proved incapable of maintaining a broad base of support among the lower and working classes. Increasingly, the JLP had also alienated powerful elements within the local business community by, inter alia, imposing higher taxes and by failing to promote more aggressively local participation in the foreign-dominated areas of the economy, particularly in bauxite, tourism, and banking.[5] It was therefore a broad, multiclass movement that in the 1972 election year rejected the decade-long rule of the JLP in favor of the PNP, led by the charismatic trade unionist Michael Manley.

At the outset, Manley's domestic economic agenda was mildly redistributive. The new government concentrated on developing the island's social infrastructure through health, education, and training programs for the poor. In addition, the administration undertook a major reform of the civil service by upgrading the salaries and status of government workers. The only major instance of direct government intervention in the economy during Manley's first two years was the creation of Jamaica Nutrition Holdings, Ltd. (JNH), a wholly owned state enterprise charged with bulk importation of basic foodstuffs. Although JNH evoked some initial criticism from local traders, it was eventually accepted as a desirable and legitimate public enterprise.[6]

The period between 1974 and 1980 is the most crucial one for understanding the growth of the state sector in Jamaica. Statism under Manley evolved from latent nationalistic sentiments among Jamaicans of almost every race, class, and political background. Manley exploited these sentiments by taking on the most visible symbols of foreign domination of the economy: the six North American bauxite producers. In 1974 he introduced a substantial increase (600 percent) in the bauxite production levy and announced the government's intention of acquiring total ownership of the aluminum companies' bauxite lands and 51 percent equity in their bauxite mining operations. Over the next five years, the government struck deals with Alcoa, Kaiser, Reynolds, Alcan, and Alpart (an intercompany venture); only one firm--Revere--chose in the end to liquidate its Jamaican assets. The government's bid for full ownership of the land and a majority share in the mining operations was successful. However, the companies won long-term supply guarantees and retained all but some nominal shares in the lucrative refining area, as well as managerial control over industry operations.[7]

The bauxite levy hike was a pivotal act, for it gave the government the financial means to accelerate its redistributive program and to secure at least a controlling interest in key national industries that were dominated by foreign companies. Although the bauxite sector was the primary target, the government also negotiated the transfer to the public sector of the national bus company, the electric power service, and the telephone company. It also purchased the cement and dairy companies, which Manley claimed had taken unfair advantage of their monopolistic positions. In the financial sector, the Manley administration acquired three banks (one foreign), with the stated objectives of providing incentives to small business and channeling more funds into productive endeavors, particularly agriculture.[8]

Toward the mid and late 1970s, the Jamaican government moved into the agriculture sector to spur the creation of new job opportunities, as well as to rescue declining sugar-refining operations. It purchased a number of large estates from international firms and then transformed them into worker cooperatives. Some sixty thousand farmers were eventually resettled on government-sponsored agricultural cooperatives.

Direct government involvement in trading and shipping activities also expanded during the Manley period. The Jamaica Merchant Marine was established in 1975 (with a Mexican shipper as a minority partner) to reduce the costs of bauxite exports and grain imports. With the strong endorsement of the trade unions, the government established the State Trading Company (STC) to handle bulk purchases of basic consumer goods and to explore new possibilities for barter trade. Once operational, the STC and its companion agency, the Export Trading Corporation, created a furor in the local private sector, where prominent leaders warned that the Manley administration was "moving the country towards total governmental control of the economy."[9]

Growing private-sector concern over the enlargement of the state sector did not deter the government from acquiring yet additional enterprises, nor from starting up new ones. By the late 1970s, however, the Manley government had to confine its acquisitions to private-sector failures--firms that because of decapitalization or lack of foreign exchange were either bankrupt or almost so. Public-sector rescue missions were undertaken to maintain employment and preserve whatever productive capacity the island could claim during the severe economic downturn of the period. Among the firms the state rescued were several sugar refineries, a textile factory, a food processor, a catering service, a car rental company, a newspaper, and a boutique.

By far the most ambitious rescue mission was of some fourteen hotels, representing about half of all hotel rooms in the country. The Manley government had become the island's reluctant innkeeper by virtue of the fact that in many cases it held the mortgages for the failed companies. Disinvestment was also a factor, as hotel owners grew increasingly fearful over the effects on the tourist industry of political violence and heightened government rhetoric. In any case, the government's takeover of these hotels was in no way underpinned by the nationalistic or strategic considerations that were used to justify, for example, the bauxite and utility nationalizations. In concrete terms, saving the hotels meant saving ten thousand jobs and keeping alive one of the few sectors of the economy that was capable of generating much-needed foreign exchange.

By the close of the Manley period, the state sector possessed an extraordinary collection of enterpriese. Only a handful of these were inherited from previous governments; the lion's share of state enterprises were actively acquired, created, or taken over by default. Table 1 reflects the range of enterprises in the state's portfolio prior to 1981. Although not an exhaustive list of all state undertakings, the table provides a useful categorical background derived from ECLA's (the Economic Commission on Latin America) classification of public enterprises. This categorization will lend greater clarity to the task of understanding the nature of the privatization program undertaken by the Seaga government.

Large-scale unemployment, uncontrolled inflation, a critical shortage of foreign exchange, massive capital flight, swollen budget deficits, and mounting foreign obligations were all evidence of the rapid decline of the Jamaican economy in the late 1970s. Completely dependent on imports of foreign energy supplies, the island never recovered from the two major oil shocks of the period. Aggravating the macroeconomic picture was the government's expansionary policies, which saw a rise in the central government deficit from 5 percent of GDP in 1972 to a high of 19 percent in 1976.[10] Official attempts to check the economic decline did not produce the results required by the IMF, with which Jamaica had begun an adjustment program in 1977. Although the IMF revised its current account targets, it proved less accommodating on the fiscal side. Ultimately, the Manley government was unable to contain expenditures, especially in the form of increases to public-sector employees. Partially as a result of this, in 1979 Jamaica had a recurrent budget deficit of 4 percent of GDP (instead of a balance) and an overall public-sector deficit of 13 percent of GDP, compared to the IMF target of 8.9 percent. This impasse was never broken, and relations between Jamaica and the IMF came to a stormy close in March of 1980.[11] During the election campaign of that year, opposition candidate Seaga pledged if elected to reenter an adjustment program with the IMF.

Privatization under the Seaga Government

Upon coming to power, Edward Seaga sought, above all, to halt the deterioration of the economy and to restore stability in order to secure new capital inflows from the IMF and later, from the international capital market and donor governments. As these capital flows were renewed, liquidity would pick up, thereby allowing the government to dismantle the import restrictions and foreign-exchange controls that had straitjacketed the island's productive capacity during the Manley years. The Seaga strategy was based on a commitment to tighter macroeconomic management, in addition to an overarching belief in the efficacy of export-oriented, private sector-led growth. In this setting, government's role would be diminished and in large part limited to activities that enhanced the environment for private capital formation. Both local and foreign capital were urged to participate in the recovery process.

Seaga's private-sector bias did not, however, represent a wholesale embrace of laissez faire capitalism. Instead, he promoted a "middle path between a simplistically applied pure capitalist market system and the completely centralized one of Marxist economies." In the Jamaican setting, Seaga explained, "central planning and state intervention must be used to guide development strategies, to balance growth with distribution, to provide opportunities for the poor, and to protect the disadvantaged." At the same time, the private sector would be "set free to operate in a climate conducive to doing business and creating jobs." He emphasized, however, that some initiatives would involve "an appropriate mix of public and private investment."[12]

Consistent with the mixed-economy approach, the Seaga government issued no sweeping plans to either denationalize industry or auction off state holdings indiscriminately. Rather, divestment policy focused on deficit-ridden public enterprises, save certain strategic holdings (for example, utilities) for which losses could be expected and tolerated. No such tolerance was voiced for public losers in manufacturing and agriculture, which registered deficits of US$22 million and US$16.3 million respectively in 1980. In that year, losses for Jamaican public enterprises totaled US$64.6 million--roughly the equivalent of a month and a half's worth of debt-service payments. This situation added an understandable element of urgency to the divestment effort.

The reprivatization of the hotels was from the onset the centerpiece of the divestment program. The state holding company National Hotels and Properties Ltd. (NHP), lost approximately US$146 million between 1979 and 1981, accruing some US$70 million in debts.[13] Next in line for sale or lease were the government-owned sugar factories, which by the end of 1981 accounted for about 70 percent of total refining on the island. If anything, government management of the factories probably accelerated the rate at which refined-sugar output was falling. Similarly, the three large agricultural cooperatives started up under Manley had also performed poorly and were slated for reorganization. In 1981 alone, the National Sugar Company (or NSC, the state holding company) lost US$45 million. By the close of that year, NSC had accumulated debts of nearly US$150 million.[14]

The remaining divestment targets were smaller enterprises that shared one key characteristic with the hotels and sugar factories: they were public losers. A good many, in fact, were relatively recent additions to the state portfolio, having been picked up by the previous government during the 1977 to 1979 rescue mission. Two exceptions--the rail and bus companies--had become state property under different circumstances. In any case, the driving force behind the nascent divestment effort was the Seaga government's need to preserve scarce revenues by turning these troubled firms over to private hands. At the same time, the government was faced with the possibility of having to close down heavily indebted enterprises that could not be privatized. In this way, the burden of government borrowing carried by the local capital market would be lightened significantly, thereby freeing up commercial credit lines for more of what the government hoped would be productive endeavors.

From the start, divestment was not undertaken in an atmosphere of panic. The head of the government divestment committee emphasized the strictly commercial nature of the undertaking in the most straightforward language: "We are not giving them away." In addition to scrutinizing the financial state of potential buyers, the committee also sought proof of managerial and technical abilities and expertise in the particular area of business. It expressed concern that irresponsible or merely speculative purchases would increase the likelihood of eventual deprivatization.[15]

Not to be obscured by the Seaga administration's preoccupation with divestment was its broad effort to deregulate the economy and, more specifically, to make governmental agencies more supportive of private capital formation. To this end, the government pledged a major rollback in import, customs, and foreign-exchange regulations to allow producers to acquire raw materials, spare parts, and equipment, as well as to satisfy consumer demand for increasingly scarce non-Jamaican goods. The government also favored a reduced role for the STC and other state marketing agencies, which had "grown beyond their optimal size" and were of dubious relevance to an economic plan developed around the concept of private initiative.[16] With regard to taxation, the Seaga government emphasized enforcement of prevailing laws, rather than the introduction of new taxes. If anything, it favored selective reductions, although fiscal considerations limited its options with respect to a proposed lowering of the bauxite levy.

Predictably, the deregulation program also contained, albeit as a more distant goal, the removal of price controls and subsidies and the realignment of wages to better reflect true production costs. The price and subsidy issue was politically treacherous, as Jamaicans had grown accustomed to sizable discounts on food and petroleum imports and a host of public sector-produced goods and services. Much of this subsidizing activity was carried out through exchange-rate policy, whereby the government allowed truly vital goods (foodstuffs and medicines) to be imported at the highly overvalued exchange rate of J$1.78 to US$1. (By comparison, the black market exchange rate at end-1981 was between J$2.20 and J$2.40 to US$1.) Devaluation, via exchange-rate unification or modification of the parallel rate, was not politically acceptable at a time when the government was attempting to marshal public support behind the adjustment program. Yet although Seaga attempted to reassure Jamaicans that adjustment would bear no unreasonable social costs, it was clear that a more realistic pricing structure would have to emerge, particularly after the island entered into a new US$650 million extended-fund agreement with the IMF in early 1981.

Divestment Problems: Micro Case Studies

Hotel Properties

From the onset, the privatization of the hotel properties was the focus of considerable effort and energy on the part of the government. The Seaga administration moved swiftly and, with minimal bureaucratic footdragging, managed to turn over six of the fourteen hotel properties to private management in just over a year. After its initial string of successes, however, this privatization process slowed considerably; by the close of 1983, only seven of the hotels had been privatized, and not one had been sold outright.

Various factors explain the government's inability to privatize the hotels as quickly--and completely--as it had hoped during the initial phase of the campaign. The prolonged worldwide recession was certainly a key factor. Economic downturns in the United States and Canada have a direct and measurable impact on Caribbean tourism, and for at least the first two years of the Seaga government, the market was simply not propitious for new investment. It should also be mentioned that the large-scale devaluation of the Mexican peso has also undermined the comparative advantage of Caribbean vacations with respect to the North American tourist market. Similarly, the strength of the U.S. dollar (to which most Caribbean currencies are pegged) has deterred European vacationers from visiting the islands.

Another major disincentive has been the generally decrepit condition of the hotel properties. By NHP's own admission, the hotels had not been maintained well under public stewardship, thus forcing potential buyers to lay out a sizable amount of capital to return them to working order. New NHP outlays for refurbishing could accomplish only cosmetic improvements; it remained largely the burden of the new management to restore the properties to commercial viability.[17]

Perhaps the most significant obstacle to hotel divestment has been the terms under which the government has been willing to relinquish the properties. Although under the Hotel Incentives Act, the government offered rather generous concessions (including ten- to fifteen-year tax holidays, customs relief for materials and equipment, and loss carry-forward provisions for a concessionary period of up to six years), prospective investors have apparently been discouraged by a distinct policy shift emphasizing long-term leasing over purchase. The leasing plan carries a minimum commitment of five years, with guaranteed returns for the government in the form of fixed rental fees (typically between 8 percent and 12 percent of the current valuation of the property) and a profit-sharing clause.

The government's public explanation of the policy shift was that the hotel properties were appreciating rapidly and that straight business considerations dictated the decision to retain public ownership.[18] Privately, some officials have also acknowledged that a not-unconnected factor has been growing uneasiness over the idea of returning the property to foreign owners, who by far composed the majority of prospective private operators (see table 2).

In any case, it is doubtless true that a less-conditional set of divestment terms would have made the hotel properties more attractive to prospective new operators. Had the government been willing to sell at heavily discounted rates, only the most run-down facilities would probably remain under NHP control. As discussed, however, the government has demonstrated an unwillingness to sell at a time when the properties are appreciating rapidly in value. Strategic control may also be a factor, particularly as tourism grows in importance as a long-term generator of employment and foreign exchange.

Sugar Refineries

The Seaga government's objectives for the sugar sector have been twofold: to reorganize and upgrade production (by among other means promoting private development and ownership), and to divest itself of the deeply troubled sugar factories, of which it owned eight at the start of 1981. During its first year in office, the Seaga government disbanded the sugar cooperatives. The sugar factories, however, have not been divested. The government immediately closed one factory, in fact, in the belief that it was not worth salvaging.

The refinery divestment effort has been troubled on many fronts. It is important, first, to understand the general problems--shared also by Jamaica's sugar-producing neighbors--such as hurricanes and poor weather conditions, crop disease, low prices, and limited market-access. The Jamaican sugar industry has been further weakened by chronic shortages of parts, equipment, and fertilizer resulting from lack of foreign exchange. Labor problems have also played a part in the decline of the sector and have apparently discouraged new private development. Tate and Lyle, the British sugar company, at one point reportedly offered to take over and manage all of NSC's possessions on the condition that the cooperatives be disbanded and the sugar workers' benefits be curbed. Although the cooperatives were abolished, the deal fell through because the government chose not to interfere with the activities of the powerful trade unions involved.[19]

The government was similarly unsuccessful in its negotiations with other large multinationals, such as Bacardi and Gulf & Western. In October 1983 the government opted to cut its losses by closing down all seven NSC sugar mills. As a result, some eleven thousand sugar-mill workers (about 1 percent of the work force) became unemployed. Although the government promised a phased reopening of the plants, local sugar experts speculated that only three plants would be reopened if conditions improved significantly.[20]

Although Jamaica's three privately owned and operated mills were not directly affected by the closure decision, it is quite possible that sugar refining may ultimately prove to be a nonviable enterprise in Jamaica and in many other small, capital-poor Caribbean nations. Accordingly, the apparent failure of the NSC divestment effort may be interpreted as a prophetic reading of the market on the part of companies that have surveyed the Jamaican situation. Quite possibly, of course, the industry's decline might not have been inevitable had the state more effectively carried out its caretaker responsibilities.

The NSC divestment effort could take a new turn if conditions in the world sugar-market brighten appreciably. More likely, the sugar lands will be sold off piecemeal to entrepreneurs interested in cultivating different crops. There is evidence that this has already begun to take place on a limited scale, although new investors will still have to confront the broader problems of finding new markets and securing reasonable shipping rates. Divesting the sugar lands will therefore remain a longer-term proposition. Privatization of the NSC refineries may not be possible.

Reverse Divestment: The Esso Case

The Seaga government's orientation toward a mixed economy was in a sense clarified by a controversial decision made in 1982. At a time of alleged state shrinkage, the government nationalized the island's sole oil refinery. The facility was purchased for US$14 million (plus US$2 million for spare parts and an additional US$41 million for oil stocks) from Esso West Indies, which had previously run the unit under a twenty-year agreement with the government.[21]

The prime minister justified the move by citing the benefits of government ownership. The main benefit was that public control would pave the way for a modification of the refining process, thus allowing Jamaica to import discounted Venezuelan and Mexican crude directly. Other reports circulating at the time suggest that Esso had pressured the government to either raise local oil prices--a move that four years earlier had sparked riots in Kingston--or provide subsidies in lieu of price increases.[22]

In either case, the decision to take over the Esso facility was based on pragmatic reasoning--of either an economic or a political nature. Coming from a figure like Seaga, who was so closely associated with private-sector interests, the decision was also a controversial one. In a public statement the prime minister admitted that the nationalization had cast some doubt on his administration's policy of state ownership, but he emphasized that the commonweal sometimes "requires public ownership of vital corporations."[23]

The Esso case is important for two reasons. First, it helps explain the selective nature of the government's divestment initiatives by showing that Seaga was not ideologically opposed to state ownership. Second, it illustrates that state shrinkage in certain sectors of an economy may be balanced, or even outweighed, by new government ventures into areas traditionally controlled by private interests.

Privatization Accomplished: Versair and the JOS

Two examples, one of a clear-cut divestment and another of a partial privatization, represent the chief success stories of the government's program. Interestingly, both examples involve private operators securing government contracts to serve rather protected markets.

Versair

Versair is a catering company that supplies food and beverages for all airlines operating in Jamaica and for restaurants and bars at both international airports. The company came under government ownership during the late 1970s, at a time when the tourist industry was severely depressed. Although Versair did not actually go bankrupt, the Manley government was sufficiently interested in maintaining its services to decide to purchase the operation. Like many other enterprises acquired by the government at the time, Versair was dreadfully managed and subject to steep financial losses.

As a divestment target, Versair was blessed by its connection to the tourist industry, which was one sector expected to rebound quickly under the new government. In late 1981, the Seaga government announced that a consortium of companies had purchased the company. The purchasers represented a highly desirable mix of local, regional, and foreign capital: Grace, Kennedy and Company (Jamaica), Goddard Company (Barbados), and the Marriot Company (United States).

The JOS

For years the Jamaica Omnibus Service (JOS) was such an unreliable form of transportation that it was blamed for the unusually high incidence of tardiness and absenteeism among workers who depended upon it. It was also a financial liability that cost the government about J$11 million a year in deficits, with cumulative losses surpassing its total equity value by 1982.

Clearly, the JOS was not prime divestment material. However, short of complete divestment, the government managed to cut its losses by curtailing the JOS's direct-carrier responsibilities and by auctioning off its primary passenger routes to private operators. These private carriers either lease JOS buses or use their own minibuses. Although the JOS survives as an administrative entity, it now serves mostly a regulatory function, supervising routes, fares, and scheduling.

This experiment in partial divestment has apparently been successful. The privatization of the JOS's direct service responsibilities is widely credited with notable improvements in national transportation over the past couple of years. Moreover, the JOS case suggests a possible alternative to complete divestment in cases in which the risks of taking over a failing government enterprise are too great for any one investor.

State Shrinkage: Other Aspects

"Simulated" Privatization

The Seaga government's efforts to reduce and reform the role of the public sector have taken on a number of guises, aside from the aforementioned attempts at privatizing state-owned enterprises. For one, there is some evidence that through "simulated" privatization public enterprises are now more closely scrutinized on the basis of their financial and managerial performance and have been made more adaptable to changes in the marketplace. For example, in late 1983 the newly reorganized Air Jamaica ceased its Trinidad and Tobago run after one trial year, on the grounds that it was "not sufficiently profitable" (doubtless an understatement). Earlier, the national airline had scrapped its London and Frankfurt routes when sizable losses were apparent. To maintain its European connections, Air Jamaica entered into an agreement with Air Florida (now defunct), by which it was guaranteed an allocation of seats on the U.S. carrier's regular London to Miami runs. The Jamaican carrier then assumed responsibility for passage from Miami to Kingston.[24] While concentrating its limited resources on more popular and well-traveled routes, Air Jamaica was thus prevented from accruing yet greater losses. Such flexibility is not characteristic of Jamaican public enterprises and can therefore be likened to the operation of a private firm.

Reducing excess employment in public enterprises is another key feature of simulated privatization that the government has undertaken to some extent. The initial reorganization of the island's bus system, for example, made over 500 JOS employees redundant. At one point in 1982, the state-owned Jamaica Frozen Foods reportedly sacked 101 of its 171 employees when raw material shortages all but brought production to a halt. Although it is difficult to generalize based on these examples alone, the government does appear to have made some headway in the mammoth task of trimming the payrolls of public enterprises. Less than total success can properly be viewed as a result of government fears of further worker dislocation in Jamaica's high unemployment environment. Perhaps more significant, there appears to be a tacit understanding between the powerful Jamaica Civil Service Association (JCSA) and the government by which the former agrees to reasonable wage adjustments in exchange for job stability.[25]

Deregulation

The project of deregulating the Jamaican economy was begun almost immediately when the Seaga government came to power. At the beginning, there was very little resistance to this effort. Forced austerity during the previous years had created a buildup in consumer demand for just about everything from corn flakes to Toyotas. Industry, too, welcomed the dismantling of the stringent import-control regime, which in many cases had made spare parts and machinery impossible to attain and at times forced plants to shut down. The reopening of the economy was welcomed by nearly all quarters.

With specific attention to import policy, deregulation has not been carried out to the full extent originally planned by the government; that is, although the import of a wide range of goods is no longer restricted by burdensome licensing procedures, de facto restrictions exist in the form of foreign-exchange quotas assigned by the National Planning Agency. The markedly decreased availability of hard currency since 1981 has made the restrictiveness of this quota system quite apparent. As during the Manley period, for example, manufacturers have been denied foreign exchange for vital inputs. Furthermore, there is evidence suggesting that the government has failed to give foreign-exchange allocations priority and has made available a disproportionate amount for the import of nonvital consumer goods at the expense of manufacturers and exporters.[26]

Finally, it is questionable whether import policy changes have effected a significant debureaucratization of the system. Complaints heard from private-sector groups suggest that the delays and red tape have simply been transferred from one government agency to another. Private-sector criticisms of the new system also focus on the government's continued inability to control "higgling" (informal trading outside customs authority).[27] These and other complaints from the business community have evolved into a movement, in some instances, for more instead of less government intervention in the trading system.

Exchange-Rate Policy

A desire to avoid extensive social hardship and the heavy political flak of a full-fledged devaluation explains the Seaga government's decision to maintain a two-tiered exchange system during its first two years in office. Although the system was not formally introduced until early 1983, it was in reality well established via the unregulated--but tolerated--black market currency trade. Once the parallel system was put into formal operation, only basic foodstuffs, petroleum, pharmaceuticals, textbooks, government supplies, and raw materials for industry could be imported at the offical rate of J$1.78 to US$1. All other goods (save for a relatively small list that could be transacted at a special CARICOM rate of J$2.25 to US$1) were subject to semiregulated commercial bank rates of J$2.46 or lower, depending on the demand for hard currency at time of purchase. With respect to imports of nonpriority goods, the Jamaican dollar had been devalued by 38.2 percent.

The system underwent several modifications before collapsing in November of 1983. For one, the government gradually narrowed the list of goods that were eligible for importation at the official rate. To combat chaotic exchange-rate fluctuation (and probably speculation), at one point the government also coaxed the commercial banks to set a joint weekly rate of exchange. This measure helped pacify the legitimate parallel market for several weeks, but it did not significantly enhance hard currency availability, nor did it fully undercut the black market. Ultimately, it was the IMF that forced the government to abandon the parallel system and devalue. Against the U.S. dollar, the Jamaican dollar fell immediately to $3.15.

Exchange-rate unification/devaluation ended the "back door" subsidizing activity that kept prices of priority import items artificially low. In this sense, it can properly be interpreted as another aspect of deregulation, although in truth the Seaga government did not voluntarily pursue the devaluation to the full extent ultimately required by the IMF as a condition for continued borrowing privileges.[28] Furthermore, in lieu of subsidization via the exchange rate, the government continues to subsidize the cost of basic food imports through tax revenues. In this case, Jamaican authorities have accepted a market-based strategy to correct external imbalances and price distortions. However, because of the continued subsidization of food costs, the government has demonstrated that its commitment to a truly unregulated system is less than absolute.

State Shrinkage: Stakeholders and Dynamics

To a considerable degree, the driving force behind the reprivatization and deregulation of the Jamaican economy has been Edward Seaga, who even as opposition leader consistently attacked the interventionist policies of the Manley government. Seaga's personal ideological leanings, however, do not fully explain the process of state shrinkage in Jamaica. Indeed, the process must be understood in the context of a broader policy milieu in which key actors or stakeholders, domestic and foreign, have proved to possess a significant amount of power to influence, in varying degrees, the policies and actions of the government.

The IMF

Undoubtedly the most powerful stakeholder outside the government is the IMF, which over the last decade has made more funds available per capita to Jamaica than to any other member nation. By renewing relations with the fund, the Seaga government committed itself to an adjustment program involving fiscal and monetary restraint, decontrol of prices, and a host of other policies aimed at bolstering the island's balance of payments situation. As described in the preceding section, the fund's intervention on the issue of exchange-rate policy was the decisive factor in the government's decision to abolish the dual rate and devalue. In addition, fund conditionality has been a major motivating force behind the government's attempts to reduce public expenditures, even though Jamaica has consistently failed to meet its fiscal deficit targets.[29] Measures that the government has taken to trim back deficit spending--limits on public-sector wage increases, selective reductions in the public payroll, removal of subsidies, price increases in government services, and the like--can rightfully be linked to the IMF agreement, particularly when viewed in light of the heavy political risks that such implementation has meant for the Seaga administration.

It is difficult to ascertain the extent to which the fund has attempted to influence specific fiscal-policy decisions in Jamaica. On the surface, at least, IMF deficit targets appear to focus on aggregate public spending, without reference to particular areas of problematic government activity. In this sense, the actual mechanics of the domestic adjustment effort remain the exclusive responsibility of Jamaican authorities. It is quite likely, however, that in private negotiations with the Jamaican government, the fund has advanced more specific prescriptions for fiscal management. This would not be unprecedented. In its negotiations with the Manley government, for example, the fund pressed for a reduction in the number of government ministries, departments, statutory boards, and state enterprises.[30]

There is no reason to believe that the fund has become any less concerned with the size and role of the Jamaican public sector under its current leadership. The IMF may therefore be more actively and directly involved in the reduction of the Jamaican state than is commonly believed.

The U.S. Government

The U.S. government under the Reagan administration represents another key stakeholder from the international community. The Reagan government took over the White House at about the same time that Seaga came to power and immediatley lent enormous amounts of aid and technical support to the Jamaican recovery effort. Besides providing bilateral grants and loans, the United States has also purchased extraordinarily large quantities of Jamaican bauxite for the national strategic stockpile. Additional, although less quantifiable, support for Jamaica is evident in the U.S. representation in regional and multilateral organizations such as the IDB, the World Bank, and the IMF.

To be sure, Seaga's unabashedly "pro-Western" political orientation helps explain the extent of Washington's support. Not to be overlooked, however, is Jamaica's embrace of private sector-led development, a strategy that the Reagan government would like to see advanced throughout the Caribbean region. In this context, the United States has a clear interest in seeing that Seaga's experiment in reprivatization is successful.

Indirectly, through a variety of programs designed to stimulate the private sector, U.S. government assistance reinforces the indigenous state-shrinking process. The Reagan administration's Caribbean Basin Initiative (CBI), of which Jamaica is a beneficiary, is a prime example of the U.S. government's commitment to the success of free enterprise in the troubled region. It would hardly be an exaggeration to assert that Jamaica is the test case of the CBI strategy. No other recipient nation has received a comparable level of official U.S. assistance. Significantly, a large percentage of this support has taken the form of USAID programs promoting the development of the private sector.

With good reason, the supportive role played by the United States has been for the most part restrained in order not to usurp local authority. Yet, the advisory and consultative component of U.S. assistance should be recognized as a powerful tool for the promotion of free enterprise and therefore for the reduction of the state sector as an economic actor. If on the whole its involvement in Jamaica has been indirect and restrained, the United States at times has become directly involved by advancing measures that would be more supportive of foreign investment and that would hasten the process of deregulation.[31]

The Local Private Sector

Jamaica's private-sector groups have had no small part in the state-shrinking process, for they are well organized, powerful, and extremely influential in top policymaking circles of the Seaga government. The private sector, however, is not homogeneous. The specific interests of traders, for instance, do not coincide on all counts with manufacturers' interests. When Seaga began loosening the controls on the economy, in fact, deep schisms within the business community became apparent. Importers profited handsomely, but manufacturers long accustomed to a protected market petitioned for relief. Exporters meanwhile complained bitterly that the foreign-exchange quota system was clearly favoring merchants over producers.

In short, the business community's initial response to the Seaga program, although largely supportive at the beginning, turned negative when the harsh realities of deregulation became apparent. The government has therefore had to accommodate these frequently conflicting interests to some degree, although bottom-line IMF targets have ultimately proved more significant determining factors in the outcome of macroeconomic policy decisions.

The divestment issue has been of less interest to the Jamaican private sector, except in comparatively few instances when local entrepreneurs found themselves in direct competition with public enterprises. Established hoteliers, for example, have stated support for NHP privatization, although it is uncertain whether the more expensive and poorly managed government properties ever posed a threat to their market share. Also, with few exceptions, existing private companies have not sought management contracts for NHP possessions.

In general, examples of local investors assuming ownership over public enterprises in areas other than hotels have been limited to the Versair case and a few small manufacturing companies, one in the frozen food area. The failure of local investors to assume control of the sugar sector is particularly apparent, although again, the risks involved in such as undertaking have had an understandable deterrent effect.

The Bureaucracy

Under JLP as well as PNP governments, the Jamaican bureaucracy has shown itself to be an extremely potent force in the policy arena. Through a multiplicity of ministries, agencies, public corporations, statutory boards, and state enterprises, the reach of the Jamaican bureaucracy extends to all reaches of national life. It is also quite independent and capable of protecting its own interests regardless of the party in power. Jamaican bureaucrats have traditionally enjoyed wide discretionary powers, which have not always been exercised in accordance with central government directives. In fact, a distinct anti-governing party tendency among bureaucratic elements has been noted by at least one keen observer of the Jamaican scene.[32]

Generally speaking, the bureaucratic predilection to resist the loss of power and authority that state shrinkage implies is clear. In Jamaica, the very nature and strength of the bureaucracy suggests an extraordinary amount of resistance from well-entrenched civil servants whose interests are effectively defended by the powerful JCSA. This is particularly true in the all-important area of job security.

On another plane, state shrinkage has also been undermined by ministerial appointees who, once empowered, have proved reluctant to cede their new authority.[33] In some cases, the behavior of boards appointed to oversee public enterprises displays similar antipolicy tendencies. In one well-publicized case, the state-owned National Commercial Bank, acting on its own initiative, purchased a hotel in Kingston at a time when the prime minister was trying to privatize the government's other tourist properties.[34]

In summary, the Jamaican public sector in its numerous organizational manifestations has demonstrated formidable strength in slowing (and even undermining) the state-shrinkage mandate of the Seaga administration. To suggest a wide-scale bureaucratic reorganization as a solution to the problem is to seriously underestimate the political difficulties of such an undertaking. For Seaga, there would be practical problems as well, not the least of which is finding a team of loyal and competent administrators willing to do battle with an established bureaucratic system that resists any incursions into its power and independence.

Concluding Assessment

From the start, the Seaga administration's effort to reduce the state's role in the economy was limited. This effort was clearly not designed to strip the state of its ownership and control over all productive activities. Instead, the Seaga administration drew rather distinct lines between enterprises that were appropriate for state ownership and those that were better suited for private proprietorship. Only in the case of the hotel properties has the government displayed ambivalence with respect to the appropriate type of privatization that should be pursued. That issue is not yet resolved, although through leasing arrangements the government has found at least an acceptable short- to medium-term solution.

Whether the hotel and sugar holdings are eventually privatized, the state's share of the nation's output will remain large, and irreversibly so. Table 3 charts the growth of government consumption as a percentage of GDP in Jamaica as well as in neighboring Caribbean countries. The measure is an admittedly crude one, but the figures nonetheless reflect the Jamaican state's relatively large share of national output. Only in Guyana, where about 80 percent of the economy is state owned, is there a higher ratio of government consumption to GDP. Note also that in Jamaica the trend of an increasingly higher government consumption-to-GDP ratio has not been reversed in the post-1980 period.

The state's spending commitments remain sizable. In the 1980 to 1982 period, the ratio of current government expenditures to GDP remained constant at about 33 percent. Capital expenditures in that period increased from 10.0 percent to 12.2 percent of GDP. Debt-service payments, which reached 29 percent of exports in 1982, have risen to the current level of about 45 percent.[35] The government is also committed to a number of infrastructural development projects that require public financing beyond whatever support is supplied through multilateral or bilateral sources. Furthermore, the government has been forced to put up venture capital for priority development projects, most notably in the area of nontraditional agriculture. Finally, spending on health, education, and social welfare continues to account for a large portion of current revenues and an increasingly high percentage of government borrowing--particularly when food subsidies and wages for nonessential government workers are factored in.

To a large extent, continued high levels of government spending and investment can be attributed to a rather gross overestimation of private capital formation during the recovery period. That this recovery effort coincided with a major downturn in the world economy should certainly not be overlooked. In any case, new foreign investment has been particularly disappointing. Despite a wide range of fiscal incentives offered, new investments from North America and Western Europe totaled only US$110 million in the three-year period from 1981 to 1983. Particularly disconcerting for the government has been its inability to secure major commitments from large U.S.

companies, including those affiliated with the U.S. Business Committee on Jamaica.[36]

The reticence--or inability--of the local private sector to lay out new capital should also be considered. Essentially, there are two schools of thought on the subject. The first theory states that the combined impact of foreign-exchange shortages and heavy debt burdens has effectively prevented local producers from considering new investment or expansions. (Jamaican producers also point out that even when concessionary financing has been made available--such as the US$100 million Export Development Fund set up by the World Bank--they have not been able to secure the requisite guarantees from commercial banks.) In this case, lack of local private initiative can be viewed as a matter of fate, not choice.

The competing theory minimizes the overall economic potential of surviving domestic producers in Jamaica. Instead, emphasis is placed on the need to attract expatriate capital (roundly estimated at one billion US dollars) that fled the island during the latter Manley years and has not returned. This theory reinforces prevailing descriptions of the local private sector as critically deficient in entrepreneurship and averse to risk to an almost irrational degree.[37] Accordingly, potential investors from this category will continue to choose safe ventures (for example, real estate in Miami) rather than commit their resources to opportunities in agriculture, manufacturing, or tourism.

Whichever theory most accurately explains the lack of local private initiative, it seems clear that Seaga's preference for private over state-led development has not been reinforced by a ground swell of local business activity. So long as Jamaican business interests remain on the sidelines with multinational capital, the state is forced to invest its own scarce resources in a variety of economic activities in order to maintain output, generate foreign exchange, and create jobs.

Historically in Jamaica, high unemployment has been one of the strongest motivating factors behind state involvement in productive activities. This is as true now for Seaga as it was for Manley in the early 1970s. Until unemployment can be reduced significantly below current levels (about 26 percent), new forms of state activity could well emerge as tools for absorbing the surplus labor force. To some extent, IMF prescription will act as a brake on new state initiatives. Nevertheless, in Jamaica, as elsewhere in the developing world, the state remains the employer of last resort. This imposes clear limits on its ability to withdraw from economic activities, even when there is overwhelming evidence that these activities could be more efficiently managed by the private sector under different circumstances.

Table 1

State Ownership by ECLA Category, 1980

ECLA Category	Nature of Enterprise
Public utilities	Electric power production and transmission
	Rail, bus, and air transportation
	Telephone and communication services
Strategic concerns	Bauxite mining
	Merchant marine service
	Cement production
	Dairy and agricultural production
	Food storage and processing
	Export and import marketing
	Banking
Expropriations	None
Rescue operations	Hotels, travel agencies, and other tourism-related companies
	Sugar refineries
	Light manufacturing companies

Table 2

Jamaican Hotel Privatization as of December 1983

Hotel	Operator(s)	Corporate Base
Trelawny Beach Club	Far East Hotels and Entertainment Ltd.	Hong Kong
Royal Caribbean Hotel	Grand Metropolitan and Holiday Inns	United States
Casa Montego	Bert Wright	Jamaica
Negril Beach Village	Village Resorts Ltd.	Jamaica
Inter-Continental	Americana Hotels	United States
Mallards Beach Hyatt	Sheraton	United States
New Kingston Hotel	Wyndam Company	United States

Table 3

Government Consumption as Percentage of GDP

Country	1960	1965	1970	1975	1980	1981	1982
Jamaica	9.2	11.0	9.5	18.2	21.3	21.4	22.9
Guyana	11.4	15.0	17.0	19.6	28.9	29.4	30.0
Trinidad	9.6	12.1	13.9	11.0	13.2	16.9	--
Barbados	--	--	--	13.0	12.0	11.9	12.5
Dominican Republic	12.6	18.3	11.6	6.1	7.8	9.5	9.8

Source: International Monetary Fund, IFS Yearbook, 1983.
Dash means no information.

Notes

I wish to acknowledge the assistance of Jane Rovira Burch of Business International, Alice Lentz of the Council of the Americas, and Richard Fletcher of the Inter-American Development Bank for their extremely valuable comments on the text.

1. World Bank, World Development Report, Baltimore, Md.: Johns Hopkins University Press, 1983, p. 56.

2. The colonial government nationalized Jamaica's rail system in 1896. The government established Air Jamaica, the national air carrier, in mid-1960 to exploit the lucrative New York to Jamaica tourist route. Originally, Air Jamaica was operated by two foreign firms, BOAC and BWIA (see Ransford Palmer, The Jamaican Economy [New York: Praeger], 1968).

3. International Monetary Fund, IFS Yearbook (Washington, D.C., 1983).

4. Terry Lacey, Violence and Politics in Jamaica, 1960-1970 (Manchester: Manchester University Press, 1977), p. 17.

5. Carl Stone, Class, Race and Political Behaviour in Urban Jamaica (Kingston: University of West Indies Press, 1973), p. 169.

6. Opposition to the JNH reportedly subsided when "competing middlemen" were reassured that their interests were not at stake. Interestingly, while playing a subsidizing role, the JNH posted a J$18 million (J$0.90:US$1) surplus in 1973 (see the Jamaica Daily News of 2 December 1977).

7. Joan Lipton, "Bauxite in Jamaica: Ownership and Control in a Partially Nationalized Industry," Office for Public Sector Studies Technical Papers series, no. 21 (Austin: Institute of Latin American Studies, 1979).

8. "National Self-Reliance Statement" (Kingston: Agency for Public Information, 19 January 1977).

9. Comments of former head of the Jamaica Manufacturers' Association, Charles Henderson-Davis, as quoted in the Daily Gleaner (25 November 1977). Both the Gleaner and the Daily News were filled with private-sector criticisms of the government's marketing ambitions. These comments underline the extreme sensitivity of the private sector to perceived government intrusion into commercial affairs.

10. Inter-American Development Bank, Economic and Social Progress in Latin America (Washington, D.C., various years).

11. For a detailed discussion of Jamaica's relations with the IMF during this period, see G. Russell Kincaid's article, "Conditionality and the Use of Fund Resources," Finance and

Development (June 1981). For an alternative view, see the article by Norman Girvan et al. entitled, "The IMF and the Third World: The Case of Jamaica," Development Dialogue 2 (1980).

12. Edward Seaga, from a speech entitled, "Harmonizing Host Country and Corporate Activities," delivered at the Stanford University Graduate School of Business, 14 January 1983.

13. Journal of Commerce (19 October 1981).

14. Canute James, "Jamaican Sugar Sector Interest U.S. Firms," Journal of Commerce (23 February 1982).

15. "Jamaica '82: New Opportunities for Investment," Wall Street Journal (supplement) (19 February 1982).

16. Edward Seaga, as quoted in the Journal of Commerce (25 October 1982).

17. See John Huey's piece, "Jamaica Hotel Scheme May Be Key to Revival of Island's Economy," Wall Street Journal (29 May 1981).

18. Tourism minister Eric Abrahams noted, "It is not a good market for second-hand hotels. We had an offer of US$20 million for a hotel that cost us US$30 million to build some years ago, but now would cost us US$70 million to replace" (Caribbean Insight 5, no. 5 [May 1982]).

19. See Caribbean Insight 4, no. 12 (December 1981) and Latin America Regional Report (Caribbean) of 20 September 1982.

20. For an analysis of the problems experienced by Caribbean sugar producers, see "Mill Closures Highlight Caribbean Sugar Industry Crisis," Financial Times of London (25 October 1983).

21. Journal of Commerce (6 October 1982).

22. Ibid.

23. Seaga's explanation was contained in his report to Parliament on 2 November 1982.

24. Accounts of Air Jamaica's reorganization were carried in Caribbean Insight (May 1981 and June 1982). See also "Airline Seeks to Regain Economic Viability," Journal of Commerce (19 October 1981).

25. Observation based on a case involving Seprod, the state-owned producer of basic goods, and the government, as reported in Caribbean Insight (July 1981).

26. "Why Jamaica's Economy May Run Aground," Business Week (10 October 1982). See also Latin America Regional Report (Caribbean) (12 June 1981) for manufacturers' views on the foreign-exchange situation.

27. The changes in the import regulation system are described in "Jamaica Implements Two-Tiered Exchange Rate to Boost Exports, Economy," Business Latin America (19 January 1983). Reactions from key private-sector figures are contained in interviews published in the Daily Gleaner (7-8 September 1983).

28. Even with the devaluation, the US$650 million extended fund agreement was terminated. At this writing, a new US$180 million standby plan is being arranged between Jamaica and the fund.

29. For example, the central government deficit for the fiscal year ending in March 1982 amounted to 17 percent of GDP, against an IMF target of around 13 percent. Deficit spending also forced the government to monopolize an extremely large portion of net domestic credit, thus further squeezing the pool of credit available for private-sector borrowing. See the chapter on Jamaica in the IDB's report for 1983, as well as S. Karene Witcher's article "Jamaica Reportedly at Odds with the IMF," Wall Street Journal (11 March 1983).

30. According to a confidential briefing paper, an IMF team sent to Jamaica in late 1979 was instructed by top fund officials to pressure the government to reduce the number of state agencies, public corporation boards, and public enterprises (see Anthony Sampson, The Money Lenders [New York: Penguin Books, 1981]).

31. For instance, in early 1982 U.S. ambassador to Jamaica Loren Lawrence reportedly criticized the Jamaican government for its lack of "a realistic economic program" and suggested, among other things, further reducing import and export controls.

32. See Carl Stone, "Class and the Institutionalization of Two Party Politics in Jamaica," Journal of Commonwealth and Comparative Politics 25 (1976): pp. 183-184.

33. Observations of Richard Fletcher, minister of state for finance and planning (1977-1980), from correspondence with me of January 1984.

34. Seaga was further disturbed by the fact that the hotel was purchased for J$2.4 million over its highest valuation (see Latin America Regional Report [Caribbean] [5 November 1982]).

35. From the IDB Report for 1983.

36. The U.S. Business Committee (the so-called Rockefeller Committee) was set up in early 1981 to marshal support among U.S. companies for the Jamaican recovery effort.

37. See, for example, Paul Chen Young's critical study, "Report on Private Investment in the Caribbean" (Kingston: Atlas, 1973).

Part III

COUNTRY EXPERIENCES ELSEWHERE

CHAPTER 10

Economic Liberalization Policies in Sri Lanka: International Pressures, Constraints, and Supports

Ronald J. Herring

Introduction

Public intervention in the economy is inevitably justified with reference to promotion of the general welfare; operationalizing the general welfare produces significant political disputes. Sri Lanka's political-economic history divides fairly neatly into one period (from independence in 1948 to the elections of 1977) in which the government was seen as the solution to increasing economic problems, and another period, from 1977 to the present, in which governmental intervention in the previous three decades is seen more as the problem than as the solution. The expansion of the functional scope of government in the economy was fairly steady until 1977, resulting in a very heavily taxed, tightly regulated system. The 1977 elections were largely a referendum on perceived failures of the "closed economy"; the champions of a liberalized "open economy" triumphed decisively.

The argument of this paper is that, despite internal and external critiques, the pre-1977 policies demonstrated concretely the possibility of significant development at very low levels of per capita income and extreme dependence. For the bottom of the income pyramid, public programs, despite well-known failings, contributed to security and well-being remarkable in comparison with other low-income nations. Post-1977 policy has not so much reduced the functional scope of government in the economy as it has curtailed certain interventions while expanding others. Sri Lanka offers a case in which the economic logic of liberalization supports a shift in governmental priorities rather than a wholesale privatization campaign. The most significant privatization is not of public assets but rather of poverty and insecurity for weaker sectors of the society; responsibility for well-being has been shifted from government to individuals and families in their interaction with market forces.

In this profound shift in priorities, international factors have been decisive: the relative success and failure of pre-1977 policies, and even their form, were dependent on structural forces in the international system--most important, the international division of labor, which was a colonial residue, and shifts in the terms of trade. Likewise, the success or failure of post-1977 liberalization policies is dependent on (in the literal sense of "hangs from") those same international forces and more than ever on particular international actors appraising Sri Lanka's domestic policy.

The Ironies of Sri Lanka's Experience as a Development Model

Sri Lanka (known as Ceylon until 1972) has received international attention disproportionate to its size as both a positive and a negative model of economic development. One of vhe world's poorest, most vulnerable, and dependent economies, classically dualistic in the separation of an export-oriented plantation enclave from a large peasant subsistence sector, the nation has traditionally depended on the sale of plantation crops in international markets to earn foreign exchange for the purchase of food imports and other necessities. At independence, half the dietary staple (rice) was imported and 90 percent of foreign exchange earnings came from three crops (tea, rubber, and coconut).

But unlike many poor and dependent societies, Ceylon developed an elaborate and expensive set of social welfare policies disproportionate to its per capita income. The official international development community widely condemned these policies as "premature welfarism" that diverted resources from investment and toward social consumption and thus retarded growth. Until the 1970s, Ceylon was frequently cited as a negative development model in which welfarism and strict public regulation of the economy hindered growth; if anything is evidence of "price distortion" it is the distribution of free food to the populace.

But in the 1970s something very close to a "paradigm shift" took place in development policy logic, at least at the symbolic level. The new paradigm redefined development itself, de-emphasizing aggregate growth in favor of measures of social well-being, particularly for the poorest of the poor (for example, World Bank 1975). There was, at least in theory, explicit recognition that rapid aggregate growth could produce a "trickling up" and marginalization as well as a trickling down.

By alternative criteria of development, such as the meeting of "basic needs" and a reduction in levels of malnutrition, disease, and inequality, Sri Lanka, somewhat ironically, became a positive rather than a negative development model relative to most poor societies and indeed relative to many not-so-poor ones as well (ibid. 1980a:90; Jayawardena 1974; Isenmen 1980). For example, if one employs the criterion of the "Physical Quality of Life Index," PQLI (composed of equally weighted measures of literacy, infant mortality, and life expectancy), Sri Lanka in the mid-1970s ranked higher than Venezuela or Chile, with a life expectancy near that of some European countries and far greater than subcontinental neighbors India, Pakistan, Nepal, Afghanistan, and Bangladesh (see table 1). For a rough comparison of these data, consider that Sri Lanka's PQLI of 82, with a GNP per capita of less than $200 annually, came closer to that of Sweden (97) or the United States (95), than to that of India (43) or Nepal (13) (see McLaughlin-ODC, 1979: table A-4). Though the PQLI is by no means unexceptionable,[1] as the aggregate measure may obscure significant differences by class, sector, gender, and region and depends on often problematic and noncomparable data, the Sri Lankan experience rightly received a great deal of international attention. The fact that the nation achieved one of the highest ratios of PQLI to per capita GNP in the world, despite classical and severe structural dependency, raises a profound developmental point: extreme national poverty need not entail mass destitution, just as national wealth is no guarantee of well-being for the bottom of the income pyramid. Extensive governmental intervention in economic decisions and processes sustained this mediation between national poverty and individual well-being.

The second irony in Sri Lanka's development experience is that, just as some international recognition was accruing to the stubborn persistence of "premature welfarism" in the face of previous international criticism, the accumulation of structural forces in the international economy began to erode the material base of those policies. Few nations have experienced so drastic and long-term a deterioration in terms of trade as did Ceylon from the mid-1950s to 1976. The data in table 2 illustrate the dilemma: over time, a given level of exports would purchase a declining quantity of imports. The volume of imports, accordingly, fell, first through severe restriction of luxury imports (automobiles, whiskey, and the like). The structure of the economy, however, limited the amount by which imports could be cut: levels of food, medicines, intermediate goods, spare parts, fertilizer, and such, could not easily be reduced without damaging the economy or the population's welfare. The gap was met by borrowing, and debt service obligations further reduced import capacity. The debt service ratio rose from negligible levels in the 1950s to over 20 percent (excluding short-term credits) in 1975. Though the economy was exporting substantially more in 1975 than in 1960, those exports had a purchasing power little more than one-third the smaller volume of exports in 1960.

The nation's deteriorating exchange position crucially conditioned the expansion of the public sector in terms of regulation, production, and welfare, but two legacies of colonial rule laid the groundwork: democratic politics and an extensive public sector before independence. The plantation economy required extensive infrastructure; the colonial state owned and developed relatively advanced railways, electrical, postal, telegraphic, telephone, and water supply services, and even held the monopoly for salt production. Quasi-public financial institutions serviced the commercial needs of the colony. Because of the colony's extreme dependence on imports and its strategic importance, the state established production units during World War II for plywood, quinine, drugs, leather, coir, paper, ceramics, acetic acid, glass, and steel (Karunatilake 1976). Welfare policies likewise began under colonial rule--a network for subsidized rice and flour distribution and rationing in 1942, for example. Free education (through the university level), poor relief, and subsidized or free medical care were all introduced in the late colonial period (Corea 1975: chaps. 5, 6; Wickremeratne 1973; Gavan and Chandrasekera 1979: 11-15; Gunatilleke 1978; Lakshman 1980: 17; Karunatilake 1975; Herring 1981). The state also took an extraordinarily active role from 1935 onwards in planning and subsidizing "colonialization schemes" to remove the landless and land-poor from the deteriorating peasant sector to free farms in new irrigated tracts (Herring 1983: chap. 5).

Public institutions create clienteles: in a political democracy, distribution and expansion of spoils (jobs, contracts, services, subsidies) become objects of partisan competition for votes and means of servicing electoral machines. While remaining a colony, Ceylon received universal franchise very early (1931); though politicians could not control essential levers of state power, they could compete in patronage and promises. A wealthy plantation economy supported such predictably popular programs as subsidized food and free farms, but as the terms of trade turned against Ceylon after independence, the economy's capacity to bear the costs was strained. Food subsidies alone claimed about 20 percent of government expenditure (World Bank 1953, part 1). When the government in 1953 attempted to reduce rice subsidies because of increasing costs during the Korean War, a well-established leftist opposition called for the "Great Hartal" (general strike), which paralyzed the nation (Wanasinghe 1980; Wriggins 1960: 75-76; Ponnambalam 1981:25). The prime minister resigned and the finance minister (currently president of Sri Lanka) lost his seat in the following elections.

As the significant reserves of the early 1950s dwindled and the nation's vulnerability to exogenous shocks became apparent, concern for import-substituting industrialization naturally developed. Indigenous entrepreneurs seemed more drawn to the plantation economy and import-export trade than to risky long-term industrial development; the state took up the slack. Through both conservative and populist regimes the economic role of government increased. As current account deficits became chronic, some nationalizations were justified by the necessity of "stemming the drain of foreign exchange and the evasion of controls" (Karunatilake 1976:183). A similar concern for private-sector leakages of foreign exchange and extensive abuses (Wickramasinghe 1974) led to the establishment of state trading concerns, tighter regulations, and export-oriented public-sector firms (petroleum products, for example). Fed by concern over shortages of imported consumer goods and the volatility of "rice politics" in a highly politicized society, governments expanded state control of distribution of necessities (both goods and services) at fair prices. Political elites found further nationalizations and controls attractive for narrowly partisan political reasons as well in a political system very evenly balanced between the major contenders (which alternated in power until 1982). By 1975 roughly one-fourth of GNP was in government or public-sector hands.

Adverse international pressures, in conjuction with a specific internal political configuration, are thus an important explanation for state intervention in the economy. Freedom for policy maneuver was extremely limited; no regime can control international prices, and an economy receiving 90 percent of its export earnings from plantation crops needs both breathing space and resources to diversify significantly. Moreover, as government revenues were heavily dependent on export taxes, deterioration in the terms of trade contributed significantly to burgeoning domestic budget deficits. Like many structurally similar poor nations in the mid-1970s, Sri Lanka faced an economic crisis largely external in origin (Kappagoda and Paine 1981: 101-110): slow growth, austerity budgets, mounting internal and external debts, high unemployment.

In 1977 elections produced a virtual rout of the political forces that had presided over these economic disasters and ushered in a regime openly committed to a radical redirection of national economic policy meant to resurrect long-suppressed market mechanisms and open the economy to foreign capital (see Warnapala 1979). Ironically, just as important elements in the international development community were having second thoughts about the reality of the "equity-growth tradeoff" and commending Sri Lanka for its achievements in meeting basic needs and reducing income inequality while maintaining a long-term growth rate respectable in comparison to subcontinental neighbors (see table 1), domestic political forces, with decisive international support, began dismantling the supporting ensemble of policies that had evolved over the previous three decades. In a final irony, in recognition of that policy shift, Sri Lanka is celebrated, almost certainly prematurely, as "an IMF success," recognizing the congruence of the strategy shift with the policy preferences of the International Monetary Fund and the sudden appearance of high growth rates after 1977.

Delegitimizing the "Closed Economy"

So severe was the economic crisis of the early 1970s that there is a sense in which the complex of policies in place at the time, and the political forces associated with them, were inescapably delegitimized in popular perception. A leftist United Front government came to power in 1970 with an overwhelming electoral mandate. That government inherited the accumulated consequences of the 1960s analyzed above--unprecedented debts and deficits--and, more proximately important, the inability of the domestic economy to generate jobs; unemployment, especially among educated youth, had become an explosive social issue. At least 14 percent of the labor force was _openly_ unemployed, though the level in some of the densely settled rural areas was much higher and young people were especially affected. Underemployment was severe and dissatisfaction with jobs "inappropriate" to level of education or expectations widespread and bitter (ILO 1971:Vol. 1: chap. 2).

The austerity budget of 1971 illustrates the extent to which the structural forces represented by deteriorating terms of trade and increasing budget deficits impinged on domestic economic policy. Political opposition prevented the government from increasing the price of flour and sugar, but the price of rice was increased 25 percent and medical subsidies were reduced. N. M. Perera, one of Ceylon's leading Trotskyites, as minister of finance laconically noted, "This has been a hard budget. It has not been a pleasant or easy task for me. Poignant memories of the past keep crowding around me. All my life I have fought to ease the burden of the poor and the humble. I am now the instrument not of easing, but of heaping additional burdens on them" (Halliday 1975:210).

Any regime would have faced similar agonizing and limited options. The Left protected its political constituency more than the Right arguably would have, but the room for maneuver was narrow. Though the government continually asked for the forebearance of the poor and unemployed and promised that the austerity measures (long suggested by the World Bank and the IMF) were temporary, an important section of the militant Left rejected both the government's program and its analysis. The JVP (Janatha Vimukhti Peramuna, or People's Liberation Front) as already mobilizing and organizing in the countryside for revolution, a process accelerated by the failure of the United Front government to produce radical structural changes (Obeysekara 1973; Wijeweera 1975). The Insurgency of 1971 was launched more in response to tactical problems relating to government suppression than from a well-conceived strategic position, but it nevertheless succeeded in wresting large areas of the island from state control until the reinforced armed forces could regroup and, with diverse international technical assistance, crush the rural youths' rebellion. The Insurgency had a profound impact on Ceylonese politics, acting as a catalyst, for example, in generating a significant land reform, which had not been mentioned in the coalition's Election Manifesto, and in increasing the urgency of job creation (partly through continuous expansion of public-sector employment) (Herring 1983: chaps. 5,8).

The land reform of 1972--which the prime minister had introduced with the stark "We are sitting on a volcano"--was based less on rational economic principles than on the need to generate symbols of social justice, food self-sufficiency, and concern for the rural unemployed. The plantation lands appropriated by the state were <u>by statute</u> to be distributed in such a way that rural youth could be provided employment with an income equivalent to that of a post usually occupied by a moderately-educated person. In 1975 the foreign-owned estates were nationalized. The two land reforms together placed a great deal of prime agricultural capital in the state's hands, in marked contrast to the symbolic posturing in redistributive agrarian policy more typical of the region. Some of that land was allocated to experiments in collective and cooperative farming, particularly for groups of unemployed youth, but the major thrust was to place the commanding heights of the national economy under state control, significantly increasing resources for the ordinary politics of patronage and partisan manipulation (ibid.: chap. 5)

Food became a major crisis for the regime; the rapid escalation in international prices resulted in widespread hunger, despair, and reduced rations. Suffering and deprivation in the 1973-1974 period were severe,[2] particularly among the plantation proletariat--the Tamil tea laborers. To illustrate the linkage between international structural vulnerability and regime constraints, one need only note that, though rice imports were cut 12.5 percent in 1973-1974 (contributing to increased malnutrition), the rice import bill increased by 166 percent. Likewise, the precipitous rise in costs of petroleum-based products dislocated the economy further and added to unemployment. Those factories that depended on imports of machinery, fuel, and raw materials were forced to lower production or shut down (Balakrishnan 1977:202, 210). Between 1973 and 1974, manufacturing value declined and capacity utilization fell to about 40 percent. The transportation system suffered, slowing commercial activity, and rising costs increased the losses of public-sector transportation operations. Paddy production suffered from bad weather, fertilizer shortages, and the government's mandatory procurement policy at prices that did not keep up with inflation in costs of production--a policy strongly conditioned by the perceived political necessity of protecting mass welfare with low rice prices and the fiscal necessity of reducing producer subsidies.

Scarcity and discretionary authority predictably produce externalities in the form of corruption, victimization, and favoritism. The United Front was widely perceived to be guilty of these and other abuses of power and eventually unraveled internally. But more important, the policies that clearly produced hardship and facilitated corruption did not seem to the public to have accomplished anything: suffering was widespread, unemployment reached 25 percent, economic growth virtually ceased, and essential goods were increasingly scarce.

Though both the external development experts and the electorate judged economic performance under the "closed economy" very harshly, it is not at all clear that alternative policies would have fared better in a small, dependent economy in the face of the extraordinarily adverse conditions--natural and economic--of the early 1970s. The economic crisis of mid-decade was genuine, and severe, but the performance of the economy over this period was not noticeably worse than that of other poor nations, even by the narrow criterion of growth rates. This is particularly true when growth rates are compared in per capita terms; Sri Lanka's extensive social welfare system has contributed to a decline in population growth rates, thus improving per capita economic performance. Moreover, measures of economic development that include some notion of physical well-being or "basic needs" decisively differentiate Sri Lanka from regional neighbors (refer to table 1). Even the World Bank, long critical of Sri Lanka's heavy expenditures on education, health, and nutrition (about 10 percent of GNP over the past two decades) commended the results in terms of "human development" and now argues that (a) the "trade-off" between human development and growth "has not been so sharp as is sometimes suggested" and (b) growth rates deteriorated "for reasons generally independent of human development spending" (largely the weather and terms of trade) (1980a:90).

Post-1977 Economic Policy: Opening the "Closed Economy"

The elections of 1977 produced a new regime and a dramatic rejection of the policies that had evolved over the previous three decades, largely as *ad hoc* efforts to alleviate the constraints and pressures of structural dependence in the context of high levels of politicization, partisan competition, and patronage expectations. The culmination had been a tightly regulated, "closed" economy in which the state became increasingly relevant to major economic decisions state participation in the economy increased through nationalization of important sectors and the proliferation of public corporations (Lakshman 1980). Imports were strictly controlled through licensing procedures, state monopolies, and rationing of hard currency. Essential commodities were rationed and offered at subsidized prices (sometimes gratis) to guarantee consumers a floor level of consumption. The widely recognized result was scarcities, corruption, and black-marketeering, as well as shortages in capital and intermediate goods and spare parts. All of these throttled growth and aggravated unemployment, particularly in the 1970s, when deteriorating terms of trade aggravated already severe constraints on imports.

The erosion of social welfare coverage set in before the sweeping 1977 UNP electoral victory (140 of 168 seats), as mentioned previously. But whereas the previous government had cut subsidies reluctantly, in response to budgetary and foreign-exchange pressures, the new regime pledged to reduce subsidies on the theory that their opportunity cost in terms of competing developmental expenditures was too high. The core assumption was that the national economy had been shackled by excessive regulation, an excess of consumption expenditure over investment, and "wasteful and complacent" public-sector enterprises. Market forces were to play a greater role in allocating resources, and public enterprises were to compete with the private sector. The Central Bank termed the new ensemble of policies "a sweeping departure from a tightly controlled, inward-looking, welfare-oriented economic strategy to a more liberalized, outward-looking, and growth-oriented one" (CBC, AR 1978:2).

The key elements of the new policy involve powerful investment incentives to foreign and domestic capital (for details, see Sri Lanka 1979), a shift in the composition of public spending, and a liberalized international trade policy, premised on export-led growth. Employment creation is a central objective, through both encouragement of domestic and foreign capital and ambitious developmental public works such as the Accelerated Mahaweli Development Scheme for bringing vast new tracts of irrigated land under cultivation while substantially increasing hydroelectric generating potential.

The role of the state is by no means minimal, and indeed the public investment program has proved overly ambitious; but the state is to play a smaller role in regulation, commerce, and production, and a greater role in developing infrastructure. The initiatives are by any measure bold and clearly captured the imagination of the external development establishment. Fiscal logic suggests that the very boldness itself is dependent on international support: if tax incentives are given business and yet the government increases infrastructural investment when budget deficits are already large and chronic, additional financial resources on a large scale must be found externally. Likewise, relaxing import controls can be expected to put pressure on the balance of payments.

International factors in the new strategy thus become critical; international support in material terms has arguably been a necessary condition for the liberalization initiatives. The international development community has provided resources to tide the regime over the potentially rocky readjustment period. The dynamics are familiar. Following a sharp devaluation of the rupee in November of 1977, the IMF announced support for "the comprehensive program of economic reform . . . in support of which the present stand-by arrangement (of SDR 93 million) has been approved" (IMF Survey 6:23, 1977). IMF approval is an important signal in international financial and development communities, and the government quickly took advantage of its new status.

In pursuit of the new strategy's emphasis on external investment capital and foreign loans, the finance minister visited groups of investors and officials of aid-giving nations and agencies across the globe. In the first full year of the new regime, official loan commitments more than doubled the 1977 level, in marked contrast to the experience of other South Asian nations at the same time. These official loans carried a grant element of 64.8 percent (World Bank 1980c: Vol. 1:191). The net flow from all lenders increased from $48 million in 1977 to $175.9 million in 1979 (ibid.:102). The finance minister was thus able to boast in his budget speech for 1981 that, "due to the confidence placed by the international cummunity in our new economic policies, we have been able to obtain greater volume of foreign aid and foreign assistance per capita than perhaps any other third world country" (Sri Lanka 1980a:2). As important, considering previous national experience with debt difficulties, the minister noted that more than a third of the assistance was in the form of outright grants, the balance as long-term loans "at minimal interest." Given the current "aid-weariness," Sri Lanka was indeed successful by its announced criterion of foreign-assisted development, and the minister acknowledged the direct connection to the new economic policy: "Without the courageous and imaginative steps we took . . . , nothing would have moved, nothing would have happened" (ibid. 1980c:2).

The marked increase in the level of international grants has allowed the economy to run unprecedented balance-of-trade deficits (a consequence of import liberalization and deteriorating terms of trade). The burden of amortization claims on export earnings was reduced not only through increases in the level of outright grants, but by the substitution of long-term subsidized loans and IMF drawings for high-interest suppliers' credits and commercial loans. The lengthening of the debt service structure was especially evident in 1979, when approximately 70 percent of the long-term loans contracted, accounting for 74 percent of loan volume, allowed a grace period of ten years or more (CBC, RE 1979:185). The position was further alleviated by the outright remission of debts equaling Rs 804 million in 1979.

The effect of international factors in facilitating a higher level of imports and, indirectly, exports (since the import component of intermediate goods is over 75 percent) extends beyond the balance of payments. Domestic capabilities of the government in so dependent an economy are in large part a function of levels and terms of international trade (for analysis of the effects of the Great Depression and Second World War in this regard, see Corea 1975). The tax revenues foregone as a result of the incentives for capital had to be made up from other sources. Taxes on individual and corporate income and profits fell from 17.5 percent of total revenues in 1976 to 9.8 percent in 1978. Similar decreases occurred in the share of taxes on property, net wealth, estates, inheritance, and gifts (IMF 1980:511). Indirect taxes thus increased, and in 1979 taxes on international trade amounted to 55 percent of total tax revenue. Without strong international support, current account deficits would necessarily curtail the level of such trade and thus force very hard political and fiscal choices on the government.

Both internally and externally, the new strategy has been hailed as a remarkable success. Such claims are based on relatively high growth rates since 1977 and require considerable qualification. First, the new strategy was launched in an unusually auspicious economic situation: the terms of trade, which had deteriorated since 1960, showed a 35 percent improvement in 1976, 31 percent in 1977; tea prices experienced an unprecedented rise of 80 percent, contributing to an unprecedented current account surplus of Rs 1,259 million. Gross national product grew at a rate of 8.2 percent in 1978, a very high rate by historical standards, then slowed to 6.2 percent in 1979, 5.5 percent in 1980, 3.9 in 1981, 5 in 1982, and 4.9 in 1983. The rate of growth in real national income has been significantly less, however, because of subsequent deterioration in the terms of trade (see table 3). Moreover, as foreign nationals have claimed larger interest, profit, and dividend factor payments, GNP growth rates have diverged from GDP growth rates. Nevertheless, the acceleration of economic activity has been significant; the more important question is whether the growth rates represent self-sustaining processes or simply reflect a combination of the effect of a large influx of external resources into a very small economy combined with initially favorable terms of trade and the short-term explosion of pent-up demand once the restrictions on imports were lifted.

The import liberalization policy, by removing constraints on imported intermediate goals, certainly contributed to growth in the manufacturing sector, but simultaneously contributed to wiping out the current account surplus very quickly. In 1978 the balance-of-trade deficit was the largest in Sri Lanka's history--and that deficit was dwarfed by the 1979 deficit, which in turn was exceeded in 1980, 1981, 1982, and 1983. As the data in table 3 indicate, in 1977 and 1978 the movement of terms of trade in Sri Lanka's favor (which began in 1976) peaked; import liberalization produced large balance-of-trade deficits over time as prices of imported goods increased much more rapidly than prices of exports. The resultant current account deficits were covered by dependence on foreign funding.

It is fair to say that domestic political elites read the international acclaim and support as carte blanche for a very ambitious development program. This was not to be the case. The 1980 budget deficit amounted to more than 21 percent of GDP and was accompanied by a rate of inflation of at least 30 percent. Officials of the World Bank and the IMF told the government that financial indiscipline was becoming a serious problem. The consortium of donors meeting in Paris in July 1980 was critical of the ambitious public works, particularly housing construction and water-supply schemes. External pressure called for cutting the current account and budget deficits and raising more resources internally. The finance minister predictably responded that "external factors beyond our control" were responsible and that cuts in the investment program would dampen the enthusiasm the government had worked so hard to instill among investors (AWSJW, 6/6/81, 7/20/81). In the 1981 budget some of the more ambitious development projects had to be cut, but a large share of the remaining deficit was still covered by international assistance. The foreign contribution to financing of the net cash budget deficit in 1976 was 32.5 percent; in 1980, 70.4 percent (CBC, RE 1979: table 10.1). The Public Investment Programme of the Ministry of Finance and Planning, 1980-1984, projected a strategy in which net external inflows would be greater than domestic sources, constituting 54 percent of total public investment over the five-year period (Sri Lanka 1980b).

This familiar pattern was repeated in meetings with the Aid Sri Lanka Consortium and IMF in the summers of 1982 and 1983; "belt-tightening" was urged, the government pleaded domestic constraints and blamed external factors, and compromises were made. In 1982 the government was particularly unwilling to cut expenditures because of the upcoming presidential elections (Samarasinghe 1983). In 1983 the IMF took an especially dim view of budget and current account deficits and urged the traditional remedies: devaluation and cuts in subsidies to mass consumption. The finance minister answered that new capital expenditure projects had been totally suspended and that construction on the Mahaweli project was vital for reducing food import costs (and thus balance-of-payments pressure). There was reluctance to cut health, education, and welfare subsidies further, as the nation's remarkable records in these areas "are our pride and we cannot afford to throw them away" (FEER, 6/23/83). As for devaluation, the minister pleaded, "We have only so much to export and any further devaluation can only make imports more expensive."

Despite initial international enthusiasm for the new policies, there are already signs of what may develop into serious problems. At the most general theoretical level, there is some evidence that massive foreign inflows may produce something like a "hothouse" effect in Third World economies, generating significant short-term growth but depressing long-term growth prospects (for a review and empirical analysis, see Bornshier, Chase-Dunn, Rubinson 1978: Bornshier 1980). Since the foreign exchange problem has been a persistent obstacle to economic development in Sri Lanka, the question of profit repatriation, debt servicing, and other outflows becomes critical. Samarasinghe (1980:14) estimates that net foreign exchange earnings from the Export Promotion Zone are only one-third of gross earnings and would be even lower if repatriation of profits and royalties, and the like, were calculated. The net deficit in national accounts for investment payments increased from Rs 10 million in 1977 to Rs 98 million in 1979 (CBC, RE 1979: appendix table 83), and increased further to Rs 432 million in 1980, Rs 1,712 million in 1981, and Rs 1,969 million in 1982 (CBC, AR 1982, table 25). At the same time, hard currency debts have quadrupled since 1977 and will eventually have to be serviced.

It is unlikely that the international community can be counted on repeatedly to make the types of concessions that greeted the new strategy initially. Vulnerability to global recession, protectionism, and terms-of-trade shifts remain the primary determinants of domestic success. Indeed, empirically, the economy is more vulnerable to exogenous shocks under the liberalized regime than under the closed economy (Jayatissa 1982). Simply from shifts in the terms of trade, Sri Lanka lost 7 percent of its real national income in 1982 and 8 percent in 1983. The global depression in primary commodity prices significantly affected government revenues (and thus budget deficits and international approval of the regime): as a striking example, rubber export volume increased by 17 percent in 1982, but export earnings fell by 20 percent and export duty revenues fell by 47 percent. Cocounts experienced a similar, less drastic, decline (CBC, AR 1982:5).

No amount of international pressure on Sri Lanka can produce policies that effectively counter these types of systemic shocks. The IMF has noted that the sharp deterioration in terms of trade from 1980 to 1983 increased the current account deficit from 5.5 percent of GDP to 16 percent (IMF Survey, 9/19/83). To cover these growing deficits, the government has resorted to more extensive commercial borrowing: the debt service ratio has risen accordingly. When short-term debt obligations and IMF transactions are calculated, the debt service ratio reached 15.2 percent in 1982 and 17.5 percent in the first half of 1983 (CBC 1982:104; CBC 1984:21). Although not high by contemporary Third World standards, the debt service ratio is now near the historic high experienced during the "oil shock" period of 1973-1974, well over 20 percent.

Privatization, Entitlements, and Discretionary Boons

Despite an economic philosophy that emphasizes the magic of the market and the disutility of state intervention in economic activity, government policy to date has not dismantled the large public sector, nor has "simulated privatization," in the sense of forcing market efficiency criteria on public-sector firms through competition, played a major role. The state has not, for example, reversed the two land reforms, which put the largest plantations into the public sector; about two-thirds of the tea acreage and one-third of the rubber remain public. Public corporations still run airports, provide insurance, manage hotels, produce traditional medicines, deal in fish, sell milk, fly tourists, build houses, transport people, and monopolize the airways, among other things. Public-sector industrial corporations include steel, petroleum products, textiles, fertilizers, tires, salt, dairy products, distilleries, oils and fats, timber and plywood, paper, cement, and ceramics. More than 60 percent of industrial production is by the public sector (CBC, RE 1982:43). Setting the index of public-sector industrial production for 1977 at 100, a fairly steady increase was evident through 1982 (index=124.6), with the only significant declines in food, beverages, and tobacco.

Public-sector firms vary in profitability, with no clear trend since the new policies took form. The rate of growth in production in public-sector enterprises has been considerably lower than in the private sector. One irony is that import liberalization--a key component in the strategy--has badly hurt the National Textile Corporation and the National Paper Corporation (ibid.:62), adding to the troublesome budget deficit. Of course, the profitability of some public-sector firms has been adversely affected by the terms of trade (for example, plantation industries and petroleum products).

Actual transfer of productive assets from the public sector to the private has been minimal--a few textile mills, some agricultural land--but the regime has significantly reduced the public sphere in terms of exclusivity. Trading monopolies, both international and domestic, have been broken, a transnational venture for flour milling has been arranged, foreign banks have been permitted (and invited) to establish branches (twenty-one as of 1982), and bus transport has been opened to the private sector. It is in the field of regulation that the state has most significantly withdrawn from economic activity, especially in the Export Promotion Zone, where a kind of frontier laissez faire attitude prevails. Not only are long-established legal protections of labor in abeyance, but even data collection and monitoring are accorded very low priority.

Food policy has been central to both domestic politics (narrowly conceived) and conflicts between Sri Lankan regimes and important international actors. A fundamental change in food policy was effected in June 1978 when the general subsidy of food consumption was restricted to households earning less than Rs 3,000 per year. Approximately 7.72 million persons--about half the population--claimed to be eligible. Further targeting accompanied a revision of the program from a ration provision to a food stamp program limited to those with incomes less than Rs 300 (currently $12) per month. About half the population remains on the rolls, despite international pressures to reduce the subsidy and domestic talk of further restrictions of coverage. In any event, the government has undercut the effect of the subsidy by refusing to revise purchasing power by indexing either the income criterion or the stamp values to counter inflation. Between the inception of the program and July 1981, the purchasing power of a typical family's food stamps had been cut in half (Sri Lanka 1981: table 3). Subsequent inflation has cut the benefits in real terms even further. An evaluation by the Food and Nutrition Policy Planning Division of the Ministry of Plan Implementation found that the effect of policy changes has been a deterioration of the nutritional status of preschool children and an increase in the number of cases of serious malnutrition (ibid.:30). That study concluded that the food stamp system, although cheaper, put more families at risk nutritionally than the older ration system.

The pressure on the government to reduce welfare expenditures has been partially successful: food subsidies, which were roughly 14 percent of government spending in 1979, and 6 percent of GDP, declined to 7 percent of expenditures and 2 percent of GDP by 1981. But the government has found it more difficult than anticipated to cut public consumption in favor of investment. Despite significant reduction in entitlement coverage under the food subsidy program in 1979, the gross food subsidy bill continued to increase because of higher import prices for wheat, flour, and rice (CBC, RE 1979, appendix, table 93). The politics of food has been turbulent in Sri Lanka: attempts to cut subsidies have been met with predictably powerful opposition, frequently forcing backtracking in policy (Ponnambalam 1981:25, 32,

48, 62, 78-79). The importance of these facts is that the social and political effects of austerity programs typically advocated by the IMF have been deflected by the extraordinary international support for making Sri Lanka a showcase of export-led growth, liberal economic policy, and openness to foreign capital. It is, however, an open question how well the services related to the physical quality of life will survive in the face of persistent and powerful external demands for greater fiscal discipline.

Income inequality has inevitably entered discussions of the liberalization program. The widely discussed reduction of income inequality between 1963 and 1973 is a matter of considerable empirical dispute (Jayawardena 1974; E. L. H. Lee 1976; 1977; Dahanayake 1979; Lakshman 1980). The dispute largely turns on the validity of the consumer finance surveys (CFS) conducted by the Central Bank in 1963, 1973, and 1978-1979 and 1981-1982. If these surveys accurately reflect real-income inequality (which is problematic because of reporting biases at the upper end and arguable evaluations of income in kind), provisional data from the 1981-1982 CFS indicate increased inequality between 1973 and 1981-1982; indeed, the Gini coefficient, which had fallen to 0.41 in 1973, and was precisely the same in 1978 as in 1963 (0.49), increased to 0.52, the highest level since the surveys began in 1953. Given the increases in property income after 1977, and tax concessions to capital, income inequality after taxes and before subsidies has almost certainly increased (compare Lakshman 1980; Samarasinghe 1980). Moreover, the real value of the most important consumer subsidies has been significantly eroded. Likewise, the management of public-sector enterprises has historically had a purposive redistributive impact (Lakshman 1980:22), which is now contrary to official policy.

Whatever the reality of apparent changes in income equality, inequalities in <u>consumption</u> were kept very low by the pre-1977 policies of subsidization and rationing of essential consumer items and severe restrictions on luxury imports and high tax rates on the wealthy. The relaxation of controls has produced a flood of luxury consumer items since 1977--electric food processors, Danish hams, Scotch whiskey, smoked herring, stereo components, television sets, automobiles, and so forth--in a society in which per capita income is still near $300 per annum. Though the share of consumer goods in total imports has remained fairly constant, luxury items make a striking impression on the visitor accustomed to the old Sri Lanka. To take but one item, imported passenger vehicles, which cost only Rs 18 million in 1975, rose to Rs 563 million in 1979 (CBC, RE 1979: table 7. 13). Although availability of all imported items has improved since liberalization, the effect has been most noticeable in terms of goods that can be purchased only by the very wealthy.

Though the government has taken a decidedly laissez faire position with regard to certain economic dynamics, the role of the state is still large. Sri Lanka has traditionally been one of the most heavily taxed poor nations. Government revenue was 26.5 percent of GDP in 1978, compared to 11 percent in India and 12 percent in Pakistan; government <u>expenditure</u> was 40.9 percent of GDP (CBC, ESS 1979: table 2.1) By 1982 government revenues were down to 19.5

percent of GDP, but spending remained near the 40 percent level (38.7) (Sri Lanka 1983: table 74). The gap between the two figures indicates the lack of financial discipline that concerns the IMF.

While the current regime was cutting some areas of public consumption, it expanded others. In 1979 a National Housing Development Authority was established to construct 100,000 living units before 1983. The program was later expanded to a target of 1,000,000 units, through both direct construction and "aided self-help" programs. An "Electoral Housing Program" undertook direct construction of 155 houses per electorate. Not surprisingly, international opinion of the IMF variety was hostile to both the diversion of investment funds from capital formation and the interest subsidies to "aided" home builders. Nevertheless, the plan was attractive to USAID, which contributed heavily, and is tailor-made for servicing government patronage interests. Not only can significant boons be selectively allocated, but ruling politicians gain attractive opportunities for skimming operations. Likewise, the massive Mahaveli (river valley) development programs provided ample opportunities for patronage, from lucrative contracts to free irrigated land for farmers.

The public investment program has been ambitious, but is not meant to increase the public sector's share of final goods production. Rather, as the finance minister stated in July 1984, "public investment is to be viewed basically as a means of providing the infrastructure facilities necessary to support private entrepreneurship" (CDN, 7/28/84). Accordingly, the capital transfers to public corporations have been heavily dominated by the Mahaveli Development Authority (irrigation, electric power), which has consumed between 50 and 70 percent of the total annual transfers; by the National Housing Development Authority; and (more recently) by the National Water Supply and Drainage Board and Air Ports Development Authority (CBC, AR 1983: appendix, table 35). Public capital expenditures as a percentage of total public expenditure increased from 21 percent in 1971-1972 to 38 percent in 1978 and to 43 percent in 1982 (CBC, RE 1982:250), though budget deficits continue to put pressure on capital spending, and it is widely acknowledged in Sri Lanka that the rapid expansion of capital spending has produced considerable waste and corruption.

Despite cuts in some programs, the net thrust of the new policies was to increase the share of investment in GDP. Gross domestic investment increased from an annual average share of GDP of 16 percent for the 1970-1977 period, to an annual average of 27.7 percent for the 1978-1983 period (see table 4). Coupled with cuts in taxes to offer incentives to private and foreign capital, the ambitious public investment program inevitably inflated budget deficits (table 5 presents a summary). Budget deficits reached 26.1 percent of GDP in 1980, 22.1 percent in 1982, contributing to mounting public debt, though the significant grant element in foreign assistance enabled the regime to escape a debilitating debt service burden. Still, by 1984 interest on the public debt--domestic and foreign--was the largest single expense in the budget, exceeding capital transfers, salaries, and subsidies and grants (ER 9:8, 1983: 116). Foreign financing has typically covered around 50 percent of the annual deficits since 1977. To understand how crucial international support for continuation of the current policies is, we may note that although the share of public investment more than doubled as a percentage of GDP in the 1978-1983 period, compared to 1970-1977 averages, international assistance (grants, loans) almost quadrupled as a percentage of GDP (table 4).

The "financial discipline" that the IMF repeatedly urges thus presents difficult dilemmas to the regime. Withdrawal of subsidies and high rates of inflation are more politically tolerable in a boom economy than in a period of declining growth rates. Economic expansion is heavily dependent on the incentives granted capital, as well as on the continued enthusiasm of external sources of hard currency. The import component of industrial raw materials hovers around 80 percent; unless the terms of trade show dramatic improvement, continued production expansion and provision of essential consumption items are likely to remain dependent on the "confidence of the international community" of which the finance minister speaks. That confidence in turn depends heavily on assessments of the IMF and thus on the degree of tolerance of that organization for fiscal indiscipline and economic heterodoxy. In crudest terms, financial discipline is likely to involve some mix of reducing business incentives (jeopardizing further investment), reducing public developmental expenditures (jeopardizing employment and growth), and reducing the social wage, directly or indirectly (threatening both social peace and improvement of the "physical quality of life" for the bulk of the population). The resultant policy mix will reflect the regime's perception of the respective tolerance levels of foreign and domestic capital, domestic consumers, and the international development establishment.

International Factors in "Opening" and "Closing" the Economy

In a political economy as dependent as that of Ceylon/Sri Lanka, analysis of domestic policy shifts of necessity incorporates extensive attention to external forces. Domestic elites (selectively) benefited greatly from the "closed" economy: the regulatory interstices and public economic activities allowed windfall profits, bribes, influence peddling, political patronage, and partisan advantage for various sections of the dominant classes. The "open economy" continues many of these political advantages while subjecting entrepreneurs to greater risk with wider opportunities. It is easy to understand in political terms why the public sector has remained large. Moreover, for elites, liberalization and cuts in the social wage are a small price to pay for concessional hard currency flows, which averaged roughly 13 percent of GDP from 1978 to 1983 (almost four times the average for 1970-1977). Domestic elites' interests may be served by a variety of policy packages; the focus of this piece has been on external forces and actors that shaped the policy environment--the complex of opportunities, pressures, and constraints that has shaped domestic policy choices. Restricted choice is of course a core element of dependency.

The roots of social welfare policies, and the potential to finance them, are found in the late colonial experience--the development of a wealthy plantation export sector, early popular representative political forms, and the development of infrastructure to service the plantation economy. The structuration of the national political economy during the colonial period simultaneously opened important opportunities for social welfare development and left that potential vulnerable to external forces in the global economy. The development of a tightly regulated, "closed" economy was a response to that vulnerability, given the domestic political necessity of protecting the mass public from immiseration through exogenous shocks. The strategies of the first three decades of independence did not alter the structural vulnerability of the economy and resulted in a genuine economic cul-de-sac of high unemployment, internal and external deficits, scarcities, slow growth, and austerity budgets when international economic forces produced unrelenting pressures over time. It was the realignment of domestic political forces, strongly influenced by the inability of ruling elites to cope with international economic forces, which allowed international actors to play a decisive role in supporting a fundamental shift in development strategy after 1977.

It is ironic that the current regime speaks of a shift from a "closed" to an "open" economy. Even in its tightly regulated, closed form, the Sri Lankan economy was in a critical sense open; the ineffectual "closing" of the economy was in part a response to its vulnerability to external forces. Whatever the validity of Cameron's (1978) argument concerning the contribution of openness of economy to expansion of the public sector in advanced industrial societies, the connections and mechanisms in the case of Sri Lanka are clear. Given a closely competitive political system, openness created the foreign exchange reserves and budgetary flexibility for the welfare state when export prices were buoyant; when the terms of trade deteriorated, openness was manifest as vulnerability, and domestic political pressures led to expansion of the welfare state and regulatory apparatus to protect the domestic population from externally induced immiseration. The IMF's argument that the resources spent on public consumption could have been better spent on investment ma¼ be true but was politically irrelevant. The comparative developmental records of regional neighbors that took the other path do not, however, support the argument that national policies were disastrous.

Effects of liberalization on the mass public have been ambivalent, but heavily mediated by external forces. Unemployment has been cut in half, fed by aid-driven expansion, but international donors are demanding higher taxes and spending cuts. Inequality has increased and the social wage deeply cut. Attracting foreign capital to create more employment depends on advertisements of a docile, inexpensive labor force, stripped of traditional legislative protections in the Export Promotion Zone; moreover, the government has demonstrated a very tough attitude toward labor. Reductions of inequalities of income and wealth are contrary to the incentives for accumulation on which the strategy depends; the government resurrects as justification Kuznets' hypothesis, that inequalities inevitably grow in the early stages of growth, then subside. The continuation of food subsidies for half the population and the introduction of a minimal unemployment dole resemble in form policies of a welfare state, but are arguably functional requisites for maintaining low wage rates and social peace, both of which are selling points in the competition to attract foreign capital.

The dismantling after 1977 of the state's direct intervention in and regulation of production and exchange, although supported domestically by dominant classes and by mass discontent with previous policies, was a necessary condition for the extraordinary international support the new regime has received, and such support is a necessary condition for sustaining the policy changes. The policy changes themselves create the conditions for future dependence on those same international actors and thus restrict the range of domestic policy options. The social welfare role of the state is in theory de-emphasized, with international approval (and pressure), though there remain tactical domestic political difficulties in a complete retreat; moreover, persistent international vulnerability (food and fuel prices, for example) introduces constraints on reducing the fiscal burden of welfare policies despite reductions in their coverage. To date, the maintenance of a regime committed to dismantling the _internal_ welfare state has required that Sri Lanka itself remain an international welfare case. As a result, whether or not the economic policy changes produce rapid growth without immiseration of the weakest sectors, or rapid growth at all, is heavily dependent on decisions made outside Sri Lanka, as well as on structural forces that, to date, have been largely kept off the global policy agenda.

Notes

1. For a discussion of alternative measures, see Hicks and Streeten (1979). The inclusion and weighting of literacy is particularly problematic in the PQLI because of the different real advantages implied by different kinds of literacy in different economic and cultural contexts; with regard to Sri Lanka on this point, see Ann Mattis (1978). On the inadequacy of traditional measures, and a defense of the PQLI, see Morris (1979). On the persistence of severe poverty in Sri Lanka despite the impressive aggregate indicators, see Marga Institute (1981); Isenman (1980); E. L. H. Lee (1976); and Pieris (1982).

2. E. L. H. Lee (1976) documents deterioration of real wages in the estate sector as well as in urban areas. Gunatilleke (1978:48-51) discusses the sources that led him to report widespread malnutrition in Sri Lanka in the mid-1970s. Nutrition data presented by Gavan and Chandrasekera (1979:table 7) indicate serious malnutrition effects, especially in the estate sector. The available nutrition data of a systematic sort relate to a period after the most severe stage of the food crisis. Paul Isemen (1980:244) presents data and analysis to link an increase in mortality, particularly on the estates, to the food crisis in 1974 (Marga Institute 1981). On Sri Lanka's international food situation, see ARTI (1976).

Table 1

Physical Quality of Life Index Scores and Growth Rates for Subcontinental Nations

	GNP/ Capita, 1978 (US$)	Literacy Rate (%)	Infant Mortality Rate (per 1000 live births)	Life Expectancy at One Year	PQLI	Average Annual Growth Rate (GNP/Capita 1960-1977)
Nepal	120	5	200	46.4	13	0.2
Afghanistan	240	8	182	47.9	18	0.2
Bangladesh	90	22	132	53.1	35	-0.4
Pakistan	230	16	121	57.0	38	3.0
India	180	34	122	55.9	43	1.3
Sri Lanka	190	81	45	70.2	82	2.0

Source: Morris and McAlpin (1980:3); GNP figures from World Bank (1980a:110); growth rates from World Bank (1979: appendix, table 1).

Table 2

Deterioration of International Exchange Position
(Index 1970=100)

	1960	1965	1970	1971	1972	1978	1974	1975
Exports (volume)	85	103	100	97	95	96	83	100
Exports (value)	103	96	100	99	100	116	181	169
Imports (volume)	130	84	100	88	86	77	55	68
Imports (value)	59	71	100	107	113	149	264	309
Terms of trade*	175	135	100	93	88	78	69	55
Purchasing power of exports	149	138	100	90	84	75	57	55
External long-term debt outstanding (Billion Rs)	.29	.49	1.58	1.80	2.39	2.80	2.88	3.71

Source: United Nations Statistical Yearbook (1978, tables on pp. 492-501; CBC, AR (1983, table 36).

$$* \text{ Terms of trade} = \frac{\text{Export Price Index}}{\text{Import Price Index}} \times 100$$

Table 3

Balance of Trade and Terms of Trade during the New Economic Policy

Year	Exports (Value Rs mln)	Imports (Value Rs mln)	Balance of Trade (Rs mln)	Export Prices (Index 1978=100)	Import Prices (Index 1978=100)	Terms of Trade (1978=100
1960	1,832	1,960	- 128	17	9	185
1975	3,968	5,196	- 1,228	29	49	58
1976	4,840	4,901	- 61	34	44	78
1977	6,569	6,061	+ 508	55	54	102
1978	13,193	15,099	- 1,906	100	100	100
1979	15,282	22,602	- 7,320	109	152	72
1980	17,595	33,942	-16,347	126	217	58
1981	21,043	36,582	-15,539	129	282	46
1982	21,454	41,946	-20,492	119	309	38
1983	25,096	45,553	-20,457	165	375	44

Source: Central Bank of Ceylon (1979b: table 7.1); CBC (1982:73-82); CBC (1983, appendix table 18; table 1.41); CBC, AR, 1983, appendix tables 67, 64.

Table 4

International Support for the
Liberalization Regime: Savings and Investment

(% of GDP, Current Market Prices)

Year	Gross Domestic Investment	Public Investment	Foreign Savings
1970	18.9	8.2	4.8
1977	14.4	7.2	-3.6
Annual Average, 1970-1977	16.0	7.7	3.3
1978	20.0	11.9	4.5
1983	29.0	15.5	12.5
Annual Average, 1978-1983	27.7	16.7	12.7

Source: Sri Lanka, Ministry of Finance and Planning, Public Investment 1984-1988.

Table 5

Budget Deficits, Foreign Finance, and Public Debt
under the Liberalization Regime
(Rs million)

Year	Budget Deficit	Foreign Finance Contribution to Covering Deficit	Public Debt Outstanding
1976	3,576	1,326	15,621
1977	3,074	1,779	22,434
1978	7,165	4,454	27,746
1979	8,791	4,237	31,512
1980	16,274	6,735	46,779
1981	14,866	8,208	58,659
1982	20,091	8,794	71,250
1983	23,385	14,024 *	98,380 **
1984	16,543 *	12,312 *	NA
1985	NA	13,500 **	NA

Source: CBC, AR (1983: table 28).
* Estimate
** Provisional

References

Abbreviations

<u>AWSJW</u>	<u>Asian Wall Street Journal Weekly</u> (New York)
ARTI	Agrarian Research and Training Institute (Colombo)
CBC	Central Bank of Ceylon (Colombo)
AR	Annual Report
RE	Review of the Economy
ESS	Economic and Social Statistics of Sri Lanka
<u>DN</u>	<u>Ceylon Daily News</u>
<u>ER</u>	<u>Economic Review</u> (People's Bank, Colombo)
<u>FEER</u>	<u>Far Eastern Economic Review</u>
ILO	International Labour Office (Geneva)
IMF	International Monetary Fund (Washington, D. C.)

ARTI. 1976. <u>Sri Lanka and the International Food Crisis</u>. Colombo.

Balakrishnan, N. 1977. "Industrial Policy and Development since Independence." In <u>Sri Lanka: A Survey</u>, edited by K. M. de Silva. Honolulu: University of Hawaii Press.

Bornshier, Volker. 1980. "Multinational Corporations and Economic Growth." <u>Journal of Development Economics</u> 7:2 (June).

Bornshier, Volker; C. Chase-Dunn; and R. Rubinson. 1978. "Cross-National Evidence of the Effects of Foreign Investment and Aid on Economic Growth and Inequality: A Survey of Findings and Reanalysis." <u>American Journal of Sociology</u> 84.

Cameron, David. 1978. "The Expansion of the Public Economy: A Comparative Analysis." <u>American Political Science Review</u> 72: 1243-1261.

Ceylon, Central Bank. 1984. <u>Economic Performance in the First Half of 1983</u>. Colombo.

Corea, Gamini. 1975. <u>The Instability of an Export Economy</u>. Colombo: Marga Institute.

Dahanayake, P. A. S. 1979. "Growth and Welfare: Some Reflections on the Effects of Recent Development Policy Reforms in Sri Lanka." CBC <u>Staff Studies</u> 9, nos. 1,2 (April/September).

Gavan, James D., and Indrani Sri Chandrasekera. 1979. "The Impact of Public Foodgrain Distribution on Food Consumption and Welfare in Sri Lanka." International Food Policy Research Institute Research Report 13. Washington, D.C.

Gunasekera, H. M. 1977. "Foreign Trade of Sri Lanka." In <u>Sri Lanka: A Survey</u>, edited by K. M. de Silva. Honolulu: University of Hawaii Press.

Gunatilleke, Godfrey. 1978. "Participatory Democracy and Dependence: The Case of Sri Lanka." Marga Quarterly Journal 5, no. 3.

Halliday, Fred. 1975. "The Ceylon Insurrection." In Explosion in a Subcontinent, edited by Robin Blackburn, pp. 151-220. Middlesex: Penguin.

Herring, Ronald J. 1981. "The Janus-faced State in a Dependent Society: Determinants of Shifts in Sri Lanka's Development Strategy." Paper presented at APSA meeting, New York.

-------. 1983. Land to the Tiller: The Political Economy of Agrarian Reform in South Asia. New Haven, Conn.: Yale University Press. (In Asia, Delhi: Oxford University Press, 1983.)

Hicks, Norman, and Paul Streeten. 1979. "Indicators of Development: The Search for a Basic Needs Yardstick." World Development 7, no. 6 (June).

International Labour Office. 1971. Matching Employment Opportunities and Expectations: A Programme of Action for Ceylon. Vol. 1, Report; Vol. 2, Technical Papers. Geneva.

International Monetary Fund. 1980. Government Finance Statistics Yearbook IV. Washington, D.C.

Isenmen, Paul. 1980. "Basic Needs: The Case of Sri Lanka." World Development 8, no. 3 (March).

Jayatissa, R. A. 1982. "Balance of Payments Adjustments to Exogenous Shocks during 1970-1981." CBC Staff Studies 12, no. 1 (April).

Jayawardena, Lal. 1974. "Sri Lanka." In Redistribution with Growth, by Hollis Chenery et al. London: Oxford University Press.

Kappagoda, Nihal, and Suzanne Paine. 1981. The Balance of Payments Adjustment Process: The Experience of Sri Lanka. Colombo: Marga Institute.

Karunatilake, H. N. S. 1975. "The Impact of Welfare Services in Sri Lanka on the Economy." CBC Staff Studies 5, no. 1 (April): 201-232.

-------. 1976. "The Public Sector in the National Economy." CBC Staff Studies 6, no. 2 (September): 179-198.

Lakshman, W. D. 1980. "Income and Wealth Distribution in Sri Lanka: An Examination of Evidence Pertaining to the Post-1960 Experience." IDCJ Working Paper No. 16. Tokyo: International Development Center of Japan.

Lee, E. L. H. 1976. "Rural Poverty in Sri Lanka, 1963-1973." World Employment Programme Working Paper. Geneva: ILO.

Lee, Edy. 1977. "Development and Income Distribution: A Case Study of Sri Lanka and Malaysia." World Development 5, no. 4 (1977).

Marga Institute. 1981. "An Analytical Description of Poverty in Sri Lanka." Colombo.

Mattis, Ann R. 1978. "An Experience in Need-Oriented Development." Marga Quarterly Journal 5, no. 3: 1-30.

McLaughlin, Martin M., and Overseas Development Council. 1979. The United States and World Development: Agenda 1979. New York: Praeger.

Morris, Morris David. 1979. Measuring the Condition of the World's Poor: The Physical Quality of Life Index. New York: Pergamon.

-------, and Michelle B. McAlpin. 1980. "Measuring Welfare in South Asia." Paper distributed for the SSRC/ICSSR Conference on South Asian Political Economy, New Delhi, 12-16 December.

Obeysekara, Jayasumana. 1973. "Revolutionary Movements in Ceylon." In Imperialism and Revolution in South Asia, edited by Kathleen Gough and Hari P. Sharma, pp. 368-395. New York: Monthly Review Press.

Oliver, Henry M., Jr. 1957. Economic Opinion and Policy in Ceylon. London: Cambridge University Press.

Pieris, G. H. 1982. Basic Needs and the Provision of Government Services in Sri Lanka. Geneva: ILO.

Ponnambalam, Satchi. 1981. Dependent Capitalism in Crisis: The Sri Lankan Economy. London: Zed.

Richards, Peter, and Wilbert Gooneratne. 1980. Basic Needs, Poverty and Government Policies in Sri Lanka. Geneva: ILO

Samarasinghe, S. W. R. de A. 1980. "Current Economic Policy: A Comment." Conference on Post-War Economic Development of Sri Lanka. Peradeniya, 16-20 December.

-------. 1983. "Sri Lanka in 1982." Asian Survey 23, no. 2 (February): 158-164.

Sri Lanka. 1979. "The New Tax Policy." Speech by the minister of finance and planning to Parliament, 4 April 1979.

-------. Minister of Finance and Planning. 1980a. "Budget Speech, 1981." Colombo.

-------. 1980b. Public Investment Programme, 1980-1984. Colombo: Ministry of Finance and Planning.

-------. 1980c. Performance. Colombo: Ministry of Plan Implementation.

-------. 1981. "Evaluation Report of the Food Stamp Scheme." Colombo: Ministry of Plan Implementation.

-------. 1982. Sri Lanka Yearbook. Colombo: Department of Census and Statistics.

-------. 1983. Statistical Pocket Book of the Democratic Socialist Republic of Sri Lanka. Colombo.

-------. 1984. Public Investment, 1984-1988. Colombo: Ministry of Finance and Planning.

United Nations. United Nations Statistical Yearbook. Annual. New York.

Wanasinghe, Sydney. 1980. "The Hartal of August 1953." Young Socialist 2 (June).

Wiswa Warnapala, W. A. 1979. "Sri Lanka 1978: Reversal of Policies and Strategies." Asian Survey 19, no. 2 (February).

Wickramasinghe, Wimal. "The Faking of Foreign Trade Declarations." CBC Staff Studies 4, no. 1 (April): 45-56.

Wickremeratne, L. A. 1973. "The Emergence of Welfare Policy, 1931-1948." In History of Ceylon, edited by K. M. de Silva, pp. 476-488. Colombo: University of Ceylon.

-------. 1977. "Planning and Economic Development." In Sri Lanka: A Survey, edited by K. M. de Silva. Honolulu: University of Hawaii Press.

Wijesinghe, Mallory E. 1976. The Economy of Sri Lanka, 1948-1975. Colombo: Ranco.

Wijeweera, Rohan (Rohana). 1975. "Speech to the Ceylon Criminal Justice Commission." In Explosion in a Subcontinent, edited by Robin Blackburn, pp. 221-251. Middlesex: Penquin.

World Bank. 1953. The Economic Development of Ceylon. Baltimore: Johns Hopkins University Press.

-------. 1975. The Assault of World Poverty. Baltimore: Johns Hopkins University Press.

-------. 1979. World Development Report, 1979. Washington, D. C.

-------. 1980a. World Development Report, 1980. Washington, D. C.

-------. 1980b. Annual Report. Washington, D. C.

-------. 1980c. World Debt Tables. Washington, D. C.

Wriggins, W. Howard. 1960. Ceylon: Dilemmas of a New Nation. Princeton: Princeton University Press.

Chapter 11

Privatization in the African Context

V. V. Ramanadham

The first section of this chapter deals with the concept of privatization in its comprehensive meaning; the second brings out the salient features of whatever privatization has been practiced in some African countries. There is a critique of the rationale of privatization in the third section, and the last one analyzes the problems and implications of the policies of privatization.

The Concept of Privatization

Privatization is a new trend in several countries and seems to be understood in different ways by different people. Let us, at the outset, delineate the concept in analytical terms.

Privatization at the enterprise level, the clearer aspect of the privatization concept, can proceed in terms of ownership changes or operational changes (see fig. 1). The former envisage, on the whole, a reduced public shareholding proportion in one way or another. That proportion becomes zero when an enterprise is denationalized (that is, transferred to the private sector), as is currently contemplated in Kenya in specific cases. In the other cases detailed on figure 1 it is useful to distinguish between domestic capital and foreign capital let into a public enterprise (the latter might be more zealously welcomed, as in Ethiopia under the 1983 proclamation on joint ventures).

The concept of operational changes is uniquely significant in the context of developing countries. Ownership changes, especially of the extreme kind (that is, denationalization), are not politically easy, yet substantive elements of privatization can be introduced in the organizational structures and in the operating criteria of the public enterprise, as in the Sudan (see later discussion). Incidentally, this angle of privatization emphasizes that the essence of the publicness of the enterprise borders on operational uniqueness rather than on mere ownership.

The macrodimension of privatization (fig. 1) refers to the fact that the proportion of private investment in the national economy expands as a sequel to government policies on investment and entrepreneurship. The microchanges cited in the preceding paragraphs themselves culminate in changes at the macrolevel, unless for every microchange increasing the private proportion of ownership in some enterprises there are offsetting developments that raise the public share of ownership in other enterprises or bring into being new enterprises under full or majority ownership.

Privatization in the macro sense is also positive when the government's entrepreneurial decisions on investment imply a relatively high share on the part of private capital--as in Egypt, where "the relative importance of the contribution of the public sector in total investment decreased from 90% in the years prior to 1973 to about 76% in 1981/82."[1]

An interesting facet of the privatization concept may be deduced from a situation in which a joint venture that has substantial public investment may nevertheless "be deemed to belong to the private sector of the economy" (for instance, in Egypt).[2] More than semantics is involved here, for, being considered a private-sector enterprise entitles the joint venture to certain exemptions from the characteristics and obligations attached to public enterprises,[3] and it correspondingly enjoys enhanced operational autonomy (it approximates figure 1's microlevel operations).

To appreciate the comprehensive connotation of privatization as presented here, one must understand the diverse strands of policy traceable in the rethinking on the size and role of public enterprises in the African context.

Privatization in Some African Countries

This section presents the salient aspects of privatization measures undertaken in recent years in some African countries--Egypt, the Sudan, Ethiopia, and Kenya. The first three represent economies subjected to almost wholesale nationalizations as a matter of socioeconomic policy, whereas Kenya has always been a mixed economy.

Egypt

The Open Door policy initiated in 1974 encouraged private investment. It is estimated that the contribution of the private sector rose from 10 percent of total investment in 1973 to 24 percent in 1981. It accounted for 48 percent of the GDP in 1981-1982.[4]

It would be interesting to look at the sectorial composition of the stimulated private investments between the plan period that has just ended and the current plan period (table 1).

The Open Door policy involved a variety of administrative and legislative measures. Law no. 43 of 1974, concerning the investment of Arab and foreign funds and the free zones, as amended by Law no. 32 of 1977, states that "projects may not be nationalized or confiscated . . . except by judicial procedures" (Article 7) and offers enterprises several privileges and exemptions. The companies coming under this law are deemed to belong to the private sector; legislation and regulations applicable to the public sector do not apply to them. For example, the conditions and procedures for electing representatives from labor to the boards of directors of public-sector enterprises do not apply to them except that the companies' own statutes shall provide for labor's participation in management by some method (Article 10). Employees and board members are exempted from the provisions of Law no. 113 of 1961, which limits remunerations (Article 11). And, the projects of the enterprises are exempted from a variety of taxes (under Articles 16 and 17). It is interesting to note that under Article 6 enterprises established "entirely with Egyptian capital and owned by Egyptian nationals" also enjoy many of the above-cited privileges. Joint ventures involving foreign capital can be so organized as to allow "majority foreign ownership and management control," with one exception, viz, banks, where the Egyptian share should be at least 51 percent.[5]

There have been other elements of privatization in government policies. As regards the enterprises that stay in the public sector--and these will be a very large number indeed--the government has developed new policies in two important directions: first, managers are provided with a greater degree of autonomy than before;[6] second, the government has determined that there was "no alternative" to a careful cost-benefit analysis of every project, to ensuring efficient implementation of investment at the lowest costs possible, to the choice of efficient technical and management systems, and to the reduction of losses at every stage of the production process. The plan document (1982-1987) is replete with such desiderata as "reconsidering the management of the public sector to raise its productivity," reducing subsidies, and fixing prices "on economic basis," and "fixing a remunerative price that ensures a reasonable rate of profit enough to finance investment."[7]

The Sudan

The Sudanese case reinforces the theme of rethinking traced in Egypt's experience. At several points we have evidence that supports the conceptual variations in the theme outlined in the opening section of this chapter.

Policies progressively favoring or encouraging private investment have raised such investment from 39 percent of the total investment in the 1955 to 1961 period to 58 percent in the 1968 to 1972 period. The 1978-1983 plan mentioned among its objectives "encouraging the private sector, both foreign and local, to play its role fully and effectively in development."[8] Many incentives have been offered to private investment--to "national" capital as well as to foreign capital.[9] For instance, exemptions have been granted from the business-profits tax for up to five years, and from export duties. Land is available at reduced prices, and electricity and transport rates are reduced. Customs duties may be increased on the imports of commodities that compete with, or that substitute for, the products of the projects concerned; or imports may be restricted for a period. Guarantee is given against nationalization, "unless the public good so requires and by virtue of a law." But in any such case fair compensation is contemplated after evaluation of property at the prices current at the time of nationalization. The evaluation as well as any remittances abroad will be promptly made. Further, the Consultative Committee set up under the Encouragement of Investment Act will include four members from the private sector.

Apart from the incentives to private investment, government policies reflect close attention to several substantive elements of privatization. Let us look at the organizational measures first. Public holding companies in the sugar, textile, and cement sectors were abolished. This, it is claimed, has led to enhanced autonomy of the operating plants and the promotion of some degree of healthy competition.

Next financial criteria of public-enterprise operations have been significantly brought under market discipline ("marketized"). For instance, prices have been revised so as to offer "incentives to production."[10] Several subsidies were eliminated. Financial arrangements within the irrigated-agriculture sector have been completely restructured, and the minimum level of revenues that the Egyptian banks should generate was agreed on with the International Monetary Fund in 1982. On the whole, a conscious attempt has been made to strengthen the finances of the public-enterprise sector.

Further, the emphasis currently placed on the use of limited resources to rehabilitate existing production potential, rather than for new projects, illustrates the shift in thinking in favor of maximizing the returns on investment or a trend toward some degree of marketization of the economy.[11]

Ethiopia

The Ethiopian case brings out but one point, viz, that a government almost committed to total nationalization of the industrial economy has begun to appreciate the need for the introduction of foreign capital, which can be private in nature. The modality is that of a joint venture, in which the foreign shareholding shall not ordinarily exceed 49 percent. Participation is between foreign capital and Ethiopian public capital only and is intended to offer Ethiopia the benefits of foreign technology.[12] The foreign investor is offered incentives in the form of certain tax exemptions and protection of "the right of ownership" of shares. In the event of the government's buying all the shares for reasons of national interest, a "fair and equitable price" will be paid. A close study of the legislation concerned indicates, however, that the joint venture can take on the characteristics of a public enterprise whose direction and decision making are vested predominantly in the hands of the majority shareholder, viz, the government.

Kenya

The current thought on the relative role of public enterprises in Kenya provides rich evidence of the multifarious modalities of privatization presented in the opening section.

The economic policies of Kenya originated from the concept of African socialism enunciated in 1965. This envisaged that "the power to control resource use resides with the State." It would be an "error of great magnitude," however, to assume that this control could be achieved only through ownership.[13]

Kenya has been a mixed economy, and the question of which enterprises to nationalize or sponsor in the public sector has always been dealt with in a pragmatic manner. The 1965 sessional paper prepared for Parliament on African socialism upheld as a critical issue, "under what circumstances and to what extent should we nationalize means of production" and supplied the following answer: Nationalization will be needed:

> (i) when the assets in private hands threaten the security or undermine the integrity of the nation; or (ii) when the production resources are being wasted; or (iii) when the operation of an industry by private concerns has a serious detrimental effect on the public interest; and (iv) when other less costly means of control are not available or are not effective.[14]

It is relevant to our theme to excerpt from the paper the following, almost conclusive, observation: "Nationalization . . . will be considered if the need is urgent, if other less costly controls are ineffective, and if it is understood that most industries nationalized will not be operated at a loss."[15]

The number of public enterprises of one kind or another has increased colossally over the years. A recent count of government investments revealed the following:

1. Total number of statutory boards	147
2. Companies:	
(a) wholly owned by the government	47
(b) in which the government has controlling interest	36
(c) in which the government/statutory boards have minority interest	93
Total government involvement	323 [16]

The sectorial spread of public enterprise has been very wide. Working from published data, I can present a cross-classification between sizes of public-sector industries and the public shares in those industry categories.[17] The upper left-hand quadrant of table 2 represents public-sector activities that are small in aggregate size and that account for small proportions of employment in those industries in the country; the lower right-hand quadrant refers to industries of large absolute size in the public sector, which constitute a major part of the concerned activities in the country. There is a wide spread between these extremes. On the whole, most of the industries that attracted relatively small government involvement are of relatively small size within the public sector, whereas the large public-sector industries account for high degrees of the concerned activities in Kenya. To put this another way, large public enterprises enjoy significant degrees of monopoly power, and several small public-enterprise activities exist that are exposed to competition from the private sector.

Kenya's public enterprises have a complex ownership structure. Some are wholly owned by the government; some are wholly owned by the government and other public enterprises; some are wholly owned by public enterprises and, in some cases, jointly with private investors; some in all these categories are majority owned and some others are minority owned by the government or public enterprises. Interesting investment relationships exist under which a major public enterprise and one of its subsidiaries hold shares in another enterprise (which thus becomes a subsidiary of both of them); in some cases the public ownership, even if minority, is diffused throughout several enterprises. It is not my purpose to explain these facts--some are just historical in significance--but it may be relevant to note them, as the next section bears out.

One other point worth noting is that public enterprises are found in almost all sectorial categories--heavy, basic, infrastructural, light, manufacturing, finance, and services. Today the government has ownership interest in textiles, shoes, sugar, tires, alcohol, pharmaceuticals, canning, mining, salt, drilling, paper, hotels, cement, batteries, vehicles, radios, fishing, engineering, beverages, and food processing.[18] And public investments constitute a "very sizeable proportion of the total capital formation in the country."[19] Working from the data found in the <u>Statistical Abstract</u>, we can deduce a clear trend toward increase in the relative contribution of the public-enterprise sector to capital formation, sector by sector and on the whole (see table 3).[20]

Let us pursue the trends of rethinking on the role and extent of public enterprise in Kenya. The Ndegwa Committee (1979), in the course of an intensive review of the public-enterprise situation, observed that the growth in this sector "has not been accompanied by development of efficient management systems to ensure that the sector plays its role in an efficient manner." It was struck by "clear evidence," in many cases, of "prolonged inefficiency, financial mismanagement, waste and malpractices." It feared "the danger of over-politicising production and production through the establishment of too many parastatals." It felt that "certain existing organizations ought to be abolished." It was evident to the committee that many public enterprises "have deviated from their primary functions," and it concluded that the shortcomings it discovered constituted "a serious threat to the economy."

It is interesting to refer to the committee's emphatic observation in 1979 that "the economic and social costs of delay in taking action" to remedy the serious problems of the public-enterprise sector "are simply unacceptable." The trend of introspection continued and was concretized into positive thought in favor of "divestiture" when the Working Party on Government Expenditures reviewed the situation in 1982. The Working Party opined that most of the public investments "are not strategic in any sense of the word" and that "government participation in commercial enterprise has been carried well beyond original conceptions." It recommended as a "matter of high priority for the government" that it "revise this trend by working out a viable programme for divesting itself of some of its investments to Kenyan investors."

The privatization plan envisaged by the Working Party is multipronged and calls for distinguishing public enterprises among four categories:

> (i) those whose retention as government agencies or enterprises is essential to accelerated and equitable national development and the regulation os the private sector; (ii) those whose objectives have been achieved and which should be discontinued; (iii) those whose functions could be absorbed by parent-ministires; and (iv) those whose functions would be more efficiently performed by the private sector.

That the government's own thinking was along similar lines may be inferred from the "Sessional Paper on Development Prospects and Policies" (1982), which spoke of "the return" of some public enterprises "to private sector operation."[21]

The recommendations of the Working Party met with government approval. The president of Kenya was convinced that "a number of these public enterprises could be made more productive and more profitable in the hands of private Kenyans as owners and managers."[22] In June 1983, he appointed the Task Force on Divestiture of Government Investment, as recommended by the Working Party, with the following terms of reference:

(1) To carry out a careful review of the parastatal sector and come up with two distinct groups of parastatals, namely, those that are public-oriented and that provide public goods and services, and those that are private-sector oriented.

(2) To study the legal, financial, and organizational characteristics of parastatals and determine

    (a) those in which government involvement, direct or indirect, should be reduced or terminated.

    (b) those whose functions can be absorbed by the parent ministries or other parastatals.

    (c) those that require legal, functional, financial, and organizational readjustment or restructuring.

    (d) methods and strategies of implementing recommendations on items 2(a)-(c).

(3) To study the existing capital market and recommend effective strategies and appropriate mechanisms through which the government should dispose of its investments.

The task force has been at work, but the work undoubtedly is quite complex.

Why Privatization?

Let us take a critical look at the factors that may have prompted thought in favor of some kind and degree of privatization in the African countries, particularly those covered in the preceding section. (I keep aside any sudden emergence of rightist ideology, which is, in fact, not relevant in the cases covered.) Figure 2 summarizes the argument in this section.

Macrofactors

(1) The first of these refers essentially to the government's decision to attract foreign capital so as to avail itself of the technology and investment opportunities that such capital provides. In the process, the overall proportion of private holding in the economy might increase, assuming that the foreign capital is private. This type is the major type of privatization in Ethiopia.

(2) An interesting connection between macroinvestment needs and privatization can be derived from the Egyptian experience. For a time the private sector, whose savings "went up enormously," did not find "open doors to absorb its savings capacity" and therefore moved toward increased consumption or speculation or investment abroad. This, the government realized, was a lost opportunity. There could be ways of catching private savings for public investment, but it was felt that they might have a "high cost if required for government investment."[23]

A similar trend of thought is perceptible at the federal government level in Kenya--an openly mixed economy. Fixed capital formation in the private sector fell seriously from 1979 to 1982. Government borrowings from the banking system led to a curtailment of lending to the rest of the economy. The president observed that "the private sector requires more funds and these can only be obtained if Government borrows and spends less."[24]

(3) Closely related to the preceding consideration is the compulsion many governments experience to curtail public expenditures as a matter of overall economic and budgeting policy. Agreements with the IMF have often included limitations on government expenditures--as in the Sudan,[25] and expenditure ceilings have been set for each ministry in Kenya, which correspondingly restrict the room for government investments in public enterprises. The area open for private investment, including foreign capital not borrowed or necessarily guaranteed by the government, expands in such a situation.

Comparative Advantage

This ought to be the main plank on which the case for privatization (or nationalization in appropriate cases) should rest. When an enterprise loses its comparative advantage in a given sector of activity by being a public enterprise, a case for its privatization (in whatever sense) is implied.[26]

(1) Under this heading fall enterprises "whose objectives have been achieved and which should be discontinued," in the words of Kenya's Working Party on Government Expenditures.[27] Units taken over when sick are eligible for privatization once the sickness is cured. Such easy examples apart, two difficult problems need to be added in the context of the "original purpose": How easy is it to determine whether that purpose is achieved; and more basic, Is the original purpose valid today? Solutions are, no doubt, easier in a mixed economy than in a predominantly public enterprise-oriented economy.

(2) Gradual diminutions in market imperfections weaken the comparative advantages of public enterprises. It is from this angle that policy statements such as the Ivory Coast's that there will be gradual relaxations in government intervention and investment should be appreciated.[28] Besides, changes in economic strategy can have a bearing on the scope of privatization. This may be evidenced from the current conditions in the Sudan. The emphasis of the Three-Year Public Investment Program is on fuller utilization and rehabilitation of the existing plant.

<u>Poor Performance</u>

The most powerful factor underlying thoughts favoring some privatization seems to lie in the poor results recorded by public enterprises across the board. These have to be considered strictly under two headings--financial and social--and a balanced view has to be taken of performance.

Let us look at the social returns first. These, in a sense, provide the major justification for a public enterprise. For one to conclude that such an enterprise has no case on these grounds one has to (1) be certain of what the social returns under review are and (2) to be able to demonstrate that the social returns realized are outweighed by the lowness of the financial results. Not only are these determinations difficult at the technical level, but they are bound to be unlikely on political grounds. We do not have much evidence under this heading, except for a finding by the Working Party in Kenya in 1982 that government joint ventures have, in some cases, led to "some de-Kenyanisation of the economy."[29]

For a stimulus for privatization on the grounds of results, we have, therefore, to concentrate on the financial returns. Here the evidence is ubiquitous. The returns are so poor that, despite valid notions of social benefit, governments have become seriously concerned. The Working Party in Kenya produced some figures to indicate that the government was receiving very low returns on an investment of about 900 million Kenyan pounds (about 450 million dollars). Data on the Sudan's public enterprises merited the official pronouncement that "their net contribution to domestic capital formation has been minimal."[30] Enterprises in many sectors--industrial and agricultural--incurred serious losses in 1978 and 1979.[31] And their indebtedness to the Bank of Sudan increased considerably between 1979 and 1981.[32] The planning document of Egypt (for 1982 to 1987) emphasizes that "there is no alternative . . . to reducing losses in every stage of production" and commends the fixing of a "remunerative price that ensures a reasonable rate of profit enough to finance investment."[33]

Although poor financial results have begun to get governments thinking about the role and performance of public enterprises, it is difficult to expect privatization in the sense of denationalization as a quick solution. Three reasons exist: first, it is difficult on political and ideological grounds; second, the deficits of some public enterprises are planned deficits--for social reasons--hence deficits are not a conclusive ground for denationalization; third, many of the enterprises can improve in net financial position if, irrespective of ownership, operating criteria are rationalized. It is in the last sense that privatization has significance--even in public enterprise-oriented (or socialist) economies. I have already noted certain structural operating and managerial changes initiated in Egypt and the Sudan.

The precise processes of privatization in this sense call for an accurate classification of the causes of deficits, for the direction of privatization varies with the cause. Inefficient management must prompt measures of marketization of managerial hiring and incentives and of arrangements of private participation through joint ventures. External interventions are of two kinds: we have to live with the socially desirable ones; the other kind ought to be curbed. Progress in privatization of ownership can help in this. But whether politicians are keen on such a result is doubtful. A major direction of privatization, which can exorcise the problem, consists of the evolution of operating criteria that bring the enterprise management close to market discipline, once the socially desired interventions are provided for. This seems to be the trend of enterprise reforms in countries like Egypt, where "the public sector continued as a pioneer in development during the last two decades [and] will continue in the future," and in the Sudan, where significant structural changes affecting holding-company structures and monopoly power, despite public ownership, are being implemented. In a clearly mixed economy such as the Kenyan, on the other hand, both structural adjustments within public ownership and denationalization are possible, as is implicit in the government pronouncement that "structural adjustment must embrace a more constructive and profitable role for essential parastatals and the return of others to private sector operation."[35]

The second term of reference set for the Task Force on Divestiture in Kenya suggests the scope of options under the principle of privatization. The most valid ground on which to think of privatization is the loss of comparative advantage on the part of a public enterprise, not just financial deficits, though the latter have, in many cases, triggered thought in this area.

One final illustration of the changing trends of thought on the role of public enterprise in the national economy may be drawn from the current development plan of Nigeria:

> Public sector investment will continue to complement private investment and be largely confined to areas where private initiative has failed to respond or responded too slowly to meet the demands of the economy. Such investment will, however, as much as possible, be undertaken in co-operation with private interests. This is to ensure that such government ventures are run along commercial lines rather than as social services. Every public venture will be expected to pay its own way even if, for social reasons, it is considered undersirable to insist on profit maximization. Apart from the defense industries and security printing, no specific area will be reserved exclusively for government.[36]

Problems of Privatization

Privatization is not as easy as it sounds. The nature of associated problems varies from country to country and depends on the precise direction in which any of the available options under that generic policy is adopted (see first section). I shall highlight the major issues that call for attention and control on the African scene.

The Denationalization and Sale Price of an Enterprise

If the enterprise has been operating at a deficit, it may not prove easy to sell it to private investors except at prices low enough to attract them. How low should the price be? Assuming that the shares are not quoted on the stock exchange, there is little of that kind of a guidance. Whether it should be sold for a price that equals the net capital worth (that is, original investment minus accumulated deficits) has no quick answer for the following reasons. A figure for accumulated deficits is the product of accounting practices of past years concerning the treatment of costs. One cannot be certain that it represents all costs, or only those costs that ought to have been charged to current operations year after year so far. This figure and therefore the net worth computation correspond to current operating profitability arising from the existing managerial structures, criteria, and practices. It is possible that changes in these, which could not be effected while the enterprise was in the public sector, can easily be effected on denationalization and can then cause a sudden increase in profitability. The present-worth basis might therefore understate the real worth of the enterprise to the new investors.

In the capital-markets circumstances prevailing in most African countries and by virtue of certain considerations restrictive of buyer potential (see later discussion in this section), denationalization may smack of a distress sale. Add to this the possibility of bargaining pressures or irregularities, and the inconclusiveness of the price is all the more certain and the economics as well as the ethics of the measure may fall into the area of doubt and controversy.

A useful guideline in this context would be that, where ameliorative steps are possible in restructuring the capital, production, and management structures, these should be implemented prior to putting the enterprise up for sale. The Kenyan policy understands the necessity of making currently unprofitable enterprises profitable "before the disposition of shares," wherever possible.[37]

Turning to a profitable enterprise marked for denationalization on grounds of comparative advantage, we encounter a pricing problem of another kind. Do the accounts reflect the enterprise's true value? Here one has to look at the implications of inflation. It is unlikely that in the state of accounting sophistication generally prevalent in the African countries the assets are appropriately revalued. So the capital worth, exclusive of revaluation reserves, turns out to be lower than the real worth of the enterprise. Add to this the intelligence of potential buyers and the sale price may prove artificially low.

An important requirement for a smooth policy of government disinvestment is the provision of a system of price determination, as opposed to ad hoc decisions. Some form of independent commission may be entrusted with this function, based on the government guidelines. An interesting example, drawn from a somewhat similar context, is the Capital Issues Commission set up in Nigeria to determine the prices at which "alien enterprises or shares of alien enterprises" are to be sold or transferred to nationals under the Nigerian Enterprises Promotion Decree (1977).

Distributional Effects of Privatization

This is an important implication of privatization, which goes beyond the narrow context of public enterprise and has particular relevance in the Africa region for various reasons: (1) income and wealth disparities are high; (2) development plans, almost everywhere, have emphasized reductions in such disparities as a major objective;[38] (3) the "elite" groups that can buy the divested assets are already rich; and (4) domestic capital potential is relatively low. Who buys the divestments therefore assumes significance. Groups of potential investors may be classified as follows: (1) African nationals, (2) nationals of non-African origin, and (3) foreigners. The first would be the most welcome group, if only it were large enough. But concentration can easily unleash undesirable consequences. It may therefore be appropriate for governments to consider the desirability of regulating the per capita ownership of the divestments or regulate them in any other way. (Precedent is not wanting in this direction. Nigeria has legislated certain provisions intended to limit individual purchase of "alien shares of firms" with the object of minimizing economic concentration through that channel.)[39] Two questions remain, however: What practical effect do such regulations have? and Do they defeat the major aim of divesting government investments in enterprises?

These questions acquire special force when we consider the second group, for they introduce the ethnic dimension. It is difficult to dilate on what impact this dimension will have in practice, though the possibility of its weakening the implementation of denationalization measures can be real from time to time.

The third group raises a different problem, namely, the degree of foreign control over the national economy. To the extent that the economy can be under the effective influence of the government, as in a joint venture in which the public shareholding is the majority (vide Egyptian and Ethiopian laws on the subject), the danger may not be serious. But there is already evidence in some countries like Kenya, where, in some cases, the practice of joint ventures has had undesirable effects.[40] It has to be recognized that the policies of privatization, for the best results, have to be accompanied by suitable measures of effective public watchfulness over the working of foreign capital holdings in partnership with the government or with local private capital or on their own. The case for such measures is indeed independent of privatization policies, but the best results of the latter for the national economy flow from them. This conclusion applies not only to the sale of a divestment (or positive denationalization) but also to the admission of private capital into a joint venture with the government in an existing or new enterprise or into an activity without public or any other local equity participation whatsoever.

Possible Changes in the Pattern of Public-Enterprise Ownership

Privatization might lead to certain changes in the pattern of public enterprise and ownership. Assume that indigenous nationals are not capable of taking over the investments that the government divests itself of but that the government is anxious that the ownership of the divested shares or enterprises should not go to "others." It probably will initiate a financial mechanism in the public sector for advancing funds to local people to enable them to bid for the divestments (as evidenced by Nigerian experience in "indigenizing" investments by aliens). Certain conditions would apply, of course, probably the show of some resource potential on the nationals' part. The net outcome might well be that, although the government disinvests certain of its investments in production units, its investments in enterprises that finance potential investors increase somewhat.

Privatization thus does not ultimately imply a net reduction in governmental or public investments equivalent to the initial divestments. On occasion, this can prove to be a problematic trend, for the government's stake is now proportional, not to the potentialities of production units, but to the capability of willingness to repay of the local borrowers. It is not uncommon for willingness to be low.

Another change in the entrepreneurial character of public enterprise that results from the introduction of privatization measures is the transfer, by and large, of the relatively profitable enterprises, the quick-yielding projects, and the downstream activities to the private sector, whereas the more basic activities and those that are likely to generate low profits or deficits for social reasons stay in the public sector. There is nothing intrinsically wrong in this, provided the financial character of these enterprises is the result of a conscious decision based on social reasons. Yet two consequences follow. First, the situation contributes to budgetary difficulties in the sense that the current flow between the public exchequer and the public-enterprise sector turns out to be unfavorable to the former. This may lead to additional taxation or deficit financing of any budgetary gap. Though such an event flows directly from the government's decision to subsidize certain activities, the impression it generates all around is that because of privatization the government is forced to resort to such measures. The fear of such criticism can operate against further measures of privatization, though the case for the latter may in fact be intrinsic, on grounds of comparative advantage.

The second consequence is more material in terms of substance. The net outcome of privatization measures that retain losses in the public sector and shift profits to the private sector will be a distributional inequity, especially in the circumstances of a less-developed country characterized by wide income disparities. The African scene, as a cross section, comes within this description. The fruits of profitable activities rest with private investors--the fewer, the less dispersed the shareholding--whereas the impact of a budget deficit begins to be reflected in (probably) regressive tax measures. Public resentment may build up slowly, but surely, against such trends, the more certainly when the profits of the privatized units have been built on the edifice of gestation losses squarely borne by the public sector in the preprivatized days. Other things being equal, social tempers may rise with a vengeance in favor of renationalization measures as time goes on. It is best to avoid such causes of policy instability, by designing orderly strategies of privatization. In other words, privatization should be a channel for productive efficiency and surplus generation but not an unlimited gift of easy profit to private investors.

Implications of Privatization for Planned Development

Privatization has two fundamental implications in the context of planned development, which happens to be the strategy of most African countries. The first concerns the sectorial areas and production functions, in respect of which privatized or private units are not under the same discipline of priorities as apply to public-sector investments. There is a need, then, for helpful, if not effective, guidelines from the government--a point clearly recognized in Egypt's current planning document. It is equally important that in the least-developed countries of Africa the competence of private investors in project formulation and operational strategies is on average not as high as one would deem necessary. This is in fact one of the original reasons for the emergence of the public-enterprise sector. It is therefore desirable for the government to promote specialist technical services under the public aegis, services that provide the needed expertise to private investors. Once again, current Egyptian planning recognizes this need.

The other implication is related to the basic conflict between the interests of growth and of distributional justice. Privatization measures are largely a product of pro-growth considerations. Yet, as

I have suggested several times, privatization leads to some concentration and some aggravation of income and wealth disparities. The latter may be considered a cost of growth. How acceptable such a cost is to the nation depends on its social ideology, development status, and current state of public finances. There can be no generalization by way of an answer. What is important to note is that some conscious answer is essential, so that the government can go ahead with the smooth implementation of whatever policy of privatization it opts for. Otherwise, practice becomes so inconsistent and ad hoc that the results may turn out to be insubstantial.

Fig. 1. The Concept of Privatization

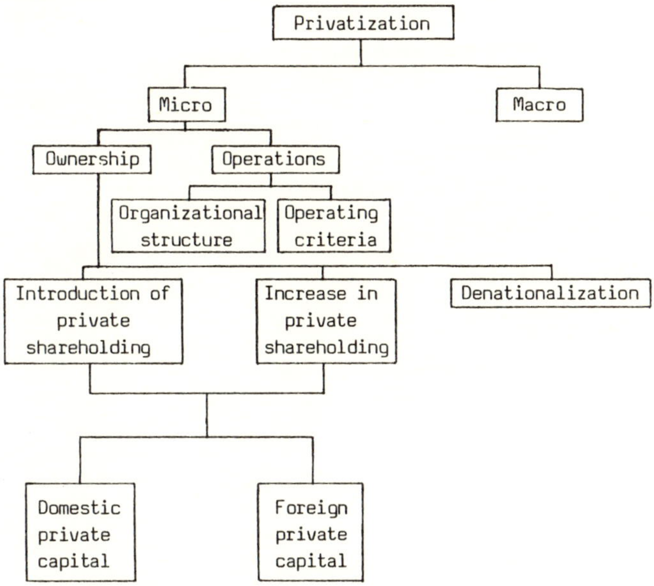

Fig. 2. The Rationale for Privatization

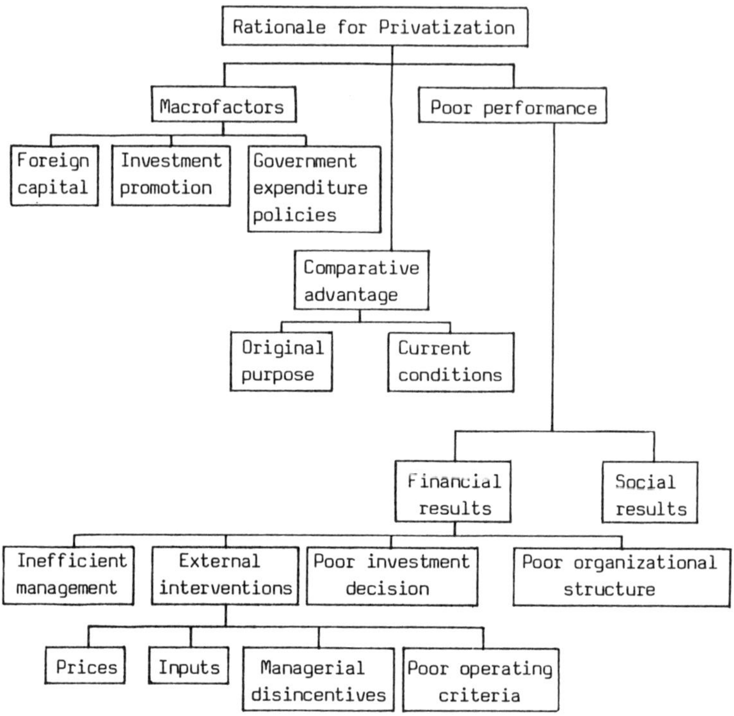

Table 1

Private Investment in Egypt

Sector	Private Investment as % of Total Investment	
	1977-1982 Planning Period	1982-1987 Planning Period
Agriculture and land reform, irrigation and drainage	29	27
Industry and metallurgy	23	21
Petroleum	-	-
Electricity	-	-
Contracting	24	54
Total commodity sector	20	20
Transport and communication	3	6
Suez Canal	-	-
Commerce, finance, insurance, and tourism	14	33
Total production-service sector	5	8
Housing	74	94
Public utilities	-	-
Education, health, other services	16	26
Total service sector	36	45
Total fixed investments	20	23

Source: Part One - The Present - The Five-Year Plan's Development Pillars and Policies 1982/83 - 1986/87 (Cairo), p. 63.
Note: A dash signifies zero.

Table 2

Size of and Monopoly in Kenya's Public-Enterprise Sector

No. of Wage Employees in Public Sector Industry	% of Public Sector Wage Employment in Industry Total					
	Below 10	10 - 25	25 - 50	50 - 75	75 - 100	100
Less than 100	Drugs and medicines Wholesale trade Retail butchering Oil and gasoline retail General retail Ocean and coastal transport Services incidental to transport Storage and warehousing "Other" insurance Property companies	Mining and quarrying				
100 - 200	Metal products Electrical contractors Food - wholesale trade "Other" passenger transport	Soft drinks			Pottery	Pipelines
200 - 500	"Other" agricultural activities General wholesale trade Freight by road	Engineering products: wholesale trade	Cotton gins Accounting, etc.			Petroleum refining

500 - 1,000	Hotels, etc.	Grain mills Printing, etc.	Insurance companies	Shipbuilding and repairing	Chemical and fertilizer Mineral mining Manufacture and repair of air-craft Financial services	Inland water transport K.P. & T. administrative services
1,000-2,000		Spinning, weaving, and finished textiles	Manufacture and assembly of motor vehicles	Slaughtering,etc. Basic chemicals Cement Painters, roof tiles, etc., in construction "Other" financial institutions		KR central administration
2,000-5,000		Ranches	Agricultural products: whole-sale trade Air transport Financial institu-tions		Supporting services to air transport Communications	Electricity Railways
5,000-10,000		Mixed farming	Food products (manufacturing)	Sugar	Water	
10,000-and above				Sugar plantations "Other" construc-tion (not build-ing)	Agricultural services	Forestry Railroad equip-ment Supporting services to water transport

Source: Basic data from <u>Statistical Abstract 1981</u> (Nairobi, 1982), pp. 240-244.

Table 3

Public-Enterprise Sector Contribution

to Capital Formation, by Industry, 1979

Sector	Contribution as % of Total 1964	1970	1979
Agriculture	7.6	4.1	11.2
Forestry	100.0	100.0	100.0
Fishing	-	-	-
Mining and quarrying	-	90.8	-
Manufacturing	2.7	36.7	27.2
Building and construction	18.2	14.2	11.1
Electricity and water	17.6	90.3	100.0
Transport, storage, communications	39.7	46.6	64.8
Wholesale, retail trade, restaurants and hotels	7.8	9.7	9.5
Finance, insurance, real estate, business services	7.8	16.3	57.6
Ownership of dwellings	51.1	42.4	52.5
Other services	1.8	0.4	5.8
Total	20.1	35.8	38.1

Source: Statistical Abstracts (Nairobi), 1970, 1975, and 1979.

Notes

The focus and interest of this chapter are technical; there is no intention to tread on ideological issues.

1. Part One - The Present - The Five-Year Plan's Development Pillars and Policies 1982/83-1986/87 (Cairo), p. 32.

2. Law no. 43 of 1974 concerning the Investment of Arab and Foreign Funds and the Free Zones, as aoended by Law no. 32 of 1977, Article 9 (Cairo, 1977).

3. See Article 10 of Law no. 43 (note 2).

4. The Five-Year Plan (Cairo), p. 32.

5. City Bank, Investment Guide (Egypt), p. 23.

6. Heba Handoussa refers to the measures of decentralization in control over public enterprises that came with the abolition of the general organizations (analogous to holding companies), and to the granting of some autonomy to managers in the areas of employment, wage payments, and pricing ("The Impact of Economic Liberation on the Performance of Egypt's Public Sector Industry," Second BAPEG Conference, Boston, 1980).

7. The Five-Year Plan (Cairo), pp. 23-27.

8. The Six-Year Plan of Economic and Social Development--1978/79 - 1982/83 V of 1 (Khartoum, 1977), p. 31.

9. The Encouragement of Investment Act 1980 (Khartoum).

10. Ministry of Finance and Economic Planning, Information Memorandum (Khartoum, 1983), pp. 4-5.

11. Ibid., p. 6.

12. A Joint Proclamation to Provide for the Establishment of Joint Venture (Negarit Gazeta, Addis Ababa, 22 January 1983).

13. "African Socialism and its Application to Planning in Kenya," sessional paper (Nairobi, 1965), p. 11.

14. Ibid., p. 27.

15. Ibid.

16. Report and Recommendations of the Working Party on Government Expenditures (Nairobi, 1982), p. 92.

17. Central Bureau of Statistics, Ministry of Economic Planning and Development, Statistical Abstract 1981 (Nairobi, 1982), pp. 240-244.

18. Working Party on Government Expenditures, p. 42.

19. Review of Statutory Boards, Report and Recommendations of the Committee (Nairobi, 1979), p. 22.

20. Statistical Abstracts, pp. 39, 36 of 1970 volume, pp. 49, 51 of 1975 volume, and pp. 47, 49 of 1979 volume.

21. Sessional Paper No. 4 of 1982 on Development Prospects and Policies (Nairobi, 1982), p. 14.

22. "Kenyatta Day: Message to the Nation," by Pres. David T. Arap Moi (20 October 1982).

23. The Five-Year Plan (Cairo), pp. 97-98.

24. Statement by the president on the current economic situation in Kenya, 21 September 1982 (Nairobi).

25. Ministry of Finance and Economic Planning, Information Memorandum, March 1983 (Khartoum), p. 5.

26. For an elaborate discussion on this issue, see V. V. Ramanadham, The Nature of Public Enterprise, part 2, section 8 (London, 1984).

27. Working Paper on Government Expenditures, p. 43.

28. L'Experience Ivoitienne de Planification (1970), p. 24.

29. Working Party on Government Expenditures, p. 41.

30. The Six-Year Plan (Khartoum), p. 31.

31. Ministry of Financial and National Economy, Economic Survey 1978/79 (Khartoum).

32. Bank of Sudan, Twenty-Second Annual Report, 1981 (Khartoum, 1982), p. 90.

33. The Five-Year Plan (Cairo), pp. 22-23, 27.

34. Ibid., p. 32.

35. Development Prospects and Policies, p. 14.

36. Fourth National Development Plan 1981-85, Vol. 1 (Lagos, 1981), p. 142.

37. Working Party on Government Expenditures, p. 43.

38. For example, "more even distribution of income among individuals and socio-economic groups" (Fourth National Development Plan 1981-85, Vol. 1 (Lagos, 1981), p. 37.

39. Some of the provisions of the Nigerian Enterprises Promotion Decrees of 1977 are cited below, rather extensively in view of their relevance to our theme:

In respect of ALL businesses listed in Schedule 1 and all businesses listed in Schedules 2 and 3 which are being operated other than as public companies (i.e. proprietorships, partnerships or private companies), no sale or transfer of interest can be effected unless the terms of sale or transfer have been approved by the Board. Alien owners of such enterprises will be allowed to submit names of prospective buyers, but the Board reserves the right to reject or vary whatever submissions are made to it;

In case of public companies the Allotment Committee of the Capital Issues Commission will be responsible for allotment of share, or stocks;

Both the Nigerian Enterprises Promotion Board and the Allotment Committee will take steps to ensure that the beneficial ownership of enterprises or shares of enterprises which are being sold for the purpose of complying with the provisions of the Decree are as widely spread as possible and deliberate efforts would be made to prevent the concentration of ownership in a few hands.

Except in the case of owner-managers, no enterprise or the entire mandatory portion of shares of any enterprise affected by the Decree would be sold or transferred to a single individual, and in no case will a single individual be allowed to have control of more than one enterprise affected by the Decree.

Except in the case of owner-managers, the maximum interest that any Nigerian citizen or non-public sector association (whether corporate or non-corporate) could be allowed to acquire in any one enterprise will be limited to 5 per cent of the equity shares being offered for sale or N50,000 worth of shares, whichever is higher. Nigerians are advised to note that the 5 per cent or N50,000 maximum rule is not as restrictive as it seems. However, any Nigerian citizen or association already holding more than the 5 per cent or N50,000 permissible maximum will not qualify for any further allotments, but will not be forced to divest any of his or its current holdings;

In considering applications from Nigerians to buy enterprises or shares of enterprises affected by the Decree, the Nigerian Enterprises Promotion Board or the Allotment Committee, as the case may be, will take into account the existing interest or shareholdings of such applicants in the enterprise or shares being sold and in any other enterprise or shares of enterprises affected by the Decree. In this connection the Nigerian Enterprises Promotion Board or the Allotment Committee, as the case may be, is not obliged to approve in whole or in part, any application from any Nigerian citizen or association (whether corporate or non-corporate) for the purchase of enterprises or shares of enterprises affected by the Decree. Besides, the Board or the Allotment Committee reserves the power to request for any information whatsoever from any Nigerian citizen or association (whether corporate or not) seeking to purchase shares or interest in enterprises affected by the Decree;

All Schedules 2 and 3 enterprises as well as enterprises complying under Section 7(1) of the Decree, are obliged to reserve not less than 10 per cent of the amount of sale for their employees. At least one-half of the 10 per cent must also be reserved for the non-managerial staff. Any lawful arrangement under which the acquisition of the shares by workers will be achieved or facilitated will be favourably considered by the Board provided that the arrangement is not obnoxious. The Nigerian Enterprises Promotion Board is always ready to advise and assist enterprises to ensure that Government objective of worker equity participation is achieved.

40. Working Party on Government Expenditures, p. 41. See also David Wainaina Gachuki, "Public Enterprise and Foreign Capital in Kenya: The Policy Environment," in The Role of Public Enterprises in Development in Eastern Africa, ed. G. K. Laws and S. E. Migot-Adholla, p. 208. (Nairobi: Institute for Development Studies, 1980): "Government participation means that the investors hold it as a hostage against the government to extract concessions to certain privileges."

CHAPTER 12

The State and Economy in Portugal: Perspectives on Corporatism Revolution, and Incipient Privatization

Eric N. Baklanoff

Introduction

Before the revolution, private-enterprise ownership dominated the Portuguese economy to a degree unmatched in other Western European countries. Not only were state enterprises conspicuous by their absence in the manufacturing sector, but private ownership totally dominated the railways, air transport, mining, electricity, petroleum refining, and telecommunications. As table 1 shows, private firms generated 99 percent or more of the value added in each of the enumerated activities in 1973, except in administration and defense, education, and health.

The military coup of April 1974, which ousted the long-lived authoritarian Salazar-Caetano regime, was rapidly transformed into a social revolution that has profoundly recast Portugal's polity and economy system. The revolutionary leadership undercut the old elite's economic base by nationalizing the banks and most of the country's heavy and medium-sized industries, expropriating landed estates in the central and southern regions, and giving independence to Angola, Mozambique, and other colonies. The last action dismantled the web of economic relationships, known as Escudo Area, through which metropolitan Portugal was linked to its "overseas provinces" and marked the dismemberment of Europe's oldest colonial empire.

The failure of a Far-Left bid for total power on 25 November 1975 halted the prolonged series of political disorders and paved the way for the establishment of a democratically elected constitutional government. In the spring of 1984, ten years after the military coup, Portugal--though still classified as a less-developed nation--has taken on a Western European cast.

The transformation of Portugal's political economy commands our attention for a number of reasons. First, Portugal--a charter member of NATO--will soon become a full participant in the European community. Second, scholars interested in the "anatomy of revolution" can compare the Portuguese experience with that of other nations that have undergone rapid systemic change. Third, Portugal's recent experiment with nationalization of industry will be of particular interest to students of public-enterprise economics.

With a per capita gross domestic product (GDP) of $2,440 in 1981 (less than half of neighboring Spain's), Portugal is the poorest country in Western Europe. Other indicators, such as the high infant mortality rate (25/1000) and the relatively large fraction of the working population in agriculture (27 percent in 1981), confirm Portugal's status as a less-developed country. Nevertheless, as a consequence of rapid economic growth and structural change from 1960 to 1973, the Organization for Economic Cooperation and Development (OECD), of which Portugal is a member, classifies it as one of eleven "newly industrializing" countries.

I shall examine the varied configurations of state intervention in the Portuguese economy: the changing functional scope of the state as both regulator of the economy and owner-manager of productive enterprises. I shall survey as well the evolution of the corporate state under the old regime and highlight the major economic problems confronting Portugal on the eve of the military coup, and I shall analyze the organizational and structural changes associated with the radical policies of the Armed Forces Movement (AFM) regimes--what I have called the "nationalization-redistribution syndrome." I shall focus on the increasing weight of the consolidated public sector in the Portuguese economy since 1973 and link state expansion to the operational, financial, and managerial problems experienced by the public enterprises. I shall consider the growing incongruity between the Marxian-oriented 1976 constitution and the moderate coalition governments that have ruled Portugal since the late 1970s--a conflict that has resulted in fundamental constitutional revisions. In the concluding section, I discuss prospects for state shrinking in the context of the constitutional reforms, moderate coalition politics, and the 1983 stabilization program supported by the International Monetary Fund (IMF).

The Political Economy of the Old Regime

For forty years, from 1928 to 1968, Antonio Salazar's political and economic doctrines were to shape Portugal's destiny. Richard Pattee (1957:205-206) describes Salazar's mental set as it would be carried into public action: "Salazar has never promised Portugal anything but hard work, rectitude, tenacity, and the kind of daily homework in economics that he imposed on his students at Coimbra. Salazar is first and foremost an extremely competent housekeeper and he has conceived of Portugal as a menage which was in dire need of being put in order, lest it fall apart."

In 1933, at the bottom of the Great Depression, Salazar promulgated the Constitution of 1933, which laid down the principles for a New State. Neither capitalist nor Communist, the philosophical foundation of the New State rested on Roman Catholic social theory, with its emphasis on a "corporate form of social life," as well as on Lusitanian integralism, a political doctrine that opposed the positivism, egalitarianism, and atheism associated with the French Revolution (Marques 1972:177-178).

The New State, a Mediterranean version of the corporate state, resembled European fascism only superficially. Significantly, Salazar purged the Portuguese Fascist elements in 1934 and specifically denounced the National Syndicalists as "inspired by certain foreign models" (Payne 1973:668-669). He declared his opposition to all the "grand heresies" of the contemporary world, including nazism, communism, and materialism. In his writings, including _Doctrine and Action_ (1939), he emphasized the fundamental distinction between the Catholic corporatism of the New State and fascism--a "pagan Caesarism" that does not recognize moral or juridical limits (Ferro 1935:96). As Howard Wiarda writes, "We must begin to recognize that the mainstreams of corporatism in the Iberic-Latin world were always fundamentally different from and opposed to nazi and fascist models and that the nations of the Iberic-Latin culture area are now nowhere served or accurately described by resort to the fascist or neofascist brands" (1972:32).

The corporative framework within which the Portuguese economy evolved combined two salient characteristics: extensive state regulation, and predominantly private ownership of the means of production. Leading financiers and industrialists accepted extensive bureaucratic controls in return for assurances of minimal public ownership of economic enterprises and certain monopolistic (or restricted-competition) privileges. There existed a close and mutually beneficial relationship between high-ranking public officials and the country's leading business groups. The largest companies often hired former cabinet ministers and other high-level government officials. Most private firms had government representatives on their boards of directors.

Under the Portuguese corporative system, employers and workers were organized in guilds and syndicates, respectively, in commerce, industry, banking, and transport. Similar organizations existed for farmers, rural laborers, fishermen; special organizations (_ordens_) existed for professional groups. The guilds negotiated collective labor contracts governing wages, hours, and working conditions. Disputes were referred to the government's labor tribunals for settlement, and the tribunals' decisions were mandatory for both parties. Strikes and lockouts were prohibited.

Within this corporative framework the state exercised extensive de facto authority regarding private investment decisions and the level of wages. A system of industrial licensing (_condicionamento industrial_), introduced by law in 1931, required prior authorization from the state for setting up or relocating an industrial plant, or for reopening a plant that had suspended operations for over two years (Associacao Industrial Portuguesa). Investment in machinery and equipment designed to increase the capacity of an existing industrial firm also required government approval. Applications for new investments had to be made to the minister of the economy and were published in the _National Bulletin of Industrial Licensing_. The objective of publication was to permit any interested party in the relevant industry to comment on or object to the granting of an application. Such broad discretionary powers for government officials in the licensing of industrial investment often strengthened the monopolistic position of existing firms, led to misallocation of capital resources, gave rise to claims of grave irregularities, and deterred investment by foreign enterprises in the Portuguese economy.

Nevertheless, under pressure of circumstance, Salazar eventually opened the way for an alternative development strategy, albeit most reluctantly. He reasoned that, to preserve Portugal's "multiracial, pluricontinental" state, it was necessary to accelerate economic development both in the metropolis and in the "overseas provinces." As economist V. Xavier Pintado (1973:7) observes, "Behind the facade of social and political immobilism under the loosening grip of an aged Salazar, Portugal knew deep and lasting changes during the 1960's."

Salazar's decision to step up the rate of development in the face of mounting defense expenditures led him reluctantly to seek outside assistance in the form of credits and direct investment. Portugal joined EFTA (the European Free Trade Association) in 1961. Against the opposition of protectionist interests, Salazar's young minister for the economy, Luis Teixeira Pinto, succeeded in bringing about some liberalization of the industrial licensing system. The last years of the Salazar era witnessed the creation of important privately organized ventures, including an integrated iron and steel mill, a modern ship repair and shipbuilding complex, vehicle assembly plants, oil refineries, petrochemical plants, pulp and paper mills, and electronics plants.

The liberalization of the Portuguese economy was given further impetus under Salazar's successor, prime minister Marcello Caetano (1968-1974). Adopting the motto "Evolution with continuity," Caetano brought a new group of technocrats into government. They set about to eliminate price controls, lower trade barriers, and remove industrial licensing requirements for new firms in many branches. Notwithstanding the emergence of a small Europe-oriented technocratic cadre within the Caetano government, it is important to point out the tenuousness of its position. In striking contrast to their counterparts in Spain--the Opus Dei group, which dominated the commanding heights of the Spanish economy and held cabinet rank--none of the Portuguese technocrats enjoyed full cabinet rank. Both Pintado, secretary of state for commerce, and Rogerio Martins, secretary of state for industry, were subject to the authority of the minister for the economy, and neither had access to cabinet meetings, where crucial political and economic questions were debated. More important, in Spain Franco's authority was unassailable; in Portugal, prime minister Marcello Caetano never was able to exert authority autonomously in the way Salazar had. Many of the powerful figures within the regime with whom Caetano had to consult reflected the views of Portugal's traditional elites on such questions as the status of the African provinces and the pace of modernization.

Portugal's commitment to the African territories continued to be the central public issue of the Caetano administration. The massive military deployment in Africa and official economic assistance for the development of Angola and Mozambique drained resources that would otherwise have been available for a more decisive development push in metropolitan Portugal. Within the Caetano government, as Lawrence Graham (1975:40-48) demonstrates, there were four broad clusters of interest that addressed themselves to the metropole's relations with its overseas provinces. Three of them--"the ultraconservatives, the integrationists, and the federalists--were broad coalitions with representatives in the civilian bureaucracy, the military, and the business community. The fourth, the developmentalists, was made up of advocates of a resolution of the African question by negotiated settlement and of European integration" (ibid:40).

Mostly economists by profession, the developmentalists considered metropolitan Portugal's involvement with the African territories as a major obstacle to the nation's full commitment to integration with Europe. Among the most prominent members of this group were Pintado and Rogerio Martins, as well as Joao Salgueiro, undersecretary of state for planning. However, as Graham makes clear, members of the developmentalist cluster "simply did not move in sufficiently large numbers into strategic positions to be able to effect meaningful change in the distribution of power within the regime" (ibid:54). By the middle of 1972, Pintado, Martins, and Salgueiro had left the government, and by early 1973, Caetano was moving back to a more traditional stance, which stressed continuity between his administration and that of Salazar.

Compared with the 1940s and 1950s, the annual growth rate of the Portuguese economy from 1960 to 1973 advanced notably. During the 1960-1970 decade, GNP growth per year averaged over 6 percent and accelerated to 7 percent from 1970 to 1973 (Baklanoff 1979:803-804). Considering that the Portuguese population actually decreased slightly between 1960 and 1973, the per capita growth performance was even more impressive. The secondary sector, including manufacturing, paced the economy's advance, with growth averaging about 9 percent annually from 1960 to 1973. Lagging behind general economic growth was the primary sector, including agriculture, fishing, and mining. Agricultural production, which grew by only 1.5 percent per annum from 1960 to 1970, slowed to less than half that rate from 1970 to 1973. Tertiary-sector growth, comprising the whole range of private and public service activities, advanced at a pace nearly equal to GNP. The rapid expansion of tourism services between 1960 and 1973 supported the growth of the tertiary sector.

The Portuguese economy changed significantly by 1973, when, compared with its position in 1961, total output (GDP at factor cost) grew by 120 percent in real terms; the secondary sector was over three times greater; the size of the tertiary sector doubled; but the primary sector, chiefly agriculture, advanced by only 18 percent. Manufacturing, the major component of the secondary sector, was three times as large at the end of the period.

The decline in the resident labor force associated with worker emigration and the military draft coincided with a healthy advance in total output. Clearly, growth in all three sectors was mainly the result of large rises in labor productivity. Because of the reduction of the Portuguese resident population and work force, the rural-to-urban migration within Portugal provided the necessary elasticity of labor supply for the labor-absorbing secondary and tertiary sectors.

From 1960 to 1973, Portuguese policy tools were mobilized in support of a shift of resources from low-productivity toward high-productivity uses, including export-oriented industries. That Portugal had indeed undergone a profound restructuring of its economy is evidenced by the changing sector-distribution of the working population and the changing composition of output (Baklanoff 1979:804-806). Between 1960 and 1973, the share of the labor force in the primary sector (agriculture, fishing, and mining) fell from 44 percent to 28 percent, that of the secondary sector (manufacturing, construction, and electricity, gas, and water) rose from 29 percent to 36 percent, and that of the tertiary sector (including transport and communications) rose from 28 percent to 35 percent. In Portugal, the shift of the working population out of agriculture involved a reduction in the number of persons engaged in that sector (a decline of about 550,000 workers between 1960 and 1973) as well as in the proportion of farm workers in the total labor force. The composition of the gross domestic product also changed markedly during the dozen years from 1961 to 1973. The share of the primary sector in GDP shrank from about 24 percent in 1961 to just under 13 percent in 1973, and the secondary or industrial sector's contribution increased from about 37 percent to 51 percent during the period. Tertiary activities accounted for a somewhat smaller share of GDP in 1973 compared with 1961, experiencing a decline from 39 percent to 37 percent.

Attracted by growing investment opportunities and favorable domestic legislation, foreign private capital became a significant factor in the establishment of new industries after 1960. Foreign-controlled firms supported expansion and diversification of Portugal's burgeoning industrial sector. By the early 1970s, foreigners held 81 percent of total equity capital in the electrical machinery industry, 72 percent in rubber products, 62 percent in transport equipment, 48 percent in chemicals, 43 percent in paper and products, and 28 percent in clothing and shoes (Donges 1980:265, table 3). Significantly, foreign investment was responsible for an estimated 41 percent of Portugal's merchandise exports from 1970 to 1974 (ibid: 267, table 5). Association with EFTA and close affiliation with multinational companies that provided venture capital, advanced technology, and market outlets contributed much to Portugal's export performance.

Under the old regime, some forty great families dominated Portugal's private sector. These industrial dynasties were allied by marriage with the large, traditional landowning families of the nobility, who held most of the arable land in the southern part of the country in great estates. Many of these dynasties had business interests in Portuguese Africa, from which they profited considerably. Within this elite group, the top ten families owned all the important commercial banks, which in turn controlled a disproportionate share of the national economy. Because bank officials were often members of the boards of directors of borrowing firms, in whose stock the banks participated, the influence of the large banks extended to a host of commercial, industrial, and service enterprises.

The concentration of business ownership and control in the hands of the financial-industrial families through conglomerate groups was brought out in an important study, <u>Sociedades e grupos en Portugal</u>, by

Maria Belmira Martins (1973). Of the 40,051 corporations operating in metropolitan Portugal in 1971, 168 (0.4 percent) had 53 percent of the total corporate net worth.

With the rapid advance of industry and the growth of cities, new channels of upward mobility were opened. Harry Makler's (1969) study of the industrial elite revealed that the typical business executive (manager or owner of a large firm) was drawn from a middle-class background. The great majority of these elite managers of entrepreneurs were sons of business executives or professionals and were highly educated. A subsequent empirial study by Makler of the Portuguese industrial elite highlights the central role of education as a vehicle for upward mobility into the world of business (1974: tables 1 and 2). Before the 1974 revolution, the largest, most technologically advanced (and recently organized) firms offered the greatest opportunity for management careers based on merit rather than on accident of birth.

The period of accelerated growth from 1960 to 1973 witnessed rapid transformation of the Portuguese economy climaxed by the conclusion of a free-trade agreement between Portugal and the EEC in 1972. Still, on the eve of the April 1974 military coup, Portugal faced four major problems: (1) an excessive rate of worker emigration and military conscription, which gave rise to critical shortages of skilled manpower; (2) a high level of defense spending, estimated at 40 percent to 45 percent of the national budget, associated with the counterinsurgency wars in Africa; (3) an anachronistic pattern of agricultural organization, which inhibited the nation's rate of growth; and (4) a high concentration of economic and political power in the oligarchy of the "forty families."

The Social Revolution: Magnitude and Configuration of the Public Enterprise Sector

In the brief period between the collapse of the old regime in April 1974, and the abortive leftist coup of November 1975, a bewildering variety of politicoeconomic models were proposed for Portugal by the provisional Armed Force Movement (MFA) governments, including the Western European, Yugoslav, and Albanian models.

In the early months following the military coup, the new Portuguese government's economic orientation could be described as moderate-reformist. The regime's economic and social program (OECD 1974:33-34), published on 15 May 1974, made no provision for large-scale nationalization of industry or agriculture. Point (e) of the program simply provided for the "adoption of new measures of government intervention in the basic sectors of the economy and particularly in the sectors of national interest, without prejudice to the legitimate interest of private enterprise"; point (m) argued for "reform of the tax system so as to rationalize it and ease the tax burden on less-well-off groups, with a view of a fairer distribution of income"; point (q) recommended measures "to stimulate agriculture and gradual reform of the land tenure system"; and point (a), within the sphere of social policy, favored introduction of "a minimum wage to be progressively extended to all sectors of activity."

The reorganization of the MFA coordinating committee in March 1975 brought into prominence a group of Marxian-oriented officers who, in league with CGTP-Intersindical, the Communist-dominated trade-union confederation, sought the radical transformation of the nation's social system and political economy. Abandoning its moderate-reformist posture, the MFA leadership set out a course of sweeping nationalizations and land expropriations. During the balance of that year, the government nationalized all Portuguese-owned capital in the banking, insurance, petrochemical, fertilizer, tobacco, cement, and wood pulp branches of the economy, as well as the Portuguese iron and steel company, the major breweries, the large shipping lines, most public transport, two of the three principal shipyards, core companies of the Companhia Uniao Fabril (CUF) conglomerate, the radio and television networks (except that of the Catholic church), and important companies in the glass, mining, fishing, and agricultural sectors. Because of the key role of the domestic banks as holders of stock, the government indirectly acquired majority or minority equity positions in hundreds of other firms. Another three hundred small-to-medium enterprises came under public management as the government "intervened" to rescue them from bankruptcy following their takeover by workers or abandonment by management.

Although foreign direct investment was statutorily exempted from nationalization, many foreign-controlled enterprises curtailed or ceased operation due to costly forced labor settlements or worker takeovers. The combination of revolutionary policies and negative business climate brought about a sharp reversal in the trend of private inflows from abroad.

A study by Maria Belmira Martins and Rosa (1979) shows that 244 private enterprises were directly nationalized during the sixteen-month interval from 14 March 1975 to 29 July 1976. Nationalization was followed by the consolidation of the several private firms in each industry into state monopolies. As an example, Quimigal, the chemical and fertilizer entity, represents a merger of five firms. Four large companies were integrated to form Petrogal (Petroleos de Portugal). Portucel brought together five pulp and paper companies. The fourteen private electric-power enterprises were joined into a single power generation and transmission monopoly, EDP (Electricidade de Portugal). With the nationalization and amalgamation of the three tobacco firms under Tabaqueria, the state gained complete control of this industry. The several breweries and beer-distribution companies were integrated into two state firms, Centralcer and Unicer, and a single state enterprise, Rodoviaria, was created by joining the ninety-three nationalized trucking and bus lines. The forty-seven cement plants, formerly controlled by the Champalimaud interests, were integrated into Cimpor (Cimentos de Portugal).

The government also acquired a dominant position in the export-oriented shipbuilding and ship repair industry. Because of foreign-investor participation, LISNAVE, the huge modern ship repair facility, was not taken over. LISNAVE is currently owned by Swedish and Dutch interests (39 percent), Jose Manuel de Melo (16 percent), and the government indirectly (28 percent) through acquisition of the banks and insurance companies, most of which were shareholders.

Former private monopolies, such as the iron and steel company, Siderurgia Nacional, the railway, Caminhos de Ferro Portugueses (CP), and the national airline, TAP, retained their company designations following nationalization.

Unlike other sectors, where existing private firms were typically consolidated into state monopolies, the commercial banking system and insurance industry were left with a degree of competition. By merging some of the small financial institutions, the number of commercial banks was eventually reduced from fifteen to nine. Notwithstanding their public status, the nine remaining domestic commercial banks have retained their individual identities and certain differences in activity. Because interest rates and commissions are fixed by the Bank of Portugal, interbank competition is based mainly on the quality of services rendered (Palha 1983:11). On the date of their nationalization, the banks held 22 billion escudos of stock in other enterprises, 161 billion escudos of commercial loans, and 235 billion escudos of deposits (Martins and Rosa 1979:15; 25.5 escudos/dollar). The three foreign-owned banks in the country--Banco do Brazil, Credit Franco-Portugais, and the Bank of London and South America--were excluded from the takeover decree. Despite this exception, the nationalized banks at the end of 1977 held 98 percent of all commercial bank capital and equal shares of commercial loans and deposits.

Although a new government agency, the Institute of State Participation (IPE), was created to oversee the operations of the public-enterprise sector, de facto supervision of the public firms has been carried out by those central ministries whose activities are most closely linked to their operations. Until 1976 intervention and the placement of governmental representatives in firms were identified with the military and civilian radicals in command of the ARM regime. Following the consolidation of a middle-of-the-road civilian regime in the form of the First Constitutional Government, personnel identified with the Socialist party moved into public-sector management positions (Graham and Wheeler 1982:234-235).

As table 1 shows, two years after the military coup, the consolidated public sector accounted for 47 percent of the country's gross fixed investment (GFCF), 30 percent of total value added (VA), and 24 percent of employment. (These shares should be compared with 10 percent of fixed investment, 9 percent of value added, and 13 percent of employment for the traditional public sector of 1973.) Expansion of the public sector since the revolution is particularly noteworthy in heavy manufacturing, public services, including electricity, gas, transport and communications, and in banking and insurance. Further, according to the Institute for State Participation, these figures do not include private enterprises under temporary state intervention, private enterprises with minority state participation (less than 50 percent of the common stock), or worker-managed firms and agricultural collectives.

Excluding the weight of "general government," Portugal's public enterprise sector--the nationalized and state-controlled firms (equity holdings of 50 percent or more)--accounted in 1978 for 18.4 percent of VA, 34.3 percent of GFCF, and 6.8 percent of the nation's employment (OECD 1981:28, table 12). The relative scope of Portugal's public enterprises in the economy was, therefore, generally greater than that of Great Britian's "nationalized industries" (Amuzegar 1981:238) under the last Labour government (11 percent of GDP, 20 percent of GFCF, and 8 percent of the work force).

Nationalized enterprises and state-controlled firms accounted in 1977 for about 25 percent of the value added in the Portuguese manufacturing sector (OECD 1981:28, table 12). However, the public firms (e.g., iron and steel, cement, petrochemicals, because of their predominantly high capital intensity accounted for a disproportionately high share of fixed investment (76 percent) in manufacturing. With respect to both production and employment, private enterprise continues to play a considerable role in Portuguese industry. The importance of private firms (including foreign-controlled enterprises) is even greater in regards to exports of manufactured products, where their share exceeds 85 percent. This is explained by the fact that major exporting industries such as food processing, textiles and clothing, footwear, wood and cork products, and electrical and nonelectrical machinery, are largely in private hands.

The relative scope of the Portuguese public-enterprise sector as outlined in the preceding discussion is based on official national statistics as presented in the OECD annual reports on Portugal. In sharp contrast to the percentages cited above, the World Bank in its 1983 World Development Report (p. 51) gives the Portuguese state-owned enterprises' share of value added in manufacturing as about 15 percent for 1976 and the nonfinancial state-owned enterprises share of GDP as about the same percentage. (In its bibliographical note [p. 131] the World Development Report informs the reader that its statistics on state-owned enterprises are predominantly from Peter Short's research for the IMF, as well as UNIDO publications and World Bank data.) Considering the massive state takeovers across a spectrum of economic activities, it would appear that the World Bank's percentages grossly underestimate the significance of Portugal's public enterprises since the revolution.

In its relative scope and sectorial configuration, the Portuguese public-enterprise sector resembles Mexico's "parastatal" sector following the nationalization of that country's private commercial banks on 1 September 1982. In both countries the state, through ownership and control of enterprises, monopolized energy, telecommunications, railways, and air transport--and dominated or monopolized a broad spectrum of manufacturing branches, particularly in the heavy industry category. Because the private banks in both countries held common stock in their clients, the nationalization of these banks resulted in indirect state ownership of hundreds of small and medium-sized enterprises.

The redistribution of the means of production from the oligarchy to the state was initially accompanied by a radical redistribution of national income from property owners, entrepreneurs, and private executives to workers (Baklanoff 1984). The newly formed labor unions, heavily influenced by the Communist party, focused on expansion of the public sector, employment guarantees, and income redistribution. A 1975 law regulated every aspect of labor-management relations and provided that all dismissals with cause must pass through courts.

Problems of Public Enterprises: The Budget Link

Since 1973 the Portuguese economy has experienced a rapid, and often uncontrollable, expansion of public expenditures--both general government and public enterprise. From modest surpluses before the revolution, the balance of current revenues and expenditures swung to a deficit of nearly 4 percent of GDP in 1980, and the overall balance to a deficit equivalent to 9.1 percent (OECD 1981:23, table 11). The public deficit grew steadily from 19.5 billion escudos in 1975 to 110 billion escudos in 1980, and Central Bank financing of a large share of these deficits has contributed importantly to Portugal's recent high inflation rates.

The increasing weight of the public sector in the Portuguese economy is largely attributable to the pervasive spread of social welfare expenditures, problems arising as a consequence of decolonization, and the nationalization of industries. The share of public expenditure in GDP, which had remained stable until the early 1970s, rose from just under 23 percent in 1973 to about 34 percent in 1980 (ibid.).

On the revenue side, the upward trend was less pronounced: the share increased from 23 percent in 1973 to 30 percent in 1980. Apart from the growing public-investment effort, the government deficit was the result of a determined effort to redistribute income, mainly through transfers and subsidies, and of the failure of revenues to match them (Schmitt 1981:9). Public-debt interest payments, associated with the growing deficit and foreign borrowing, grew from 0.4 percent to 3.2 percent of GDP between 1973 and 1980, thus showing the fastest advance of any category of public expenditure.

The steep increase in subsidies (averaging 54 percent annually from 1974 to 1980) can be attributed in part to the operations of the public-enterprise sector; state enterprises have also absorbed a large share of capital transfers and account for practically all capital endowments (ibid.:27). Notwithstanding the large subsidies received by the public-enterprise sector, its contribution to the nation's net savings in both 1981 and 1982 was negative (Banco de Portugal 1983:220-221). Further, the rapid buildup of Portugal's external debt from $5.4 billion in 1978 to $13.5 billion at the end of 1982 is largely associated with the public enterprises, whose share in the foreign debt expanded from 37 percent in 1978 to 57 percent in 1982 (OECD 1982:23; and Banco de Portugal 1983:153).

It is not surprising that numerous nationalized enterprises have experienced severe operating and financial difficulties. State operations have entailed considerable uncertainty as to the goals of public enterprises, with negative implications for decision making, often at odds with market criteria. For example, among the conditions stated in Decree-Law no. 442/76 that may lead to state intervention is the "failure of management to meet social responsibilities towards workers, the state, social well-being and local authorities" (Balassa 1976:11). In many instances, managers of public firms have been less able than their private-sector counterparts to resist strong wage demands from militant unions (Banco de Portugal 1981:193). Further, public-firm managers may be required for reasons of political expediency to maintain a redundant labor force and freeze prices or utility rates for long periods in the face of rising costs. Overstaffing has been particularly flagrant at Petrogal (the national petroleum monopoly) and Setenave (the wholly state-owned shipbuilding and repairing enterprise). Setenave's work force, which rose from only fourteen hundred in 1973 to sixty-two hundred in 1977, is the major recipient of public industrial subsidies. The nationalized banks had to absorb the more than seven thousand bank employees who returned from the former Portuguese colonies, a requirement that significantly raised their labor costs after 1975 (Banco de Portugal 1982:8). The failure of the public-transportation firms to raise fares during a time of accelerating inflation has resulted in substantial operating losses and the obsolescence of the sector's capital stock.

The dismemberment of the Portuguese overseass empire also adversley affected several other state enterprises: TAP, the national airline, suffered a sharp decline in income and was left with unsuitable aircraft designed for the African trade that accounted for 40 percent of its prerevolution earnings. Further, a number of nationalized industries--notably iron and steel and chemicals--lost their privileged markets in Angola and Mozambique after decolonization.

The failure of most public enterprises to turn a profit is reflected in their unsatisfactory debt ratios. A sample of thirty-three public enterprises revealed an overall debt ratio (assets/liabilites) of only 0.37 in 1979 (ibid. 1981:194). This figure falls short of the prudent minimum ratio of 0.5 and has probably deteriorated since 1979. The failure of most public enterprises to generate internal savings has exacerbated the problem of the overall government deficit.

Apart from special cases, as in iron and steel, where the economies of scale are optimal for very large firms, the desirability of establishing national monopolies is questionable. In Portugal, the elimination of competition following the official takeover of such industries as cement, breweries, pulp and paper, and trucking, may have reduced managerial incentives for cost reduction and technical advance.

The nine nationalized banks, as I have noted, continue to compete with one another. Still, they are constrained by government-imposed salary limits and changes in their boards of directors every three years, including the naming of numerous political appointees lacking in banking or general financial expertise. A senior (unrotated) director, who can earn no more than one million escudos a month (about one thousand four hundred dollars in the summer of 1982), is receiving less than one half the real income he or she enjoyed in 1973.

The heavy drain on managerial and technical expertise sustained by the nationalized firms has compounded the problem of goal ambivalence that characterizes the public-enterprise sector. The income-leveling measures of the MFA, together with the "anti-Fascist" purges in factories, offices, and large agricultural estates, induced an exodus of human capital. By the end of 1975, an estimated eighty thousand skilled workers, technicians, professionals, and business executives had left Portugal for Brazil alone (Keefe 1977:138).

The most detailed analysis of Portugal's loss of managerial resources is based on Harry M. Makler's follow-up of a survey of 306 enterprises that he conducted in July 1976, and again in June 1977. His (1979) study makes clear, as I have indicated, that nationalization was greater in the modern, large, technically advanced industries than in the traditional industries such as textiles, apparel, and construction. In small enterprises (fifty to ninety-nine employees), only 15 percent of the industrialists had quit, as compared to 43 percent in the larger. In the giant firms (one thousand or more employees), more than half had quit. His calculations show that the higher the socioeconomic class origin, the greater the likelihood that the industrialist had left the firm. "But, the more upwardly mobile also were more likely to have quit than those who were downwardly socially mobile" (ibid.155). Significantly, a much larger percentage of professional managers (52 percent) compared with owners of production (founders, 18 percent; heirs, 21 percent; and owner-managers, 32 percent) had left their enterprises. Further, these managers, when Makler originally interviewed them in 1965, were earning between $17,500 and $35,000, compared with most founders, who reported earnings of $9,000 or less a year. Shortly after the revolution, the regime established a maximum income of $12,000 a year, from all sources (World Bank 1978). (As a result of official measures affecting wages and salaries, the average pay gap between unskilled workers and managers shrank from 1/7.3 in 1973 to 1/4.3 in 1975.) Wittingly or unwittingly, the revolutionary regime had moved against the bulk of the technocratic class: the professional managers of the large recently founded and technically advanced firms that became the targets of nationalization.

Reforming the Revolution

On 2 April 1976 a new democratic constitution was promulgated, on 25 April Portuguese voters chose a parliamentary body, the Assembly of the Republic, and on 27 June a president in free elections. Formulated during a period of revolutionary fervor by the representatives to a constituent assembly, the 1976 Constitution combined elements of Western democratic experience with Marxian rhetoric. As Paulo de Pitta e Cunha (1979:523) makes clear, Article

89 attributes a residual role to private enterprise as a form of historically precarious property, allowed only in the "transitional stage toward socialism." Unlike other Western European constitutions, the Portuguese constitution subordinated the private sector to the overall objectives of "building up a socialist economy" (Article 91) and "progressive and effective socialization of the economy" (Article 105).

As foreseen in Article 85, Law 46/77 of 8 July 1977 defined the industries in which private enterprise is not permitted. These included banking, insurance, air, rail and urban transport, iron and steel, cement manufacture, mail and telecommunications, electricity production and distribution, petroleum refining and basic petrochemicals, fertilizers, and the arms industry. The law states that all nationalization effected after 25 April 1974 (the date of the military coup) is "considered to be the irreversible victory of the working class."

Led by prime minister Mario Soares, Portugal was governed from 1976 to 1978 by the Portuguese Socialist party--PS--whose deputies, however, failed to command a majority in the Assembly. Under the socialist governments, Portugal (1) formally applied for full membership in the European Economic Community, (2) promulgated a new Foreign Investment Code designed to restore foreign business confidence, (3) established the basic legislative framework for compensation for assets that were nationalized or expropriated, (4) enacted a law delineating the boundaries of the public and private sectors, and (5) agreed to an IMF-sponsored stabilization program. During his trips abroad, Soares also persuaded some exiled business executives to return to Portugal. In the case of the enterprises previously intervened by the state, several deemed economically viable were returned to private hands. In 1979 the Socialists were instrumental in the formation of the General Union of Workers (UGT), a democratic alternative to Intersindical.

The Socialist government's decision to implement the IMF stabilization program, a condition for the release of a $750 million consortium loan pledged by fourteen industrial countries to Portugal, was to have a significant impact on the allocation of national resources and the functional distribution of income (Schmitt 1981; Stuart 1981). The effect of the stabilization program, along with official measures taken earlier, was to shift economic resources from domestic consumption to investment and exports. From 1977 on, the authorities took several measures to slow nominal wage growth below the increase in the general price level, with the result that real wages declined. The government also relaxed the rules for worker dismissal, placed a ceiling on public-sector employment, and eliminated price controls on many items. The considerable reduction in real wages in factories and fields after 1976 contributed to the restoration of Portugal's competitive posture in foreign markets; exports, including tourism services, increased from 16.5 percent of domestic expenditure in 1976 to an average of 27 percent in the 1979 to 1980 period. Further, total consumption, which had exceeded domestic expenditure by two percentage points in 1975, averaged just under 89 percent from 1979 to 1980. With renewed private saving and a much-improved climate for investment, capital formation (gross investment) rose sharply from a low of 13.6 percent in 1975 to average over 24 percent in the 1979 to 1980 period.

Overall, the pattern of functional income distribution shifted considerably, and by 1979 the wage bill in national income (averaging 54.7 percent) was again much the same as in 1973 (51.6 percent). Unlike the early 1970s--years during which Portugal experienced an acute labor shortage--the late 1970s and early 1980s were marked by very high levels of unemployment. It should be remembered that metropolitan Portugal's civilian labor force rose by an estimated 10 percent between 1974 and 1976 (OECD 1977:12) because of the absorption of the 500,000 retornados from the former colonies and the demobilization of the African expenditionary forces. Notwithstanding labor's greatly enhanced political influence, high unemployment levels have depressed wages.

Elections in 1979 and 1980 gave Portugal a Center-Right coalition government with an absolute majority in the Assembly. Known as the Democratic Alliance (AD), the coalition emerged from the October 1980 elections with an 18-seat majority in the 250-seat parliament. The coalition partners were intent on finding enough common ground with the democratic opposition--which included the Socialists and Independent Social Democrats--to purge the 1976 Constitution of its Marxian bias and to extinguish the Revolutionary Council, the military's post revolutionary vehicle for demonstrating political power.

Amending the constitution required that two thirds of assembly deputies present and voting must approve any change, and amendments were to include no veto for the president or the Revolutionary Council. In advance of the constitutional debate, the AD government made four attempts to reopen commercial banking and insurance to private enterprise, only to have these rejected by the Revolutionary Council on allegedly constitutional grounds. In October 1980 the Portuguese government implemented the compensation program by issuing the first Compensation Certificates owed on a total of nearly 226,000 claims.

The growing conservative cast of Portuguese society, several years after the revolutionary turmoil, is revealed in a survey supported by the Rockefeller Foundation and administered for Thomas Bruneau (1981:418-423) by a local research group. This survey, concluded in the spring of 1978, and more recent surveys indicate that, although most Portuguese citizens value their recently won political liberties, their view of the revolution is on balance negative. As an example, when asked, "Which of these aspects should we be proud of?" pride in historical (the discoveries) and cultural factors ranked high. By contrast, the results of the revolution--that is, the 1976 Constitution, the government, and decolonization--received little support. Similarly, when asked, "Which government or regime governed best?" the 1978 survey revealed that Caetano ranked far above Soares, the leader of the Socialist party--and this preference for the former prime minister was widespread among the middle, lower-middle, and lower classes.

The country's shift toward the Right was also reflected in the growing assertation of employer groups. Major economic confederations, including the Confederation of Portuguese Industry, the Confederation of Portuguese Agriculturalists, and the Confederation of Portuguese Commerce, held congresses in January 1979, and again in April 1981. They demanded fundamental revision of the constitution, particularly in matters dealing with the organization and direction of the economy.

After a long debate, the 1976 Constitution was revised in September 1982. The constitutional revisions backed by the AD government, with the Socialists providing the necessary votes for a two-thirds majority, (1) eliminated the Revolutionary Council in favor of a civilian constitutional court, (2) limited the power of the president, and (3) excised most of the Marxian rhetoric of the original document, thereby signaling more space for the private sector.

On 10 June 1983, following the April 1983 parliamentary elections, a new coalition government of the Socialists, who received 36 percent of the vote, and the Social Democrats (who finished second with 27 percent) took office. Headed by Mario Soares, this Center-Left government--the first since the revolution--enjoys a two-thirds majority in the Assembly.

The new government inherited a financially troubled economy characterized by excessive spending, both at home and abroad. The current account in Portugal's balance of international payments shifted from near equilibrium in 1979 to deficits of 5 percent of GDP in 1980, 11.5 percent of GDP in 1981, and 13.2 percent of GDP in 1982 (IMF 1983:334-335). These current external deficits were financed through substantial international borrowing, mainly by the public-sector enterprises. As a consequence, Portugal's external debt had risen to over $13.5 billion by the end of 1982. Whereas general government revenue equaled about 31 percent of GDP in 1982, public-sector expenditures reached just under 43 percent of GDP. The resulting overall public deficit of 12.6 percent of GDP contributed to a sharp increase in domestic monetary expansion, as well as to the growth of Portugal's external indebtedness.

To cope with the overheated economy, the Soares government put in place an economic stabilization program in October 1983 with the support and guidance of the International Monetary Fund. The main economic objective of the stabilization or adjustment program is to reduce the current account in the balance of payments deficit to a level that does not give rise to financial difficulties and that allows significant reduction in the external debt service burden in the medium term. Specifically, the government aimed at reducing the current account deficit to 9.3 percent of GDP in 1983, and to 6 percent of GDP in 1984 (ibid.:334). The strategy to achieve targeted adjustment in Portugal's external position is centered on budgetary restraint. The 1984 austerity fiscal budget aims at reducing the overall public deficit to 6 percent of GDP from a level of 12.6 percent of GDP in 1982.

A strengthening of the financial condition of the public enterprises is to complement budgetary restraint on the part of the general government. Their resort to domestic and external credit is to be contained through a cutback in their investment program and through measures to increase their self-financing. The latter is to be accomplished through realistic pricing policies and a determined effort to contain costs and raise productivity. As steps in this direction, public transportation fares were raised by 30 percent on 1 September 1983, and wage settlements in the public enterprises were concluded at rates significantly below the rate of inflation.

Meanwhile the Center-Left government has introducted two structural measures that should strengthen Portugal's economic performance in the long run. First, a law enacted in October 1983 increases the flexibility of the country's labor market by easing the conditions of hiring and dismissing workers. The labor law permits public firms to lay off unneeded workers subject to government approval on a case-by-case basis. When implemented, this law could result in layoffs of between 30 percent and 40 percent of the 250,000 employees in state enterprises. Second, legislation has also been passed to open to private initiative, both domestic and foreign, a number of industries that hitherto had been reserved exclusively for the state.

Conclusions and Prospects

Antonio Salazar's political and economic doctrines shaped Portugal's destiny over four decades, from 1928 to 1968. The corporate framework under which his New State evolved combined two salient characteristics: extensive state intervention in the economy, and private ownership of the means of production. The state exercised extensive de facto authority over labor-management relations and over private investment decisions. Nevertheless, under the pressure of circumstances that included the outbreak of guerrilla warfare in Portugal's African territories, Salazar agreed to modify his nation's introverted and interventionist posture. During the closing years of his rule, from 1961 to 1968, international credits were solicited, direct foreign investment was encouraged, and the state's regulation of industrial investment was relaxed. The liberalization of the Portuguese economy continued under Salazar's successor, prime minister Marcello Caetano.

Paced by industrial growth and exports, Portugal experienced accelerated economic development and structural change from 1960 to 1973. Nevertheless, on the eve of the 1974 coup, Portugal was still a poor country by Western European standards. And its economy, pushed to the limit by the enormous budgetary outlays associated with the counterinsurgency wars in Africa, was dominated by a handful of powerful financial-industrial family groups.

Before the Portuguese revolution, private-enterprise ownership dominated the Portuguese economy to a degree unmatched in other Western European countries. In 1978, four years after the military coup, the scope of the Portuguese public-enterprise sector exceeded the relative importance of the United Kingdom's nationalized industries under the last Labour government. State intervention, through ownership and control of enterprises, was prompted by mixed motives. The reorganization of the MFA Coordinating Committee in March 1975 brought into prominence a group of Marxist-oriented officers who, in league with CGTP-Intersindical, the Communist-dominated trade-union confederation, sought the radical transformation of the nation's social system and political economy. Beyond Marxian ideology (whose base has always been confined to a small minority), a more popular motive--the elimination of the power of the "forty families" oligarchy--explains the nationalization of the family-owned commercial banks and insurance companies and the "commanding heights" of the economy.

Unlike the nationalization/expropriation policies in countries like Mexico, Argentina, and Peru--which reflected mainly economic nationalism--in Portugal, foreign investors were statutorly exempt from government takeovers. It is an irony that Law 46/77, passed in 1977, denied to private enterprises of national origin access to the enumerated industries reserved to the state, while admitting the continued existence of foreign-controlled firms established before the revolution.

The direct nationalizations that affected nearly 250 large and medium-sized firms was massive and broad in its sectorial scope: the Portuguese government took over the privately owned railways, the national airlines, trucking and bus lines, and urban transport, as well as electricity generation and transmission and telecommunications. Within the industrial sector, the state acquired a monopoly over iron and steel, petroleum refining, petrochemicals and chemicals, cement, pulp and paper, breweries, and tobacco, and a dominant position in the nation's shipbuilding and ship repair industry. Because of the key role of the large family-owned banks as holders of stock in their client firms, the bank nationalizations gave the state an "unanticipated" interest in hundreds of small and medium-sized firms. More, the government also gained control by intervening hundreds of other enterprises that had been abandoned by their owners or seized by their workers.

Most nationalized and intervened enterprises have experienced severe operating and financial problems. Consequently, as a group they have contributed to the large government budget deficit and the associated inflationary pressures, as well as to Portugal's large external public debt. In a highly politicized environment, public firm managers have often been required to yield to militant labor unions' demands for excessive wage increases, to maintain redundant labor forces, and to freeze prices, (especially utility rates) at below market levels. Compounding these operating difficulties has been the heavy drain through emigration of managerial and technical expertise sustained by the large technically advanced, and recently nationalized enterprises.

During the radical leftist phase of the revolution, it was feared that Portugal would be integrated into the Soviet political orbit.

The failure of a Far-Left bid for total power in November 1975 halted the prolonged series of political disorders and paved the way for constitutional government. Formulated during a period of revolutionary fervor on the part of representatives to a constituent assembly, the 1976 Constitution combines elements of Western democratic experience with a Marxian bias and defines Portugal as a "republic--engaged in the formation of a classless society." Unlike other Western European constitutions, the original document subordinated the private sector to the objectives of "building up a socialist economy." "The Portuguese," in the words of Francisco Sarsfield Cabral, an incisive Lisbon observer, "have basically exchanged the paternalism of a dictatorship with the paternalism of socialism" (Hoelterhoff 1984:30).

The growing conservative cast of Portuguese society several years after the revolutionary turmoil is revealed in opinion surveys and is also reflected in the rising assertion of employer groups. Since 1979 moderate coalition governments have emerged in Portugal whose platforms have been incongruent with the economic principles codified in the 1976 constitution. In September 1982 these moderate elements joined forces to revise the constitution fundamentally. One significant outcome of constitutional reforms is likely to be a redrawing of the frontier between public and private enterprise in favor of the latter.

What, then, are the prospects for privatization or state shrinking in Portugal? First, under the current Center-Left coalition government, we may anticipate acceleration of the return of seized or intervened property to its original owners in the hope that they will make their firms profitable again. Second, with IMF support and guidance, the government intends to reduce the nation's public deficit sharply by, among several measures, subjecting the state-owned enterprises to market discipline; that is, "simulated privatization" through enhanced management autonomy and attention given to cost-effectiveness criteria will increasingly shape the behavior of the nationalized firms. Third, recently enacted legislation allows private domestic and foreign companies to compete against public enterprises in the banking, insurance, cement, and fertilizer industries, and joint ventures are permitted with state companies in steel, petroleum, refining, chemicals, and arms manufacture. Other industries will undoubtedly join the list in the near future. Finally, following Mexico's example, the Portuguese government may decide to divest itself of the hundreds of small and medium-sized firms in which the nationalized banks currently hold stock.

Holders of Compensation Certificates are encouraged to invest the proceeds in Portuguese ventures. This provides a mechanism whereby privatization of the economy can be funded. About two dozen foreign banks, including several major U.S. institutions, have in the past four years set up offices in Portugal in anticipation of government approval of private banking. Most of these have expressed interest in setting up full branch operations in Portugal.

In sum, a decade after the 1974 revolution, a policy of cautious "privatization" has replaced the "irreversible nationalizations" posture associated with the original 1976 constitution.

NOTE

I am indebted to a number of persons who provided helpful comments on an earlier version of this paper: Lawrence S. Graham, Thomas Bruneau, and Juergen B. Donges. I also wish to thank the University of Alabama Research Grants Committee and the Board of Visitors of the Graduate School of Business for their financial assistance in support of my research in Portugal.

Table 1

Participation of Public Sector in Portugal's Economy before and after the Revolution
by Industry or Branch
(Percentage of Total)

	Traditional Public Sector (1973)			Public Sector after Revolution (1976)		
	Value Added	Gross Fixed Investment	Employment	Value Added	Gross Fixed Investment	Employment
Agriculture and fisheries	0.5	19.9		1.5	24.9	
Mining	1.1	2.9		4.5	15.5	
Manufacturing	-	-		13.5	51.0	
Construction	-	-		4.7	21.0	
Electricity, gas, water	0.1	2.7		99.9	99.6	
Commerce	-	-		1.9	5.3	
Banking, insurance, real estate	-	-		63.2	23.5	
Transport and communication	0.3	17.4		75.1	85.9	
Administration and defense	100.0	100.0		100.0	100.0	
Education	88.6	96.9		88.6	96.9	
Health	68.4	92.8		69.5	94.2	
Other services	0.2	-		3.1	45.4	
Total public sector	8.9	10.2	13.4	29/6	47.2	23.7

Source: Instituto Nacional de Estadística (INE), National Accounts, cited in OECD (1979), p. 40, table 13.
Note: No employment data available for individual industries.

References

The literature on Portugal's old regime, including the central place of Salazar, is extensive and includes works by Baklanoff (1978, 1979, 1980, 1984), Martins (1973), Ferro (1935), Graham (1975), Graham and Makler (1979), Kay (1970), Keefe et al. (1977), Makler (1969, 1974), Marques (1972), Pattee (1975), Payne (1973), and Wiarda (1973, 1977).

A number of writers, including Baklanoff (1984), Bruneau (1981), Graham and Makler (1979), Graham and Wheeler (1982), Harsgor (1976), Maxwell (1976, 1983), Morrison (1981), and Macedo and Serfaty (1981), have analyzed the Portuguese revolution from different perspectives.

Amuzegar, Jahangir. Comparative Economics. Cambridge, Mass.: Winthrop, 1981.

Associaçao Industrial Portuguesa. Guide to Investment in Portugal. Lisbon, 1968.

Baklanoff, Eric N. The Economic Transformation of Spain and Portugal. New York: Praeger, 1978.

---. "The Political Economy of Portugal's Old Regime: Growth and Change Preceding the 1974 Revolution." World Development 7, no. 9/9 (1979): 799-811.

---. La transformación económica de España y Portugal: La economía del Franquismo y del Salazarismo. Madrid: Espasa-Calpe, 1980.

---. "Reforming the Portuguese Revolution: Perspectives on the Nationalization-Redistribution Syndrome." Reform and Revolution in Latin America: SECOLAS Annals. Vol. 15 (March 1984), pp. 35-53.

Balassa, Bela. "Industrial and Trade Policy in Portugal." Paper prepared for Conference on the Portuguese Economy, German Marshall Fund and the Gulbenkian Foundation, Lisbon, 11-13 October 1976.

Banco de Portugal. Report of the Board of Governors for 1980. Lisbon, 1981.

---. Relatorio de 1982. Lisbon, 1983.

Bruneau, Thomas C. "Patterns of Politics in Portugal since the April Revolution." In Portugal since the Revolution: Economic and Political Perspectives, edited by Jorge Braga de Macedo and Simon Serfaty, pp. 1-24. Boulder, Colo.: Westview, 1981.

---. "Portugal in the 1970's: From Regime to Regime." Ibero-Amerikanisches Archiv 7, no. 4 (Autumn 1981): 389-424.

Donges, Juergen B. "Foreign Investment in Portugal." Segunda Conferencia Internacional sobre Economia Portuguesa, Lisbon, 1980.

Ferro, Antonio. Oliveira Salazar: El hombre y su obra. Madrid: Ediciones FAX, 1935.

Graham, Lawrence S. Portugal: The Decline and Collapse of an Authoritarian Order. Comparative Politics Series, no. 01-053. Beverly Hills, Cal.: Sage, 1975.

---, and Harry M. Makler, eds. Contemporary Portugal: The Revolution and Its Antecedents. Austin: University of Texas Press, 1979.

---, and Douglas L. Wheeler, eds. In Search of Modern Portugal: The Revolution and Its Consequences. Madison: University of Wisconsin Press, 1982.

Harsgor, Michael. Portugal in Revolution. The Washington Papers, Vol. 3, no. 33. Beverly Hills, Cal.: Sage, 1976.

Hoelterhoff, Manuela. "Singing a Fado over Portugal's Sad Fate." Wall Street Journal, 24 January 1984.

International Monetary Fund. IMF Survey. Washington, D.C., 24 October 1983.

Kay, Hugh. Salazar and Modern Portugal. New York: Hawthorn, 1970.

Keefe, Eugene K., et al. Area Handbook for Portugal. Washington, D. C.: GPO, 1977.

Macedo, Jorge Braga de, and Simon Serfaty, eds. Portugal since the Revolution: Economic and Political Perspectives. Boulder, Colo.: Westview, 1981.

Makler, Harry M. A "elite" industrial portuguesa. Lisbon: Instituto Gulbenkian de Ciencia, 1969.

---. "Educational Levels of the Portuguese Industrial Elite." International Studies of Management and Organization 4, no. 1-2 (Spring/Summer 1974): 41-65.

---. "The Portuguese Industrial Elite and Its Corporative Relations: A Study of Compartmentalization in an Authoritarian Regime." Economic Development and Cultural Change 24, no. 3 (April 1976): 495-526.

---. "The Portuguese Industrial Elite." In Contemporary Portugal: The Revolution and Its Antecedents, edited by Lawrence S. Graham and Harry M. Makler, pp. 147-165. Austin: University of Texas Press, 1979.

Marques, A.H. de Oliveira. History of Portugal. Vol. 2. New York: Columbia University Press, 1972.

Martins, Maria Belmira. Sociedades e grupos en Portugal. Lisbon: Editorial Estampa, 1973.

---, and Jose Chaves Rosa. O grupo estado: Analise e listagem completa das sociedades de sector publico empresarial. Lisbon: Editora SOJOURNAL, 1979.

Maxwell, Kenneth. "The Thorns of the Portuguese Revolution." Foreign Affairs 54, no. 2 (January 1976): 250-270.

---. "The Emergence of Democracy in Spain and Portugal." Orbis (Spring 1983): 151-184.

Morrison, Rodney J. Portugal: Revolutionary Change in an Open Economy. Boston: Auburn House, 1981.

OECD. Economic Survey: Portugal. Paris, 1974, 1977, 1979, 1981, 1982.

---. Investing in Developing Countries. Paris, 1983.

Palha, Ana Maria de Castro. The Banking and Financial System in Portugal. Discussion Paper, no. 3/1. Lisbon: Banco de Portugal, 1983.

Pattee, Richard. Portugal and the Portuguese World. Milwaukee, Wis.: Bruce, 1957.

Payne, Stanley. A History of Spain and Portugal. Vol. 2. Madison: University of Wisconsin Press, 1973.

Pintado, V. Xavier. Portugal's Economy and Profit Opportunities. Lisbon: Banco Portugues de Atlantico, 1973.

de Pitta e Cunha, Paulo. "Portugal and the European Economic Community." Economia 3, no. 3 (October 1979): 511-532.

Salazar, Antonio de Oliveira. Doctrine and Action. London: Faber & Faber, 1939.

Schmitt, Hans. Economic Stabilization and Growth in Portugal. Occasional Papers of International Monetary Fund, no. 2. Washington, D.C., April 1981.

Stuart, Brian C. "Stabilization Policy in Portugal, 1974-78." Finance and Development 18, no. 3 (September 1981):25-29.

Wiarda, Howard J. "Corporatism and Development in the Iberic-Latin World." In The New Corporatism: Social-Political Structures in the Iberian World, edited by Fredrick B. Pike and Thomas Stritch, pp. 3-33. Notre Dame, Ind.: University of Notre Dame Press, 1973.

---. Corporatism and Development: The Portuguese Experience. Amherst: University of Massachusetts Press, 1977.

World Bank. *Portugal: Current and Prospective Trends*. Washington, D.C., 1978.

---. *World Development Report 1983*.

CHAPTER 13

Privatizing Public Enterprise: The Record of The UK Conservative Government, 1979-1983

David Steel and David Heald

Introduction

The privatization of public enterprises was one of the most important and distinctive features of the record of the 1979-1983 Conservative government. No fewer than twelve statutes were enacted empowering ministers to sell assets or shares and to relax statutory monopoly powers. Progress in implementing these provisions was more limited but, nonetheless, by the dissolution in May 1983, the government had already effected the most radical shift since 1951 in the boundary between the public and private sectors of industry.

The _Conservative Manifesto_ for the 1979 general election provided little guidance as to the scale or scope of this program. It contained only four pledges:

(1) To offer to sell back to private owners British Shipbuilders and British Aerospace and to give their employees the opportunity to purchase shares;
(2) To sell shares in the National Freight Corporation to the general public in order to achieve substantial private investment in it;
(3) To relax bus licensing to enable new services to develop, particularly in rural areas, and to encourage new private operators;
(4) To review all the activities of the British National Oil Corporation.[1]

In practice, however, the government went a great deal further than this. By May 1983, firm proposals had been announced for over twenty enterprises (the only major omission being the National Coal Board) and many of them had been implemented successfully. Indeed, most unusually, the government's enthusiasm for this radical cause gathered momentum, rather than waned, as its term of office progressed.

The government's record, in this as in other areas, marks a significant break with past Conservative practice. The 1951-1955 government denationalized only steel, which had only recently been nationalized, and road haulage (and parts of both industries remained in public ownership). The 1970-1974 government talked ambitiously about denationalization before it took office but actually achieved no more than minimal changes. The 1979-1983 government's break with precedent reflects the important change of direction that occurred in Conservative economic policy generally and in its attitude toward the public sector in particular during its period in opposition between

1974 and 1979. The focus of this chapter is on the scope of the program and on the methods adopted and difficulties encountered in implementing it. First, however, it will be helpful to outline briefly the context in which the privatization program has been pursued and the arguments ministers have adduced in its support (no attempt will be made here to assess their validity).[2]

Why Privatize?

The government's policies toward public enterprises were part of its general program of reducing state activities and freeing market forces. In this context, privatization has two main elements: denationalization--the sale of assets or shares, regardless of whether the state retains a partial holding in an enterprise; and liberalization--the relaxation or abolition of statutory monopoly powers. This distinction and the definition of these terms are important because the word privatization, scarcely heard in the UK before 1979, has come to be used so frequently and in such diverse contexts that its meaning has become imprecise. Almost any policy designed to reduce the scale or limit the scope of the public sector or to encourage private provision of services that were previously supplied publicly is now labeled as "privatization." In relation to central and local government, it sometimes means selling assets (for example, the sale of highway service areas and of land and buildings), but more often it refers to the contracting out to the private sector of the provision of services that continue to be financed by the taxpayer (for example, local authority refuse collection and disposal services and the ancillary services of the National Health Service, NHS). Privatization has also been applied to the policy of transferring the financing of public services from taxes to charges (for example, in relation to public-sector housing).[3]

As these examples illustrate, the government has been sympathetic to privatization in all parts of the public sector. However, it has approached the privatization of public enterprises with particular enthusiasm and determination. In part this reflects the greater ease with which such a policy can be applied to already-freestanding units. More important has been the undisguised hostility of most Conservative politicians toward the nationalized industries, which stands in contrast to their much greater ambivalence about the public nonmarket sector (seen, for instance, in their declarations on the NHS during the first half of 1983).

The unpopularity of the nationalized industries among Conservative politicans is not new. In the past, however, they have been content to criticize the industries' record and to resist strongly any proposals to extend public ownership, but they have not engaged in significant denationalization. The tougher line that developed during the 1970s can be attributed to two developments. First, external criticism of the industries intensified and some of their problems increasingly came to be regarded as insoluble. Thus, during this period, the industrial-relations problem of the UK economy transferred from its traditional home in private manufacturing to the public sector, especially the nationalized industries.[4] In such a climate, the serious problems of certain undertakings, notably the British Steel Corporation, have had reverberations for other public enterprises, irrespective of their own performance. Second, there was a significant shift in the Conservative party as its leaders renounced the pragmatism of their predecessors and espoused the revived doctrines of monetarism and free-market economics. This change in both the substance and style of Conservative politics is crucially important to an understanding of the emphasis laid on privatization and of the determination with which it has been pursued. It is therefore important to look briefly at the arguments that ministers have used in support of their proposals.

Four recurring arguments can be identified, although not all of them apply to each case of privatization. Three, concerning efficiency, economic freedom, and pay bargaining, relate to both elements of privatization--denationalization and liberalization; the fourth, concerning public sector borrowing, to denationalization only.

The first, and probably the most widely used, argument in favor of privatization concerns efficiency. Ministers believe that public enterprises are intrinsically less efficient than private enterprises because they are insulated from the disciplines of the capital and product markets. They do not have to compete for capital in the open market, nor do most of them have to meet consumers' wishes to remain in business. With the sanctions of bankruptcy and takeover removed, and with no private shareholders to satisfy, managers of public enterprises are alleged to have little incentive to promote the efficient use of the resources at their disposal. In any case, government intervention in pursuit of macroeconomic and income-redistribution objectives has frequently frustrated their efforts to do so. Privatization is advanced as a solution to all these problems. The abolition or relaxation of statutory monopolies will, ministers claim, promote efficiency through competition in the marketplace; denationalization will restore market disciplines; and partial denationalization will, by introducing pressures to attract and maintain private capital, increase incentives to operate efficiently and make government intervention more difficult because of the private interests involved.

Second, the government argues that public ownership threatens economic freedom. Insofar as public enterprises enjoy statutory monopoly powers or are able to use their market strength to compete "unfairly," they limit consumers' freedom of choice. In addition, the very fact of public ownership impinges on economic freedom because the government is depriving individuals of income or capital and forcing them to hold "implied shareholdings," which they might not privately choose. Based on this argument, freedom is fostered by extending competition and by reducing the public sector so as to allow individuals to keep a higher proportion of their wealth in the form they themselves choose.[5] Similarly, part of privatization's appeal to the government relates to the latter's desire to boost wider share ownership among the population and among an enterprise's employees in particular. The government sees this as a means of increasing the stability of the private-enterprise system as a whole and of individual companies. Indeed, Nicholas Ridley, MP, the financial secretary to the treasury in 1982, claimed that privatization, rather than nationalization, would lead to "real public ownership--that is ownership by the people."[6]

Third, there is a more pragmatic argument concerning pay bargaining in the public sector. This problem has been given prominence by many Conservative politicians since the conflict with the miners in 1974, which precipitated the fall of the Heath government. They argue that, whereas trade unions in the private sector know that an excessive pay award may lead to bankruptcy, no equivalent constraint exists in the public sector. This has led many Conservatives to believe that it would be impossible to withstand pay claims in those sectors in which workers have the power to hold the nation "by the jugular vein" and that the problem can be solved only by removing access to Exchequer funds.[7] Denationalization potentially can remove such access; liberalization also contributes to the solution of this problem by making it more difficult for managers to pass on excessive pay increases to consumers by raising prices.

Fourth, the government's determination to arrest monetary growth has led it to pay great attention to reducing public-sector borrowing. Denationalization can contribute to this process in two ways: the sale of public assets generates an immediate cash flow to the Exchequer; and the creation of hybrid enterprises (those in which the state retains a partial shareholding) enables their borrowing to be defined out of the Public Sector Borrowing Requirement (PSBR). Under present conventions, the borrowing of the nationalized industries is included in the PSBR regardless of the source of such borrowing.[8] In contrast, although practice is rather confused, the borrowing of publicly owned companies (irrespective of the proportion of their shares held by the state) has in the past usually been excluded. Thus the external finance from nongovernment sources of Rolls-Royce, although wholly owned by the state, has never been included in the PSBR. However, when public corporations have been converted into companies registered under ordinary-companies' legislation, they have been excluded only after the share sale, not on incorporation. The new test is said to be the question of whether effective control has passed out of the government's hands (though the proportion of shares retained makes this in itself problematical).[9]

An evaluation of the government's case for privatizing public enterprises is outside the remit of this chapter, which concentrates on the implementation of the program. We have outlined the principal arguments only to explain the enthusiasm that ministers have shown for privatization and the determination with which they have sought to overcome the practical problems that have arisen in putting it into practice. These arguments are, however, also relevant to the final section's assessment of the government's success at the end of its first term of office in achieving its objectives.

The Government's Record

The appendix to this chapter outlines the privatization program of the 1979-1983 government in a form that utilizes the distinction we made earlier between denationalization and liberalization (with the result that several enterprises appear in both parts). Its length provides a rough indication of the scale of the program.[10] By May 1983, the government had either privatized or taken steps in this direction in relation to all or part of no fewer than twenty-five public enterprises.

In assessing the significance of this record, three qualifications need to be made. First, some of the undertakings involved, such as Amersham International (formerly the Radiochemical Centre) and the British Sugar Corporation, are of minor importance in relation to the public sector of industry as a whole. Second, several of the larger enterprises were affected only marginally. Thus the Post Office's letter monopoly was relaxed only in areas such as express mail and the transfer of mail between document exchanges, and it was solely the subsidiary activities of British Rail, such as hotels, shipping, and property, and of British Leyland that were included. Third, less progress was made in implementing many of the most far-reaching proposals affecting major public enterprises, such as the sale of British Gas's oil interests and the abolition of its monopoly rights over the purchase of North Sea gas and its sale to industry, and the sale of 51 percent of British Telecommunications (British Telecom). Nonetheless, during its first four years in office, the government succeeded in raising 1,440 million pounds through sales of public-enterprise assets,[11] in converting four major undertakings into companies with just under 50 percent public shareholding, and in making significant reductions in the restrictions on entry into two important sectors of the economy.

In the most important cases, denationalization has only been partial. Earlier denationalizations, such as steel and road haulage in the 1950s, were outright in the sense that public assets were simply sold to private bidders. On this occasion, however, the entire assets of an enterprise or all of its shares have been sold in only a few instances, such as Amersham International, most of British Rail's hotels, and some of the National Enterprise Board's subsidiaries (e.g., Ferranti, International Computers, and Fairey Holdings). The more usual approach has been to introduce private capital through the creation of hybrid companies in which the government has retained a holding of just under 50 percent. This happened in the case of British Aerospace, Cable & Wireless, the oil-producing side of the British National Oil Corporation (Britoil), and the British Transport Docks Board (Associated British Ports), and was planned for British Airways (for which legislation was enacted in 1980) and British Telecom (for which legislation was introduced in the final session of the 1979-1983 Parliament but which lapsed at the dissolution). [12] This approach was also intended for the National Freight Corporation (although the government planned to retain at most only a very small shareholding); however, the recession, which hit the road transport industry very severely, caused postponement of the corporation's flotation, and eventually the government sold it instead to a consortium of its employees, backed by a group of major banks.

As far as liberalization is concerned, the main developments have occurred in two sectors: transport and telecommunications. Route licensing in the bus industry has been eased, making the entry of private operators on to profitable routes much easier and allowing both public and private bus operators to compete more vigorously with British Rail, notably in the provision of intercity express services. The government has also taken steps toward deregulating domestic air routes, with private operators such as British Midland being granted licenses for routes hitherto reserved for British Airways. The most far-reaching changes, however, have been in the telecommunications industry, where, at the same time as technological changes are challenging the exclusive position of British Telecom, the government has progressively made further inroads into its statutory monopoly, starting with the supply, installation, and maintenance of most equipment and later extending to the resale of British Telecom's network for value-added services and to the provision of competing transmission services (the first rival system, run by the Mercury Consortium for business users, received a license in February 1982).

Implementation of the Program

Only a very limited privatization program had been declared as Conservative policy before the government took office in 1979. However, more far-reaching proposals had been made in 1978 by a Conservative party research group under the chairmanship of Nicholas Ridley, whose unpublished report was leaked to The Economist.[13] Its recommendations, which caused some embarrassment to the Shadow Cabinet at the time, resemble much more closely than the Conservative Manifesto the program that actually evolved between 1979 and 1983. In fact, the program appears to have developed in a rather piecemeal and ad hoc manner. Important questions, such as the proportion of shares to be retained in hybrid companies, received little prior attention. Indeed, the government has never really provided a proper justification for its decision to retain about 50 percent, especially as the logic of its general arguments in favor of privatization suggests that the process should be complete. Ministers have, however, on a number of occasions pointed to British Petroleum (in which the government had had a stake of about 50 percent since 1914) as a successful model.[14] The capacity of the market to take up large share issues was also an argument for limiting the size of any one sale and for moving in stages in those cases in which ministers stated that the government holding might be reduced further in the future.

Two examples provide clear illustration of the way in which the program evolved. In the case of the British National Oil Corporation (BNOC) the government displayed considerable indecision. Its first proposal--to sell some of its offshore assets--had to be abandoned amidst almost universal condemnation. Two different methods of injecting private capital then emerged: one, to issue revenue bonds to the public, the return on which would be related to revenues from specified BNOC fields in the North Sea; the other, to divide BNOC into two parts, trading (which would remain wholly stated-owned) and production (part of which would be sold to the public). The latter proposal was first announced in late 1979, but the introduction of legislation was twice delayed, ostensibly because of congestion in the parliamentary timetable but more likely in the face of formidable practical difficulties in splitting the corporation and opposition from within the cabinet (notably from the Treasury and the Foreign Office). As a result, the revenue bond proposal was adopted and preparations were made for the launching of the scheme in the autumn of 1981. However, the appointment of Nigel Lawson to replace David Howell as secretary of state for energy in September 1981 resulted in a last-minute reversion to the more radical option, reflecting Lawson's determination to overcome the practical and political obstacles that had daunted his predecessor.

The second example is British Telecom. Initially, the government's approach to liberalization was cautious, proposing only to end British Telecom's monopoly of the supply, installation, and maintenance of equipment other than the subscriber's first telephone. However, prompted by two reports it commissioned from enthusiastic supporters of liberalization (Professors Michael Beesley and Stephen Littlechild), it became increasingly radical, first authorizing private operators' use of British Teleom's network to supply services to third parties and the provision of competitive transmission services (Beesley), and later deciding to end the first telephone monopoly and to permit competition in international communications (Littlechild).[15] In this case, too, the government showed indecision over methods of injecting private capital. After prolonged discussions, the chancellor announced in his 1982 budget that agreement had been reached for British Telecom to raise funds through the issue of revenue bonds. Within a matter of weeks, however, this plan had been abandoned in favor of the more drastic option of privatizing British Telecom through the sale of equity shares.

On the methods of privatization, there are also clear signs of haste and improvisation. Little, if any, preparatory work appears to have been undertaken, and officials did not have any blueprints to take down from the shelves. Although each of the denationalization schemes followed a broadly similar pattern, there are a number of interesting variations on such questions as whether the government should appoint directors to serve on the boards of hybrid companies (for example, in British Aerospace and Britoil but not Associated British Ports and British Airways) and the setting of a statutory ceiling on the public stake in such companies (in British Airways only), which cannot be explained in terms of the special circumstances of particular enterprises. Similarly, with regard to liberalization, surprisingly little prior thought seems to have been given to important issues, such as who should regulate the new competitive regime in the gas and telecommunications industries: the minister, the public enterprise itself, or a special regulatory body. Moreover, it was widely regarded as unsatisfactory that the Littlechild Report and the government's conclusions on its recommendations were published only during the committee stage of the Telecommunications Bill.

In a few cases the government was able to sell shares under existing powers (for example, the sale of its shareholding in the British Sugar Corporation and part of its holding in British Petroleum). Generally, however, legislation was required to effect both denationalization and liberalization: for the former, to establish companies registered under the Companies Act to which the assets of existing public corporations could be transferred and to provide for the sale of shares; for the latter, to repeal statutory restrictions upon entry and to lay down a framework for future competition.

Both processes have proved to be extremely complex and to involve a large number of legal and practical issues. To a certain extent, enabling legislation simplified the task and left ministers to fill in the details later, a device that also suited the government's tight timetable.[16] Nonetheless, either in the legislation itself or during the passage of the legislation through Parliament, ministers were required to provide a considerable amount of detail about their intentions, for example, in relation to the constitutions of the new companies and about methods of regulation. In this, as well as at the later stage of offering shares for sale, the government depended heavily upon a wide array of well-paid advisers, notably lawyers and merchant bankers. The split of BNOC posed special difficulties because of the complex participation agreements the corporation had concluded with private oil companies and because everything had to be resolved in three-way negotiations between the Department of Energy and the two successors of the original corporation (BNOC and Britoil), each backed by its team of legal and financial advisers.

In this process, the government was helped to a considerable extent by the cooperation of the affected enterprises. In only a few cases did their boards oppose the substance of the government's proposals (in rather more, they expressed concern about timing and, in relation to liberalization proposals, about safeguarding the position of public suppliers). In 1979 a spirited campaign by the board of BNOC, led by its founder chairman, Lord Kearton, persuaded the government not to sell profitable oilfields and to accept instead forward sales of oil as its contribution toward the reduction of the PSBR in 1979-1980. However, this rebuff led ministers to search hard to find a new chairman who was enthusiastic about privatization. They eventually recruited a City financier, Mr. (now Sir) Philip Shelbourne, who, in conjunction with Nigel Lawson, played a key role in the launching of Britoil.

The most successful case of opposition to date has been the British Gas Corporation. Under the leadership of its formidable chairman, Sir Denis Rooke (whom the government reappointed in 1981), it has resisted the government's attempts to privatize <u>parts</u> of its undertaking. It has required ministers to issue formal directions and succeeded in stalling the disposal of its showrooms and the sale of its 50 percent interest in the Wytch Farm oilfield in Dorset (for which a direction was issued in October 1981 but which had still not been sold at the dissolution) and of its offshore oil interests.[17] British Telecom and British Shipbuilders also voiced opposition to privatization, particularly insofar as it endangered the integrity of their undertakings. Otherwise, resistance has been exceptionally weak. In many cases, privatization has been welcomed as a means of escaping the harsh financial controls being exerted by the government over profitable nationalized industries. Moreover, the recruitment of

Shelbourne is not the only example of the government using its powers of appointment to further its policy objectives (for example, appointing Sir John King as chairman of British Airways and Ian MacGregor as chairman first of British Steel and later of the National Coal Board and not reappointing union leader Clive Jenkins, the general secretary of the Association of Scientific, Technical, and Managerial Staffs, to the board of BNOC).

In legislative terms, the government's record in obtaining endorsement of its proposals is impressive. In four parliamentary sessions, it introduced thirteen privatization bills (table 1), and all but one of them reached the statute book (the exception being the Telecommunications Bill, which was lost only because of the early dissolution) virtually unscathed. In two cases, a guillotine motion had to be introduced, but this was indicative only of the opportunities parliamentary procedures provide for the opposition to delay progress (including an eleven-hour speech by John Golding, MP, on the Telecommunications Bill) and not of any difficulties the government experienced in winning comfortable majorities for its proposals.

The government's record in this respect reflects its large majorities in both houses of Parliament and the enthusiasm of its own supporters, not least in midterm when the macroeconomic outlook was bleak and privatization provided a valuable tonic for dispirited backbenchers. It was further helped by the unprecedented weakness of the Labour opposition, which seemed more interested in its own internal divisions than in effective opposition to controversial legislation on the details of which ministers were often vulnerable. The attitude of the House of Lords, which caused the 1974-1979 Labour government serious problems with aircraft and shipbuilding nationalization, was significant. The fact that the government extended its program far beyond its 1979 manifesto was not greeted by the chorus of protest that would occur were a Labour government to push through nationalization measures outside its manifesto commitments.

In contrast, the government's progress at the second stage of denationalization--that of actually selling shares--was much less impressive. With only a few exceptions, the sales were delayed, in most cases for a substantial period. For this and other reasons, too, the proceeds from this source were significantly lower than ministers intended and fell short of the targets that were set for special sales of assets as part of the drive to reduce the PSBR (see table 2, discussed in the next section).

A major reason for this shortfall was the poor financial health of some of the leading candidates for denationalization, caused by the severity of the recession and various special problems affecting particular enterprises. Poor financial health led the government to abandon the plan to sell shares in the National Freight Company to the public (instead it was sold to its staff); to postpone the flotation of British Airways indefinitely, for which legislation had been enacted in October 1980; to delay the sale of shares in Associated British Ports substantially (which occurred seventeen months after the necessary legislation received the Royal Assent); and to delay and modify the proposal to denationalize British Shipbuilders (ironically one of the few commitments included in the 1979 manifesto).[18] Problems such as these encouraged the government to bring forward some of the commercially strongest enterprises, such as Cable & Wireless and Britoil, to which its general arguments appeared much less applicable. Moreover, the sale of Britoil--the largest to date--in a highly depressed oil market resulted in proceeds only about half of the initial forecast.

For other reasons, too, the government experienced difficulties in raising as much as it might have hoped. The management of new issues is never easy, and various special factors, largely but not entirely beyond its control, compounded these problems. The size of most of the offers and the publicity surrounding them, not least as a result of the Labour party's threats of renationalization either with no compensation or "with compensation of no more than that received when the assets were sold,"[19] meant that the government and its City advisers were working in virgin territory. The government itself also imposed various restrictions on most of the sales, for instance to limit foreign purchases and to secure wide dispersal of ownership.

Problems such as these exacerbated the difficulties of deciding on the best method of sale. The government's desire to help the small investor led it to choose a fixed-price offer for the first three flotations: British Aerospace, Cable & Wireless, and Amersham International. In one sense, these sales were highly successful in that they were heavily oversubscribed (2.4 times for British Aerospace, 4.6 for Cable & Wireless, and 24.6 for Amersham); however, each oversubscription, together with the premium at which the initial dealing took place, suggests that the selling prices could have been fixed at a higher level and that assets were disposed of at less than market value. Indeed, this aspect of the Amersham sale in particular caused the government considerable embarrassment, and the Public Accounts Committee in April 1982 criticized its methods of selling shares.[20]

These criticisms led the government to decide that the largest sale to date, that of Britoil, should be by tender but with special arrangements for small investors. Again, however, it was embarrassed by the outcome. Only just over 25 percent of the shares were taken up, the remainder being left in the hands of the underwriters as a result of last-minute nerves on the part of the financial institutions about the prospects for the oil market. Two months later, the government's problems were compounded by a thirty-five-times oversubscription for the shares of Associated British Ports for which it had reverted to a fixed-price offer.

Despite these problems, ministers could claim with some justification that the conclusion of these sales was in itself a considerable achievement. If the transfer of ownership is more important than the price secured, this is a fair claim. Moreover, as far as Amersham and Britoil were concerned, last-minute changes in the market's assessment of the offers were the government's undoing, and in the latter case ministers argued that the "loss" was borne by the underwriters rather than the taxpayer, as it was they who were left with the bulk of the offer in their hands and the Exchequer received in full the money it had expected at the time of the offer for sale.

One potential problem that did not materialize during this first phase of the privatization program was effective trade union opposition. With higher unemployment, falling membership (but not union densities), anti-trade-union legislation, and hostile public opinion, the unions have not been looking for additional battlefields. Thus, although opposed to privatization in principle, most unions appeared to accept the inevitable and did little to resist the implementation of the government's plans. Only in two cases did the threat of significant industrial action materialize: there were one-day strikes against the disposal of gas showrooms and against the government's plan to sell a 51 percent stake in British Telecom. Both were well supported, and the showrooms action was claimed to have met with some success. However, it was management opposition that was decisive in persuading ministers to delay (officially, on the grounds that new safety legislation would be needed first).

The government embarrassed the unions by skillfully exploiting highly popular concessionary issues of employee shares. Although a negligible proportion of the total, they are rich in public-relations value. There were also two special cases of employee involvement: a management-led consortium, but with more extensive employee shareholding and the support of four of the five unions involved (but not the largest, the Transport and General Workers' Union), bought the National Freight Company in 1982; and the National Union of Railwaymen (NUR) became a shareholder in Gleneagles Hotels, a company established to run three of British Rail's Scottish hotels--a tactic designed to protect its negotiating rights and that, although not welcomed by the government, had the effect of compromising the union's opposition to privatization.[21]

Assessment of the Government's Record

As befits a controversial program, the government's record in privatizing public enterprises during its first term of office has been the subject of widely differing verdicts. Some, both supporters and opponents, have regarded the scale of the program as impressive, going far beyond anything previously achieved, whereas others have expressed disappointment that after four years the core of the "problem," the public-enterprise heartland such as coal, electricity, gas, and railways, has remained largely unscathed. The share flotations have been heralded as successful, or at least satisfactory, by some financial commentators and condemned as disastrous, and even scandalous, by others. As for implementation generally, ministers have been both congratulated on their good fortune (for example, in the lack of effective parliamentary and trade union opposition) and commiserated with on their bad luck (for example, in the volatility of the stock market and the economic recession). It is as yet premature to attempt a comprehensive assessment of the government's record, for the program is by no means completed, as the 1983 <u>Conservative Manifesto</u> and subsequent ministerial speeches indicate.[22] Moreover, many of the effects will be apparent only in the long term. Nonetheless, it is useful to look at experience up to May 1983 in order to gauge the progress that the government had made in achieving the objectives that it had set for the program.

Of the four aims outlined earlier, the reduction of the PSBR was prominent during this first phase of the program. Given the government's preoccupation with the PSBR, it is not surprising that denationalization appeared as an attractive option, especially as an alternative to making cuts in public spending. This goal strengthened ministers' resolve to overcome the many practical problems that confronted them and influenced the order in which proposals were implemented. However, the amounts actually raised were trivial in the context of public expenditure totals.

For each fiscal year, the government fixed a target for "special sales of assets." Table 2 sets out these targets and the outturns achieved. The government's definition of "asset sales" extends beyond the privatization of public enterprises. The table, therefore, has been broken down to distinguish between those sales that form part of the privatization program as it has been defined here (section 1 of the table) and other asset sales (section 2). Section 1 shows that over four fiscal years just 1,147 million pounds (cash) was raised, of which just over 50 percent accrued from the BP and Britoil sales. To this total, there need to be added the proceeds of various sales that have remained within the businesses concerned, such as British Rail and British Steel, even if effectively offset by equivalent reductions in Exchequer finance.[23]

Assessment of the government's record in terms of its own targets is complicated.[24] In 1979-1980 the outturn appears to have been remarkably close to the target. However, the figures were manipulated by the inclusion of the proceeds of forward sales of BNOC's oil (section 3), which accounted for over 60 percent of the sums raised. Moreover, this device simply shifted cash flow forward, causing negative figures when the practice ceased such that, although in 1981-1982 the asset sales achieved (sections 1 and 2) were in line with the government's target, they were more than offset by this factor. The outturn in other years was also influenced by the inclusion of rather dubious items such as the premiums on North Sea oil licenses (which in 1980-1981 accounted for almost 50 percent of asset sales) and the sale of oil stockpiles.

Quite apart from the delays that have occurred and the depressed state of the oil market, the benefit to the Exchequer has been limited because of the need to provide certain companies with new capital (for example, British Aerospace) and to fund deficiencies in pension funds (of the National Freight Company, for example). In the longer term, privatization may also have some adverse budgetary implications for the Exchequer. If denationalization leads to a rationalization of activities, the PSBR could be increased as a result of redundancy payments and unemployment pay.[25] Liberalization is also likely to have the effect of limiting the ability of public enterprises to continue the practice of cross-subsidization. Many of the advocates of privatization see its elimination as a major gain. However, the government's position is ambivalent, reflecting the political pressures, not least from Conservative MPs, to maintain services such as those in rural areas, which are generally believed to be cross-subsidized. If competition diminishes the profitability of those parts of a business that have financed cross-subsidization in the past, the government will have either to incur higher public expenditure on explicit subsidies or build continued cross-subsidization into the new arrangements (as it is doing in the case of British Telecom's license), if it is to avert a drastic reduction in the provision of unprofitable "social" services.

The program further contributed to reducing the PSBR through the creation of companies--both hybrid and wholly private--whose borrowing, as soon as flotation occurred, was excluded from the PSBR. By May 1983, four enterprises--British Aerospace, the National Freight Company, Britoil, and Associated British Ports--had been excluded. As Cable & Wireless and the Radiochemical Centre (now Amersham International) were Companies Act companies before privatization, only that part of their external finance that came from the Exchequer was ever included. Again, therefore, the effect upon the PSBR was modest. It should also be noted that the same result could have been achieved with rather less difficulty simply by altering the definition of the PSBR, a change that has been widely advocated and that would bring the UK into line with a number of other countries. Indeed, the government has itself demonstrated that the rules are not immutable. Traditionally, as has been mentioned, those public enterprises taking the Companies Act company form even with 100 percent state shareholding had their external finance from nongovernment sources excluded from the PSBR. On that basis, once a public corporation became a Companies Act company, it should have been excluded. However, the Treasury has decided that the new companies should be excluded only after control has passed to the private sector (understood to occur after a 50 percent share sale). Such a ruling has enabled ministers to claim that the "benefit" of reducing the PSBR can be achieved only in this way.[26]

An attempt to secure wider share ownership influenced the government's choice of method of sale and led it to give preferential treatment to small investors in the allocation of shares. However, in no case was the proportion of shares held by small shareholders significant (although it would of course have been lower but for the government's action). Moreover, in the case of British Aerospace, there was a dramatic 83 percent fall in the number of shareholders in the ten months following flotation.[27] The slide in the price of Britoil shares to 157p (1.52 dollar/pounds) in February 1983 (compared with the striking price of 215p) must also have caused ministers some embarrassment, as the shares that were taken up went almost exclusively to private individuals who, unlike the financial institutions, were less able to respond to the last-minute fears about the future of oil prices.[28] The government met with greater success in its attempt to promote employee shareholding. Around 100,000 employees took advantage of the opportunities that were offered, representing about 90 percent of the total eligible work force. However, the proportion of the total equity acquired by employees was negligible, ranging from 4.3 percent in Associated British Ports to just 0.1 per cent in Britoil.[29]

In the longer term, the success or failure of the program will be judged by its effects upon the quality and efficiency of service provision. As far as consumer choice is concerned, there is no question that the program has in various sectors, notably buses and telecommunications, opened up new opportunities. However, the government's success in promoting competition can only be assessed once the market has settled down. In the bus industry, for example, relaxation of the licensing system brought in a large number of new operators but many of them have already gone out of business.

In other sectors, a serious conflict has emerged between the government's denationalization and liberalization objectives. Whether denationalization of itself will lead to more competition or less depends heavily on each case's circumstances, such as the technology of the industry and the prevailing market structure. Moreover, to raise as much money as possible from denationalization, there are obvious attractions in selling an enterprise to a company already operating in the relevant sector and in providing the new operator with a degree of protection. Ministers have recently demonstrated a growing awareness of these tensions within the privatization program and have asserted the primacy of the liberalization objective.[30]

However, the government's record casts doubt on such assertions. Various decisions, such as British Steel's joint ventures with the private sector and the merger between Seaspeed and Hoverlloyd, former competitors in the provision of cross-Channel hovercraft services, have limited competition. Similarly, liberalization of the provision of telecommunications networks has been extremely hesitant, with just one rival to British Telecom being granted a license and with a guarantee that no further networks will be licensed until 1990 at the earliest. Most embarrassing of all to those ministers who espouse competition must have been European Ferries' bid for British Rail's subsidiary, Sealink. Instead of rejecting it immediately on the grounds that it would have given European Ferries 80 percent of the cross-Channel market, the government reached this decision only after it had received an adverse report from the Monopolies and Mergers Commission. Such tensions between denationalization and liberalization arise even more seriously in relation to a number of the current front-runners for flotation, such as British Airways and British Telecom, and will test to the full the relative priority the government attaches to these two objectives.

The question of whether privatization will lead to greater efficiency can also be answered only in the long term. The present evidence on the respective merits of private and public enterprise is far from conclusive.[31] Certainnly a belief in the superiority of the private sector is widely held. However, it is difficult to isolate the effects of ownership from other factors, such as size. Moreover, the turnaround in the finances of a number of public enterprises since 1979 suggests that quality of management may be crucial. In any case, a policy of selling off the most profitable or efficient enterprises, thus leaving the public sector with the troublesome lossmakers, has clear implications for the future imag and performance of the nationalized sector.

A particular aim of the government in this area has been to fre public enterprises from ministerial intervention. Only experienc will tell whether privatization will have this effect. Problems ar particularly likely to arise in relation to the new hybri companies.[32] Despite the continuing substantial publi shareholding, ministers insist that they will not intervene in suc companies' commercial affairs other than in exceptional circumstances, such as an attempt to alter the articles of association so as to permit a higher proportion of foreign ownership. It remains to be seen, however, whether this stance will hold in the face of political and economic pressures. There have already been a few signs of parliamentary pressure on ministers to take a closer interest, and in fact almost all of the new hybrids operate in sectors such as defense, energy, and communications in which ministers retain major responsibilities.

Another source of pressure to intervene is likely to come from industrial relations. The weakening of public-sector trade unions has been an important strand in the privatization program. Since 1979, however, the effects of high levels of unemployment on union activity have moderated its salience. In addition, those enterprises privatized during the government's first term of office were not those with a record of difficulty in industrial relations. As privatization moves into areas of potential confrontation, such as telecommunications, gas, and electricity, where there is the prospect of disrupting the entire economy, it will be seen whether governments will be able to resist the pressures on them to become involved in the resolution of disputes.

This brief analysis provides some indication of the complexity of reaching a full assessment of the government's record, especially since the program is incomplete and before many of the longer-term consequences have emerged. Nonetheless, a few concluding observations can be made. First, the government has demonstrated that, with sufficient determination, it is possible to overcome the practical difficulties of implementing privatization. Its achievements by the end of its first term of office exceeded the expectations of virtually all informed commentators. On the other hand, except in telecommunications and oil, the changes that it had effected by May 1983 in the industrial public sector may reasonably be regarded as limited. The 1983 _Conservative Manifesto_ and developments since the general election make it clear that the government intends to take the program considerably further but, as it digs deeper into the core of this sector, the problems of implementation will increase.

Table 1

Privatization Legislation

Title	Date of Commons Second Reading	Date of Royal Assent	Enterprises Affected
British Aerospace Act 1980	November 1979	May 1980	British Aerospace
Civil Aviation Act 1980	November 1979	November 1980	British Airways
Industry Act 1980	November 1979	June 1980	National Enterprise Board, Scottish & Welsh Development Agencies
Transport Act 1980	November 1979	June 1980	National Freight Corporation, National Bus Company, Scottish Transport Group, & municipal operators
Atomic Energy (Miscellaneous Provisions) Act 1981	February 1981	July 1981	Radiochemical Centre
British Telecommunications Act 1981	December 1980	July 1981	Post Office (posts & telecommunications), Cable & Wireless
Iron and Steel Act 1981	March 1981	July 1981	British Steel Corporation
Transport Act 1981	January 1981	July 1981	British Railways Board, British Transport Docks Board
Oil and Gas Enterprise Act 1982	January 1982	June 1982	British Gas Corporation, British National Oil Corporation
Transport Act 1982	February 1982	October 1982	National Bus Company
British Shipbuilders Act 1983	November 1982	May 1983	British Shipbuilders
Energy Act 1983	November 1982	May 1983	Electricity Boards
Telecommunications Bill 1982	November 1982		British Telecommunications

Table 2

Proceeds from Special Sales of Assets

(Millions of Pounds Cash)

	1979-80	1980-81	1981-82	1982-83
TARGET[a]	1,000	500	500	600
1. PRIVATIZED NATIONAL INDUSTRIES AND PUBLIC SHAREHOLDINGS[b]	336	126	305	380
Sale of shares in British Petroleum	276		8[c]	
Sale of shares held by National Enterprise Board	37	83	2	
Sale of shares in British Aerospace		43		
Sale of shares in Cable & Wireless			182	
Sale of shares in British Sugar Corporation			44	
Sale of shares in Amersham International			64	
Sale of shares in National Freight Company			5	
Sale of shares in Britoil (first installment)				334[d]
Sale of shares in Associated British Ports				46
Sale of shares in other companies	23			
2. OTHER ASSET SALES	34	279	189	108
Sale of land and buildings owned by various public bodies[e]	34	56	88	31
Sale of highway service area leases		28	19	4
Receipts from seventh and eighth rounds of offshore oil licensing		195		33
Sale of oil stockpile			63	33
Sale of other stocks			19	7
TOTAL (1+2)	370	405	494	488
3. REVENUE OFFSETS				
Advance payments to BNOC for oil	622	(49)	(573)	-
Stamp duty and VAT	7			
GRAND TOTAL (1+2+3)	999	356	(79)	488

Sources: Targets--HM Treasury, *Economic Progress Report*, no. 145 (May 1982)
Outturns--Cmnd 8789, *The Government's Expenditure Plans 1983-84 to 1985-86* and *Hansard* (27 July 1983), Col. 453.

Notes:

a. Comparison of actual proceeds against target is complicated by the switch from volume to cash planning in the 1982 Public Expenditure White Paper (Cmnd. 8494). The target figures listed in the table ignore this complication, as have government pronouncements. They are taken from the Treasury's _Economic Progress Report_ and do not in all cases agree with the figures in successive Public Expenditure White Papers.

b. To these totals need to be added the proceeds of various sales that have remained within the business concerned, for instance, British Rail and British Steel, even if effectively offset by equivalent reductions in Exchequer finance.

c. The government's nil-paid rights in the 1981 rights issue.

d. Includes repayment of a debenture of 88 million pounds with interest. The second installment of 293 million pounds (investors paid for their shares in two installments) was received in April 1983.

e. New towns, water authorities, Property Services Agency, Crown Agents, Forestry Commission.

Notes

This paper deals only with the privatization program of the 1979-1983 Conservative Government. Since 1983 the program has been extended significantly and a number of major changes have been made in its character. For more up-to-date information see Steel and Heald, eds., Privatising Public Enterprises: Options and Dilemmas (London: Royal Institute of Public Administration, 1984).

1. Conservative party, The Conservative Manifesto 1979 (1979).

2. Such an assessment is provided in D. A. Heald and D. R. Steel, "Privatising Public Enterprise: An Analysis of the Government's Case," Political Quarterly 53 (1982):333-349.

3. These four uses of the term "privatization" are discussed in D. A. Heald, Public Expenditure: Its Defence and Reform (Oxford: Martin Robertson, 1983), chap. 13.

4. See, for example, the figures published by the Department of Employment in Hansard (25 November 1982), cols. 571-572.

5. It is an argument that raises fundamental issues about the relationship between markets and freedom, issues that are beyond the scope of this paper but that are thoroughly discussed in Heald, Public Expenditure.

6. Quoted in Economic Progress Report, HM Treasury (May 1982), p. 1.

7. See, for example, the report of a Conservative research group whose unpublished conclusions were leaked to The Economist (27 May 1978).

8. Present practice is set out in the report of the Treasury and Civil Service Committee on the financing of the nationalized industries (HC 348, 1980-81, Appendix 18).

9. There has been almost no public discussion of the implications of different levels of public shareholding for public control. At first sight, it might appear that ministers regard 50 percent as the crucial threshold. However, the government has not adhered to this view in every case, sometimes stating that control would pass out of its hands despite the retention of a 51 percent stake and at other times insisting on the sale of significantly more than 50 percent for this to occur. Moreover, no one would suggest that in the private sector control cannot be exercised unless a single shareholder holds more than 50 percent of the voting shares.

10. Despite the efforts made here to define privatization, the boundaries of the program remain rather imprecise. For example, public bodies sold surplus assets, such as land, long before privatization was conceived and for reasons unconnected with the present arguments. Similarly, various developments, such as thg

creation of joint ventures, can--and have--been regarded in some quarters as extensions rather than reductions in the public sector ("creeping nationalization").

11. During the fiscal years 1979-1980 to 1982-1983, 1,147 million pounds were raised (table 2) and a further 293 million pounds in April 1983.

12. In March 1983, the government shareholding in Cable & Wireless fell to just over 45 percent when the company issued additioncl shares in connection with the purchase of shares in the Hong Kong Telephone Company. Following the general election the government share was further reduced to 22 percent when it decided to sell half of its remaining stake. In April 1984, the government disposed of its residual shareholding in Associated British Ports.

13. _The Economist_ (27 May 1978). Ridley was then a backbencher but he has been a minister in the government since 1979 and, since 1981, he has had responsibilities in relation to privatization, first as financial secretary to the treasury and, from October 1983, as secretary of state for transport.

14. Ironically, they have done this at the same time as they were taking steps to reduce the government's stake in BP (from 51 percent to 46 percent in 1979, to 39 percent in 1981, and to 32 percent in September 1983).

15. M. E. Beesley, _Liberalisation of the Use of British Telecommunications' Network_ (London: Department of Industry, 1981); S. C. Littlechild, _Regulation of British Telecommunications' Profitability_ (London: Department of Industry, 1983).

16. This device was adopted most dramatically in the most complicated case, that of Britoil. The relevant parts of the Oil and Gas Enterprise Act are very short (just four pages) and use was made of "scheme-making" powers modeled on those of the Transport Act 1968.

17. At an early stage in the row, Rooke challenged the government to privatize the entire corporation rather than to dismember it. After the 1983 general election, there were reports that his bluff was going to be called.

18. Instead of denationalizing British Shipbuilders as a whole, the government has been considering the sale of only its profitable parts, notably the naval shipyards.

19. Confusion as to the Labour party's intentions reflected the strains between the Parliamentary Labour party (PLP) and the Annual Conference and within the PLP itself. The phrase quoted here is from the party's 1983 manifesto, _The New Hope for Britain_.

20. Tenth Report from the Committee of Public Accounts (HC 189, 1981-1982).

21. This course of action was too expensive to repeat in the other cases in which the NUR's efforts were focused on preserving as far as possible its negotiating rights and protecting its members' interests rather than on outright opposition to the sales.

22. See, for example, the speech made by the financial secretary to the treasury, John Moore, MP, at the annual conference of stockbrokers, Fielding, Newson Smith, on 1 November 1983.

23. For example, in 1982-1983, 35 million pounds were raised from the sale of British Rail hotels and 60 million pounds from British Airways' subsidiary, International Aeradio (Hansard, [27 July 1983], col. 453).

24. See note a to table 2.

25. A. T. Peacock and G. K. Shaw make this point in The Public Sector Borrowing Requirement, University College at Buckingham Occasional Papers in Economics, no. 1 (1981). Interestingly, this study was commissioned by the Centre for Policy Studies and a first draft was presented to a seminar organized by the Prime Minister's Policy Unit and chaired by Professor Alan Walters, then the prime minister's economic adviser.

26. Perhaps the most overt abuse of the PSBR argument for denationalization can be found in Patrick Jenkin's statement on the future of British Telecom, reproduced in The Future of Telecommunications in Britain, Cmnd. 8610, 1982.

27. Tenth Report from the Committee of Public Accounts (HC 189, 1981-1982), Appendix 2.

28. The price subsequently improved (although the shares were still at a 41p discount at the time that the second installment was due), and by the time of the general election the discount had been reduced to 9p.

29. Speech of the financial secretary to the treasury, 1 November 1983, press release, p. 11; Hansard (29 July 1983), cols. 731-732.

30. Speech of the financial secretary, p. 16.

31. A recent review of the evidence is provided by R. Millward, "The Comparative Performance of Public and Private Enterprise," in Lord Roll, ed., The Mixed Economy (London: Macmillan, 1982), pp. 58-93.

32. These problems are discussed in D. R. Steel, "Government and the New Hybrids: A Trail of Unanswered Questions," Fiscal Studies 5, no. 1 (1984):87-97.

Appendix

Privatization of Public Enterprise, 1979-1983

DENATIONALIZATION

Proposal	Progress
BRITISH AEROSPACE: Conversion into Companies Act company and sale of about 50% of its shares	Legislation enacted in May 1980; conversion into company in January 1981; sale of 51.6% shares in February 1981
BRITISH AIRWAYS: Conversion into Companies Act company and sale of "a substantial minority shareholding" (probably 49%)	Legislation enacted in November 1980; implementation delayed by BA's financial problems at least until 1984; among measures to raise cash, sale of subsidiary, International Aeradio, in 1982
BRITISH GAS CORPORATION: Sale of (1) British Gas's 50% interest in Wytch Farm oilfield in Dorset, (2) its 900 showrooms, and (3) its offshore oil business	(1) Direction issued in October 1981, sale repeatedly delayed, now due in 1984; (2) & (3) legislation enacted in June 1982, sale of (3) planned for 1983-84 but sale of (2) postponed because of need for additional legislation on safety of appliances and their installation
BRITISH LEYLAND: Sale of various subsidiaries	Sales to date include Prestcold (refrigerators), agricultural tractor and forklift truck businesses
BRITISH NATIONAL OIL CORPORATION: Originally sale of offshore assets: later, division into trading and production and sale of majority stake (initially 51%) in production business; restricted role for BNOC	Original proposals abandoned in 1979; legislation enacted in June 1982; split of BNOC and creation of Britoil in August 1982 and sale of 51% shares in November 1982; various restrictions effected
BRITISH PETROLEUM LTD.: Sale of 10% of state shareholding	Sold in November 1979, reducing combined Treasury and Bank of England holding from 51% to 46%; further reduced to 39% by 1981 rights issue

Appendix--continued

DENATIONALIZATION

Proposal	Progress
BRITISH RAIL: Transfer of subsidiaries (hotels, ferries, hovercraft, and nonoperational property) to holding company and sale of at least a majority interest (timing and manner of sale to be decided by British Rail)	British Rail Investments Ltd. created in November 1980; legislation permitting sale of shares enacted in July 1981; merger of Seaspeed (BR) and Hoverlloyd in October 1981; sale (in most cases outright) of property, laundries, and 26 (of 29) hotels with 2 others leased pending estate development; sale of Sealink to European Ferries blocked by Monopolies Commission
BRITISH SHIPBUILDERS: Partial privatization whether by sales of subsidiaries or joint ventures with private sector	Legislation enacted in May 1983
BRITISH STEEL CORPORATION: Sale of between 15% and 25% either through specific sales of subsidiaries or by way of joint ventures with private sector (Operation Phoenix)	Legislation enacted in July 1981; three joint ventures launched in 1981 and 1982; sale of Redpath Dorman Long in 1982
BRITISH SUGAR CORPORATION: Sale of government's 24% shareholding	Sold in July 1981
BRITISH TELECOMMUNICATIONS: Conversion into Companies Act company and sale of 51% of its shares	Telecommunications Bill lost at dissolution in May 1983
BRITISH TRANSPORT DOCKS BOARD: Conversion into Companies Act company (called Associated British Ports) and sale of about 50% of its shares	Legislation enacted in July 1981; conversion into company in December 1982; sale of 51.5% shares in February 1983
CABLE & WIRELESS LTD.: Sale of just under 50% of its shares	Legislation enacted in July 1981; sale in October 1981

Appendix--*continued*

DENATIONALIZATION

Proposal	Progress
NATIONAL BUS COMPANY: Joint ventures with private sector in express coach and holiday businesses and in certain property developments and improvements	Legislation enacted in October 1982
NATIONAL ENTERPRISE BOARD: Sell 100 million pounds assets in 1979-80 and generally dispose of its shareholdings "as soon as commercially practicable"; powers to be severely restricted; merge with National Research Development Corporation and rename as British Technology Group (thus confirming its revised emphasis on assisting new high technology ventures)	Released from obligation to sell 100 million pounds in 1979-80; legislation enacted in June 1980; by May 1983 sales amounting to over 150 million pounds, of which the most important were Ferranti, International Computers, and Fairey Holdings; transfer of British Leyland and Rolls-Royce to Department of Industry in 1980-81; new guidelines issued in August 1980; operational merger in July 1981
NATIONAL FREIGHT CORPORATION: Conversion into Companies Act company and sale of "all or virtually all" of its shares	Legislation enacted in June 1980; conversion into company in October 1980; following delay in flotation due to recession, company sold to consortium of managers and employees backed by group of major banks in February 1982
RADIOCHEMICAL CENTRE LTD. (renamed Amersham International Ltd.) Sale of up to 100% of its shares (held by UK Atomic Energy Authority)	Legislation enacted in July 1981; sale of all shares in February 1982

EXTENDING COMPETITION

Proposal	Progress
BRITISH GAS CORPORATION: Abolition of British Gas's monopoly rights over purchase of North Sea gas and its sale to industry	Legislation enacted in June 1982

EXTENDING COMPETITION

Proposal	Progress
BRITISH TELECOMMUNICATIONS: Initially liberalization of supply, installation, and maintenance of all equipment other than first telephone and maintenance of private branch exchanges (1); . . . following Beesley Report (1981, use of BT network by private companies to supply services to third parties (2) and provision of additional transmission services (3); following Littlechild Report (1983), abolition of "first telephone" monopoly and greater freedom in use of BT network (4); creation of office of director general of telecommunications to supervise telecommunications industry (5)	Legislation enacted in July 1981; (1) to be phased in between 1981 and 1984; (2) private companies permitted from October 1981 to use BT circuits to supply special services that BT is not ready to supply and to supply all such services (but not merely to-sell capacity) from April 1982; (3) Mercury Consortium licensed in February 1982 to provide independent telecommunications system (designed for business users); (4) and (5) included in Telecommunications Bill, which fell at dissolution in May 1983
BUS AND COACH SERVICES: Relaxation of licensing controls to permit greater competition with municipal and nationalized operators (National Bus Company, Scottish Transport Group)	Legislation enacted in June 1980; new system in force in October 1980
ELECTRICITY: Encouragement of private generation of electricity by empowering private firms to sell electricity to local electricity boards on fair terms and to use National Grid, and by repealing statutory prohibition on generation as a main business activity	Legislation enacted in May 1983
POST OFFICE: Limited relaxations of postal monopoly (e.g., express mail, bulk mail between document exchanges)	Legislation enacted in July 1981; express mail monopoly ended in November 1981; licenses permitting document exchanges to transfer mail and charities to carry Christmas cards issued in late 1981

Part IV

CONCLUSIONS

Chapter 14

State Shrinking: Problems and Prospects

William P. Glade

"Neoconservative" is the characterization most often used in the United States for the policy stew concocted of deregulation, decentralization, supply-side economics, and monetarism (the mixture more colloquially referred to as Reaganomics). In our context, it focuses mainly on deregulation (i.e., reducing the indirect intervention of the state), paring the coverage of social administration, pruning the bureaucracy, and other fiscal retrenchment. There has been some devolution of programs to the states, but little privatization (i.e., curtailing the direct intervention of the state) inasmuch as parastatal firms are a relatively unobtrusive part of the U.S. economic setting.[1]

"Neoliberal" is the term customarily used in Latin America for kindred policies, though the monetarism of the three Southern Cone military governments gave a uniquely sinister cast to the first attempts to evacuate the state from portions of the extensive policy space it had come to occupy since the revival of interventionism earlier in the century. In Latin America, as in most of the rest of the world, privatization in one or more of its versions is very much in the picture. Under the pressure of IMF-approved adjustment programs, deregulation has been tried as well, while Mexico, Chile, and Peru have also made some stabs in the direction of decentralization.

If there is a common denominator running throughout these and other national variations, it is, if not an abandonment of the former faith in the general efficacy of government intervention, at least a greater awareness of its practical limitations and its circumstantial constraints. "Neoskeptical" may be a more exact description of the current turn of policy than either neoconservative or neoliberal--for it reminds us, as we need to be reminded, that there was also a "paleo" skepticism, the loss of faith in the efficacy of the market that swept the corridors of policy establishments around the world with the debacle of the Great Depression.

To be sure, the scope of intervention had been spreading since soon after the Cobden-Chevalier treaty, which marked, perhaps, the high tide of laissez-faire, especially in its liberal trade policy aspects, or what was then called economic liberalism. Thereafter, diverse influences--ranging from the canny political calculations of Bismarck, who anesthetized currents of worker protest with his innovative social programs, to the emerging exigencies of an urban-industrial life that relied on new public goods--virtually ensured that the expansion of the public sector would be relentless. In essence, there was a growing practical awareness (even before theoreticians got around to the matter) of the phenomenon of "market failure."

From the 1930s through the 1950s, the enlargment of the state sector even seemed to gain momentum, starting with the policy expedients cobbled together to deal with the Great Depression and, in short order, the draconian measures devised to handle the wartime mobilization of resources. By the end of the 1940s, the Keynesian policy revolution had been installed as the new common sense of the industrialized world, and copied by many less-developed economies in addition. Currents akin to democratic socialism were then, or soon thereafter, in the ascendant in key countries (e.g., the United Kingdom, New Zealand, Canada, India, and decolonized British Africa), while in Latin America the U.N. Economic Commission for Latin America and, later, the Alliance for Progress both came down heavily on the side of development planning, partly (though only partly) inspired by the spectacular success of Marshall Plan economic programming in Western Europe. The Marshall Plan itself carried over into France's indicative planning system and spawned a different version of business-government collaboration in Germany's social market economy. Postwar Japan's unique marriage of recombined business conglomerates with the Ministry of International Trade and Industry looked to be the very apogee of managed capitalism. Meanwhile, of course, the centrally planned model of development had been imposed by force of arms on great portions of Eurasia and by the 1960s had even jumped the Atlantic to Cuba.

Given the longevity and breadth of this long-wave of interventionist policy and, hence, its presumed social functionality, to dismiss the role of the state with the seigneurial casualness of the more exuberant market devotees would seem incautious at the very least. Yet, as the papers in this volume make plain, a rather different policy style now seems to be in the making. How durable and far-reaching is it likely to be?

It is obviously not possible to come up with a conclusive appraisal of a policy alteration that, considering the historical context, is at most yet in its infancy. Nevertheless, three sources of information can usefully be brought to bear in gauging the prospects for privatization: the critique that has been building in recent times on shortcomings of the public sector, the practical problems that have been encountered in the privatization process thus far, and a reprise of the factors that may continue to push in the direction of the secular trend of public sector growth.

Public Sector Deficiencies: The Accumulating Evidence

The authoritative *World Development Report* for 1983 showed, on the basis of a careful empirical analysis, that among developing countries there has been an inverse relationship between economic controls and economic growth, between regulated economic systems and the capacity to weather externally induced shocks. A number of other studies sharply critical of interventionist development strategies in the Third World have also appeared in recent times, among them works by Bauer, Johnson, Krueger, Lal, Krauss, not to mention the development policy counsel that has been purveyed for a much longer period by advisers of the so-called Chicago School persuasion.[2] These however, are only the tip of the iceberg in a burgeoning literature on the more baleful aspects of interventionism. So vast is this literature nowadays, though, that we should greatly overleap the boundaries of what is appropriate in a volume of this sort were we to essay more than a mention of different segments of the field of criticism.

To begin with the most extreme forms of intervention, those associated with the operations of a Soviet-style system, it is worth recalling that a socialist economist, Oskar Lange, was one of the earliest serious critics through his elaboration of a theory of market socialism, but later critics of the traditional planning approaches have added much to the doubt that such systems can, at present, work very effectively. Among these, Janos Kornai has been particularly influential ever since the publication in the late 1950s of his _Overcentralization in Economic Administration; A Critical Analysis Based on Experience in Hungarian Light Industry_. But Czech theoreticians and planners--e.g., Miloslav Kohoutek and Ota Sik--made important advances, as did, of course, Yugoslav economists. During the 1960s and 1970s, many Western scholars--among them Granik, Morgan, Spulber, Portes, and Marschak--shed additional light on the reasons that central planning was generally falling so far short of its stated aims.[3]

Meanwhile, the scholarly spotlight has been focused no less intensively on the economic conditions that have undermined the old Keynesian consensus in the West, and a growing body of what may be called scholarly advocacy has been providing a larger rationale for policies in the state-shrinking vein. As far back as the 1940s, Hayek and Mises had enjoyed a limited but dedicated following among those fearful of statism, while the gloomy prospects foretold by Schumpeter in his _Capitalism, Socialism, and Democracy_ were scarcely calculated to inspire hope in the future of welfare capitalism. In time, like-minded spirits began to appear in other quarters, advancing arguments that, from a number of directions, cast growing doubt on the efficacy of interventionism, even before supply-side economists began to make their pitch for the same cause, that of market-guided economy.[4] The work of Friedman in this respect scarcely needs mention, _Free to Choose_ having reached even more people than Hayek's foreboding _The Road to Serfdom_ Olson's _Rise and Decline of Nations_ is somewhat more technical in its argumentation than either of these semi popular works, but its vision is no less sweeping so that it is, in some respects, a latter-day parallel to Schumpeter's global scenario.

Beyond these examples and other like-minded individual scholarly analyses, one can even go on to identify several of the main institutional platforms with which many of these critics have been associated, a sign, as it were, of a growing commonality of vision and of concerted efforts to refine the social diagnostic power of the new analysis. Of these, some can be best described as schools of thought not necessarily confined to a single organizational center. Such, for instance, is what is, in some respects, the grandfather of the lot, the Austrian School, which has been so ably, if briefly, reviewed by Littlechild.[5] Similar in policy orientation, though not in methodology, would be the many economists associated with the Chicago School (including its UCLA offshoot among other parts of the Chicaco diaspora), the Virginia School of writers on public choice,[6] those working on the New Resource Economics, participants in the Carnegie-Rochester Public Policy Conferences and in the Interlaken Conferences on Analysis and Ideology,[7] and members of the Mt. Pelerin Society, which began its work in 1947.

Over the years, a good many policy research and policy advocacy centers have been established to develop critical analyses that in one way or another would be supportive of the state-shrinking agenda. Abroad some of the more important are the Fraser Institute in Canada, the Institute of Economic Analysis in London, and the newer (1977) Adam Smith Institute, which is also in London. The major centers of this inspiration, however, are to be found in the United States and would include the Hoover Institution (Stanford), the American Enterprise Institute for Public Policy Research (Washington, D.C.), the Cato Institute (San Francisco), the Institute for Contemporary Studies (San Francisco), the Center for the Study of Public Choice (at George Mason University), the Center for Research in Government Policy and Business (at the University of Rochester), the Manhattan Institute for Policy Research (in New York City), the Pacific Institute for Public Policy Research (San Francisco), the International Institute for Economic Research (Los Angeles), and the Heritage Foundation (Washington, D.C.).[8] Newest among the policy study centers of this general orientation are a couple targeted on privatization per se, the Center for Privatization in Washington, D.C., a private-sector organization set up under USAID auspices, and the Privatization Research Organization of the Center for Management at Baruch College, City University of New York.

From these and other scholarly redoubts has been mounted a formidable assault on the intellectual foundations of state-managed capitalism and socialism. Of particular interest for us, however, has been the unsparing search for organizational weaknesses. Scarcely a stone has been left unturned in the quest to highlight the blemishes of the mixed economy and the assorted types of planned systems. Some have provided instructive insights by harkening back to the classical economists' observation that government might be the main source of monopoly and misallocation of resources;[9] others, by carrying this hoary wisdom to new heights of theoretical elegance.[10] A number have advanced our understanding by harsh, but not necessarily partisan, assessments of the welfare and regulatory programs of the modern state.[11] Several recent studies have pointed out that government has gorwn so sprawling that it now overflows the boundaries that conventionally define the public sector.[12] Of particular usefulness for undertaking the impetus toward state shrinking are studies that have pointed to such intractable problems as the self-serving manipulation of information flows (and, by derivation, the policy process) by government entities. In this connection, Yudof's meticulously researched contribution is outstanding, for in the context of an "information society," information management extends by far the implications of the bureaucratic behaviors detailed by the scholars mentioned below.[13]

Much light has been shed on the thorny problems of public policy formation and implementation by students of modern bureaucracy, who laid to rest years ago the illusion that a Weberian bureaucracy rationally, efficiently, and submissively carries out the orders of a democratically organized polity. Whether conducted by bitter critics, by the realistically sympathetic, or from still other points of view, most contemporary studies paint a rather different picture of the phenomenon, revealing the goal substitution and deflection that result from bureaucratic politics, disparities between the bureaucratic preference function and idealized notions of the general welfare, the role of bureaucracies (and their constituencies) as vested interests, and so on.

Now approaching the status of classics in this field of study are Michel Crozier, _The Bureaucratic Phenomenon_, William Niskanen, _Bureaucracy and Representative Government_, Anthony Downs, _Inside Bureaucracy_, Francis Rourke, _Bureaucracy, Politics, and Public Policy_, Dwight Waldo, _The Administrative State_, Aaron Wildavsky, _The Politics of the Budgetary Process_, Peter Blau and Marshall Meyer, _Bureaucracy in Modern Society_, Gordon Tullock, _The Politics of Bureaucracy_, and Joseph LaPalombara, ed., _Bureaucracy and Political Development_.[14]

In respect of the LDCs, one finds there a still greater basis for misgivings about the beneficent operations of the bureaucratic state. The proliferation of agencies and parastatals has made regulation and direct management of resources the crux of government action but, for a variety of reasons, made it less and less possible to exercise real legislative authority over this economic government. Even supervision and control by the central executive are, not uncommonly, woefully lacking, while judicial oversight is virtually undreamt of. La Palombara provided, more than twenty years ago, a masterful statement of what is still the essence of the problem:

> Among other things, we know that some policy implications are [contained] . . . in all significant administrative behavior and that the power and influence-seeking groups of a society, sensing this, will cluster about decision points, hoping in this way to exert some leverage over the quite clearly political decisions that emanate from the bureaucracy. What is true of the more advanced countries is probably accentuated in developing nations, where the bureaucracy may be the most coherent power center and where, in addition, the major decisions regarding national development are likely to involve authoritative rule making and rule application by governmental structures.[15]

In an environment in which _amistad_ (friendship) shades quickly into _amiguismo_ (cronyism) and outright venality, in which political turnover and governmental instability often inhibit the development of experienced professional management, or in which authoritarian cliques and parties monopolize the exercise of power, the situation is fraught with possibilities for the misuse of resources.[16] The catalogue of other associated problems is lengthy and runs through a sacrifice of the internal consistency or coherence of governments, systemic suboptimization, regulatory rigidity as a source of disincentives for producers, arbitrary control, civil disobedience, and so on down the line. The growing literature on implementation has also revealed the vulnerability of public policy to deflection of purpose and distortion once it leaves the legislature, for interests other than those at whom the policies ostensibly aim shape program implementation in ways unintended in the formal design of the legislation. As Peters has put it in a recent discussion of overload, "The sheer bulk and inertia of bureaucracy, combined with its needs for external political support from clientele groups, tends to fragment control and divert attention from problems of governance to problems of organizational survival."[17]

The gravamen of these critical studies is, taken _tout ensemble_, certainly not a tale of unrelieved delinquency and disaster, and not all of these specialists, by a long shot, would be willing to sign up for membership in the Mt. Pelerin Society. A good many studies, indeed, point toward constructive developmentalism as one of the achievements of which public bureaucracies are, for all their shortcomings, at times capable.[18] At times, as in Mexico, Turkey, and Egypt, it would even seem that state bureaucracies must take the lead in starting development because alternative sources of leadership appear even less able. Yet each study in its own way, backed up by a host of others, provides important evidence to support a deeper, and ever more robust, theoretical case that the "market failure" literature is easily offset, in a troubling dialectic of failure, by "public sector failure."[19] Although, on the one hand, there is a clear case for the kind of corrective, remedial action the United Nations has taken in a multitude of missions and publicized in a number of specialized reports, on the other the literature just surveyed establishes a fairly strong case for taking a judicious look at the possibilities for deregulation, selective fiscal retrenchment, and one or another of the forms of privatization.

Problems of Implementation

Straight off it must be recognized that there is a world of difference between the privatization that is carried out in the advanced industrial economies and that which is being attempted in the less-developed countries. In the former, capital markets and information systems are well developed and the transfer of enterprises, even substantial conglomerates, is a routine operation. There is very little about the removal of a firm from the public sector to the private sector that distinguishes it from the sales, mergers, branching out, and company reorganizations that go on all the time. Ample support systems are in place to assist in handling all of these processes, and liquidation, too, where that is called for. By the same token, the conversion of firms to mixed enterprises involving public and private capital is not uncommon outside the United States and, for that matter, not unknown even in the United States. Peripheral privatization is likewise simple to arrange, and where the state decides to improve the management of its business holdings few, if any, real barriers seem to stand in the way.

By contrast, on any number of counts, the situation in which privatization takes place can be, and usually is, far from propitious in the case of the less-developed countries, starting with a number of contradictions that afflict the process right at the outset. As recent history shows, not the least of these contradictions is that of timing. On the one hand, the pressure or need to begin divestment has been felt most acutely in a period of economic crisis, for it is then that the fiscal burden of the parastatals weighs most heavily on the state. On the other, it is precisely then that the local private sector, struggling to maintain its own solvency, is least able to absorb these firms, whose prospects are in any case darkened by the general economic adversity. In more than one country, in fact, the economic crises has meant that failing private firms have been taken under the protective custody of the state even while public enterprises are being hawked at home and abroad.

Still more is the transfer of firms to private investors a difficulty when the public enterprises being put up for sale are large, troubled by mismanagement (or a recalcitrant work force), inadequately capitalized, handicapped by improper or worn-out (or poorly maintained) plant and equipment, uneconomically located, carrying a substantial load of debt, or some combination of these fairly common liabilities. Even in the best of times capital markets tend to be thin and the supply of skilled management and technical personnel quite limited. When the economies have been going through the wringer, as they have been of late, the problems of rescue and rehabilitation are compounded. In scarcely more than ten years, for example, some of the Chilean banks nationalized by Allende have been privatized, temporarily renationalized or "intervened" when they were going under, and then put up for sale again. In the worst cases, there may simply be no local takers for the firms put on the block.

It can, of course, be argued that, whereas domestic investors are not able to take on the problems of the state firms, foreign investors might, for several reasons, have a sporting chance at putting their affairs in order and making a go of it. Debt-equity swaps and outright sale are both being used to place state-owned enterprises in the hands of foreign management in order to salvage productive assets. No doubt a great deal more can be done along this line, given the strength and versatility of multinational corporations. But on a very large scale such a policy runs a clear risk of provoking an eventual nationalistic reaction. The state as Esau--as responsible for alienation of the national patrimony--has already put in its appearance as a theme in Mexican and Chilean political debate; it is sure to recur as a leitmotif in other national arenas as time goes by. At the very least, therefore, prudence would seem to call for opting for the joint venture form so as to bring local interests--public or private--into the partnership.

There is a second sense in which timing presents governments with a contradiction, again because privatization tends to occur in periods of slack in the economy. In most cases the firms of the parastatal sector have been operated to attain a multiplicity of objectives that might be characterized as noneconomic. Work relief for a part of the labor force, sheltered markets for the output of national companies, subsidized inputs for other national firms, economic opportunity for lagging regions, even sinecures for the well connected--such are among the political and social compromises that typically affect the operating mode of state-owned companies.

As it goes almost without saying that the less influential members of a society ordinarily have little at stake in parastatal operations, it follows that those whose interests are bound up with the aforementioned compromises are groups that have some measure of political clout. Put differently, there is often a political equilibrium as well as an economic equilibrium to consider when state-shrinking programs are being launched, and the larger the privatization project the more numerous are likely to be the constituencies of the parastatals being put up for disposition. Further, this will tend to be the case whether the government is contemplating a shutdown of some relic of obsolete technology, closing an operation that for some other reason is judged to be unsalvageable, or selling to private investors a business that might show promise when put on a commercial footing.

For would-be purchasers, this web of commitments to the "rent-seekers" in society needs to be pondered and assessed for the ability of the latter to resist enterprise reorganization and oppose a new management's changed policies. Since conditions of recession are virtually guaranteed to produce a heightened attachment to privilege, what retaliatory mischief might be done in the longer run as well as more immediately must obviously figure in the calculations. But government, too, must reckon with this in its planning, for more often than not in times of an economic slump its political base is already eroded. Under the circumstances it can ill afford to take on still more opponents unless the payoff for so doing is likely to be considerable, or unless it can in some sense convincingly plead *force majeure* as an exculpating factor (for example, compulsion from the IMF, or, in the case of oil-producing countries, a sharp fall in the market price of their petroleum exports).

On top of the timing contradictions there is a fiscal contradiction that must be confronted as well. From the standpoint of reducing the government's deficit, the strategy called for would seem to be that of selling off the loss-ridden companies (those not closed down altogether) and hanging on to the profitable ones. From the standpoint of the market, however, it is the profitable companies that are most readily sold; the "dogs" may even require a protracted period of rehabilitation, including injections of new capital, to make them attractive to possible purchasers. The net result might be, therefore, to increase the shortfall in public finance, leaving aside the nonrecurring income that comes from the sale of parastatal firms. Where the government has to relieve the firms put up for sale of some portion of their debts in order to induce investors to buy, this leads to another version of the adverse impact on government's budgetary position, insofar as the government takes on a direct debt obligation while passing the income-producing assets over to others.

As the foregoing considerations hint, a further point of social policy is inextricably bound up with implementing a country's privatization program, one that involves a quite legitimate public concern that some countries have tried to address by instituting special employee stock-ownership provisions in their privatization programs. Others have tried to deal with the issue by setting limits on individual purchases of newly issued shares. The issue in question is, of course, that of the concentration of economic power. Almost always an acute problem in developing countries, the concentration of wealth and income runs a very real risk of becoming greater if large blocs of public assets are simply given over to whoever locally has the wherewithal to purchase them, whether outright privatization or semiprivatization be involved. Interestingly, by now a fair number of Latin American public utility companies enjoy assured and growing markets and have succeeded in indexing their rates so as to avoid the problems that formerly afflicted them. Under the circumstances, their shares could become important instruments for broadening and strenghtening local capital markets, pulling in institutional and individual investors alike. To date, however, few of these have been inducted into the privatization process; most of the firms that have been put up for conversion involve greater risks of one sort or another, a circumstance that tends to militate against broader participation in their ownership. One can venture the opinion, therefore, that if heed is not paid to the question of economic concentration now, it is only a matter of time before it will reverberate much more troublesomely in the political process of the countries involved. Already, for instance, Chile's privatization program, which has seemed bent on establishing a perverse kind of apostolic succession with Hilferding's Finanzkapital, has ensured that such will come to pass the moment the military relinquish political power.

Once past these hurdles, a welter of others may remain, starting, perhaps, with complications in asset valuation. What, for example, is the replacement value of an asset that, with hindsight, one wouldn't reproduce? Again, the LDCs are often at a disadvantage in that there may simply not be a functioning market for some types of properties, a situation that may create ambiguities, to say nothing of heated public controversy, about how firms are priced. Even if there is an organized capital market of sorts, it will normally be so weak and erratic that it cannot serve as a reliable check on whether the issue price of shares in a particular privatized firm was too low. Further, the small number of possible buyers in many cases augments the likelihood that oligopsonistic power may be exercised in what will often amount to a distressed sale in the first place, stirring up charges of favoritism and corruption in the political arena. The larger the number of enterprises dumped on the market in a brief period, the greater will be the probability that these complications become more acute, notwithstanding the valuable assistance that can be obtained from foreign investment-banking houses, accounting firms, underwriting companies, management consultants, and the like.

There is some basis for believing that suspicions and accusations of preferential treatment may also attend the sharing of ownership when parastatal firms are semiprivatized. And no less damaging is the political acrimony that results from public misunderstanding when public enterprises have been so poorly run that their net asset value is quite small, realistically appraised, and when they are then sold at these realistic valuations. Moreover, it also seems to be the case that public opinion may not even understand the logic of closing, during a period of widespread joblessness, an unsalvageable firm, especially one employing a great many workers, or, in the case of firms put under private management, of discharging the redundant portion of the labor force. To be sure, in many instances such complaints can be disregarded, but where political systems are fragile, such tensions, even when baseless in terms of strict economic logic, linger and later create turbulence in the business environment. Since this possibility is not ordinarily overlooked by investors in their planning, the upshot is that initial sales prices must be more steeply discounted (hence, less return to the treasury and a greater likelihood of public controversy) as investors seek to secure a higher short-run return by way of compensation for the risk.[20]

At this point, a set of larger conflicts may enter the picture. The price fetched on companies put up for sale is, of course, not unrelated to their prospective earnings under new management. From this perspective, then, the treasury has a vested interest that coincides with the private buyers' interest in higher profits, and neither can, in these circumstances, be enamored of deflationary policies. But complications do not stop here. Inasmuch as the operating environment of the private sector in most LDCs has been one constructed out of an extraordinary range of interventionary measures, especially protectionist ones, the immediate interest of treasury and private owners alike may well run counter to the other state-shrinking policy of deregulation. Particularly is this so when a lowering of tariffs and a dismantling of other regulatory and supportive stratagems exposes a newly privatized industry to more severe competition from abroad--or from within when other regulated privileges are dispensed with. If, meanwhile, fiscal cutbacks have brought on deflation and recession, the basic recuperative power of the local private sector as well as its capacity to absorb the parastatals and reorganize for stronger foreign competition will all suffer.

In embracing the basic long-run economic logic of rationalization and privatization, therefore, one should not lose sight of the fact that a probably substantial portion of the profitability of the private-sector assets in place in LDCs is attributable to protective measures and other forms of subsidy. The parastatal sector's losses, after all, have their functional counterpart in the monopoly profits of the private sector. In the former, the operating inefficiencies and other distortions are covered by borrowing, in the latter, by heavier extractions from the customers in a captive market. Although in the NICs civil society is no longer as weak as it once was vis a vis the state, it is still wide of the mark to conclude that many of the various sectors of society can be painlessly weaned from the whole structure of state-sanctioned privilege in which they have grown up, the business sector included. Local awareness of this is what no doubt tempers the enthusiasm of not a few Third World business communities for any all-out program of privatization, deregulation, and fiscal retrenchment.[21] Indeed, whenever local business resistance to a consistent state-shrinking project joins forces with the state bourgoisie that has nested in the machinery of government and the parastatal sector, one may well come to discover that the modern state has been, in effect, Sanforized.

At the micro level, experience suggests that the road may be equally rocky. For one thing, debt is not the only contractual obligation that hampers putting the privatized firms on a new footing. Labor severance indemnities and contracts with both suppliers and customers may all stand in the way of any quick conversion to profitability and, even where not contractual, pricing policy may also be a matter that new management cannot change freely.[22] Better management of accounts receivable may also require a protracted period of adjustment. Nevertheless, the behavioral expectations of the domestic private firms that, it is hoped, will acquire the parastatals are customarily based on relatively short-term profit horizons.

What is worse, there is evidence that in some cases--Mexico comes to mind--government may even be reluctant to give either public or private management a free hand to reorganize the major troubled firms instead of providing the bolder facilitation that is actually needed: i.e., nullification of the contractual relations that frustrate the attainment of solvency. In yet other cases, governments have been reluctant to let state firms rid themselves of various unsuitable assets, thereby either improving their own commercial standing or preparing the way more effectively for a sale to the private sector. The reason for all this, however, is not simple ignorance. Since parastatals have, as was pointed out earlier, often been used to implement the political and social agenda of governments, their fate is intensely political and it is in a good many cases highly unlikely that any wholesale devolution of state companies to the private sector will occur without some exercise of government's residual interest in these firms. Be that as it may, any constraints placed on the privatized concerns will ordinarily make it that much more difficult for them to compete in the open capital market for funding--and, equally, harder for them to bring down costs for effective competition in product markets.

Additional impediments derive from current market conditions, such as the difficulty local private entrepreneurs face in raising additional capital, either at home or, even moreso, abroad, to replace outmoded plant and equipment and otherwise rehabilitate the undercapitalized firms they are taking over from the parastatal sector. Though an imaginative development of mutual funds might provide part of the answer, such would require much more in the way of information disclosure, certified auditing, and legal protection for minority shareholders than most LDCs and even NICs are at this time able, or perhaps prepared, to offer. The selection of marketing strategies may also become a problem, if, for instance, privatization lends to cream skimming (i.e., the provision of service only to profitable segments of the market), so that new public agencies must be set up to serve the poorer segments of the market, as in the case of rural electrification. To cite yet another problem, administrative procedures and record keeping have sometimes been so careless that unexpected third-party claims have on occasion arisen to plague the new management of privatized firms. (Not altogether facetiously, one could argue that privatization may be advantageous in Latin America in that it makes heavy use of two of the region's comparatively abundant resources: lawyers and accountants.) Perhaps surprisingly, given all the attention that has been devoted to the informal sector and the supposed flourishing of microenterprises, rather little has been done in Latin America to encourage peripheral privatization (sometimes called microprivatization) by contracting out, thereby broadening the distribution of economic opportunity. Somewhat more, one gathers, has been done along this line in Africa, but the evidence is fragmentary.

Out of the evolving experience of our times, still other problems are coming to light to indicate that even where government indecision and policy paralysis are not the source of difficulty, privatization programs have a long way to go to come up with satisfactory solutions for the circumstances in which most LDCs and NICs find themselves today. Just where all this will lead is still obscure, but at the moment it looks as if Latin American countries at least will tend to reserve outright privatization for firms that are smaller or otherwise less critical to their development programs and for larger and more strategic public enterprises employ either semiprivatization or simulated privatization. Not all parastatal management there has been discredited and some has exhibited a remarkable dynamism, particularly in firms that adhere, more or less, to a profit orientation already. What is more, a burgeoning generation of better-educated younger technicians, administrators, and other specialists is now coming to the fore and enhancing the possibility for enterprise reform and regeneration _in situ_, sectorally speaking. Given a halfway satisfactory operating environment, the accumulation of professional on-job experience should put such enterprises in a position to realize increasing gains of the x-efficiency type.

From a political point of view, too, the likely emphasis on semi-privatization and simulated privatization seems not to be misplaced, for it involves, in many cases, not only working from strength (i.e., with the better-managed parastatals) but also in a form that is relatively compatible with the Latin tradition of social organization. Less-statist forms of privatization may be more suitable for Africa and Asia, but a case could be made that in the Latin American context, the semi- and simulated versions, along with a good dose of peripheral privatization, should suffice and that the main correctives for gross resource misallocation lie in any case more in the area of deregulation and debureaucratization. Given a sufficiently aggressive program on this last front and sounder macroeconomic management, all firms, private and parastatal alike, would tend to operate at much higher levels of efficiency--provided, of course, that the public enterprises were also largely deprived of access to treasury borrowing.

Government in Retreat?

There is, lastly, the matter of the concert of factors that historically have made for an expansion of the public sector. The literature on this subject is well known and covers a broad spectrum of forces that have enlarged the scope of government's economic role. Though theories of public goods and of market failure have helped to illuminate part of this process and though the empirical evidence is exceedingly rich from almost all vantage points, the fact remains that a fully acceptable comprehensive or general theory of state expansion has yet to be devised. Much can be explained by remarking urban-industrial society's reliance on a growing range of public goods, the ever-denser array of externalities (both negative and positive) generated by a well-articulated industrial economy, and the usefulness of social programs in stabilizing the investment environment, politically and economically, while all but the purest monetarists would admit the utility of conscious macroeconomic management, however much it stands in need of improvement. Wagner's Law, fiscal sociology, and similar formulations may, under some conditions, explain a bit more. Nevertheless, the great synthesis is still in the future.

For the less-developed economies--or, more accurately, the late-industrializing countries--additional theoretical insights have been constucted by Eckstein, Gerschenkron, and others on the basis of the structural requirements of "catching up," refining, as it were, some of the glimmerings that, however crudely formulated and misspecified, were adumbrated much earlier in the works of Veblen (in his essays on Japan and Germany) and of economists of the German historical and cameralist schools. As a neoclassical interpretation might have it, state intervention has been portrayed as being efficient for accelerating, or even effecting, the major structural changes that the market would tend to generate more slowly, or not at all, while the market has consistently, save in the areas of "failure," proved far more efficient in incremental shifts of resources. Whether or not this can be established conclusively, it seems a not unreasonable presumption at this point and would indicate, if it were valid, which countries are "readier" than others for creeping--or perhaps even trotting--privatization, i.e., those in which the major structural alterations have been accomplished and in which there is now more scope for market incrementalism to work its way.

What is appropriate to keep in mind, however, is that the relation between the theories of "market failure" and "public failure" is complementary, not substitutive, and that just as the conditions that inspired the turn toward interventionism did not "repeal" the validity of the market in its sphere (as, for instance, Lange perceived but Stalin's henchmen did not), neither do all the revelations of disordered administration, waste, and bureaucratic ineptitude and self-aggrandizement remove the _raisons d'etre_ of much of government's economic and social ministrations. If the vast encampment of bureaucrats that constitutes modern government threatens to lurch out of control, the answer would, in this perspective, seem to be to discipline it with deregulation, fiscal retrenchment, decentralization, privatization (in whichever form might be most suited to the circumstances), and further administrative reform rather than what might be described as self-indulgent fantasizing that the modern public sector can somehow be vanquished.

Georges Bernanos, in his Diary of a Country Priest, probably expressed best the advice to which our country case studies seem to point. The priest's fanatic housekeeper, he wryly commented, went astray because, not content to keep the dust under control, she thought she could abolish it. State shrinking, in other words, has a useful role to play, but employed as a broom and not as an instrument of sectoral annihilation.

Notes

1. Though the FNMA was privatized some years ago and COMSAT was set up even earlier (in the 1960s) to privatize the satellite communications field, not a great deal of headway has been made since. Neither CONRAIL nor AMTRAK has been successfully privatized, much less the TVA, the Exim Bank, or other government enterprises. As for the fiscal and bureaucratic reductions that seemed to be called for by the findings of the Grace Commission, the actual accomplishment has been the slowing of the rate of expansion of the public sector rather than its outright contraction.

2. See, for example, Peter T. Bauer, *Reality and Rhetoric: Studies in the Economics of Development* (Cambridge: Harvard University Press, 1984), which excoriates mainstream development economics; idem, *Dissent on Development* (Cambridge: Harvard University Press, 1976); Harry G. Johnson, *Economic Nationalism in Old and New States* (Chicago: University of Chicago Press, 1967); idem, *Economic Policies towards Less Developed Countries* (Washington, D.C.: Brookings, 1967); A. D. Krueger, *Liberalization Attempts and Consequences* (New York: National Bureau of Economic Research, 1978); Deepak Lal, *The Poverty of Development Economics* (Cambridge: Harvard University Press, 1985); Melvyn B. Krauss, *Development without Aid: Growth, Poverty, and Government* (New York: McGraw-Hill, 1983); Arnold C. Harberger, ed., *World Economic Growth* (San Francisco: Institute for Contemporary Studies, 1984).

3. For examples of different facets of this literature, see David Granick, "Some Organizational Problems in Decentralized Planning," *Co-Existence*, no. 5 (1966): 169-172; Theodore Morgan, "The Theory of Error in Centrally-Directed Economic Systems," *Quarterly Journal of Economics* (August 1964): 395-419. A. Lawrence Chickering, ed., *The Politics of Planning* (San Francisco: Institute for Contemporary Studies, 1976), takes a particularly searching look at a broader array of planning systems.

4. Paul Craig Roberts, *The Supply Side Revolution* (Cambridge: Harvard University Press, 1984).

5. Stephen C. Littlechild, *The Fallacy of the Mixed Economy* (San Francisco: Cato Institute, 1979).

6. Here, of course, James Buchanan and Gordon Tullock are the key figures but the scholars who work in this line of inquiry are dispersed far beyond the Buchanan-Tullock study center, which was formerly at Virginia Polytechnic Institute and has moved to George Mason University, also in Virginia.

7. See, e.g., Karl Brunner, ed., *Economics and Social Institutions* (Boston: Martinus Nijhoff, 1979).

8. There are, of course, a good many other "conservative" policy organizations, such as the National Forum Foundation (which concentrates on national security and social policy), but the foregoing represent most of the major institutions addressing economic policy issues.

9. See, e.g., Yale Brozen, *Is Government the Source of Monopoly? and Other Essays* (San Francisco: Cato Institute, 1980).

10. James M. Buchanan, Robert D. Tollison, and Gordon Tullock, eds., *Toward a Theory of the Rent-Seeking Society* (College Station: Texas A&M University Press, 1980).

11. See, e.g., R. Emmett Tyrrell, Jr., ed., *The Future That Doesn't Work: Social Democracy's Failures in Britain* (New York: Doubleday, 1977); James S. Larson, *Why Government Programs Fail: Improving Policy Implementation* (New York: Praeger, 1980); Fritz Machlup, *The Political Economy of Monopoly* (Baltimore: Johns Hopkins, 1952); Charles Murray, *Losing Ground: American Social Policy, 1950-1980* (New York: Basic Books, 1980); Gordon Tullock, *Welfare for the Well-to-Do* (Dallas, Tex.: Fisher Institute, 1983); Melvyn B. Krauss, *The New Protectionism: The Welfare State and International Trade* (New York: NYU Press, 1978); Neil Gilbert, *Capitalism and the Welfare State: Dilemmas of Social Benevolence* (New Haven: Yale University Press, 1983). Irving Howe, ed., *Beyond the Welfare State* (New York: Schocken, 1982), is useful as a collection of leftist indictments of the flaws of the welfare state.

12. Murray Weidenbaum, *The Modern Public Sector; New Ways of Doing the Government's Business* (New York: Basic Books, 1969); James T. Bennett and T. J. DiLorenzo, *Underground Government: The Off-Budget Public Sector* (San Francisco: Cato Institute, 1983); Richard Rose, *Understanding Big Government* (Beverly Hills: Sage, 1984). Written from an explicitly state-shrinking view is Arthur Selden, ed., *The Taming of Government* (London: Institute of Economic Affairs, 1979).

13. Mark Yudof, *When Government Speaks: Politics, Law, and Government Expression in America* (Berkeley & Los Angeles: University of California Press, 1983).

14. Michel Crozier, *The Bureaucratic Phenomenon* (Chicago: University of Chicago Press, 1964); William Niskanen, *Bureaucracy and Representative Government* (Chicago: Aldine, 1971); Anthony Downs, *Inside Bureaucracy* (Boston: Little, Brown, 1967); Francis Rourke, *Bureaucracy, Politics, and Public Policy* (Boston: Little, Brown, 1969); Dwight Waldo, *The Administrative State* (New York: Knopf, 1948); Aaron Wildavsky, *The Politics of the Budgetary Process* (Boston: Little, Brown, 1974, 2d ed.); Peter Blau and Marshall Meyer, *Bureaucracy in Modern Society* (New York: Random House, 1971, 2d ed.); Gordon Tullock, *The Politics of Bureaucracy* (Washington, D.C.: Public Affairs Press, 1965). Not a classic but certainly a hard-hitting recent detailing

of bureaucratic misdeeds in the United States is J. Peter Grace's popularization of an official inquiry, Burning Money: The Waste of Your Tax Dollars (New York: Macmillan, 1984); and Joseph LaPalombara, ed., Bureaucracy and Political Development (Princeton: Princeton University Press, 1963).

15. LaPalombara, Bureaucracy, p. 15.

16. Again, the relevant literature is huge, but a few illustrations may suffice to indicate the range. Milovan Djilas, author of the much-discussed The New Class (1957), returned to the theme of bureaucratic exploitation in The Unperfect Society: Beyond the New Class (New York: Harcourt, Brace and World, 1969), as an expose of the Marxian style of dictatorship, a more primitive version of which is depicted in Paulette Pierce, Monocapitalist Development: The Struggle to Nationalize the Guayanese Sugar Industry (Totowa, N.J.: Rowman and Littlefield, 1984). The problems of institutional weakness and a basic lack of accountability in less-repressive settings of underdevelopment have been skillfully dealt with and diagnosed by Merrilee S. Grindle, Bureaucrats, Politicians, and Peasants in Mexico (Berkeley & Los Angeles: University of California Press, 1977); Edward J. Schumacher, Politics, Bureaucracy and Rural Development in Senegal (Berkeley & Los Angeles: University of California Press, 1975). David Ronfeldt's Atencingo (Stanford, Cal.: Stanford University Press, 1973) is also instructive in how the bureaucracy of parastatals is able to deal with a disadvantaged work force. See also Jeffrey Brannon and Eric N. Baklanoff, "Goal Ambivalence of a Semi-Autonomous Public Enterprise: CORDEMEX," Journal of Interamerican Studies and World Affairs 22, no. 4 (1980): 441-462.

17. B. Guy Peters, The Politics of Bureaucracy (New York: Longman, 1984), p. 187.

18. An early study of this genre is Sanford Mosk's Industrial Revolution in Mexico (Berkeley & Los Angeles: University of California Press, 1950), but the cases of South Korea, Japan, Taiwan, Brazil, and several others come to mind as instances in which state entrepreneurship acted as a constructive force.

19. Typical of the contributions to this theorizing stream are Charles Wolf, Jr., "A Theory of Non-Market Failure: Framework for Implementation Analysis," Journal of Law and Economics 22 (April 1979): 107-112; William Mitchell, "The Anatomy of Public Failure: A Public Choice Perspective," Los Angeles: International Institute for Economic Research, Original Paper #13, 1978; and H. W. Gottinger, "Public Failure: Some Reflections on the Management of Large Public Programs" (mimeographed); see J. D. Gwartney and Richard Stroup, Economics: Private and Public Choice (New York: Academic Press, 1983), chap. 30, for an introductory overview.

20. In the United Kingdom, labor's threats to renationalize notwithstanding, divestiture has met with such receptivity on the part of many buyers that one must conclude that the threats to undo Conservative Government policy are not being taken seriously. Similar revanchist movements are afoot elsehere, but if opponents cannot somehow be mollified, the only alternative for governments in such cases would seem to be to shove them aside in hopes that subsequent development will confirm the wisdom of such policies. The stable authoritarianism of Mexico, for example, would seem to permit some combination of both, and Brazil, too, has proved adept at compromising such differences. More problematic are countries like the Argentine, where the political system tends chronically toward disequilibrium.

21. Some twenty years ago both Albert Lauterbach and Frank Brandenburg pointed out the attachment of Latin American business to the prevailing scheme of governmental favor, a situation that gave rise to decidedly ambivalent attitudes among members of the formally organized business community to intervention and regulation. A fair number of country-focused studies have, over the years, provided additional documentation of this point. With maturation has come restiveness, but probably not, at least as yet, a full-blown willingness to shuck off the mantle of state protection, as, for instance, revealed in the difficulty Mexico has faced in developing sufficient policy consensus to go into the GATT. The rise of an underground economy (the now almost-legendary informal sector) has provided some evidence of more self-reliant business undertakings, but in policy formation it is still the formal business sector that counts.

22. The sticky nature of these contracts, be it remembered, may be tied in with the pivotal position of parastatals in the distribution system for political favors--including, in some countries, their use for the personal enrichment of the ruling clique.

Special Acknowledgment

Four people from the staff of the Institute of Latin American Studies must be given special praise for their help in seeing this project through to the end.

Pat Boone, who had worked energetically and effectively in organizing the conference, labored tirelessly (and cheerfully) to prepare the final copy for publication--all in addition to her substantial daily duties as the Institute's administrative assistant. In this she was ably assisted by Kathy Bork who with her superb command of an editor's skills fashioned some sort of stylistic coherence out of the individually different papers and did an amazing amount of polishing in the process.

Abraham Torres, with his customary aplomb, skillfully managed the production process and put together the marketing program for the volume. Shirley Burleson, the ILAS financial offficer and dean of the staff in terms of seniority, worked miracles in tandem with Ms. Boone in expediting all the bureaucratic paperwork associated with the conference and the subsequent publication. In Texas that is no mean job, for surely Austin--saddled with both the state government and the university--will be one of the last places on earth to experience debureaucratization.